Unreal Development Kit Game Programming with UnrealScript
Beginner's Guide

Create games beyond your imagination with the Unreal Development Kit

Rachel Cordone

PUBLISHING

BIRMINGHAM - MUMBAI

Unreal Development Kit Game Programming with UnrealScript
Beginner's Guide

First published: December 2011

Production Reference: 1081211

Published by Packt Publishing Ltd.
Livery Place
35 Livery Street
Birmingham B3 2PB, UK.

ISBN 978-1-84969-192-5

www.packtpub.com

Cover Image by Tom Mooney (tomofnz@gmail.com)

Credits

Author

Rachel Cordone

Reviewers

Edward Davies

Dave Voyles

Acquisition Editor

Wilson D'Souza

Development Editor

Meeta Rajani

Technical Editors

Pramila Balan

Kavita Iyer

Llewellyn Rozario

Project Coordinator

Kushal Bhardwaj

Proofreaders

Mario Cecere

Chris Smith

Indexer

Hemangini Bari

Graphics

Manu Joseph

Production Coordinator

Arvindkumar Gupta

Cover Work

Arvindkumar Gupta

About the Author

Rachel Cordone is a designer and self-taught UnrealScript programmer, who has been working with the Unreal Engine since 1999. She has worked for various game and simulation companies since 2003, including Pipeworks Software and Parsons Brinkerhoff, and has started up her own game company, Stubborn Horse Studios, to make independent games with the Unreal Development Kit. Stubborn Horse's first project, Prometheus, won several awards in Epic Games' Make Something Unreal Contest.

I would like to thank my crazy goat for his love and support while writing this book!

About the Reviewers

Edward Davies is in the final year of his Game Art and Animation degree at the University of Glamorgan. He has a strong interest in game design, particularly the Unreal Development Kit, concept art, and 3D modeling and texturing. More of Edward's work may be seen at www.kungfoowiz.deviantart.com/gallery.

Dave Voyles is a Managing Editor and Podcast Producer for Armless Octopus. He covers Xbox LIVE Indie Game, Xbox Live Arcade, and Playstation Network news, reviews, and developer interviews. He holds a BS in Communication Studies from SUNY Oneonta, and is currently attending the New York Institute of Technology to work on his MBA in Management of Information Systems. His additional work within the gaming community includes working as the Coordinator of the Indie Games Summer Uprising, which looks to promote the most outstanding titles on the Xbox LIVE Indie Games platform. Dave is also an Unreal Script programmer for two titles that will be released on PC and iOS, at the end of 2011. Most notably, he is the founder of the New York City-based UDK meetup group, where he works with other developers to collaborate on endeavors in a physical environment, as well as provide tutorials. You can find more of his work by visiting his sites http://www.DaveVoyles.wordpress.com or http://www.ArmlessOctopus.com.

www.PacktPub.com

Support files, eBooks, discount offers, and more

You might want to visit `www.PacktPub.com` for support files and downloads related to your book.

Did you know that Packt offers eBook versions of every book published, with PDF and ePub files available? You can upgrade to the eBook version at `www.PacktPub.com` and as a print book customer, you are entitled to a discount on the eBook copy. Get in touch with us at `service@packtpub.com` for more details.

At `www.PacktPub.com`, you can also read a collection of free technical articles, sign up for a range of free newsletters and receive exclusive discounts and offers on Packt books and eBooks.

`http://PacktLib.PacktPub.com`

Do you need instant solutions to your IT questions? PacktLib is Packt's online digital book library. Here, you can access, read, and search across Packt's entire library of books.

Why Subscribe?

- Fully searchable across every book published by Packt
- Copy and paste, print and bookmark content
- On demand and accessible via web browser

Free Access for Packt account holders

If you have an account with Packt at `www.PacktPub.com`, you can use this to access PacktLib today and view nine entirely free books. Simply use your login credentials for immediate access.

Table of Contents

Preface

Welcome to *Unreal Development Kit Game Programming with UnrealScript*! This book teaches you how to program using the UnrealScript language so you can create your own game projects using the UDK. Instead of using dry, hypothetical code you will use the topics learned in each chapter to build an actual working game. By the end of the book, you will be comfortable enough with the language to start working on projects of your own.

What this book covers

Chapter 1, Project Setup and Test Environments, guides you through the installation and setup of the Unreal Development Kit as well as ConTEXT and UnCodeX, two programs that we will use to write our code. We also examine the directory structure of the UDK and take a look at the configuration files.

Chapter 2, Storing and Manipulating Data, covers the different types of variables we can use in the UDK as well as the flow control statements we can use to react to our changing environment.

Chapter 3, Understanding the Class Tree, examines the class tree so we can understand the relationship between objects in the world. We learn about inheritance and function overriding to customize our object's behavior.

Chapter 4, Making Custom Classes, focuses on the creation of classes of our own. The core classes for any UDK project are discussed, and we create our own versions of them for our game. We change how the camera works, what the rules of the game are, and how the player is controlled.

Chapter 5, Using Functions, covers the use of functions to expand our game. Here we learn how to pass information from one object to another, and how to manipulate that data and return it to the original object. Custom functions are created for our objects to create functionality that didn't exist in the original UDK classes.

Chapter 6, Using States to Control Behavior, covers states and how they can be used to organize and control complicated behavior such as enemy classes for our game. Creating states, changing states, and working with functions within states are discussed.

Chapter 7, Working with Kismet, discusses the use of Kismet in UDK games as well as the creation of custom actions and events. These are used to demonstrate the power of Kismet to tailor the gameplay to each individual level's needs.

Chapter 8, Creating Multiplayer Games, covers running a server and a client on a single machine for multiplayer testing. We also cover the fundamentals of networking code and how to design your game with multiplayer in mind.

Chapter 9, Debugging and Optimization, discusses common errors encountered when compiling and running UnrealScript as well as solutions to these problems. Different ways of optimizing code to make your game run faster are also discussed.

Chapter 10, Odds and Ends, covers the use of Components to customize the visual look of objects in our game. The use of DLLBind to communicate with programs outside of the UDK is also discussed.

What you need for this book

A computer capable of running the UDK is required for this book, see `http://udn.epicgames.com/Three/DevelopmentKitFAQ.html` for the minimum requirements. ConTEXT and UnCodeX are included in the files with the book. See `http://www.packtpub.com/` for downloading code files.

Who this book is for

This book is for people who are new to the Unreal Development Kit and who wish to create their own game projects using UnrealScript. The information here is also useful to programmers having experience in another language and who wish to expand their knowledge by learning UnrealScript.

Conventions

In this book, you will find several headings appearing frequently.

To give clear instructions of how to complete a procedure or task, we use:

Time for action – heading

1. Action 1

2. Action 2

3. Action 3

Instructions often need some extra explanation so that they make sense, so they are followed with:

What just happened?

This heading explains the working of tasks or instructions that you have just completed.

You will also find some other learning aids in the book, including:

Pop quiz – heading

These are short multiple choice questions intended to help you test your own understanding.

Have a go hero – heading

These set practical challenges and give you ideas for experimenting with what you have learned.

You will also find a number of styles of text that distinguish between different kinds of information. Here are some examples of these styles, and an explanation of their meaning.

Code words in text are shown as follows: "We can play the example game that comes with it to get an idea of what the UDK can do by going into C:\UDK\UDK-AwesomeGame\Binaries\Win32 (or Win64 if we have a 64-bit operating system) and running UDK.exe"

A block of code is set as follows:

```
Class AwesomeActor extends Actor
    placeable;
defaultproperties
{
    Begin Object Class=SpriteComponent Name=Sprite
        Sprite=Texture2D'EditorResources.S_NavP'
    End Object
    Components.Add(Sprite)
}
```

When we wish to draw your attention to a particular part of a code block, the relevant lines or items are set in bold:

```
Begin Object Class=SpriteComponent Name=Sprite
    Sprite=Texture2D'EditorResources.S_NavP'
HiddenGame=True
End Object
Components.Add(Sprite)
```

New terms and **important words** are shown in bold. Words that you see on the screen, in menus or dialog boxes for example, appear in the text like this: "Let's click on **Return to Desktop** for now."

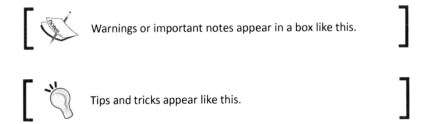

Warnings or important notes appear in a box like this.

Tips and tricks appear like this.

Reader feedback

Feedback from our readers is always welcome. Let us know what you think about this book—what you liked or may have disliked. Reader feedback is important for us to develop titles that you really get the most out of.

To send us general feedback, simply send an e-mail to feedback@packtpub.com, and mention the book title via the subject of your message.

If there is a book that you need and would like to see us publish, please send us a note in the **SUGGEST A TITLE** form on www.packtpub.com or e-mail suggest@packtpub.com.

If there is a topic that you have expertise in and you are interested in either writing or contributing to a book, see our author guide on www.packtpub.com/authors.

Customer support

Now that you are the proud owner of a Packt book, we have a number of things to help you to get the most from your purchase.

Downloading the example code

You can download the example code files for all Packt books you have purchased from your account at `http://www.PacktPub.com`. If you purchased this book elsewhere, you can visit `http://www.PacktPub.com/support` and register to have the files e-mailed directly to you.

Errata

Although we have taken every care to ensure the accuracy of our content, mistakes do happen. If you find a mistake in one of our books—maybe a mistake in the text or the code—we would be grateful if you would report this to us. By doing so, you can save other readers from frustration and help us improve subsequent versions of this book. If you find any errata, please report them by visiting `http://www.packtpub.com/support`, selecting your book, clicking on the **errata submission form** link, and entering the details of your errata. Once your errata are verified, your submission will be accepted and the errata will be uploaded on our website, or added to any list of existing errata, under the Errata section of that title. Any existing errata can be viewed by selecting your title from `http://www.packtpub.com/support`.

Piracy

Piracy of copyright material on the Internet is an ongoing problem across all media. At Packt, we take the protection of our copyright and licenses very seriously. If you come across any illegal copies of our works, in any form, on the Internet, please provide us with the location address or website name immediately so that we can pursue a remedy.

Please contact us at `copyright@packtpub.com` with a link to the suspected pirated material.

We appreciate your help in protecting our authors, and our ability to bring you valuable content.

Questions

You can contact us at `questions@packtpub.com` if you are having a problem with any aspect of the book, and we will do our best to address it.

Project Setup and Test Environments

1

Introducing the Unreal Development Kit (UDK)

Epic Games' Unreal Development Kit is a powerful tool, but like any complicated piece of software it can be overwhelming at first. This book will guide you through the structure of the UDK and the basic principles of UnrealScript, and by the end you will have the skills you need to start making your own games. Let's get started!

It's a great time to get into the UDK and UnrealScript. With the release of the UDK, Epic Games has opened up a great way for indie developers to make high quality games without high quality budgets. With hard work and dedication even a small team of people can make a great game in their spare time, and with digital distribution platforms such as Steam, it's become much easier to self-publish and build a community of fans, and being able to sell your game doesn't hurt either.

With constant updates to the UDK, Epic provides the latest features of the Unreal Engine for free if you're just looking at game development as a hobby. If you're aiming to start up your own development studio, the licensing terms for the UDK fit even in the smallest of budgets. If you're looking for AAA quality, the UDK is where you'll find it.

Being an UnrealScript programmer is the most important job in a UDK project. Even without artists you can build prototypes and demonstrate your gameplay using UnrealScript and placeholder artwork using the assets included with the UDK. As they say, actions speak louder than words, and having a fun game which people can play will help attract the art talent to give your project the visual quality you need.

So with that, let's take a look at the Unreal Development Kit!

Before we start cooking let's set the table. There are a few things we need to do before we write our first line of code.

In this chapter we will:

♦ Install the UDK and take a look at its directory structure.

♦ Learn what external programs we can use to code UnrealScript.

♦ Set up our first project.

♦ Compile and test a Hello World program.

Let's see what our computer needs to run the UDK.

System requirements

It doesn't take a top of the line computer to work with the UDK, but like any software there are system requirements that we need to meet. According to the UDK website they are as follows:

Minimum requirements:

♦ Windows XP SP2 or Windows Vista

♦ 2.0+ GHz processor

♦ 2 GB system RAM

♦ SM3-compatible video card

♦ 3 GB free hard drive space

Make sure the computer we're working on meets these requirements, and then we can install the UDK!

Time for action – Installing the UDK

Epic's official UDK website is the best place to stay up to date with the latest UDK releases and features, so we'll be heading there for the download.

1. Go to `http://udk.com/download` and get the latest release.

2. Run the installer. It will ask us to accept the license agreement and where we want to install the UDK. By default, it will use the UDK version for the installation, but to help keep things organized it's better to use a project name. This helps if you have more than one project using the same UDK version. In this book we will be calling our project **Awesome Game**, so let's change the installation directory.

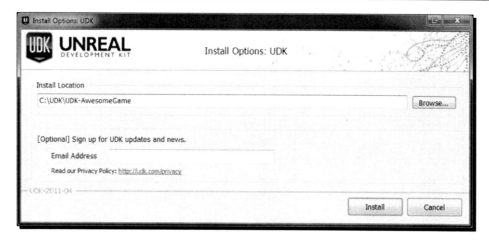

3. After installing the prerequisites and the UDK, the installer will ask us what to do next. Let's click on **Return to Desktop** for now.

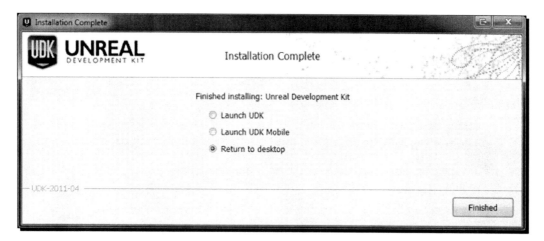

What just happened?

Now we have a working copy of the UDK installed on our computer. We can play the example game that comes with it to get an idea of what the UDK can do by going into `C:\UDK\UDK-AwesomeGame\Binaries\Win32` (or Win64 if we have a 64 bit operating system) and running `UDK.exe`. Take a few minutes and look through the game's menus and play the Deathmatch map DM-Deck to get an idea of what the UDK is capable of.

Now we're ready to take a peek under the hood of the UDK. Where are the files that the UDK uses to make our game work?

Directory overview

Let's take a look at the folders in the UDK install to see how everything is organized.

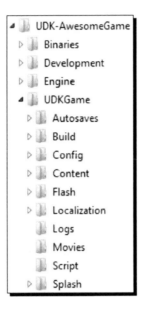

Binaries

The first folder, `Binaries`, holds the game executables and tools for artists and animators. We won't be working with the art tools in this book, but it's helpful to know what they do.

- ◆ `ActorX`: Provides plugins to export static and animated game objects from 3D modeling programs like 3ds Max and Maya.

- ◆ `FaceFXPlugins`: Lip syncing and facial animation tools for characters.

- ◆ `GFx`: Tools used to make Scaleform menus for the interface and player HUD.

- ◆ `SpeedTreeModeler`: Used to quickly make trees and other vegetation to fill game environments.

Development

The next folder, `Development`, is where most of our work will take place. You may have heard people talk about a game's source code before. The `Development\Src` folder is where our game's source code will go. If we look in the `Src` folder we see that it isn't empty, there are a lot of folders already in there. Epic provides the source UnrealScript files for reference, to make it easier to learn how to make our own code. As Indiana Jones might say if he were a programmer, "Seventy percent of programming is reading the source code." One important thing to remember: NEVER ALTER EPIC'S SOURCE CODE! A lot of the files have C++ code behind the scenes, and altering these files could break them since we don't have access to the C++ code. All the work we do will be creating our own files to work with.

Engine

The `Engine` folder holds resources and configuration files for the game and editor, and will rarely need to be touched even by experienced UnrealScript programmers.

UDKGame

The next folder is where the heart of a UDK project resides. `UDKGame` is where all of the content for our game is found, where the configuration files are, even where the splash screen is. Let's take a look at each folder individually. The next two folders are:

♦ `Autosave`: This folder doesn't exist when you first install the UDK. When you open the editor and start creating a level, the editor will periodically save a copy of your map to this folder. If the editor freezes up or your computer crashes, you would be able to retrieve a recent version of the map you had been working on without losing a lot of work.

♦ `Config`: We use the `INI` files in here to change settings that the game uses to run, as well as giving the player a way to change settings for our custom game. The game's resolution and keyboard settings are in here as an example. `INI` files can be opened with any plain text editor such as Notepad. Here is an example of keybinds that can be found in the `DefaultInput.ini` file:

```
.Bindings=(Name="E",Command="GBA_Use")
.Bindings=(Name="LeftMouseButton",Command="GBA_Fire")
.Bindings=(Name="RightMouseButton",Command="GBA_AltFire")
.Bindings=(Name="C",Command="GBA_Duck")
.Bindings=(Name="Escape",Command="GBA_ShowMenu")
```

- ◆ `Content`: Maps, sounds, characters, environment art, it's all here. The directory structure inside this folder is divided up to create separate areas for mobile content if we were working on an iOS project, to keep it separate from the normal PC content. The exact directory structure here doesn't matter much, we can organize our content however we like. As long as it's in the `Content` folder the game will be able to find it.

- ◆ `Flash`: This folder holds the source files for our Scaleform menus and any HUDs our game uses.

- ◆ `Localization`: If we were releasing our game in different languages, this is where we would put all of our translated text. As with `INI` files, `INT` files can be opened with a plain text editor.

- ◆ `Logs`: The files here record game events and any debugging code that we put in, and are very helpful when trying to fix broken code. The `LOG` files can be opened with a plain text editor.

- ◆ `Movies`: Any cutscene videos we create would go in here, as well as the game loading and level loading movie files.

- ◆ `Script`: Once our source code is compiled, the `.u` file ends up here. These are the files that the game uses and the ones that are distributed with our game, the source code is only used to create these and aren't included.

- ◆ `Splash`: In addition to the images that are shown when the game or editor are starting up, there are links to the Epic forums and the Unreal Developer Network in here. Both are valuable resources for learning how to use the UDK.

Not too complicated! In this next section we'll be taking a closer look at the `Development` folder by installing and setting up a few programs we can use to making coding in UnrealScript easier. Let's get to it!

Using external programs to code

There are two things we need to look at when deciding what programs to use to help us write UnrealScript code. The first, obviously, would be something we can use to write the code itself. Script files can be opened and written in a plain text editor like Notepad if we prefer, but there are free programs out there we can use to make our lives easier.

ConTEXT

ConTEXT is a freeware text editor designed to make working with various programming languages easier. It has text highlighting to make reading code quicker, and tools to make compiling code as easy as pressing a button. Let's install it so we can use it in our project.

Time for action – Installing ConTEXT

Find the installer included with this book, or go to http://www.contexteditor.org and download the latest version.

1. Run the installer. It will ask what language to use.

2. The installer will ask where we want to install the program. The location doesn't matter, choose a convenient location or leave it at the default.

3. The installer will ask if you would like to add shortcuts or **Replace Windows Notepad**. Let's leave this at the default for now unless you don't need the shortcuts.

4. Review the settings and click on **Install** to finish the installation.

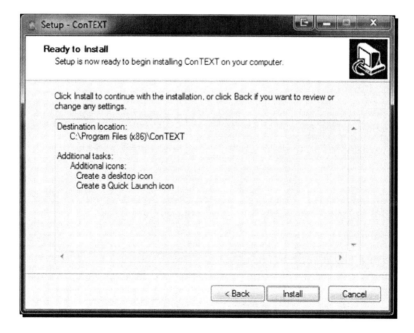

5. After ConTEXT is finished installing, let's run it!

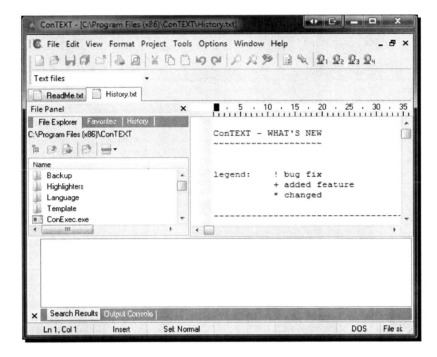

What just happened?

With ConTEXT installed we have a simple, but powerful tool to make our coding lives easier. We can drag files from the `Development\Src` folder directly onto ConTEXT to open them, or use the File Explorer pane on the left to browse through the directories. However, before we're ready to use it for programming, we need to configure a few things.

Time for action – Configuring ConTEXT

Now we'll set up ConTEXT to make reading UnrealScript easier, and use it to compile scripts with a single button press.

1. Click on **Options** in the top toolbar, then Environment Options. In the first tab, **General**, set **When started** to **Open last file/project**. That way any files that we're working on will automatically open the next time we use ConTEXT.

2. Make sure that **Remember editing positions** is checked. This makes the files we're working with open in the same position the next time we open ConTEXT. This saves a lot of time remembering where we left off.

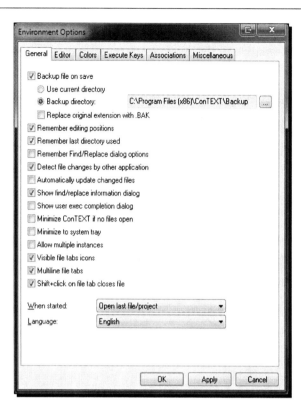

3. In the **Editor** tab, uncheck **Allow cursor after end of line**. This will keep our code clean by preventing unnecessary spaces all over the place.

4. Uncheck **Smart tabs**. Part of writing clean code is having it lined up, and **Smart tabs** tends to move the cursor to the beginning of words instead of a set number of spaces.

5. Make sure that **Line numbers** is checked. When we start compiling, any errors that show up will give us a line number which makes them easier to find and fix. This also helps when we search through our code as the searches will also give us line numbers.

6. Finally for this tab, set **Block indent** and **C/Java Block Indent** to **4**. This comes down to personal preference but having four spaces instead of two makes it easier to quickly scan through code and find what you're looking for.

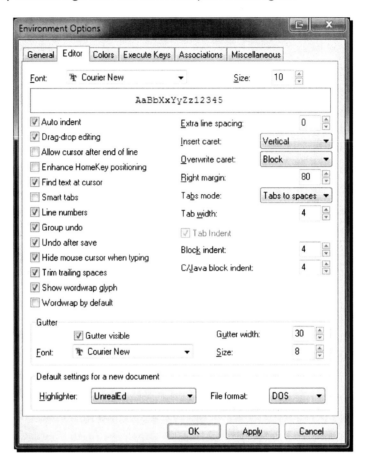

7. Now we're going to set up ConTEXT to compile code. On the **Execute Keys** tab, click on **Add**, then type .uc into the **Extensions** field that comes up.

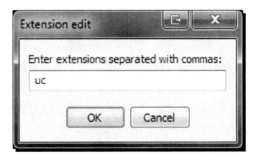

8. Once that's done four keys, *F9* through *F12*, will show up in the **User Exec Keys** window. Let's click on **F9** to make it convenient. Once clicked the options on the right become available.

9. For the **Execute** line, click on the button to the right of the field and navigate to our UDK installation's `Binaries\Win32` folder, and select `UDK.exe`. For **Start In**, copy the **Execute** line but leave out `UDK.exe`.

10. In the **Parameters** field, type "make" without the quote marks. This tells `UDK.exe` that we want to **compile code** instead of opening the game.

11. Change **Save to All Files Before Execution**. This makes sure that all of our changes get compiled if we're working in more than one file.

12. Check **Capture Console Output** and **Scroll Console to the Last Line**. This lets you see the compile progress at the bottom of ConTEXT, and any compiler errors will show up there as well.

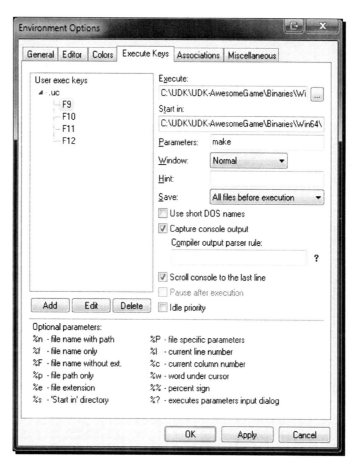

13. Now we're going to set up an UnrealScript highlighter. Highlighters make code easier to read by color coding keywords for a programming language. Since each language has different keywords, we need a highlighter specific to UnrealScript. Close ConTEXT and find the `UnrealScript.chl` file included with this book, or head to `http://wiki.beyondunreal.com/ConTEXT` and follow the instructions for the UnrealScript highlighter. Once you have your `.chl` file, place it in ConTEXT's Highlighters folder.

14. Open ConTEXT again. In the top toolbar there is a drop-down menu, and our UnrealScript highlighter should show up in the list now. Select it and we're done setting up ConTEXT!

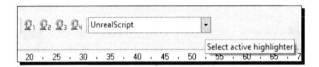

What just happened?

ConTEXT is now set up to compile our UnrealScript files; all we have to do is press *F9*. The first time we do this it will also recompile Epic's UnrealScript files, this is normal. The compiler may also show up in a separate window instead of at the bottom of ConTEXT, this is also normal.

```
R:\UDK\UDK-AwesomeGame\Binaries\Win64\UDK.exe
[0009.20] Analyzing...
[0009.39] Scripts successfully compiled - saving package 'R:\UDK\UDK-AwesomeGame
[0009.47] --------------------OnlineSubsystemPC - Release--------------------
[0009.47] Analyzing...
[0009.53] Scripts successfully compiled - saving package 'R:\UDK\UDK-AwesomeGame
[0009.59] --------------------OnlineSubsystemSteamworks - Release--------------
[0009.59] Analyzing...
[0009.71] Scripts successfully compiled - saving package 'R:\UDK\UDK-AwesomeGame
[0009.79] --------------------UDKBase - Release--------------------
[0009.80] Analyzing...
[0010.04] Scripts successfully compiled - saving package 'R:\UDK\UDK-AwesomeGame
[0010.19] --------------------UTEditor - Release--------------------
[0010.19] Analyzing...
[0010.21] Scripts successfully compiled - saving package 'R:\UDK\UDK-AwesomeGame
[0010.28] --------------------UTGame - Release--------------------
[0010.28] Analyzing...
[0017.68] Scripts successfully compiled - saving package 'R:\UDK\UDK-AwesomeGame
[0018.44] --------------------UTGameContent - Release--------------------
[0018.44] Analyzing...
[0018.91] Scripts successfully compiled - saving package 'R:\UDK\UDK-AwesomeGame
[0019.28]
[0019.28] Success - 0 error(s), 0 warning(s)
[0019.29]
Execution of commandlet took: 18.84 seconds
```

Starting to feel like a programmer yet? Now that we're able to compile code we just need an easy way to browse through Epic's UnrealScript source code, and to do that we're going to install another small program, UnCodeX.

UnCodeX

We can write our own code with ConTEXT, but now we need something to make sense of the `Development\Src` folder. There are over 2,000 files in there! This is where UnCodeX comes in. UnCodeX organizes the files into a class tree so that we can easily browse through them and see their relationship to each other. It also allows us to quickly search through the source code, which is where the line numbers in ConTEXT come in handy when we're searching through our own code.

Time for action – Installing UnCodeX

Find the installer included with this book, or head to `http://sourceforge.net/projects/uncodex` and download the latest version of UnCodeX.

1. Run the installer. It will ask you to accept the agreement. Read through it and accept.

2. Choose where you want to install the program. The location doesn't matter so choose a place convenient for you.

3. The default setting for the components is fine, so let's use a **Full Installation**. This will give us a graphical interface and some extra help files if we need them.

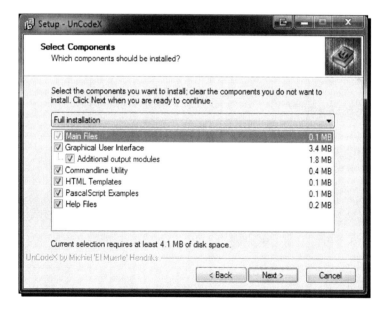

4. UnCodeX will ask whether you would like to add a Start Menu folder. Select your options and continue.

5. Select where you would like shortcuts placed and click on **Next**.

6. Review the installation settings and click on **Install**!

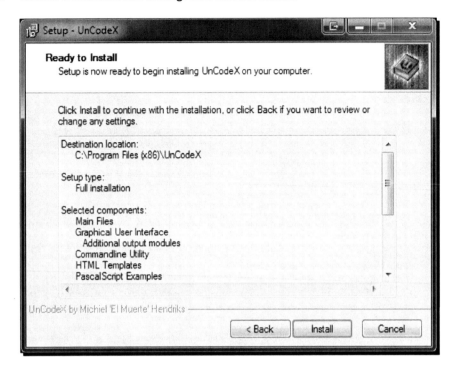

7. When the installation finishes, exit without running UnCodeX.

What just happened?

With UnCodeX installed we have a great way to browse through and search Epic's source code, as well as our own when we start creating it. UnCodeX is also very useful for debugging broken code. Now that it's installed, we need to set it up to work with our UDK directory.

Time for action – Configuring UnCodeX

UnCodeX needs to know where our source code is before we can search through it. Let's set up UnCodeX now.

1. Open UnCodeX. It will automatically detect that this is the first time we've run it and ask if we want to edit the settings. Choose **Yes**.

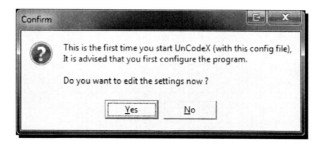

2. The UnCodeX window will pop up with the **Source Paths** tab open. This is where we will add our source code directory. Click on **Add**.

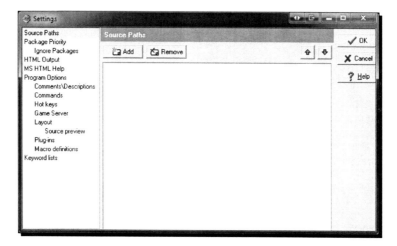

3. Navigate to our UDK installation's `Development\Src` folder and select it.

4. The directory will show up in the window below the **Add** button. That's all we need to do here, so click on **Ok**. UnCodeX will ask if we want to scan the directory. Click on **Yes**.

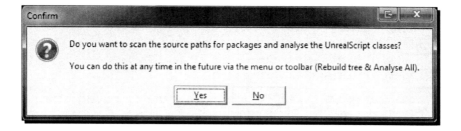

5. That's all we need to do! UnCodeX will scan and organize all of the files in the `Src` folder and display them.

What just happened?

UnCodeX is now configured and ready for us to use. Let's take a look at what it's showing us.

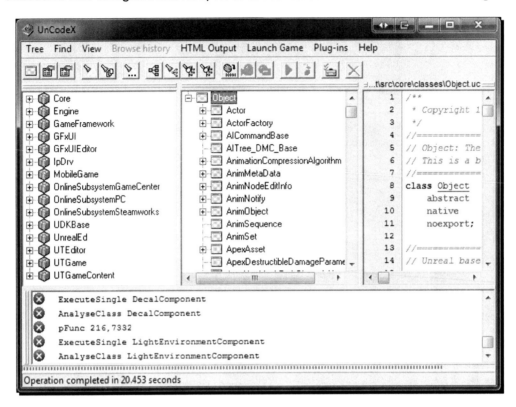

- The left window shows each package and the classes in them, which is basically like a folder in Windows. The middle window shows the class tree, which organizes all of the files to show their relationship to each other. The right window shows the contents of the file we have selected. You'll notice that some words are highlighted. Clicking on them takes you to the file or function with that name. This is convenient for finding out how things interact with each other in UnrealScipt.

- Changing projects in UnCodeX is easy. Simply go to **Tree**, click on **Settings**, and **Add** or **Remove** directories as needed. Later, go to **Tree** and click on **Rebuild and Analyse** or use the keyboard shortcut *Ctrl + B*. It will rebuild the package and class tree the same as our initial setup.

- We will be using ConTEXT and UnCodeX in this book, but there are other programs we could use when working with UnrealScript. Let's briefly discuss them, and then start setting up our own project!

nFringe

nFringe is an IDE (Integrated Development Environment) that allows programmers to work with UnrealScript in Microsoft Visual Studio 2005 or 2008. It includes a debugger that allows us to stop the game while it is running to see what is happening in script. There is a free version available for non-commercial work, but if you'd like to use it for commercial projects there is a licensing fee. If you have Visual Studio and would like to try it out, head over to `http://pixelminegames.com` and get the latest version!

WOTgreal

WOTgreal was originally created by Dean Harmon for the Unreal Engine based Wheel of Time game. The program works with all Unreal Engine games though, and is like ConTEXT and UnCodeX combined. There is a small licensing fee for the standard or professional version of the program. Head over to `http://www.wotgreal.com` to check it out!

For the most part the choice of program to use when working with UnrealScript comes down to personal taste. The Unreal Editor itself will detect changes in the source code and ask if you want to compile when it opens. Some programmers use Notepad to write and a DOS prompt to compile, using the same `make` command that ConTEXT uses. Try out the various programs to see what works best for you.

Setting up a project

Now we have the programs, we need to start working on our own project, but where do we start? Looking back at the UDK directory structure, there are really only three folders we would need to create. The first would be our own folder in the `UDKGame\Content` directory to contain any assets our project needs. Any artists or animators on the project would put their files in that directory. The second would be a folder in `UDKGame\Content\Maps` for our project's levels. This keeps everything organized and separated from Epic's assets so we know what's ours. For programmers though, there is only one folder we really need to worry about.

Time for action – Setting up AwesomeGame

The last folder we need for our own games is the one we'll be doing most of our work in as programmers. It's the place we'll be keeping all of our source code.

1. In the `Development\Src` folder, create a folder called `AwesomeGame`. Inside that, create a folder called `Classes`. This is where all of our source code will go.

When code is compiled, the final `.u` file's name is the same as the folder, so in our case when we compile a file called `AwesomeGame.u`, it will show up in the `UDKGame\Script` folder. Empty folders are ignored, so let's create our first class so we have something to work with. We'll create a simple class we can place in a level to have the game run the code that we write.

2. Create a text file and name it `AwesomeActor.uc` (make sure file extensions are shown in your folders so you don't accidentally name it `AwesomeActor.uc.txt`).

Open the file in ConTEXT and type the following code into it.

```
Class AwesomeActor extends Actor
    placeable;

defaultproperties
{
    Begin Object Class=SpriteComponent Name=Sprite
        Sprite=Texture2D'EditorResources.S_NavP'
    End Object
    Components.Add(Sprite)
}
```

Downloading the example code

You can download the example code files for all Packt books you have purchased from your account at http://www.PacktPub.com. If you purchased this book elsewhere, you can visit http://www.PacktPub.com/support and register to have the files e-mailed directly to you.

Make sure all of the punctuation is correct, particularly the opening and closing brackets after defaultproperties. The compiler is very particular about those brackets; they have to be on their own lines for anything inside them to work correctly.

The first line of our class defines the name of our object and its relationship to other objects in the game. The name of the file has to be the same as the name we type here; otherwise the compiler will give us an error. In this case both are AwesomeActor. The extends Actor part makes our AwesomeActor a child of Actor. In a way the class tree can be seen as a family tree, with classes inside the tree being children of the ones further up the chain.

The second line makes it so our class can be placed in the editor. Things like lights, path nodes, vehicles, all of these have placeable in their .uc file so the editor will let us place them. Other things like projectiles or explosions wouldn't be set as placeable since they are created while the game is running.

The section in the default properties creates a sprite so that we can see the actor in the editor and in the game.

Now, before we compile we need to let the game know about our AwesomeGame folder.

3. Open UDKGame\Config\DefaultEngine.ini and add our package AwesomeGame to the end of the EditPackages list.

```
[UnrealEd.EditorEngine]
+EditPackages=UTGame
+EditPackages=UTGameContent
+EditPackages=AwesomeGame
```

4. Save DefaultEngine.ini and close it.

What just happened?

Now we've created a folder for our code to go in called AwesomeGame, which is in the Development/Src folder. In it we've created our first code file, AwesomeActor.uc. We then edited DefaultEngine.ini so the game would recognize our new code package.

The folders in the Development\Src directory aren't automatically detected. The main reason for this is that in some cases we may not want or need the classes inside it. For instance, we may have different folders for a PC project and an iOS project. Both of them would be in the Development\Src folder, but the PC version of our game wouldn't need the iOS code and vice versa. Remember when we went over the directory structure and we talked about the Config folder? That folder contains all of the settings for our game. Let's take a look.

The file we added to, DefaultEngine, contains things like the game's resolution and texture detail. It also contains the EditPackages list we added to, which tells the game which packages to compile and in what order.

```
[UnrealEd.EditorEngine]
+EditPackages=UTGame
+EditPackages=UTGameContent
```

As you can see, the names in this list can also be found as folders in the `Development\Src` directory:

The list in `DefaultEngine.ini` seems kind of short though, doesn't it? Well, much like the class we created is a child of Actor, `DefaultEngine.ini` also has a parent. If we look at the top of DefaultEngine we can see this:

```
[Configuration]
BasedOn=..\UDKGame\Config\DefaultEngineUDK.ini
```

This `.ini` file is actually based on another one, its parent `DefaultEngineUDK.ini`. Let's close `DefaultEngine.ini` and take a look at `DefaultEngineUDK.ini`'s EditPackages list.

```
[UnrealEd.EditorEngine]
EditPackagesOutPath=..\..\UDKGame\Script
FRScriptOutputPath=..\..\UDKGame\ScriptFinalRelease
+EditPackages=UDKBase
+EditPackages=UTEditor
;ModEditPackages=MyMod
AutoSaveDir=..\..\UDKGame\Autosaves
InEditorGameURLOptions=?quickstart=1?numplay=1
```

That's a bit better. UDKBase and UTEditor are two more folders in our `Development\Src` directory. But there are a lot more folders there, so what's the deal? Let's see if we can go higher up the ini tree to find out. At the top of `DefaultEngineUDK.ini` we see that this file also has a parent:

```
[Configuration]
BasedOn=..\Engine\Config\BaseEngine.ini
```

Let's close `DefaultEngineUDK.ini` and take a look at `BaseEngine.ini`, which is in the `Engine\Config` directory.

```
EditPackages=Core
EditPackages=Engine
EditPackages=GFxUI
EditPackages=GameFramework
EditPackages=UnrealEd
EditPackages=GFxUIEditor
EditPackages=IpDrv
EditPackages=OnlineSubsystemPC
EditPackages=OnlineSubsystemGameSpy
EditPackages=OnlineSubsystemLive
EditPackages=OnlineSubsystemSteamworks
```

That's better! It looks like all of the folders are accounted for now, except for MyMod which is an empty example folder. And if we look at the top of `BaseEngine.ini` we can see that this is the end of the chain, BaseEngine doesn't have a parent.

So how does the game use these files? If you haven't run the game or compiled the code when we installed ConTEXT, run the game real quick and exit out of it at the main menu. The first time the game is run, it uses all of the Default and Base ini files to generate the ones the game actually uses in the `UDKGame\Config` directory:

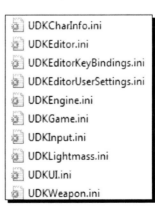

So the obvious question is why are there so many files? Well, let's take another look inside `BaseEngine.ini` to see why. About two-thirds of the way down the file we can see a list of system settings:

```
MotionBlur=True
MotionBlurPause=True
MotionBlurSkinning=1
DepthOfField=True
AmbientOcclusion=True
Bloom=True
bAllowLightShafts=True
Distortion=True
```

These settings control some of the visual effects in the game like motion blur and bloom. What would happen if we changed them? It would change the game's visual effects of course, but here's another question. While playing the game, in the **Settings** we're able to revert back to the defaults. If we changed the settings in these files, how would the game know what the default was? The game uses the Base and Default ini files to create the UDK ones, that way the player can change things like the resolution or keybinds, but the game will still have the known safe default settings available if it needs them. It may seem a bit complicated but it's pretty easy to work with. As the game's developer we would work in the Default and Base ini files to make the game work the way we want by default, and the player can change the settings if they want to.

Now that AwesomeGame has been added to the EditPackages list we'll be able to compile it. But why did we have to add AwesomeGame to the very end of the list? The way the compiler works is that it goes down the EditPackages list in order and looks for any changes to the files in the `Development\Src` directory. If any `.uc` files are changed it recompiles that package. It's also important to know that any package that our classes are dependent on has to be compiled before ours. As an example, let's take a look at `DefaultEngine.ini` again. One of the EditPackages listed is `UTGameContent`. In the `UTGameContent` folder we can see a class called `UTJumpBoots`. If we wanted to make our own jump boot class with `UTJumpBoots` as its parent, we have to make sure that `UTGameContent` is compiled before our package, otherwise the compiler won't know about that class yet and will give us an error saying our class' parent doesn't exist.

Have a go hero – More editing of ini files

Among the settings in `DefaultGame.ini` are the default time limits for maps. See if you can find and change it from 20 minutes to 15 minutes.

That takes care of our initial project setup! Now that everything is in place, we can start compiling and testing some code. Let's get to it!

Compiling and testing

We'll be using ConTEXT to compile the code we wrote, and to test it we'll be using the Unreal Editor. Don't worry if you have no knowledge of the editor, we don't need to be experts to be able to use it to test our code.

Time for action – Compiling and testing AwesomeActor

1. Open ConText and press *F9*, which we set up earlier to compile our code. If we typed everything in correctly, it should give us a **Success** message at the end!

   If there are any warnings or errors, look over the code again to make sure everything is spelled correctly and the punctuation is correct. The error message itself should provide a clue as to where to look. It will also give you a line number where the error happened.

2. Now that our code is compiled, let's add our AwesomeActor to a level. If you don't have an editor shortcut or can't find it in your **Start** menu, it's easy to make one. Go into UDK-AwesomeGame\Binaries\Win32 and right-click on UDK.exe. Click on **Send To** and then **Desktop (create shortcut)**. Right-click on the shortcut it created and click on **Properties**. In the **Target** field, add **editor** to the end without quotes:

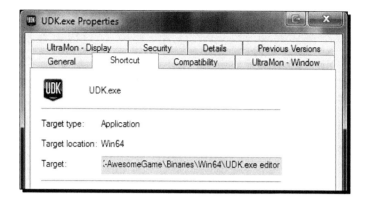

3. Now let's open the editor!

4. Close the **Welcome Screen** and **Content Browser**, and let's take a look at the editor real quick. To try out our code we're going to need a test map, so go to **File**, and click on **Open**, and select `ExampleMap.udk` to open it.

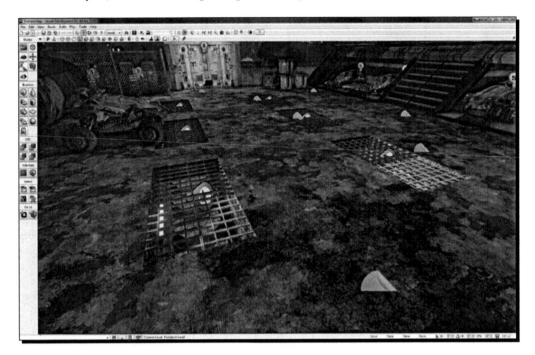

One thing we'll notice immediately is that there seems to be a lot of strange objects floating around the level. These are Actor classes that are normally invisible in game, but have sprites that can be seen in the editor. Remember the sprite we added to the default properties of our AwesomeActor? This is where it gets used.

Now let's add our AwesomeActor.

5. Click on the **Content Browser** button to open it up again.

6. The **Content Browser** will show the tab with game assets like textures and meshes at first, but we need to take a look in the **Actor Classes**, so select that tab in the top.

7. This looks a lot different than the class tree in UnCodeX though. Classes can be put into **Categories** so they're more organized in the editor, but right now we just need to see a normal class tree, so uncheck **Show Categories**.

There's our AwesomeActor class!

8. Select **AwesomeActor** and close the **Content Browser**. In the 3D viewport, right-click on the floor and near the bottom click on **Add AwesomeActor Here**.

There's the AwesomeActor, showing the sprite that we put in the default properties of our class! Normally these sprites won't show up in the game, but we didn't put any restrictions on the one in our default properties so we'll be able to see it for now.

9. Click on the **Play** button to run the game in a new window.

10. After you're done checking out the AwesomeActor in the level, close the game window.

11. Now let's save the map so we can keep using it to test. We don't want to save over `ExampleMap` so let's save it in our own folder. Create a new folder in the `Content\Maps` directory called `AwesomeGame`, and in the editor save the map as `AwesomeMap.udk` inside that folder.

12. Close the editor.

So we have our class set up, but is there anything more we can do with it? Usually the first task when learning a new programming language is to make a Hello World program, so let's do that now. Open up our `AwesomeActor.uc` file in ConTEXT. Let's add some more code.

The first thing we'll do while we're here is make it so our actor doesn't show up in the game but still shows in the editor. We can do this with a simple one line addition to our default properties.

13. Add a new line in the default properties and write the following:

```
Begin Object Class=SpriteComponent Name=Sprite
    Sprite=Texture2D'EditorResources.S_NavP'
HiddenGame=True
End Object
Components.Add(Sprite)
```

14. Now let's add our Hello World. This will go before the default properties section.

```
function PostBeginPlay()
{
    `log("Hello World! ==========");
}
```

`PostBeginPlay` is a function that is run when an Actor is first created, so it's a good place for our Hello World. The log line we put inside that function will output to a text file so we can see that our class is running correctly. So now, our class should look like this:

```
class AwesomeActor extends Actor
    placeable;

function PostBeginPlay()
{
    `log("Hello World! ==========");
}

defaultproperties
{
    Begin Object Class=SpriteComponent Name=Sprite
        Sprite=Texture2D'EditorResources.S_NavP'
        HiddenGame=True
    End Object
    Components.Add(Sprite)
}
```

Before we compile, make sure the editor is closed. The compiler can't delete the old
.u file if it's still in use by the editor and we'll get an error.

15. With the editor closed, compile the code by hitting *F9* in ConTEXT.

16. Now open the editor, and open AwesomeMap.udk.

We don't need to do anything to our AwesomeActor, changes we make to our
compiled classes automatically affect any of the actors we've placed in our levels.

17. Run the game by clicking on the **Play** button in the top as before. We'll see that our
AwesomeActor is invisible now, so the line we added to the default properties is
working. But where's our Hello World?

18. Close the game window and exit the editor. Go into the UDKGame\Logs folder and
take a look at the files in there.

There should be Launch.log, Launch2.log, and any number of backups
depending on how many times the game, editor or compiler has run. When they
run, they create a backup of the existing Launch.log file and start a new one.
Whenever more than one is run at the same time, as in the case of us running a
game window from the editor, it creates a second file called Launch2.log and so
on. So, since we were testing our code from a game window in the editor, let's take
a look at Launch2.log.

19. Open Launch2.log in the UDKGame\Logs folder.

```
[0008.05] Log: Game class is 'UTGame'
[0008.24] Log: Primary PhysX scene will be in software.
[0008.24] Log: Creating Primary PhysX Scene.
[0008.26] Log: Bringing World UEDPCAwesomeMap.TheWorld up for
play (0) at 2011.05.19-15.15.52
[0008.28] ScriptLog: Hello World! =========
[0008.28] Log: Bringing up level for play took: 0.193269
```

Towards the end of the file we can see our Hello World shows up!

Now you can see why we added a bunch of equal signs in our code. It's pretty easy for our
logs to get buried with everything else that's going on, so using some kind of unique marker
like we did makes them easier to find.

A quick note about comments

One of a programmer's essential tools are comments. They serve two purposes. First, since they're ignored by the compiler, they can be used to write notes to yourself in your code. Doing this lets you remember what your code does, which can be helpful when you come back to it months later. If you're working with other programmers, writing comments is good programming practice so others can see what your code does.

Second, comments are a quick way to remove sections of your code without permanently deleting it or relying on undo, since you may have to make changes over several days or weeks and repeatedly close and open the files.

There are two ways to write comments. The first way is to write to slash marks, which comments out a line or part of a line:

```
// This entire line is a comment.
SomeCode(); // This is a comment at the end of a line.
4 + 5; // + 6; We've commented out "+ 6;" here to test something.
```

The second way to write comments is to use a slash and asterisk. This comments out entire sections of code.

```
/* This line is commented out.
This line is commented out as well.
The slash and asterisk at the end of this line end the comment. */
```

Note that these cannot be nested as it will break the code. For example, this works:

```
/* Commenting out some code.
// Having a double slash comment inside here is fine.
Ending the comment.  */
```

While this would not work:

```
/* A comment.
/* A comment inside a comment like this would not work. */
Ending the comment. */
```

As you're working on your own projects, don't forget to comment your code! It makes it easier to read and understand.

Pop quiz – Files and directories

1. Which folder in the `UDKGame` directory does a game's level go in?

   a. `Build`

   b. `Content`

   c. `Localization`

   d. `Src`

2. What file is the highest in the chain of `DefaultEngine.ini`?

   a. `DefaultEngineUDK.ini`

   b. `BaseEngine.ini`

   c. `UDKEngine.ini`

3. What does `placeable` do in a class file?

Summary

We learned a lot in this chapter about how the UDK works and how to set up our own game project.

Specifically, we covered:

- The UDK directories and what goes into each folder. We know which folders we'll be working in as programmers as well as the ones any artists or designers on the project would be using.

- Which programs we can use to work with UnrealScript. We know that there are two aspects to programming, writing the code and being able to easily browse the existing source code.

- How to set up our own project and compile and test code that we've written. We know how to use UnrealEd and the Logs folder to help us test and make sure our code is running correctly.

Now that we've learned about the UDK, we're ready to start learning more about the UnrealScript language by taking a look at variables and operators—which is the topic of the next chapter.

2
Storing and Manipulating Data

Variables are a Programmer's Best Friend

If someone asked if it were raining, or which bag had more apples in it, it would be a pretty simple conversation. But how do you have that same conversation with a computer? In this chapter we're going to take a look at how to use variables and flow control to get our code to react to what's going on in the game.

In this chapter we will:

- ◆ Discuss different types of variables including booleans, structs, enums, and arrays.
- ◆ Learn how to set default properties for variables and how to let level designers change them.
- ◆ Use operators on variables to add, subtract, and more.
- ◆ Learn about using flow control to do different things under different circumstances.

Let's get started by learning about the different types of variables!

Variables and arrays

There are many different types of variables. Choosing which one we want to use depends on what we want to do with it. Knowing whether it's raining or not (true/false) is different from say, knowing a character's name ("Big McLargeHuge"). Let's take a look at some of the variables we can use and what they're used for.

Booleans

Quick, is it raining? Boolean variables, or bool for short, are your basic true/false questions. They're used for everything from asking if the player is driving a vehicle, to if the game has started, to whether or not an object can collide with anything.

It's standard for boolean variables' names to start with a lower case "b". This isn't required, but it's good to follow the guidelines to keep code consistent and easily readable.

Let's take a look at how we can use booleans in our code by adding to our AwesomeActor class.

Time for action – Using booleans

The first thing we need to do is tell the game about our variable. This is called declaration. Variables need to be declared before they can be used. Our declaration tells the game what type of variable it is as well as its name.

We'll continue with our "is it raining?" scenario for this experiment. In a game we might want to use this variable to check whether we should spawn rain effects or make changes to the lights, and so on.

Variable declaration in UnrealScript happens after the class declaration line, and before any functions. Let's add a variable to AwesomeActor.uc to see if it's raining or not.

1. Open up our AwesomeActor.uc class in ConTEXT and add this line after our class declaration:

    ```
    var bool bIsItRaining;
    ```

    The var tells the game that we're declaring a variable. After that, is the variable type, in this case bool for boolean. After that, we tell the game our variable's name, bIsItRaining. Spaces can't be used in variable names, but underscore characters (_) are allowed. The semicolon finishes the line. It's important never to forget the semicolon at the end of the line. Without it the compiler will think any lines after it are part of this line and will look at us confused, as well as give us an error.

2. Now let's add a log to our PostBeginPlay function to see our variable in action. Change the PostBeginPlay function to this (don't forget the tilde):

    ```
    function PostBeginPlay()
    {
        'log("Is it raining?" @ bIsItRaining);
    }
    ```

This will output our text as well as tell us the value of `bIsItRaining`. The `@` operator combines the text with the value of the variable into one sentence which the log uses. This is known as concatenation and will be discussed later in the chapter.

Our `AwesomeActor` class should look like this now:

```
class AwesomeActor extends Actor
    placeable;

var bool bIsItRaining;

function PostBeginPlay()
{
    'log("Is it raining?" @ bIsItRaining);
}

defaultproperties
{
    Begin Object Class=SpriteComponent Name=Sprite
        Sprite=Texture2D'EditorResources.S_NavP'
        HiddenGame=True
    End Object
    Components.Add(Sprite)
}
```

3. Now let's compile it. If we get any errors go back and make sure everything is spelled correctly and that we haven't missed any semicolons at the end of lines.

   Open the editor and open our test map with the AwesomeActor placed, and run the game. Nothing obvious will happen, but let's close the game and see what our `Launch2.log` file looks like:

   ```
   [0008.59] ScriptLog: Is it raining? False
   ```

   Our variable is working! As we can see, even without doing anything to it our variable has a default value. When created, booleans automatically start out false. This is a good thing to know when creating variables, especially booleans. It's best to avoid words like **Not** or **No** in boolean names to avoid having double negatives. For example, if we had a `bool` named `bIsNotActive`, and it was False, would the object be active or not? In this case it would be active, but to avoid confusion it would be better to have a variable named `bIsActive` so it would be easier to tell what it means when it's true or false.

4. Now that we have our bool, how do we change it? Let's add a line to our `PostBeginPlay` function.

```
bIsItRaining = true;
```

Now our function should look like this:

```
function PostBeginPlay()
{
    bIsItRaining = true;
    'log("Is it raining?" @ bIsItRaining);
}
```

5. Compile and run the game again, and we should see the change in the log:

```
[0007.68] ScriptLog: Is it raining? True
```

There we go!

6. We can also change it back just as easily. Let's add a line after our log to change it to false, and then add another log to see the change.

```
bIsItRaining = false;
'log("Is it raining?" @ bIsItRaining);
```

Now our PostBeginPlay function should look like this:

```
function PostBeginPlay()
{
    bIsItRaining = true;
    'log("Is it raining?" @ bIsItRaining);
    bIsItRaining = false;
    'log("Is it raining?" @ bIsItRaining);
}
```

7. Let's compile and test out the changes!

```
[0007.65] ScriptLog: Is it raining? True
[0007.65] ScriptLog: Is it raining? False
```

What just happened?

There isn't much to use in booleans; they're the simplest type of variable in UnrealScript. Don't underestimate them though, they may be simple, but a lot of the variables we'll be working with will be bools. Anything where we only need a simple true/false answer will fall under this category.

Integers and floats

Next in our tour of UnrealScript variables are integers and floats. Both store numbers, but the difference is that integers (int for short) store whole numbers without a decimal point like 12, while floats can store fractions of numbers, like 12.3. Let's take a look at how to use them.

Time for action – Using integers

Let's make an Int.

1. Declaring an integer is similar to what we did with bools, so let's replace our bool declaration line with this:

```
var int NumberOfKittens;
```

We can see that we have the same `var` text that declares our variable, and then we tell the game that our variable is an `int`. Finally, we set the name of our `int` to `NumberOfKittens`.

The name of the variable should give a hint as to the difference between ints and floats, and why we need ints to begin with instead of using floats for everything. Since we don't want to hurt any defenseless kittens we should only be using whole numbers to represent the number of them. We don't want to have half of a kitten.

2. As with our bool variable ints have a default value, in this case zero. We can check this by changing our `PostBeginPlay` function:

```
function PostBeginPlay()
{
    'log("Number of kittens:" @ NumberOfKittens);
}
```

Now our `AwesomeActor.uc` class should look like this:

```
class AwesomeActor extends Actor
    placeable;

var int NumberOfKittens;

function PostBeginPlay()
{
    'log("Number of kittens:" @ NumberOfKittens);
}

defaultproperties
{
```

```
        Begin Object Class=SpriteComponent Name=Sprite
            Sprite=Texture2D'EditorResources.S_NavP'
            HiddenGame=True
        End Object
        Components.Add(Sprite)
    }
```

3. Let's compile and run the game to test it out!

```
[0007.63] ScriptLog: Number of kittens: 0
```

Notice there is no decimal place after the 0; this is what makes an int an int. We use this type of variable for things that wouldn't have fractions, like the number of kills a player has made in deathmatch or the number of people in a vehicle.

4. Now let's see what happens when we change the variable. At the beginning of our PostBeginPlay function add this:

```
NumberOfKittens = 5;
```

Now the function should look like this:

```
function PostBeginPlay()
{
    NumberOfKittens = 5;
    'log("Number of kittens:" @ NumberOfKittens);
}
```

5. Let's compile and test!

```
[0008.07] ScriptLog: Number of kittens: 5
```

6. What would happen if we tried to add a fraction to our int? Only one way to find out! Change the line to this and compile:

```
NumberOfKittens = 5.7;
```

7. Well, it compiles, so the engine obviously doesn't care about that .7 of a kitten, but what actually happens? Run the game and then check the log to find out.

```
[0007.99] ScriptLog: Number of kittens: 5
```

Interesting! We can see that not only did it ignore the fraction, but also truncated it instead of trying to round it up to 6. This is important behavior to remember about ints. Ints will also act this way when we use math on them.

8. Change the line to this:

```
NumberOfKittens = 10 / 3;
```

This should end up as 3.333333, but with the truncation, we can see that it ignores the fraction.

```
[0007.72] ScriptLog: Number of kittens: 3
```

What just happened?

Ints are one of the ways the game stores numbers, and we use it when we don't need to worry about fractions. Usually we use them when we're just trying to count something and not trying to perform complex math with them. For that, we would use floats. Let's take a look at those now.

Time for action – Using floats

Floats are used when we need something that doesn't have nice neat values, like how far away something is or how accurate a weapon is. They're declared the same way as our bools and ints, so let's make one now.

1. Replace our int declaration with this:

```
var float DistanceToGo;
```

2. Floats have a default value of 0.0. Let's change our `PostBeginPlay` function to check this.

```
function PostBeginPlay()
{
    'log("Distance to go:" @ DistanceToGo);
}
```

3. Compile and test, and our log should look like this:

```
[0007.61] ScriptLog: Distance to go: 0.0000
```

4. We can see that unlike ints, floats will log with a decimal place. Let's see if we can change the value. Add this line to the beginning of our `PostBeginPlay` function:

```
DistanceToGo = 0.123;
```

5. Compile and test, and we should see the fraction show up in the log:

```
[0007.68] ScriptLog: Distance to go: 0.123
```

6. Let's see what happens when we use the same line we did for our int. Change the line to this:

```
DistanceToGo = 10 / 3;
```

7. Compile and test, and our log should look like this:

```
[0007.68] ScriptLog: Distance to go: 3.3333
```

What just happened?

Floats are used when we need precision in our numbers, such as calculating the distance between two points or the time remaining in a game. We also use them for complex math since they can have fractions.

Strings

No, these are not strings for our kittens to play with. In programming, strings store a series of characters, be it letters, numbers, symbols, or a combination of them. We can use them to hold the name of our character, messages to display on the screen, or the name of the weapon we're holding. Let's take a look at how to use them.

Time for action – Using strings

Well, by now we know the drill, so let's declare a string!

1. Change our float declaration to this:

```
var string DeathMessage;
```

2. By default, strings are empty. We can see this... or not see this, rather, by changing our `PostBeginPlay` function:

```
function PostBeginPlay()
{
    'log("Death message:" @ DeathMessage);
}
```

3. Compile and test to see that nothing shows up:

```
[0007.74] ScriptLog: Death message:
```

Well that doesn't help much. Let's change that.

4. Add this line to our PostBeginPlay function:

```
DeathMessage = "Tom Stewart killed me!";
```

Now it looks like this:

```
function PostBeginPlay()
{
    DeathMessage = "Tom Stewart killed me!";
    'log("Death message:" @ DeathMessage);
}
```

5. Compile and run the code, and check the log.

```
[0007.67] ScriptLog: Death message: Tom Stewart killed me!
```

What just happened?

There's not much to strings either, and they're not used nearly as much as other types of variables. They're mostly used for things that need to be made readable to the player like character or weapon names, or messages on the HUD. A few are used for other things like telling the game which level to load.

Enums

Enumerations (enums for short) are an odd variable type. They function as a list of possible values, and each value can be represented by its name or number. This allows them to be put in an order and compared with other values much like integers. As an example, if we had an enum called Altitude, we might write it like this:

```
enum EAltitude
{
    ALT_Underground,
    ALT_Surface,
    ALT_Sky,
    ALT_Space,
};
```

As we can see from the order these are in, ALT_Space would be "greater than" ALT_Surface if compared to it. Sometimes we might use enums where we don't care about the order. An example of this would be the EMoveDir enum from Actor.uc:

```
enum EMoveDir
{
    MD_Stationary,
    MD_Forward,
    MD_Backward,
```

```
        MD_Left,
        MD_Right,
        MD_Up,
        MD_Down
    };
```

This enum describes the directions an actor can be moving, but in this case we only care that the variable can only have one value. The order of the elements doesn't matter in this case.

Enum values can also be used as bytes. If we looked at our example enum, this means that they would have the following values:

```
    ALT_Underground = 0
    ALT_Surface = 1
    ALT_Sky = 2
    ALT_Space = 3
```

Now the order makes sense, and we know why we can compare them to each other like integers. But then why not just use ints instead of enums to represent the values? For readability, mostly. Would you rather see that an actor's Altitude variable has been set to ALT_Sky, or 2?

Time for action – Using enums

That's all well and good, but how do we use them? Let's set one up in our AwesomeActor class.

1. Add the enum below our class line.

```
enum EAltitude
{
    ALT_Underground,
    ALT_Surface,
    ALT_Sky,
    ALT_Space,
};
```

The E isn't necessary, but it helps to follow standard guidelines to make things easier to read.

2. Now we need to declare a variable as that enum type. This is similar to declaring other variables.

```
var EAltitude Altitude;
```

3. Now we have a variable, `Altitude`, that's been declared as the enum type `EAltitude`. Enums default to the first value in the list, so in this case it would be `ALT_Underground`. Let's see if we can change that in our `PostBeginPlay` function.

```
function PostBeginPlay()
{
    Altitude = ALT_Sky;
    'log("Altitude:" @ Altitude);
}
```

Now our class should look like this:

```
class AwesomeActor extends Actor
    placeable;

enum EAltitude
{
    ALT_Underground,
    ALT_Surface,
    ALT_Sky,
    ALT_Space,
};

var EAltitude Altitude;

function PostBeginPlay()
{
    Altitude = ALT_Sky;
    'log("Altitude:" @ Altitude);
}

defaultproperties
{
    Begin Object Class=SpriteComponent Name=Sprite
        Sprite=Texture2D'EditorResources.S_NavP'
        HiddenGame=True
    End Object
    Components.Add(Sprite)
}
```

4. Compile and test, and we'll see the enum show up in the log:

```
[0007.69] ScriptLog: Altitude: ALT_Sky
```

5. To see how they compare to each other, let's add another log after our first one:

```
'log("Is ALT_Sky greater than ALT_Surface?");
'log(EAltitude.ALT_Sky > EAltitude.ALT_Surface);
```

6. Doing a comparison like this will come back with a boolean true or false for the answer, which we'll see in the log when we compile and test:

```
[0007.71] ScriptLog: Altitude: ALT_Sky
[0007.71] ScriptLog: Is ALT_Sky greater than ALT_Surface?
[0007.71] ScriptLog: True
```

There we go!

What just happened?

Enums aren't normally something you'd start using when you're new to UnrealScript, but knowing how they work can definitely save time and jumbled code later on. If you were making a card game for example, representing the four different suits as an enum would make it a lot easier to read than if you had numbers representing them. They're not used often, but when they are they're a great help.

Arrays

Now let's take a look at some more complicated uses of variables. Let's say we have several baskets full of kittens, and we wanted to keep track of how many were in each basket. We could make a variable for each basket like this:

```
var int Basket1;
var int Basket2;
var int Basket3;
```

But that would get really messy if we had dozens to keep track of. How about if we put them all on one line like this?

```
var int Basket1, Basket2, Basket3;
```

UnrealScript lets us put more than one variable declaration on one line like that, as long as they're the same type. It saves space and keeps things organized. But in this case we'd run into the same problem if we had dozens of baskets. For something like this, we'd need to use an array.

Time for action – Using arrays

Arrays act as a collection of variables, and when we declare one you'll see why.

1. Change our variable declaration line to this:

```
var int Baskets[4];
```

This will create an array of four baskets. That's easy enough, but how do we change their values?

2. In our `PostBeginPlay` function, add these lines:

```
Baskets[0] = 2;
Baskets[1] = 13;
Baskets[2] = 4;
Baskets[3] = 1;
```

One important thing to remember about arrays is that they start at 0. Even though we have 4 elements in our array, since it starts at 0 it only goes up to 3. If we tried to add a line like this to our function:

```
Baskets[4] = 7;
```

We would get an error.

3. Let's go ahead and add the line to see what happens. It will compile just fine, but when we test it in the game we will see the error in the log file:

```
[0007.53] ScriptWarning: Accessed array 'AwesomeActor_0.Baskets'
out of bounds (4/4)
    AwesomeActor UEDPCAwesomeMap.TheWorld:PersistentLevel.
AwesomeActor_0
    Function AwesomeGame.AwesomeActor:PostBeginPlay:0046
```

The out of bounds error lets us know that we tried to access an element of the array that doesn't exist. It takes a bit of getting used to; just remember that the first element of our array will always be 0.

4. Let's take that line out of our function, and change the log line to look like this:

```
'log("Baskets:" @ Baskets[0] @ Baskets[1] @ Baskets[2] @
Baskets[3]);
```

Now our `PostBeginPlay` function should look like this:

```
function PostBeginPlay()
{
    Baskets[0] = 2;
    Baskets[1] = 13;
    Baskets[2] = 4;
```

```
    Baskets[3] = 1;
    'log("Baskets:" @ Baskets[0] @ Baskets[1] @ Baskets[2] @
Baskets[3]);
}
```

5. Let's compile and test. In our log file we should see this:

```
[0007.53] ScriptLog: Baskets: 2 13 4 1
```

Success!

6. Now for something a bit more complicated. We can also access the elements of our array with an int. Let's see if we can do that. Let's declare an int:

```
var int TestNumber;
```

7. Then set it at the beginning of PostBeginPlay:

```
TestNumber = 2;
```

8. Now let's access the array with it and log the result.

```
'log("Test Basket:" @ Baskets[TestNumber]);
```

So now our class should look like this:

```
class AwesomeActor extends Actor
    placeable;

var int Baskets[4];
var int TestNumber;

function PostBeginPlay()
{
    TestNumber = 2;

    Baskets[0] = 2;
    Baskets[1] = 13;
    Baskets[2] = 4;
    Baskets[3] = 1;

    'log("Test Basket:" @ Baskets[TestNumber]);
}

defaultproperties
{
    Begin Object Class=SpriteComponent Name=Sprite
```

```
         Sprite=Texture2D'EditorResources.S_NavP'
         HiddenGame=True
    End Object
    Components.Add(Sprite)
}
```

9. Now compile and test, then look at the log.

```
[0007.99] ScriptLog: Test Basket: 4
```

We can see that it logged the value of Basket[2], which is 4.

What just happened?

We can start to see how powerful arrays can be. We can make an array out of any variable type except for booleans, but there are ways around that. If we used an array of ints and used 0 for false and 1 for true, it could act as a boolean array.

Now we know how to make an array with a specific number of elements, but what if we don't know the number of baskets, or want to change how many baskets there are while the game is running? In that case we'll want to use a dynamic array.

Dynamic arrays

Dynamic arrays sound complicated, but they're pretty easy to work with. They're simply an array that we can change the size of when we need to. Let's take a look at how they're used.

Time for action – Using dynamic arrays

Dynamic arrays are declared a bit differently than static arrays. Let's declare one now.

1. Change our variable declaration line to this:

```
var array<int> Baskets;
```

As we can see, with dynamic arrays we don't put a number anywhere in it; it can be whatever size we need it to be. By default they're completely empty, so if we tried to log any of its values we would get an out of bounds warning similar to our experiment with static arrays.

2. We can, however, assign values any time we want, so let's add this line to our PostBeginPlay function:

```
Baskets[3] = 9;
```

3. Then log the value like this:

```
'log("Baskets:" @ Baskets[3]);
```

Now our function should look like this:

```
function PostBeginPlay()
{
    Baskets[3] = 9;

    'log("Baskets:" @ Baskets[3]);
}
```

4. Compile and test, and we can see that the value logs fine, and we didn't get any warnings.

```
[0007.82] ScriptLog: Baskets: 9
```

When we assign a value, the size of the array automatically changes to that value. As with before, if we tried to access `Baskets[4]` we would get an out of bounds warning.

Now that we have our dynamic array, there are a few things we need to know about so we can use them properly. The first thing that would be nice to know is the size of the array. Just how many baskets are there anyway? To find out we can use the length of the array.

5. Change our log line to look like this:

```
'log("Basket array length:" @ Baskets.length);
```

Now our function looks like this:

```
function PostBeginPlay()
{
    Baskets[3] = 9;

    'log("Basket array length:" @ Baskets.length);
}
```

6. Compile and test, and check the log file.

```
[0007.67] ScriptLog: Basket array length: 4
```

Remember that arrays start out at 0, so when we assigned a value to Basket[3] it's the fourth element in the array.

Now that we know the length of the array, we can use it to add values to the end of it. In our example, the length of the array is 4, with `Baskets[3]` being the last one. If we wanted to add another one to the array, it would be `Baskets[4]`. Since 4 is the length of our array right now, we would simply put that in the index.

7. Let's add these three lines to the end of our function:

```
Baskets[Baskets.length] = 23;
'log("Basket array length:" @ Baskets.length);
'log("Last basket:" @ Baskets[Baskets.length - 1]);
```

Our function should look like this now:

```
function PostBeginPlay()
{
    Baskets[3] = 9;
    'log("Basket array length:" @ Baskets.length);


    Baskets[Baskets.length] = 23;
    'log("Basket array length:" @ Baskets.length);
    'log("Last basket:" @ Baskets[Baskets.length - 1]);
}
```

The value 23 will now be assigned to the next element in the array, which now expands to five elements.

Remember that the length is one higher than the last index, so to see what the last value is we need to subtract 1 from the array length. In this case the length would be 5, so to check the last one, Basket[4], we need to use 5-1.

8. Compile and test, then check the log.

```
[0008.46] ScriptLog: Basket array length: 4
[0008.46] ScriptLog: Basket array length: 5
[0008.46] ScriptLog: Last basket: 23
```

And it works! The first line in our function changes the array length to 4 by giving Basket[3] a value of 9. Next we assign a value of 23 to `Baskets.length`, which is 4, making Baskets[4] = 23. This also increases the size of the array to 5 which is shown in the log.

What just happened?

Dynamic arrays are very useful when we don't know how many elements we need ahead of time, or the number of elements in the array needs to change during gameplay. As an example, the player's weapons could be held in an array of Actor classes, since they may pick up or lose some during the game.

Have a go hero – Copy an array

Let's say we had an array and `PostBeginPlay` set up like this:

```
var int TestArray[3];
var array<int> CopyArray;

function PostBeginPlay()
{
    TestArray[0] = 9;
    TestArray[1] = 5;
    TestArray[2] = 6;
}
```

Without using numbers, how would we copy the `TestArray` values into the `CopyArray`? Think about our experiment on adding to the end of arrays for hints, and when you are ready; check the following code for the answer.

```
var int TestArray[3];
var array<int> CopyArray;

function PostBeginPlay()
{
    TestArray[0] = 9;
    TestArray[1] = 5;
    TestArray[2] = 6;

    CopyArray[CopyArray.length] = TestArray[CopyArray.length - 1];
    CopyArray[CopyArray.length] = TestArray[CopyArray.length - 1];
    CopyArray[CopyArray.length] = TestArray[CopyArray.length - 1];
}
```

If you tried `TestArray[CopyArray.length]` at first, you probably noticed an out of bounds error in the log. Why is that? Well, an important thing to know about dynamic arrays is that assigning a value to the end of the array increases the size of the array first, before assigning the value. By the time the code reaches the right-hand side of the equals sign, the array's length has already increased by 1.

Structs

The best way to describe a struct would be to call it a variable holding a bunch of other variables. It can be called a collection of variables. As an example, let's take a look at one from `Object.uc`:

```
struct Cylinder
{
    var float Radius, Height;
};
```

As we can see, this struct contains two floats, Radius, and Height. Structs themselves can be used as variables, like this:

```
var Cylinder MyCylinder;
```

To change variables inside a struct, we would use a period in between the struct name and the variable name like this:

```
MyCylinder.Radius = 50;
```

Structs can contain variables, arrays, and even other structs. Let's take a closer look and make our own struct to learn more about them.

Time for action – Using structs

Going back to our basket of kittens example, what if there were other things in the basket besides kittens? How would we represent them?

1. Let's create a struct at the top of our AwesomeActor class and put a few things in it.

    ```
    struct Basket
    {
        var string BasketColor;
        var int NumberOfKittens, BallsOfString;
        var float BasketSize;
    };
    ```

    Now we have two types of items in the basket as well as some variables to describe the basket itself.

2. Now we need a variable of that struct so we can use it:

    ```
    var Basket MyBasket;
    ```

3. Now we can change the values in our PostBeginPlay function.

    ```
    function PostBeginPlay()
    {
        MyBasket.NumberOfKittens = 4;
        MyBasket.BasketColor = "Yellow";
        MyBasket.BasketSize = 12.0;
        MyBasket.BallsOfString = 2;
    }
    ```

    That seems easy enough to handle. Let's try something a bit more complex.

4. I heard you like structs, so we'll Inception-ize it by adding a struct inside a struct.

```
struct SmallBox
{
    var int Chocolates;
    var int Cookies;
};
```

5. Now let's put a box inside our basket struct.

```
struct Basket
{
    var SmallBox TheBox;
    var string BasketColor;
    var int NumberOfKittens, BallsOfString;
    var float BasketSize;
};
```

Now our class should look like this:

```
class AwesomeActor extends Actor
    placeable;

struct SmallBox
{
    var int Chocolates;
    var int Cookies;
};

struct Basket
{
    var SmallBox TheBox;
    var string BasketColor;
    var int NumberOfKittens, BallsOfString;
    var float BasketSize;
};

var Basket MyBasket;

function PostBeginPlay()
{
    MyBasket.NumberOfKittens = 4;
    MyBasket.BasketColor = "Yellow";
    MyBasket.BasketSize = 12.0;
    MyBasket.BallsOfString = 2;
}

defaultproperties
{
    Begin Object Class=SpriteComponent Name=Sprite
```

```
        Sprite=Texture2D'EditorResources.S_NavP'
        HiddenGame=True
    End Object
    Components.Add(Sprite)
}
```

6. Now we're getting somewhere. How would we access the struct inside a struct? Using the same method as before, we would access the box like this:

```
MyBasket.TheBox
```

So accessing variables inside the box struct would look like this:

```
MyBasket.TheBox.Chocolates = 2;
```

7. Easy enough. It would work the same way with arrays. Let's say we added a static array of fortune cookie messages to our basket. Our new struct would look something like this:

```
struct Basket
{
    var string Fortunes[4];
    var SmallBox TheBox;
    var string BasketColor;
    var int NumberOfKittens, BallsOfString;
    var float BasketSize;
};
```

8. To assign a value to one of them, we would use the same method as before:

```
MyBasket.Fortunes[2] = "Now you're programming!";
```

What just happened?

Structs are a powerful tool in UnrealScript, and they're used extensively in the source code. A lot of the code you'll make will involve structs. As an example, think about the one thing that every actor in the game has: A location. How is an actor's location stored? A variable appropriately called Location, which is declared as a 3D position using a Vector variable. If we look in `Actor.uc`, we can see how a Vector is defined:

```
struct immutable Vector
{
    var() float X, Y, Z;
};
```

This leads nicely into our next topic...

Vectors

Simply put, a vector is a 3D coordinate. It may be used to represent an actor's location, velocity, or even the angle of a surface. They're used a lot in UnrealScript, so even though they're just a struct, there are a lot of things we can do with them on their own. Let's take a look.

Time for action – Using vectors

Since we already know that an actor's Location is a vector, let's play around with our AwesomeActor's location.

1. First we'll declare a vector of our own at the top of our class.

```
var vector LocationOffset;
```

2. Vectors have their X, Y, and Z values set to 0.0 by default. We'll give ours a new value and add that to our actor's current location in our PostBeginPlay function.

```
function PostBeginPlay()
{
    LocationOffset.Z = 64.0;
    SetLocation(Location + LocationOffset);
}
```

When used as a location, the Z float inside a vector represents the up and down axis. Making the values of Z greater means moving it up, lower or more negative means moving it down. In our example we're going to move the actor up 64 units. We use the function in the second line, SetLocation, to tell the game to move our AwesomeActor. Since we already know its current location with the Location variable, we just add our LocationOffset to move it up 64 units.

3. There's one thing we need to do before we test this out. When we first created our AwesomeActor, we made it invisible in game. Let's change that so we can see what happens. In the default properties of our actor, delete this line:

```
HiddenGame=False
```

Now our AwesomeActor should look like this:

```
class AwesomeActor extends Actor
    placeable;

var vector LocationOffset;

function PostBeginPlay()
{
    LocationOffset.Z = 64.0;
```

```
    SetLocation(Location + LocationOffset);
}

defaultproperties
{
    Begin Object Class=SpriteComponent Name=Sprite
        Sprite=Texture2D'EditorResources.S_NavP'
    End Object
    Components.Add(Sprite)
}
```

4. Let's compile and test! In the editor, we can see our AwesomeActor still halfway stuck in the floor:

5. Run the game from the editor, and we can see that our code has worked! The AwesomeActor has moved up:

6. That seems like a bit too much code just to add two vectors together. Luckily, there's a much simpler way to use vectors to do what we want here. Vectors can be created and assigned a value at the same time that we're using it in code, like this:

```
vect(X value, Y value, Z value)
```

So if we just wanted to move our actor up 64 units, we could do it all on one line.

7. Let's get rid of our `LocationOffset` variable line and change our `PostBeginPlay` to look like this:

```
function PostBeginPlay()
{
    SetLocation(Location + vect(0,0,64));
}
```

8. Compile and test, and we get the same result!

Another useful function we can use with vectors is called VSize. If you remember your old geometry lessons, Pythagoras' Theorem lets us find the hypotenuse of a triangle by using the two sides. We can use a 3D version of the same equation to find the length of our vector.

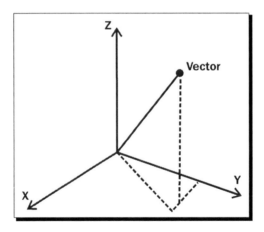

With that diagram, the length of Vector would be expressed as this:

```
Length = √(X² + Y² + Z²)
```

With VSize, all of that is done for us:

```
Length = VSize(Vector)
```

So with that in mind, let's find out how far our `AwesomeActor` is from the world origin (0,0,0).

9. Let's change our `PostBeginPlay` function to this:

```
function PostBeginPlay()
{
    'log("Distance:" @ VSize(Location));
}
```

10. Compile and test, and the answer shows up in the log!

```
[0007.88] ScriptLog: Distance: 2085.2571
```

If we wanted to find out the distance between two actors, we would use their locations like this:

```
Distance = VSize(A.Location - B.Location);
```

The order doesn't matter inside the `VSize`, we could also find the distance like this:

```
Distance = VSize(B.Location - A.Location);
```

What just happened?

Vectors are the struct we'll be using the most in UnrealScript, especially since they're used to hold an actor's Location. As we can see from the `VSize` and `vect` examples, vectors go beyond being just a struct and have their own functions dedicated exclusively to them.

One other variable to discuss also has functions dedicated to it.

Rotators

In the same way vectors are defined as a struct, rotators are as well.

```
struct immutable Rotator
{
    var() int Pitch, Yaw, Roll;
};
```

Rotators define a rotation in 3D space. To visualize it it helps to think of an airplane flying in the sky.

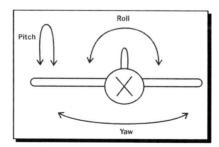

Pitch would be the airplane tilting forwards and backwards to climb or descend. Roll would be the plane tilting sideways, and Yaw would be the plane rotating horizontally, like a spinning frisbee.

In addition to a Location vector, every actor in the game has a rotator variable called Rotation that tells the game what direction it's facing. Rotating a wall in the editor changes that static mesh's rotation value. The player's view rotation is held in a rotator. They're not used as often as vectors, but they're obviously still important. Let's take a look at them.

Time for action – Using rotators

Before we use rotators on our AwesomeActor, we need to add some visual clue to let us know that it's actually rotating. To do that we're going to add another bit to our default properties like the sprite, but this time it will be an arrow we'll be able to see in the editor.

1. Below the sprite in the default properties, add this:

```
Begin Object Class=ArrowComponent Name=Arrow
End Object
Components.Add(Arrow)
```

2. We're going to log our actor's current rotation, so inside our PostBeginPlay add this:

```
'log("Rotation:" @ Rotation);
```

Our class should now look like this:

```
class AwesomeActor extends Actor
    placeable;

function PostBeginPlay()
{
    'log("Rotation:" @ Rotation);
}

defaultproperties
{
    Begin Object Class=SpriteComponent Name=Sprite
        Sprite=Texture2D'EditorResources.S_NavP'
    End Object
    Components.Add(Sprite)

    Begin Object Class=ArrowComponent Name=Arrow
    End Object
    Components.Add(Arrow)
}
```

3. Compile and take a look in the editor. Our actor now has an arrow to indicate its current rotation.

4. By default we know its current rotation is going to be (0,0,0), so let's rotate it in the editor. Click on the `AwesomeActor` to select it, and then press the *Space bar* once to change to the rotation tool.

5. Now click and hold anywhere on the blue part of the rotation tool. We're going to change our actor's Yaw, so move it as close to 90 degrees as you can get. Don't worry if it's not perfect.

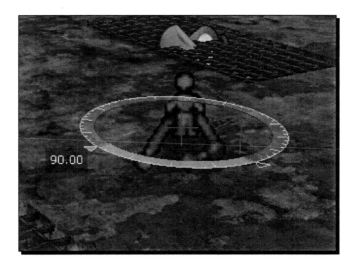

6. Save our map, and then run it in the game. Exit and check the log for our rotation value.

```
[0008.33] ScriptLog: Rotation: 0,16160,0
```

It's logging, but why is the value so high? That's definitely not 90. Internally, the ints that make up rotators are 32 bits and have a range of 0 to 65535. Therefore, in Unreal's unit system, 360 degrees = 65536. That would make 90 degrees = 16384, which is close to what was logged.

Rotators can be created the same as we did with vectors. You can make a var like this:

```
var rotator MyRot;
```

And then change the individual components in the `PostBeginPlay` function.

```
MyRot.Yaw = 2000;
```

You could also create a rotator as it's being used, like we did with vectors. The names of the functions we use for this are specific to rotators though:

```
SetRotation(Rotation + rot(0,0,4000));
```

What just happened?

Rotators, like vectors, are important structs to be examined on their own. Every actor in the game has a rotation, and the most noticeable use of rotators is in the player's camera, to tell the game where we're looking.

We've talked a lot about variables in this chapter. Next we're going to discuss ways we can change how they work.

Variable properties

Now we know what different types of variables are available to us and how to work with them. There are a few different variable properties that we need to know about to be able to use them to their fullest, first up, default properties.

Default properties

We know how to change a variable's value in our `PostBeginPlay` function, and that integers for example start out at 0 by default. But is there a better way to set an initial value? We've used it before, so you may have guessed that the default properties block at the end of our class is where we do this. Let's take a look at an example.

Time for action – Using the default properties block

1. Let's start by defining some variables in our `AwesomeActor` class.

```
var string MyName;
var int NumberOfKittens;
var float DistanceToGo;
```

2. In our default properties block, we can give these variables initial values. These are assigned before any of the code is run.

```
Defaultproperties
{
    MyName="Rachel"
    NumberOfKittens=3
    DistanceToGo=120.0
}
```

3. In our `PostBeginPlay` function, instead of changing the values we'll just log them to see the default properties in action.

```
function PostBeginPlay()
{
    'log("MyName:" @ MyName);
    'log("NumberOfKittens:" @ NumberOfKittens);
    'log("DistanceToGo:" @ DistanceToGo);
}
```

Now our class should look like this:

```
class AwesomeActor extends Actor
    placeable;

var string MyName;
var int NumberOfKittens;
var float DistanceToGo;

function PostBeginPlay()
{
    'log("MyName:" @ MyName);
    'log("NumberOfKittens:" @ NumberOfKittens);
    'log("DistanceToGo:" @ DistanceToGo);
}

defaultproperties
{
    MyName="Rachel"
    NumberOfKittens=3
    DistanceToGo=120.0

    Begin Object Class=SpriteComponent Name=Sprite
        Sprite=Texture2D'EditorResources.S_NavP'
    End Object
    Components.Add(Sprite)
}
```

4. Now let's look at the log.

```
[0008.73] ScriptLog: MyName: Rachel
[0008.73] ScriptLog: NumberOfKittens: 3
[0008.73] ScriptLog: DistanceToGo: 120.0000
```

5. Arrays have a slightly different syntax in the default properties. When used in code we use brackets to define the index, like MyArray[2]. In the default properties, we use parentheses instead.

```
MyArray(0)=3
MyArray(1)=2
```

You'll also notice that none of the lines in the default properties block have a semicolon at the end. The default properties block is the only place where we don't use them. You'll also notice that there are no spaces before or after the equal sign. This is also a quirk of the default properties block. If the formatting isn't correct you may get a compiler error or even worse, it may compile but ignore your default properties altogether. Make sure to follow these guidelines for the formatting, including having the curly brackets on their own lines. Some programmers like to have the opening curly bracket on the same line, but with UnrealScript's `defaultproperties` block, this would cause it to ignore all of the default properties.

6. Moving on! For structs, we define the default properties right inside the struct, not in the `defaultproperties` block. So taking our example struct from earlier, we would define the defaults for it like this:

```
struct Basket
{
    var string BasketColor;
    var int NumberOfKittens, BallsOfString;
    var float BasketSize;

    structdefaultproperties
    {
        BasketColor="Blue"
        NumberOfKittens=3
        BasketSize=12.0
    }
};
```

You may notice that I didn't define a default for BallsOfString, and that's perfectly fine. Any variable you don't make a default for, will use that variable type's default; in that case BallsOfString would default to 0.

This is good for structs of our own making, but what about predefined ones like vectors and rotators? Once we declare a variable of those types we can change their default properties in our default properties block, all on the same line. If we had a vector called MyVector for example, the syntax for the default property would look like this:

```
MyVector=(X=1.0,Y=5.3,Z=2.1)
```

This is true for any struct where we've declared a variable of that struct type.

What just happened?

The `defaultproperties` block is a convenient place to keep the defaults for our variables, we could use functions like `PostBeginPlay` to set values, but it's cleaner and more convenient to have them all in one place. In addition, even if we change the variable during play we can always find out the default value by using this code:

```
'log(default.BasketSize);
```

If we wanted to get rid of any changes we've made, we would just reset the variable to its default.

```
BasketSize = default.BasketSize;
```

Editable variables

Now we know how to set defaults for variables, so how do we let the level designer change them in the editor?

Time for action – Editable variables

1. This one's simple. To make a variable changeable in the editor, add a set of parentheses after var, like this:

    ```
    var() int MyEditableInt;
    ```

2. Add that variable to our class, then compile and open the editor. Double-click on the **AwesomeActor** to open up its properties, and we'll see the variable show up.

3. We can also put it in a specific category if we wanted to separate our variables into groups. Let's see what it would look like in the Physics tab.

    ```
    var(Physics) int MyEditableInt;
    ```

4. Let's compile and take a look.

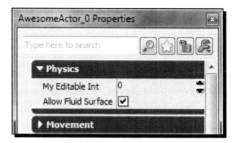

What just happened?

The level designers don't need to know about every variable an actor has, but some may need to be exposed this way. This is how lights have their brightness and color changed, for instance. When creating an actor class, it's best to give some thought to what a level designer might need to change and give them access to it.

Config variables

That's good for the level designer, but what about the player? Sometimes we want to let the player themselves change a variable. For instance, which hand the character holds the weapon in or the amount of bob as the player walks. We briefly discussed this in the first chapter, but now we'll cover it more in depth. Remember the INI files in the Config folder?

Time for action – Creating config variables

1. To let the game know that our class needs to save config variables, first we need to let it know which file to use.

```
class AwesomeActor extends Actor
    placeable
    config(Game);
```

This tells the game that our class' config variables will be defined in the Game ini files as opposed to Engine or Input and so on.

2. Now, let's make a config variable.

```
var config int MyConfigInt;
```

Config vars can have parentheses to let level designers change them, but they can NOT be put in the default properties block. Doing so will give a compiler error. Instead, we define their default properties in the INI file we specified. Since we used Game, we would put the default in DefaultGame.ini. Let's open that up now.

3.   In `DefaultGame.ini` we can see a bunch of different sections, starting with a line surrounded by brackets. The inside of these brackets specifies the package and class that the section is defining defaults for, like this:

```
[Package.Class]
```

4.   In our case our package name is `AwesomeGame`, and the class we need to define is `AwesomeActor`. At the end of `DefaultGame.ini`, make a new section surrounded by brackets.

```
[AwesomeGame.AwesomeActor]
```

5.   Right after that we can define any default values we need.

```
MyConfigInt=3
```

Once we're done, our section should look like this:

```
[AwesomeGame.AwesomeActor]
MyConfigInt=3
```

6.   Let's see if it works! In `AwesomeActor.uc`, change `PostBeginPlay` to log `MyConfigInt`.

```
var config int MyConfigInt;

function PostBeginPlay()
{
    'log("MyConfigInt:" @ MyConfigInt);
}
```

7.   Compile and run, then check the log file.

```
[0008.66] ScriptLog: MyConfigInt: 3
```

Have a go hero – Editable configurable variable?

Knowing what you know about different ways to define default values for variables, what do you think would take precedence: The config file or a value set by the level editor? Try adding a variable that's both configurable and editable and logging the result.

What just happened?

If we look in UDKGame.ini, we can see that the variable has shown up there as well. Remember that the UDK.ini files are built from the Default.ini files, and instead of changing the Default.ini files, the player and the game work with the UDK.ini ones. That way the game always has a fail safe with the Default.ini files. If the player or a setting menu in the game changed MyConfigInt to 5 for example, then the player changed their mind and used a settings menu to reset everything to the default value, we would be able to do that by using the Default.ini value for that variable.

Now that we've learned about the different types of variables and ways to set their values, let's take a look at some common operators we can use on our variables.

Common operators

Beyond simple arithmetic there are many ways of dealing with our variables, each with its own syntax and effects on the different variable types. Let's discuss some of the most commonly used operators and variable functions.

Standard arithmetic

Addition (+), subtraction (-), multiplication (*), and division (/) work on all of the variable types we discussed, but have different effects on them. For floats and ints they work as we'd expect, but with multiplication and division, keep in mind the truncating that happens when working with ints.

It's also possible to use floats and ints together.

Time for action – Math!

1. As an example, take a look at this code.

```
var float Float1, Float2;
var int Int1;

function PostBeginPlay()
{
    Float2 = Int1 / Float1;
    'log("Float2:" @ Float2);
}

defaultproperties
{
    Int1=5
    Float1=2.0
}
```

2. We can divide an int by a float or vice versa, and we get the result we expect:

```
[0008.10] ScriptLog: Float2: 2.5000
```

However, if we divide an int by an int and assign it to a float, what would we expect the result to be?

3. Let's take a look at this code:

```
var float Float1;
var int Int1, Int2;

function PostBeginPlay()
{
    Float1 = Int1 / Int2;
    'log("Float1:" @ Float1);
}

defaultproperties
{
    Int1=5
    Int2=2
}
```

With that it looks like we'd expect the same result. Let's take a look at the log:

```
[0007.66] ScriptLog: Float1: 2.0000
```

When dividing ints, the truncating happens before assigning the result, even if it's a float. Depending on what we're doing this may be what we want, but it's good to keep that in mind.

4. Two other operators that can be used for simple math are increment (++) and decrement (−).

```
Int1 = 5;
Int1++;
'log("Int1" @ Int1);
```

This would give us 6 in the log.

5. For vectors and rotators, the arithmetic works with each element of the struct individually. For example, with the following code:

```
var vector Vect1, Vect2, VectResult;

function PostBeginPlay()
{
    VectResult = Vect1 + Vect2;
```

```
        'log("VectResult:" @ VectResult);
}

defaultproperties
{
    Vect1=(X=1.0,Y=4.5,Z=12.0)
    Vect2=(X=2.0,Y=4.0,Z=8.0)
}
```

We get the following result in the log:

```
[0007.74] ScriptLog: VectResult: 3.00,8.5,20.00
```

As we can see, each individual element has been worked with separately. X added to X, Y to Y, and Z to Z.

6. Vectors can also be multiplied or divided by floats and ints. This has the effect of changing the vector's VSize while keeping the direction the same.

What just happened?

The basic arithmetic operators are simple stuff, but when working with different types of variables it's important to remember how they'll respond to the operators.

Modulo

Modulo (%) returns the remainder after division. It's a pretty obscure and not commonly used operator, but when needed it can save many lines of code.

Time for action – Using modulo

1. Let's look at an example.

```
var int Int1, Int2, IntResult;

function PostBeginPlay()
{
    IntResult = Int1 % Int2;
    'log("IntResult:" @ IntResult);
}

defaultproperties
{
    Int1=28
    Int2=5
}
```

28 divided by 5 is 5 with a remainder of 3.

2. Let's look at the log:

```
[0008.12] ScriptLog: IntResult: 3
```

What just happened?

You may be asking yourself, when will this ever come in handy? Let's say you wanted to know how many bullets a player had in their gun, but you only had the gun's clip size and the player's total number of bullets to work with. A line of code like this would work:

```
CurrentBullets = TotalBullets % ClipSize;
```

Instead of having to do any complicated math to figure it out you would be able to use modulo to save some headaches.

Comparisons

Comparing one variable to another is one of the essential tools of any programming language, and UnrealScript is no different. Comparisons give you a boolean true or false. If we wanted to know if two variables were the same, we would use a double equal sign.

```
Variable1 == Variable2
```

Why a double equal sign? What does it mean? Well, UnrealScript needs a way to assign variables as well as compare them. Using a single equal sign denotes assignment, like this:

```
Variable1 = 5;
```

We need a different operator for comparison, so UnrealScript uses the double equal sign. Let's write some example code.

Time for action – Comparisons

1. Let's take a look at two ints and the various comparison operators we can use on them.

```
var int Int1, Int2;

function PostBeginPlay()
{
    'log(Int1 == Int2);
}

defaultproperties
{
    Int1=5
    Int2=5
}
```

Setting both of them to the same value and using the equal comparison gives us
True in the log:

```
[0007.79] ScriptLog: True
```

If the variables weren't exactly the same, we would get False.

2. The opposite of this comparison is "Not Equal", which is denoted by an exclamation
    point followed by an equal sign. If we wanted to know if two variables weren't the
    same, we would use this.

```
var int Int1, Int2;

function PostBeginPlay()
{
    'log(Int1 != Int2);
}

defaultproperties
{
    Int1=3
    Int2=5
}
```

Since they have different values, we'll get True in the log again:

```
[0007.70] ScriptLog: True
```

Equal or not equal also apply to vectors and rotators. Each element in those structs
is compared to each other, and it will return False if any of them are different.

3. For greater than or less than, we would simply use those symbols.

```
var int Int1, Int2;

function PostBeginPlay()
{
    'log(Int1 < Int2);
    'log(Int1 > Int2);
}

defaultproperties
{
    Int1=3
    Int2=5
}
```

And the log:

```
[0007.60] ScriptLog: True
[0007.60] ScriptLog: False
```

4. The same works for "greater than or equal to" and "less than or equal to", we simply follow it with an equal sign:

```
var int Int1, Int2;

function PostBeginPlay()
{
    'log(Int1 <= Int2);
    'log(Int1 >= Int2);
}

defaultproperties
{
    Int1=5
    Int2=5
}
```

The log for this:

```
[0007.45] ScriptLog: True
[0007.45] ScriptLog: True
```

Greater than or less than do not apply to vectors or rotators and the compiler will give an error if we try to use them.

5. A special comparison operator for floats and strings is the "approximately equal to" operator, denoted by a tilde followed by an equal sign (~=). For floats, it returns true, if they are within 0.0001 of each other, useful for making sure complicated equations don't have to return the exact same result, just close enough to account for rounding errors.

```
var float Float1, Float2;

function PostBeginPlay()
{
    'log(Float1 ~= Float2);
}

defaultproperties
{
    Float1=1.0
    Float2=1.000001
}
```

This returns True in the log:

```
[0007.94] ScriptLog: True
```

6. For strings, the "approximately equal to" operator is a case-insensitive comparison.

```
var string String1, String2;

function PostBeginPlay()
{
    'log(String1 ~= String2);
}

defaultproperties
{
    String1="STRING TEST"
    String2="string test"
}
```

The log:

```
[0007.74] ScriptLog: True
```

As long as the letters are the same it will return true even if different letters are capitalized.

What just happened?

Comparisons, like arithmetic operators, are one of the basic things to know about a programming language. They'll be used all the time, and like arithmetic it's good to know how they interact with each variable type.

Logical operators

In logical operators, AND is expressed by two "and" signs (&&), OR by two vertical bar or "pipe" characters (||), and NOT is expressed using an exclamation point (!). To understand logical operators, think about how we use those words in sentences. As an example, take a look at this sentence:

```
If it's not raining and we have enough money...
```

Expressing this in code with logical operators would look like this:

```
!bRaining && CurrentMoney > RequiredMoney
```

We can see the use of the NOT and AND logical operators. NOT raining AND current money > required money. Let's take a look at another example:

```
Tuesday or Thursday
```

In code that would look like this:

```
Day == "Tuesday" || Day == "Thursday"
```

Time for action – Using logical operators

1. Let's put our first example in code.

```
var bool bRaining;
var float CurrentMoney, RequiredMoney;

function PostBeginPlay()
{
    'log(!bRaining && CurrentMoney > RequiredMoney);
}

defaultproperties
{
    CurrentMoney=20.0
    RequiredMoney=15.0
}
```

Remembering that bools are false by default, let's take a look at the log:

```
[0007.94] ScriptLog: True
```

Even though bRaining is False, we're asking the code if it's NOT raining, which is True. You can see why naming booleans is important now. If our variable were called bNotRaining, working with logical operators would get messy pretty quickly.

2. Let's look at our second example.

```
var string Day;

function PostBeginPlay()
{
    'log(Day == "Tuesday" || Day == "Thursday");
}

defaultproperties
{
    Day="Monday"
}
```

Since the day variable is neither of those two, we'll get False in the log:

```
[0007.79] ScriptLog: False
```

3. One final operator to discuss is the EXCLUSIVE OR, denoted by two carets (^^). This will return true if one and only one of our statements is true. Let's look at the following code:

```
var string Day, Month;

function PostBeginPlay()
{
    'log(Day == "Tuesday" ^^ Month == "January");
}

defaultproperties
{
    Day="Tuesday"
    Month="January"
}
```

If we were using a normal OR, this would return true, but since both of them are true, an EXCLUSIVE OR returns false:

```
[0007.60] ScriptLog: False
```

What just happened?

We can see how intertwined logical operators are with normal comparisons. We used the equal and greater than comparisons in our examples. When working with them, the best way to figure out how to write a statement is to say it out loud first and take note of words like AND, NOT, and OR in your sentence. This will help you figure out how to construct a logical operator statement.

Have a go hero – Writing logical statements

How would you write the following statement with logical operators?

```
If the sun is shining and we're not wearing sunblock.....
```

Answer: The operator would look something like this:

```
if(bSunShining && !bWearingSunblock)
```

Concatenation

Concatenation is a fancy word for "join two strings together". There are two concatenation operators, let's take a look at them.

Time for action – Concatenation

The good news is we've been using concatenation for awhile now, in our log lines. The two operators are the at symbol (@) and the dollar sign ($). The only difference between the two is whether or not we want a space in between the strings we're joining.

1. Let's write some code.

```
var string String1, String2, AtSign, DollarSign;

function PostBeginPlay()
{
    AtSign = String1 @ String2;
    DollarSign = String1 $ String2;
    'log("At sign:" @ AtSign);
    'log("Dollar sign:" @ DollarSign);
}

defaultproperties
{
    String1="This is"
    String2="a test."
}
```

Looking at the log shows us the minor difference between the two:

```
[0007.77] ScriptLog: At sign: This is a test.
[0007.77] ScriptLog: Dollar sign: This isa test.
```

The choice between them is as simple as the space between the joined strings.

2. The concatenation operators can also be used with equal signs to shorten the code and get rid of the need for extra variables. The @ code could also be written like this:

```
var string String1, String2;

function PostBeginPlay()
{
    String1 @= String2;
    'log("String1:" @ String1);
}

defaultproperties
{
    String1="This is"
    String2="a test."
}
```

The log ends up the same:

```
[0007.56] ScriptLog: String1: This is a test.
```

What just happened?

Concatenation is specific to strings and easy to remember. There are instances when you'd want to use the dollar sign and ones where the @ symbol is needed, it just depends on what we're trying to do with the string. As an example, death messages often use the @ symbol to join the player name to the death message so there is a space in between them, while strings that tell the game which level to load use the dollar sign specifically to avoid spaces.

Variable functions

There are many other variable functions we can use; some of them are handy to know. Let's go over a few.

Ints

- `Rand(int Max)`: Returns a random int between 0 and the maximum number specified. Note that this will never return Max itself. As an example, `Rand(10)` would return a random number 0-9.

- `Min(int A, int B)`: Returns the smaller of the two ints. `Min(5, 2)` would return 2.

- `Max(int A, int B)`: Returns the higher of the two numbers. `Max(3, 8)` would return 8.

- `Clamp(int V, int A, int B)`: Clamps V to be between A and B. If V is lesser than A it would return A, if it were greater than B it would return B. If it were already in between, V would stay the same. `Clamp(3, 5, 8)` would return 5 while `Clamp(5, 2, 9)` would return 5.

Floats

- `FRand()`: The same as Rand, but returns a random float between 0.0 and 1.0.
- `FMin(float A, float B)`: The float version of Min.
- `FMax(float A, float B)`: The float version of Max.
- `FClamp(float V, float A, float B)`: The float version of Clamp. Floats and ints can be used in either version of these three depending on whether or not we want the result to be truncated.

Strings

- `Len(string S)`: Returns the length of the string as an int. This includes spaces and any symbols.

- `InStr(string S, string T)`: Returns the position of string T in string S, or -1 if T can't be found in S. This is useful for figuring out if a string has a certain word in it, since we can check if the result is >= 0 to indicate that the word is there.

- `Left(string S, int I)`: Returns the left I number of characters. `Left("Something", 3)` would return "Som".

- `Right(string S, int I)`: Returns the right I number of characters. `Right("Something", 3)` would return "ing".

- `Mid(string S, int I, optional int J)`: Returns a string from position I. `Mid("Something", 2, 3)` returns "met". If J isn't specified this has the same effect as Right.

- `Caps(string S)`: Returns the string in all caps.

- `Locs(string S)`: Returns the string in all lowercase.

- `Repl(string S, string Match, string With, optional bool bCaseSensitive)`: Replaces Match with With in string S. `Repl("Something", "Some", "No")` would return "Nothing". The optional bool specifies if you only want it to replace With if letters have the same case as Match.

Vectors

- `Vsize(vector A)`: Returns the size of the vector as a float.

- `Normal(vector A)`: Returns the same vector, except scaled to be exactly 1.0 unit in length. This is useful when we only want a direction and want to use multiplication to come up with our own size.

- `VRand()`: Returns a random vector.

Rotators

- `RotRand()`: Returns a random rotator.

This list is by no means complete, other variable operators can be found by reading through `Object.uc` in the `Core\classes` folder.

Flow control

We learned about comparisons and logical operators earlier. Now what do we do if we want different things to happen depending on the results of those comparisons? Flow control helps us do exactly that. Let's learn how we can specify what happens under different circumstances.

If else

If/else is the basic flow control statement. Let's look at this sentence:

```
If it's raining I'll take an umbrella.
```

Using an if statement, that sentence would be written like this:

```
if(bRaining)
{
    bUmbrella = true;
}
```

We could also add an else statement to it:

```
If it's raining I'll take an umbrella, otherwise I'll wear short
sleeves.
```

That would be written like this:

```
if(bRaining)
{
    bUmbrella = true;
}
else
{
    bShortSleeves = true;
}
```

We can also use Else If for other conditions.

```
If it's raining I'll take an umbrella, or if it's cold I'll wear a
coat, otherwise I'll wear short sleeves.
```

We could write that like this:

```
if(bRaining)
{
    bUmbrella = true;
}
else if(Temperature < ComfortableTemperature)
```

```
{
    bCoat = true;
}
else
{
    bShortSleeves = true;
}
```

The important thing to remember about else/if is, that only one of these conditions will run. If it's raining and cold, only the bRaining section of the code will run, not bRaining and Temperature < ComfortableTemperature.

Time for action – Using if/else

Let's write some code to see if/else in action for ourselves.

1. Take the following code:

```
var int Int1, Int2;

function PostBeginPlay()
{
    if(Int1 > Int2)
        'log("Int1 is greater than Int2");
    else if(Int1 == Int2)
        'log("Int1 is equal to Int2");
    else
        'log("Int1 is less than Int2");
}

defaultproperties
{
    Int1=5
    Int2=2
}
```

2. What would we expect the result to be? Let's look at the log for the answer:

```
[0007.72] ScriptLog: Int1 is greater than Int2
```

What just happened?

We can see that the if statement is executed and not the else if or else statements. Notice that in this example we didn't use the curly brackets in our statements. If there is only one line after the if, else if, or else statements brackets aren't necessary. However, if there are two or more lines, we would need to use brackets.

For

For is a different kind of control statement called an iterator. It will execute the code we write a specific number of times until a condition is met. Let's take a closer look at it.

Time for action – Using the for statement

1. Let's examine the following code:

```
var int m;

function PostBeginPlay()
{
    for(m = 0; m < 3; m++)
    {
        'log("Stop hitting yourself." @ m);
    }
}
```

This is a simple way of writing the following code:

```
m = 0;
'log(m);
m = 1;
'log(m);
m = 2;
'log(m);
```

It might not seem like it's saving much time in this simple example, but consider a case where we would want to run the loop a hundred times. Putting it in a for loop would save a lot of unnecessary code!

If we write the PostBeginPlay function above into our AwesomeActor.uc class and compile it, then take a look at the log, we can see that it executed the code inside the for loop three times:

```
[0007.57] ScriptLog: Stop hitting yourself. 0
[0007.57] ScriptLog: Stop hitting yourself. 1
[0007.57] ScriptLog: Stop hitting yourself. 2
```

What just happened?

The first part of the for statement lets us set a variable to an initial value. Most of the time it will be 0, but there may be times when we need a different value, for example if we wanted to count down instead of up. The second part of the statement tells the for loop when to stop. Once the condition is false the loop exits, in this case once m reaches 3. The third part of the statement runs every time a loop finishes. In this case, the ++ operator is used to increment m by 1 each time.

While

While is similar to a **for** loop, but there is no initializing or incrementing. While loops are dangerous; if used improperly, it could lead to an infinite loop which crashes the game.

Time for action – Something

1. As an example of what NOT to do, let's take this code.

```
var int Int1;

function PostBeginPlay()
{
    Int1 = 5;

    While(Int1 > 0)
    {
        Int1 = 5;
    }
}
```

2. When we run the game with this code, it will crash.

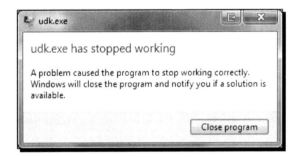

It is EXTREMELY IMPORTANT to always make sure the "while" condition will be met to avoid infinite loop crashes.

3. Let's take a look at the right way to use it:

```
var int Int1;

function PostBeginPlay()
{
    While(Int1 < 5)
    {
        'log("Int1" @ Int1);
        Int1++;
    }
}
```

In this case, Int1 will keep incrementing until it reaches 5, and the While loop will exit.

4. We could also use a statement called break to exit the loop:

```
var int Int1;

function PostBeginPlay()
{
    While(Int1 < 5)
    {
        'log("Int1" @ Int1);
        Int1++;
        if(Int1 == 3)
            break;
    }
}
```

In this case, the loop will exit when Int1 reaches 3 instead of continuing until it hits 5.

5. Another statement we can use is called continue. Instead of exiting the loop completely, it just skips to the next cycle.

```
var int Int1;

function PostBeginPlay()
{
    While(Int1 < 5)
    {
        'log("Int1" @ Int1);
        Int1++;

        if(Int1 == 3)
            continue;

        'log("This will not log if Int1 is 3");
    }
}
```

In this case, the loop will keep going until `Int1` hits 5, but when it's equal to 3 the continue statement will cause it to skip the rest of the code for that loop and move on to the next loop.

What just happened?

Using **while** statements can be handy when you don't know the number of loops you'll need beforehand, or if it would change during play. You always have to make sure the loop will be able to finish though; crashing the game is a very real concern when using while loops.

Do until

Do until is basically another way of using a while loop, and it carries the same concerns of infinite loops. An example of how to write one would be this:

```
do
{
    'log("Int1" @ Int1);
    Int1++;
} until (Int1 > 5);
```

Switch

Switch is used as a more complex form of the if/else statement, and in certain cases it can lead to cleaner code. It also has the ability to execute more than one statement for a condition.

Time for action – Using switches

1. Let's take a look at an example of a Switch statement.

    ```
    var int Int1;

    function PostBeginPlay()
    {
        Int1 = 2;

        switch(Int1)
        {
            case 1:
                'log("Int1 == 1");
            case 2:
                'log("Int1 == 2");
            case 3:
    ```

```
            'log("Int1 == 3");
        default:
            'log("Int1 isn't any of those!");
    }
}
```

2. Running the code, the log looks like this:

```
[0007.97] ScriptLog: Int1 == 2
[0007.97] ScriptLog: Int1 == 3
[0007.97] ScriptLog: Int1 isn't any of those!
```

What just happened?

Why did the other lines log? Unlike if/else statements, switches will continue executing the next steps after the condition is met. Sometimes we'll want it to do that, but if not we can use the break statement here too.

```
var int Int1;

function PostBeginPlay()
{
    Int1 = 2;

    switch(Int1)
    {
        case 1:
            'log("Int1 == 1");
            break;
        case 2:
            'log("Int1 == 2");
            break;
        case 3:
            'log("Int1 == 3");
            break;
        default:
            'log("Int1 isn't any of those!");
    }
}
```

The log file for this would have our desired behavior.

```
[0007.69] ScriptLog: Int1 == 2
```

Return

Return simply exits out of a function. This is most commonly combined with other flow control statements like if/else. Take the following code:

```
var int Int1;

function PostBeginPlay()
{
    if(Int1 == 5)
    {
        'log("Int1 equals 5");
        return;
    }

    'log("This will not log");
}

defaultproperties
{
    Int1=5
}
```

We can see what happens in the log:

```
[0007.83] ScriptLog: Int1 equals 5
```

Once the code reaches the `return` statement, it stops running any more code in that function.

Goto

Goto jumps to a specific place in a function. If we had the following code:

```
function PostBeginPlay()
{
    'log("PostBeginPlay");

    goto EndOfFunction;

    'log("This will not log");

EndOfFunction:
    'log("This will log.");
}
```

The log would look like this:

```
[0007.55] ScriptLog: PostBeginPlay
[0007.55] ScriptLog: This will log.
```

Like Return, Goto isn't really useful on its own and is more commonly combined with other flow control statements.

Pop quiz – Variable madness!

1. What is the difference between an integer and a float?

2. What type of variable is a vector?

3. How do we make a variable changeable in the editor?

   a. Add it to a config file.

   b. Add parentheses after var.

   c. Add it to the default properties.

4. How would we write "If there's no water we will be thirsty" using logical operators?

Summary

We learned a lot in this chapter about the different types of variables and how to use them.

Specifically, we covered:

- The different types of variables including ints and floats, strings, vectors, and rotators.

- How structs and arrays are created and how to use them.

- How to set default properties for variables and use config files.

- Common operators used with variables.

- The various flow control statements to do different things under different circumstances.

Now that we've learned about variables, we're ready to start learning about the class tree and the commonly used classes in a UDK project. By the end of the next chapter we will be running our own custom game!

3
Understanding the Class Tree

Who is your daddy and what does he do?

In the last two chapters we've been using classes to write and test our code. But what is a class exactly? What is the importance of the class tree, why use one at all? In this chapter we're going to take a closer look at what it means when we say that UnrealScript is an object-oriented programming language.

In this chapter we will:

- Discuss the class tree and the principles of object-oriented programming
- Talk about inheritance and what it means to the class tree
- Use function overriding to change the behavior of our classes
- Talk about casting and how to use it on our classes
- Go over the different class properties that can be used
- Discuss the difference between Actors and Objects

Let's start by talking about classes, what they are and how to use them.

What is a class?

If you were coming out with a new line of cars, you would want every one of them to be exactly the same, that way you'd know what to expect. To do that you would need a schematic. It's no different in programming. We want each instance of a projectile, vehicle, or weapon to start out exactly the same as any other, and to do that we use classes as our blueprints. Each class contains the variables, functions and other properties that define that object's behavior. Like cars, objects created from a class can be changed after they are created, but the starting point is always the same.

Time for action – All classes are created equally

What does this mean for us in practical terms? Let's take a look at our friend AwesomeActor to see if he can help demonstrate.

1. Write the following code in our `AwesomeActor` class:

```
class AwesomeActor extends Actor
    placeable;

var() int MyInt;

function PostBeginPlay()
{
    `log(self @ MyInt);
}

defaultproperties
{
    MyInt=4

    Begin Object Class=SpriteComponent Name=Sprite
        Sprite=Texture2D'EditorResources.S_NavP'
        HiddenGame=True
    End Object
    Components.Add(Sprite)
}
```

We'll use an editable `MyInt` variable to see class behavior.

2. Compile the class and open up the editor. Next to our existing `AwesomeActor`, place another one.

3. Save the map and run it from the editor, then close out the game and editor.

4. Now let's take a look at our `Launch2.log` file:

```
[0010.61] ScriptLog: AwesomeActor_0  4
[0010.61] ScriptLog: AwesomeActor_1  4
```

We can see that class instances are created with the class name and then a number added to the end. Remembering that in programming everything starts with 0, in our case we have `AwesomeActor_0` and `AwesomeActor_1`. Since we haven't changed anything about them yet, both have the default value of `MyInt`, 4.

5. How do we know which one's which? A handy bar at the bottom of the editor can help us. Reopen the editor and click on one of the AwesomeActors to select it. At the bottom of the editor we can see that instance's name.

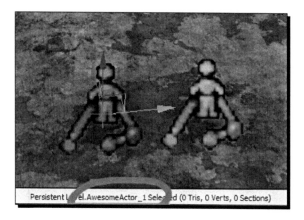

Persistent Level.AwesomeActor_1 Selected (0 Tris, 0 Verts, 0 Sections)

6. From our log we can see that each instance of `AwesomeActor` has been created in the same manner. Now let's change one of them. Double-click on one to open up its properties, and change `MyInt` to `23`.

7. Save the map and run the game, then exit and take a look at `Launch2.log`.

```
[0007.76] ScriptLog: AwesomeActor_0 4
[0007.76] ScriptLog: AwesomeActor_1 23
```

What just happened?

We can see that even though both instances were created from the same class blueprint, we can change them after they have been created. This is an important principle of object-oriented programming. Having classes lets us quickly create objects of the same type without having to have a separate file or code for each instance we're going to use. An object is created from the class with all of that class' properties, and then we can change them after they have been created.

Inheritance

Another important principle of object-oriented programming is inheritance. Let's say our game had four different kinds of weapons: Pistols, machine guns, sniper rifles, and laser cannons. A lot of the functionality of those guns would be the same. They would each have ammo, damage, accuracy, and so on. Instead of having to duplicate all that code, they could all inherit the basic functionality of a weapon and change the properties they needed to to get their specific functionality.

Time for action – Examining inheritance

1. We can see an example of this by taking a look at the class tree in UnCodeX, under **Actor | Inventory | Weapon | UDKWeapon**. Expanding **UTWeapon** we can see the different types of weapons provided as examples in the UDK:

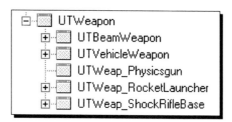

   We can see that `UTBeamWeapon` (like the plasma gun we start with when running the game), `UTWeap_RocketLauncher`, and `UTWeap_ShockRifleBase` are amongst our weaponry. Each of these behaves differently, but all of them have common functionality.

2. Clicking on `UTWeapon`, we can see some of its variables.

```
/** Initial ammo count if in weapon locker */
var int LockerAmmoCount;

/** Max ammo count */
var int MaxAmmoCount;

/** Holds the amount of ammo used for a given shot */
var array<int> ShotCost;
```

What just happened?

Things like `MaxAmmoCount` and `ShotCost` are common to all of the weapons, so instead of having to duplicate the variables to all of the subclasses, they're declared in all of the weapons' parent class, `UTWeapon`. Indeed, if we look at `UTWeapon`'s subclasses like `UTWeap_RocketLauncher`, we won't find `MaxAmmoCount` or any of `UTWeapon`'s other variables declared in any of them.

Speaking of weapons, I think it's time we started having a little fun with our code. AwesomeActor has been good to us so far, but he doesn't really do a lot besides sit there and send out log messages. Let's make a weapon.

Time for action – Making a custom weapon

The best way to learn about inheritance is to see it in action, and the most basic way to see it is through a game's weapons. They're easy to modify and are a good starting point for learning about the UDK's classes.

1. Create a new `.uc` file in our `AwesomeGame/Classes` folder and call it `AwesomeGun.uc`. Write the following code in it:

```
class AwesomeGun extends UTWeap_RocketLauncher_Content;

defaultproperties
{
    FireInterval(0)=0.1
    ShotCost(0)=0
}
```

2. Compile our class. Now here's where we would ask, "How did it compile? I didn't declare any variables, but we're putting some in our default properties!" This is how inheritance works. We already saw the `ShotCost` variable in `UTWeapon` on line 27:

```
/** Holds the amount of ammo used for a given shot */
var array<int> ShotCost;
```

If we look higher up in the class tree at Weapon, we can see `FireInterval` on line 44 (as of the October 2011 build):

```
/** Holds the amount of time a single shot takes */
var()        Array<float>        FireInterval;
```

When we create our class, any variables, properties, and functions of the classes higher in the tree are automatically created inside our class. This saves a lot of duplicated code, as anything that's going to be common to all of the subclasses only needs to be declared once. Remember when I said that a lot of programming is reading through the source code? This is why. To understand what functionality is already there and what variables we can already use, it's important to read through the classes higher up in the tree to see what they can do. This also prevents us from reinventing the wheel as it were, writing code to do something that already exists.

In our case, using the already existing `FireInterval` and `ShotCost` keeps us from having to write any code at all to change the way our gun works. We can just change the default properties in our class.

3. Open up the editor. To use our new weapon, we're going to need to place a weapon factory. In the **Actor Classes** browser, make sure **Categories** is unchecked, then browse down to **NavigationPoint | PickupFactory | UDKPickupFactory | UTPickupFactory | UTWeaponPickupFactory**. Place a **UTWeaponPickupFactory** on the floor where our AwesomeActors are, and delete our AwesomeActors.

4. Double-click on the factory to open its properties, and change its **Weapon Pickup Class** to our **AwesomeGun**.

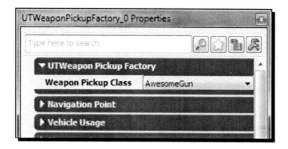

5. One minor thing to do, unrelated to our programming. Since the weapon factory we placed is a navigation point, we need to rebuild paths in the editor to prevent us from getting warnings about it when we open up the map again later. Click on the build paths icon in the top toolbar, and then close the window that comes up afterwards.

6. Save the map and test it out. Run over to the weapon factory to pick up our custom gun, and then spray the level down with rockets.

What just happened?

Boosh! And/or kakow! The changes we made were simple, but we can easily see how they affected the game. Changing the ShotCost to 0 effectively gave us infinite ammo, since firing a rocket consumes 0 ammo. Changing the FireInterval to 0.1 made it so that we fire ten rockets per second.

It's important to remember that variables and functions that are inherited only come from classes directly above ours in the class tree. As an experiment, let's create a subclass of our AwesomeGun.

Time for action – Experiments with inheritance

Let's add a variable to our AwesomeGun class and see how it works with another class we'll create.

1. Add an int to our AwesomeGun class called MyInt. Our code should now look like this:

```
class AwesomeGun extends UTWeap_RocketLauncher_Content;

var int MyInt;
```

```
defaultproperties
{
    FireInterval(0)=0.1
    ShotCost(0)=0
}
```

2. Now create another class in our `AwesomeGame/Classes` folder called `AnotherGun.uc`. Type the following code into it:

```
class AnotherGun extends AwesomeGun;

defaultproperties
{
    MyInt=4
}
```

3. Compile the code. We'll see that it compiles fine as our `AnotherGun` is inheriting `MyInt` from `AwesomeGun`.

4. Now let's change the class we're extending from to be the same as AwesomeGun's parent class:

```
class AnotherGun extends UTWeap_RocketLauncher_Content;

defaultproperties
{
    MyInt=4
}
```

5. Now when we compile, we'll get a warning:

```
Warning, Unknown property in defaults: MyInt=4
```

What just happened?

Even though the classes extend off of the same class, inheritance only happens when the class we want to use the variable in is inside the one that declares the variable in the class tree. We can change the default property of the variable for our class, and this is how we get different functionality out of them such as our example with the firing rate.

Function overriding

In addition to variables, functions declared in parent classes are also inherited by their children. This lets us change behavior that goes beyond simple variable changes. For example, two pickups under **Inventory | UTInventory | UTTimedPowerup** in the class tree, UTBerserk and UTUDamage, have the same function called GivenTo which is inherited from Inventory. Even though the function name is the same, they give the inventory items their unique behavior. UTBerserk's GivenTo function calls a function that increases the player's weapon firing rate, while UTUDamage's GivenTo function increases the player's DamageScaling variable. These functions also set different sound effects and overlays for the two different items.

To experiment with function overriding we're going to expand our AwesomeGame classes to include a custom GameInfo and PlayerController class. The GameInfo controls the rules of the game and is what makes Deathmatch different from "Capture the Flag" for example. A custom GameInfo is one of the most important classes when creating our own game, and most of the time it is the first class created in a new project.

The PlayerController is the brain behind the player's character running around on screen. It processes our input, controls the player's viewpoint, and passes and receives messages to and from other players among many other things. It is another important class in a custom game, and taking the time to read through it will help you understand how a lot of things are done in a UDK game.

So with that, let's make a custom game!

Time for action – Creating a custom GameInfo and PlayerController

Creating a custom GameInfo class is simple enough; it's just knowing where to let the game know that you want to run it. First up, let's create the class.

1. Create a new file in our AwesomeGame/Classes folder called AwesomeGame.uc. Type the following code into it:

```
class AwesomeGame extends UTDeathmatch;

defaultproperties
{
}
```

UTDeathmatch is a good place to start for a custom GameInfo, even for games that don't involve killing anyone, or for single player games. UTDeathmatch and its parent classes have a lot of functionality in common with those types of games including the player spawn behavior.

2. Now let's create a custom `PlayerController`. Create a new file in our `AwesomeGame/Classes` folder called `AwesomePlayerController.uc`. Type the following code into it:

```
class AwesomePlayerController extends UTPlayerController;

simulated function PostBeginPlay()
{
    super.PostBeginPlay();
    `log("AwesomePlayerController spawned!");
}

defaultproperties
{
}
```

We are almost done with the code part. One other thing that a `GameInfo` class does is control what type of `PlayerController` is spawned. If you wanted to have a class-based game you could do it by creating more than one custom `PlayerController` class and using your custom `GameInfo` to spawn the one the player selects.

3. For `AwesomeGame` we're only using one type of `PlayerController`, so let's set that in the default properties.

```
class AwesomeGame extends UTDeathmatch;

defaultproperties
{
    PlayerControllerClass=class'AwesomeGame.
AwesomePlayerController'
}
```

Remember that the first part of the property, `AwesomeGame`, depends on what you named your folder under `Development\Src`.

`PlayerControllerClass` is a variable declared in `GameInfo` and inherited by all subclasses of `GameInfo` including our `AwesomeGame`.

4. Compile the code.

5. The map we've been using up until now has been fine for our purposes, but we're going to need something with a little more room to experiment from now on. If you're familiar with the editor then create a simple flat map with a player start at the center and lights so we can see. If you'd rather just get to the programming, place the file called `AwesomeTestMap.udk` included with the book into the `UDKGame/Content/Maps/AwesomeGame` folder that we created in Chapter 1.

6. Time to run our game! Since the editor can't be open while we compile, and starting up the editor takes a bit of time, I prefer to use batch files to run test maps. It saves a lot of time and they're easy to set up. Create a text file anywhere that's convenient for you and call it `Awesome Test Map.txt`. Write the following in it:

```
C:\UDK\UDK-AwesomeGame\Binaries\Win32\UDK.exe AwesomeTestMap?GoalS
core=0?TimeLimit=0?Game=AwesomeGame.AwesomeGame -log
```

Make sure all the punctuation is correct, there are only two spaces after `UDK.exe` and before `-log`. If you've installed the UDK in a different location or under a different name, be sure to write down your correct path to `UDK.exe`. This file is also included with the book if you're unsure of the format. Once again remember that the first part of `AwesomeGame.AwesomeGame` refers to the name of the `.u` file you have compiled.

7. Save the text file, and then rename it to change the extension from `.txt` to `.bat`.

8. Double-click on the file to run the test map. You'll notice that the DOS window that pops up looks really familiar. Adding `-log` to the end of our batch file makes it so that we can see the log being written as it happens. If we look carefully at it, or shut down the game and open `Launch.log` (not `Launch2.log`, we're not running the editor now), we can see our log show up:

```
[0005.67] ScriptLog: AwesomePlayerController spawned!
```

Awesome!

What just happened?

Now we know that our code is working correctly. The batch file is telling the game to use our custom `GameInfo` class, which is telling the game to use our custom `PlayerController`. When setting up a new UDK project these are usually the first two classes that get created, so now we have a good starting point for creating a custom game. So what can we do now?

Time for action – Experiments with function overriding

Let's get to our experiment with function overriding by changing the way the player's camera works. If you've ever played any overhead view games like Gauntlet you'll know what we're going to do. In games like that, the camera stays in a fixed position high above the player's head, looking down towards the player. To do that, we're going to override the `GetPlayerViewPoint` function.

1. We know from our look at vectors in the previous chapter that we can get the location of actors in the world. If we wanted to move our camera away from the player, we'll need the player's location and an offset that we can use to make sure the camera stays in the same location relative to the player, like in the following diagram:

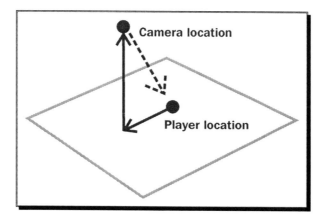

We could just directly add the values in the function, but to keep things organized it's usually a good idea to keep variables like that in the default properties where they can easily be found and changed if desired. We may also want to use this value for other purposes, so it's good to keep it all in one variable instead of having to track down and change each time we use it.

Let's add our offset and its default property to our code.

```
class AwesomePlayerController extends UTPlayerController;

var vector PlayerViewOffset;

defaultproperties
{
    PlayerViewOffset=(X=-64,Y=0,Z=1024)
}
```

The Z value will make it, so our camera is above the player. You can set this value to whatever feels right to you, but for now I'm using 1024. We've also put a value in for X to make it so the camera is moved to the side a bit and not completely straight down. But why is it negative? This value was chosen so that the radar on the default HUD stays aligned with our current direction. Other than that it's really arbitrary, there's no reason it couldn't be positive or even moved to the Y value if we wanted.

2. Now for the `GetPlayerViewPoint` function. Looking at where it's declared in `Controller.uc`, we see it needs to be written like this:

```
simulated event GetPlayerViewPoint(out vector out_Location, out
Rotator out_Rotation)
```

So let's place the function in our `AwesomePlayerController` to override it.

```
simulated event GetPlayerViewPoint(out vector out_Location, out
Rotator out_Rotation)
{
}
```

3. The first thing we need to do is call the parent class' version of the function. We'll cover the super, more in the next chapter, but basically when we're overriding functions, calling the super makes the code in our parent class' version of the function we're overriding to be also executed. For `GetPlayerViewPoint` this is important because otherwise the camera wouldn't work at all. Let's add the line to our function:

```
simulated event GetPlayerViewPoint(out vector out_Location, out
Rotator out_Rotation)
{
    super.GetPlayerViewPoint(out_Location, out_Rotation);
}
```

4. At this point nothing has changed, if we compiled now and ran the game it would still be a first person viewpoint. Now we'll apply our offset. Add these lines after the call to the super:

```
if(Pawn != none)
{
    out_Location = Pawn.Location + PlayerViewOffset;
    out_Rotation = rotator(Pawn.Location - out_Location);
}
```

This is a fair bit of code, so let's go through it one step at a time. The `if` statement you should recognize from the section in the last chapter about flow control. In this case we're checking to see if our `PlayerController` has a `Pawn`.

In the UDK, a `Pawn` is the physical representation of the player, the actual object in the world, with the `PlayerController` being its brain in a sense. In the game the `PlayerController` doesn't move, and indeed if we log our `AwesomePlayerController`'s location in the `GetPlayerViewPoint` function we'll see that once spawned it stays at the same location. In order for our camera to follow the player, we need to follow the Pawn since that is the actual visual actor of the player.

Inside the if statement, the first line gets our `Pawn`'s location and adds our `PlayerViewOffset` variable to it. Wherever the `Pawn` is, the camera will stay locked to it with this offset.

The next line is a bit of math to figure out the camera's rotation. We want it to always point toward the player, so we subtract our camera's location from the Pawn's to get a vector that points toward the player, and then turn that vector into a rotator that the function can use. This is a handy vector equation. The best way to remember it is to visualize two vectors, A and B. If we wanted to figure out what vector C was in the following diagram:

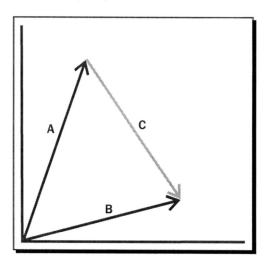

If we only have A and B, we can figure out what C is, by moving backwards along A, and then forwards along B as in the following diagram:

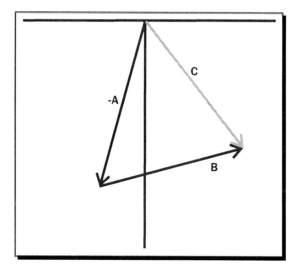

This would give us C = -A + B, or C = B − A. In our code B would be the Pawn's location and A would be the camera's, giving us our line of code:

```
out_Rotation = rotator(Pawn.Location - out_Location);
```

5. Compile the code and run it.

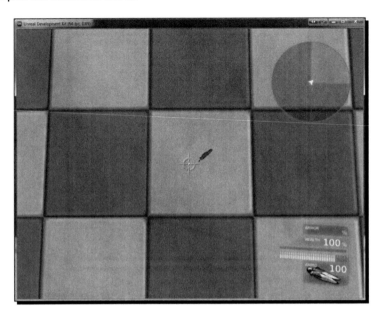

What in the world is going on here? We seem to be invisible except for a floating gun, and we're shooting at the ground. A big part of programming is knowing that your code isn't going to work perfectly the first time you write it. I call this process "breaking it towards completion". It might be broken right now, but it's a lot closer to what we wanted than when we first started. Let's see if we can make it better, starting with the invisible player.

6. By default you can't see your own Pawn. This might not make sense at first. We can see our arms and the gun in our hands, so what am I talking about? The things we see in first person view are actually different actors attached to us, usually cut off above the elbows so we only see the arms and the weapon in our hands. If we were able to see our own Pawn, the animation of it running would frequently obscure the camera's view and make it look like a polygon factory exploded on our monitor. To prevent this, meshes have a variable called bOwnerNoSee. When that's set to True, the owner of that actor can't see it. This is what we'll change in our function. Add a new line to the top of our if statement:

```
Pawn.Mesh.SetOwnerNoSee(false);
```

Our function should now look like this:

```
simulated event GetPlayerViewPoint(out vector out_Location, out
Rotator out_Rotation)
{
    super.GetPlayerViewPoint(out_Location, out_Rotation);

    if(Pawn != none)
    {
        Pawn.Mesh.SetOwnerNoSee(false);

        out_Location = Pawn.Location + PlayerViewOffset;
        out_Rotation = rotator(Pawn.Location - out_Location);
    }
}
```

7. Compile and run the code.

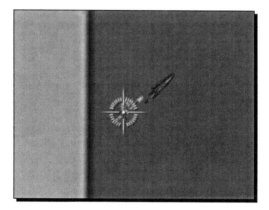

That's better. We can see our `Pawn` now. We're a bit obscured by the crosshair, but we can ignore that for a minute. We have a bigger problem right now. If anyone attacked us we'd be totally screwed because we're shooting at the ground. Let's fix that next.

8. In a normal FPS game on the UDK, when a weapon fires it asks the
`PlayerController` which direction we're facing so it knows what to shoot
at. Normally the `PlayerController` tells the weapon to use our camera's
rotation. This isn't going to work in our case, as we've changed it, so the camera
is always pointing toward the ground. To fix this we're going to override another
function called `GetAdjustedAimFor`. Write the following code after our
`GetPlayerViewPoint` function:

```
function Rotator GetAdjustedAimFor( Weapon W, vector StartFireLoc
)
{
    return Pawn.Rotation;
}
```

This tells the weapon to use our Pawn's rotation instead of the camera's rotation.
Since the Pawn never changes its pitch value (otherwise when we looked up it
would look like we were lying on our back), this will make sure that we always shoot
straight ahead. Our class should now look like this:

```
class AwesomePlayerController extends UTPlayerController;

var vector PlayerViewOffset;

simulated event GetPlayerViewPoint(out vector out_Location, out
Rotator out_Rotation)
{
    super.GetPlayerViewPoint(out_Location, out_Rotation);

    if(Pawn != none)
    {
        Pawn.Mesh.SetOwnerNoSee(false);

        out_Location = Pawn.Location + PlayerViewOffset;
        out_Rotation = rotator(Pawn.Location - out_Location);
    }
}

function Rotator GetAdjustedAimFor( Weapon W, vector StartFireLoc
)
{
    return Pawn.Rotation;
}

defaultproperties
{
    PlayerViewOffset=(X=-64,Y=0,Z=1024)
}
```

9. Compile and run the game again.

Much better! Now let's see if we can take care of that crosshair.

10. Whether or not to show the crosshair is stored as a `config` bool in the `PlayerController` class. This means we can't just change it in the default properties, since we can't set `config` variables in the defaults. This means we can change it one of three ways. We can remove the crosshair from the Scaleform HUD file, but Scaleform is a bit out of the scope of this book. We can change the `config` value in the INI files, but if the player were to change it the crosshair would appear again. For a more permanent solution, we can change the `bNoCrosshair` variable in an overridden `PostBeginPlay`.

11. Change our `PostBeginPlay` function to look like this:

```
simulated function PostBeginPlay()
{
    super.PostBeginPlay();
    bNoCrosshair = true;
}
```

Our class should now look like this:

```
class AwesomePlayerController extends UTPlayerController;

var vector PlayerViewOffset;

simulated function PostBeginPlay()
{
    super.PostBeginPlay();
    bNoCrosshair = true;
```

```
    }

    simulated event GetPlayerViewPoint(out vector out_Location, out
    Rotator out_Rotation)
    {
        super.GetPlayerViewPoint(out_Location, out_Rotation);

        if(Pawn != none)
        {
            Pawn.Mesh.SetOwnerNoSee(false);

            out_Location = Pawn.Location + PlayerViewOffset;
            out_Rotation = rotator(Pawn.Location - out_Location);
        }
    }

    function Rotator GetAdjustedAimFor( Weapon W, vector StartFireLoc
    )
    {
        return Pawn.Rotation;
    }

    defaultproperties
    {
        PlayerViewOffset=(X=-64,Y=0,Z=1024)
    }
```

12. Compile and run the code.

Almost there! Now what's with that giant gun? Remember when I talked about the first person view, and how the arms and weapon we see are different than the ones everyone else sees. The giant floating gun is what we would normally see in first person view, so let's hide it.

13. In our `GetPlayerViewPoint`'s if statement, let's add this bit of code:

```
if(Pawn.Weapon != none)
    Pawn.Weapon.SetHidden(true);
```

Now our code will check if we're holding a weapon and if so, hide it. Our function should now look like this:

```
simulated event GetPlayerViewPoint(out vector out_Location, out
Rotator out_Rotation)
{
    super.GetPlayerViewPoint(out_Location, out_Rotation);

    if(Pawn != none)
    {
        Pawn.Mesh.SetOwnerNoSee(false);
        if(Pawn.Weapon != none)
            Pawn.Weapon.SetHidden(true);

        out_Location = Pawn.Location + PlayerViewOffset;
        out_Rotation = rotator(Pawn.Location - out_Location);
    }
}
```

14. Compile and run.

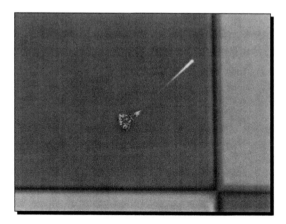

Perfect!

What just happened?

We've overridden a few functions in our quest to get things how we want. Overriding functions allows us to take the functionality that already exists and tweak it to fit our purposes. We could do a lot of different things with the `GetPlayerViewPoint` function for instance. With the right code it could be turned into an RTS click-to-move type of camera that isn't focused on our Pawn, or a sidescroller, or a third person over the shoulder camera.

Function overriding is the main reason why I say it's important to read through the source code. Knowing what already exists will help you figure out what you need to change to get the functionality you want out of the game. The two classes we've already subclassed, `GameInfo` and `PlayerController`, are good places to start reading, as well as Actor and Object for general functions available to all classes.

Next up we're going to take a look at how to use actor classes themselves as variables.

Actors as variables

In our discussion of variables in the last chapter, I purposely left out the one that's used most often, but now that we've had a chance to take a look at how classes work and are created, we can talk about how to use Actor classes themselves as variables. We've poked around a little bit in it when we made our Pawn visible and hid the giant floating gun, but let's explore it further.

Time for action – Experiments with Actors as variables

For this experiment we're going to bring back our old friend the `AwesomeActor`. We'll use him as a variable in our `AwesomePlayerController`.

1. For this experiment we'll need `AwesomeActor` to be visible, so let's make sure our default properties are set up for that. Our `AwesomeActor` class should look like this:

```
class AwesomeActor extends Actor;

defaultproperties
{
    Begin Object Class=SpriteComponent Name=Sprite
        Sprite=Texture2D'EditorResources.S_NavP'
    End Object
    Components.Add(Sprite)
}
```

Since we'll be spawning `AwesomeActor` during gameplay we don't need it to be placeable, and we're not going to do anything more with it once it's spawned so we don't need the `PostBeginPlay` function for now.

2. In our `AwesomePlayerController`, we're going to use the function that's called when we click the left mouse button to fire, called `StartFire`. Let's add that to our class:

```
exec function StartFire( optional byte FireModeNum )
{
    super.StartFire(FireModeNum);
}
```

The `FireModeNum` in this function is used for weapons that have more than one firing mode, like the plasma bolts versus the beam of the Link Gun. We don't need to worry about that variable for our experiment though, let's just make sure it calls the super so we don't completely override the function and our gun still works.

3. Now let's declare a variable of our `AwesomeActor` type at the top of our `AwesomePlayerController` class.

```
var AwesomeActor MyAwesomeActor;
```

4. We talked about the defaults of all of the other variables in the previous chapter, but what is the default for a variable of an Actor class? Only one way to find out! Let's log it in the AwesomePlayerController's PostBeginPlay function.

```
simulated function PostBeginPlay()
{
    super.PostBeginPlay();
    bNoCrosshair = true;

    `log(MyAwesomeActor @ "<-- Default for MyAwesomeActor");
}
```

5. Our `AwesomePlayerController` should now look like this.

```
class AwesomePlayerController extends UTPlayerController;

var AwesomeActor MyAwesomeActor;

var vector PlayerViewOffset;

simulated function PostBeginPlay()
{
    super.PostBeginPlay();
    bNoCrosshair = true;

    `log(MyAwesomeActor @ "<-- Default for MyAwesomeActor");
}
```

```
exec function StartFire( optional byte FireModeNum )
{
    super.StartFire(FireModeNum);
}


simulated event GetPlayerViewPoint(out vector out_Location, out
Rotator out_Rotation)
{
    super.GetPlayerViewPoint(out_Location, out_Rotation);

    if(Pawn != none)
    {
        Pawn.Mesh.SetOwnerNoSee(false);
        if(Pawn.Weapon != none)
            Pawn.Weapon.SetHidden(true);

        out_Location = Pawn.Location + PlayerViewOffset;
        out_Rotation = rotator(Pawn.Location - out_Location);
    }
}


function Rotator GetAdjustedAimFor( Weapon W, vector StartFireLoc
)
{
    return Pawn.Rotation;
}


defaultproperties
{
    PlayerViewOffset=(X=-64,Y=0,Z=1024)
}
```

Now you can see how code can get long and complicated, we're only doing simple stuff so far and look at all the code in this class! This is why it helps to have variables and functions with very descriptive names. A lot of the time you can get an idea of what's going on in the code just by reading it out loud to yourself. A descriptive name also makes it easier to search in UnCodeX to find out where things are being used.

6. Compile our code and run it. In Launch.log we can find out what the default for Actor variables is.

```
[0008.17] ScriptLog: None <-- Default for MyAwesomeActor
```

7. As we can see, the default for Actor variables is None. Where have we seen that before? We already have an example of how to use Actor variables in flow control statements in our code right here!

```
if(Pawn.Weapon != none)
    Pawn.Weapon.SetHidden(true);
```

In this case, our `Pawn` has an `Actor` variable called `Weapon`. If we look at where that's declared in the Pawn class:

```
/** Weapon currently held by Pawn */
var        Weapon              Weapon;
```

So the Pawn's `Weapon` is a variable of the `Actor` type of Weapon. It can be confusing when you're looking at code to see whether something's referring to a variable or a class, especially when the variable has the same name as the class it's a type of, so I wouldn't recommend doing this in your own code. That's why we named our `AwesomeActor` as `MyAwesomeActor`. It still lets us easily tell what type of Actor it is while avoiding the confusion of the exact same name as the class.

In the flow control statement using the Pawn's Weapon variable, we can see that we're checking to see that it's not equal to none. For Actor variables, this checks if this variable is referencing any Actor. If it is, then it won't be none and the flow control statement can continue.

One important thing to remember is that this does not mean that every Actor in the game is a variable or is assigned to one, or that declaring a variable of an Actor type automatically creates that Actor in the world. Actor variables are simply a way for us to store a reference to an Actor in the world. An Actor can be referenced by more than one variable in any number of different classes, or it may not be referenced by any variables. For instance, when we were first testing our `AwesomeActor` class, we were placing them directly in the level in `UnrealEd`. There was no `AwesomeActor` variable in any other class that was referencing them.

8. So how DO we assign things to our Actor variables? There are a few different ways of doing that. The first is by copying it from another variable that already has the reference stored. Let's say we created a variable of the type Weapon in our `AwesomePlayerController`:

```
var Weapon AnotherWeaponVariable;
```

9. `PostBeginPlay` is a bit too soon in the game's start up sequence to try and assign a reference to our weapon, so let's do it when we fire the gun. Let's change our `StartFire` function to look like this:

```
exec function StartFire( optional byte FireModeNum )
{
    super.StartFire(FireModeNum);
    AnotherWeaponVariable = Pawn.Weapon;
    `log(AnotherWeaponVariable);
}
```

10. Compile the code and run it. While in game, fire the gun (more than once is fine, it won't hurt anything). Exit and let's take a look at the log.

```
[0005.79] ScriptLog: UTWeap_LinkGun_0
```

The format may look familiar, the underscore with a number after it also showed up in the editor during our `AwesomeActor` tests in the first chapter.

Another thing that we'll notice is that even though the variable is declared as the Weapon class, a `UTWeap_LinkGun` actor was logged. Actor variables can reference either an actor of the variable type or any of its subclasses. This makes writing code more convenient, since we only need one variable to hold the player's Weapon instead of a different variable for every weapon class.

Now that we have the reference, we can manipulate it the same way we would `Pawn.Weapon`. For instance, our if statement in `GetPlayerViewPoint`:

```
if(Pawn.Weapon != none)
    Pawn.Weapon.SetHidden(true);
```

Could be changed to this:

```
if(AnotherWeaponVariable != none)
    AnotherWeaponVariable.SetHidden(true);
```

One important thing to remember about this though is that even though we assigned `AnotherWeaponVariable` to `Pawn.Weapon`, we only did it once. If `Pawn.Weapon` changed, `AnotherWeaponVariable` wouldn't automatically change to match it. For example, say your favorite color was purple. If I said my favorite color was your favorite color, mine would be purple as well. If you changed your favorite color to blue, mine would still be purple unless I said my favorite color was your favorite color again. Make sense?

11. The second way of getting a reference to an Actor is by spawning that Actor ourselves. Using our `AwesomeActor` as an example, let's change our `StartFire` code to this:

```
exec function StartFire( optional byte FireModeNum )
{
    super.StartFire(FireModeNum);
    MyAwesomeActor = spawn(class'AwesomeActor',,, Pawn.Location);
    `log(MyAwesomeActor @ "<-- MyAwesomeActor");
}
```

If we look at where the spawn function is declared in Actor.uc we can see how it's used:

```
native noexport final function coerce actor Spawn
(
    class<actor>        SpawnClass,
    optional actor       SpawnOwner,
    optional name        SpawnTag,
    optional vector      SpawnLocation,
    optional rotator     SpawnRotation,
    optional Actor       ActorTemplate,
    optional bool        bNoCollisionFail
);
```

The function line may look confusing, but the important part for us right now are the parameters. We tell it what class to spawn and the rest is optional. The only thing we're giving it for now is a location, which is our Pawn's location to make it easy to tell when the `AwesomeActor` has been spawned.

12. Compile the code and test it out. When we fire our weapon, an `AwesomeActor` should appear in game as well as the log. Fire the weapon a few times while moving around so we can see what happens.

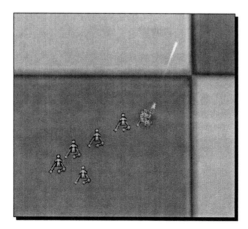

Our AwesomeActors are spawning! Now let's take a look at the log:

```
[0007.76] ScriptLog: AwesomeActor_0 <-- MyAwesomeActor
[0008.11] ScriptLog: AwesomeActor_1 <-- MyAwesomeActor
[0008.52] ScriptLog: AwesomeActor_2 <-- MyAwesomeActor
[0008.81] ScriptLog: AwesomeActor_3 <-- MyAwesomeActor
[0021.36] ScriptLog: AwesomeActor_4 <-- MyAwesomeActor
```

We can see that as each `AwesomeActor` was spawned, it was assigned to our `MyAwesomeActor` variable, but when a new one was spawned the reference was replaced with the new one. We can also see that this doesn't mean the old one was destroyed just because MyAwesomeActor's reference changed.

13. Another way we can get a reference to an Actor is by using what's called an iterator. There are a few functions in `Actor.uc` we can use that will cycle through all of the actors currently in the level and let us sort through them to find what we want. Before we do this we need to place an `AwesomeActor` in the level ourselves so we can see if we can get a reference to it. Change AwesomeActor's code to read the `placeable` keyword:

```
class AwesomeActor extends Actor
    placeable;


defaultproperties
{
    Begin Object Class=SpriteComponent Name=Sprite
        Sprite=Texture2D'EditorResources.S_NavP'
    End Object
    Components.Add(Sprite)
}
```

14. Compile the code, then open our test map in the editor and place an `AwesomeActor` near the player start. Save the map and close the editor.

15. Now for the iterator function. We can do this in `PostBeginPlay`, so let's put it there:

```
simulated function PostBeginPlay()
{
    super.PostBeginPlay();
    bNoCrosshair = true;

    foreach DynamicActors(class'AwesomeActor', MyAwesomeActor)
        break;

    `log(MyAwesomeActor @ "<-- MyAwesomeActor");
}
```

The way iterators work is that for every Actor in the map it finds that is either the class we specify (AwesomeActor in this case) or a subclass of that class, it will assign it to the variable we specify (MyAwesomeActor) so we can do things to it or check things about it. The break line right afterward makes it exit the loop after the first one it finds, but the `MyAwesomeActor` variable will keep the reference to it. Let's try it out.

16. Compile the code and test. Close the game and take a look at the log:

```
[0004.62] ScriptLog: AwesomeActor_0 <-- MyAwesomeActor
```

The code found it!

What just happened?

Using Actors as variables is an important concept to grasp in UnrealScript. Without them objects in the world would have a hard time interacting with each other and it would be difficult to have any kind of complexity without them. As with any other type of variable we can use logical operators on them such as == or != to test if two variables are the same or not. They can also be made editable, since Actors placed in the world already exist and getting a reference to another one is as simple as typing its name into the property. They can't however be used in the default properties, since our classes are just blueprints for objects that haven't been created yet.

Before we move on to our next subject, let's try a challenge.

Have a go hero – Keeping references to spawned actors

In our experiment with getting a reference to an Actor as we spawned it, every time a new one was spawned the reference was replaced. But, if we had an array of our class declared like this:

```
var array<AwesomeActor> MyAwesomeActors;
```

How would we rewrite the `StartFire` function to keep a reference to every `AwesomeActor` that we spawned instead of just the latest one?

Hint – Remember our lessons on adding elements to dynamic arrays.

Casting

Another important principle in object-oriented programming in UnrealScript is typecasting, or casting for short. We know that when creating subclasses we can add functions or variables that don't exist in the parent class. We also know that when we have an actor variable that it can reference a subclass of that actor. So if we have a subclassed actor referenced in our variable, how do we use the variables or functions that are unique to that subclass?

Time for action – Casting Actor variables

The answer of course is casting. Let's set up a subclass of `AwesomeActor` and see how we can use it.

1. Create a new file in our `AwesomeGame/Classes` folder and call it `UberActor`. Type the following code into it:

```
class UberActor extends AwesomeActor
    placeable;

function UberFunction()
{
    `log("UberFunction was called!");
}

defaultproperties
{
}
```

We're extending off of `AwesomeActor` and adding a function called `UberFunction` that will log when it is called. Remembering our inheritance, we don't need the sprite in the default properties because we will inherit it from `AwesomeActor`.

2. Compile the code and open the editor. If we take a look in the Actor browser we'll see our `UberActor` underneath `AwesomeActor` in the class tree.

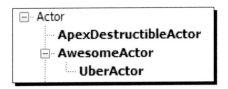

Close the editor for now; we'll be spawning the `UberActor` directly so we can get an easy reference to it.

3. In our `AwesomePlayerController` class, add the `StartFire` function again and spawn an `UberActor` into our `MyAwesomeActor` variable:

```
exec function StartFire( optional byte FireModeNum )
{
    super.StartFire(FireModeNum);
    MyAwesomeActor = spawn(class'UberActor',,, Pawn.Location);
    `log(MyAwesomeActor @ "<-- MyAwesomeActor");
}
```

And since we've made a lot of changes these past few pages, let's make sure our `AwesomePlayerController` classes match:

```
class AwesomePlayerController extends UTPlayerController;

var AwesomeActor MyAwesomeActor;

var vector PlayerViewOffset;

simulated function PostBeginPlay()
{
    super.PostBeginPlay();
    bNoCrosshair = true;
}

exec function StartFire( optional byte FireModeNum )
{
    super.StartFire(FireModeNum);
    MyAwesomeActor = spawn(class'UberActor',,, Pawn.Location);
    `log(MyAwesomeActor @ "<-- MyAwesomeActor");
}

simulated event GetPlayerViewPoint(out vector out_Location, out
Rotator out_Rotation)
{
    super.GetPlayerViewPoint(out_Location, out_Rotation);

    if(Pawn != none)
    {
        Pawn.Mesh.SetOwnerNoSee(false);
        if(Pawn.Weapon != none)
            Pawn.Weapon.SetHidden(true);

        out_Location = Pawn.Location + PlayerViewOffset;
        out_Rotation = rotator(Pawn.Location - out_Location);
    }
```

```
}

function Rotator GetAdjustedAimFor( Weapon W, vector StartFireLoc
)
{
    return Pawn.Rotation;
}

defaultproperties
{
    PlayerViewOffset=(X=-64,Y=0,Z=1024)
}
```

4. Compile and run the code, shoot the gun a few times, then shut down the game and take a look at the log:

```
[0007.73] ScriptLog: UberActor_0 <-- MyAwesomeActor
[0008.52] ScriptLog: UberActor_1 <-- MyAwesomeActor
[0009.52] ScriptLog: UberActor_2 <-- MyAwesomeActor
```

As expected, even though MyAwesomeActor has been declared as an AwesomeActor type, our subclass can still be used and referenced by MyAwesomeActor.

5. Now what do we do if we want to call UberFunction? Let's try calling it directly in our StartFire function:

```
exec function StartFire( optional byte FireModeNum )
{
    super.StartFire(FireModeNum);

    MyAwesomeActor = spawn(class'UberActor',,, Pawn.Location);
    `log(MyAwesomeActor @ "<-- MyAwesomeActor");

    if(MyAwesomeActor != none)
        MyAwesomeActor.UberFunction();
}
```

That should work, right? Since our MyAwesomeActor variable references an UberActor, we should be able to just call the function right?

6. Compile the code.

```
Error, Unrecognized member 'UberFunction' in class 'AwesomeActor'
```

Well that's no good. Since we declared `MyAwesomeActor` as an `AwesomeActor` type, the game will treat it as one when we try to call functions and variables directly on it. Any functions and variables in the subclass won't be available to us. This is where casting comes in handy.

7. Let's change the `StartFire` function a little bit.

    ```
    exec function StartFire( optional byte FireModeNum )
    {
        super.StartFire(FireModeNum);

        MyAwesomeActor = spawn(class'UberActor',,, Pawn.Location);
        `log(MyAwesomeActor @ "<-- MyAwesomeActor");

        if(UberActor(MyAwesomeActor) != none)
            UberActor(MyAwesomeActor).UberFunction();
    }
    ```

8. Now let's try compiling:

    ```
    Success - 0 error(s), 0 warning(s)
    ```

    That's better!

9. Now let's run the game, fire the weapon, and see what happens in the log:

    ```
    [0006.59] ScriptLog: UberActor_0 <-- MyAwesomeActor
    [0006.59] ScriptLog: UberFunction was called!
    ```

    There we go, our `UberFunction` was called successfully! But what happens if we run this code with a `MyAwesomeActor` that isn't an `UberActor`? Let's try that out.

10. Let's change the `StartFire` function again to spawn a normal `AwesomeActor` instead of an `UberActor`:

    ```
    exec function StartFire( optional byte FireModeNum )
    {
        super.StartFire(FireModeNum);

        MyAwesomeActor = spawn(class'AwesomeActor',,, Pawn.Location);
        `log(MyAwesomeActor @ "<-- MyAwesomeActor");

        if(UberActor(MyAwesomeActor) != none)
            UberActor(MyAwesomeActor).UberFunction();
     else
         `log("MyAwesomeActor is not an UberActor.");
    }
    ```

We've also added an else to our flow control statement, if it's not able to call `UberFunction` the log will let us know.

1. Compile and run the code, fire the weapon, and then exit and take a look at the log.

   ```
   [0008.80] ScriptLog: AwesomeActor_1 <-- MyAwesomeActor
   [0008.80] ScriptLog: MyAwesomeActor is not an UberActor.
   ```

   The code went through to our else statement, so it's working correctly. Our `MyAwesomeActor` isn't an `UberActor` now. But what's going on with the `MyAwesomeActor` variable exactly?

2. Let's change `StartFire` again. This time we'll add two logs, one normal and one with casting.

   ```
   exec function StartFire( optional byte FireModeNum )
   {
       super.StartFire(FireModeNum);

       MyAwesomeActor = spawn(class'AwesomeActor',,, Pawn.Location);

       `log(MyAwesomeActor @ "<-- MyAwesomeActor");
       `log(UberActor(MyAwesomeActor) @ "<--
   UberActor(MyAwesomeActor)");
   }
   ```

   What do you think the typecast log is going to show? Let's find out.

3. Compile and run the game, fire the gun, and exit to look at the log:

   ```
   [0008.65] ScriptLog: AwesomeActor_1 <-- MyAwesomeActor
   [0008.66] ScriptLog: None <-- UberActor(MyAwesomeActor)
   ```

   That makes sense. An actor variable can either reference an object that actually exists in the level, or else it will be "none". When we're casting a variable, if the actor referenced by our variable isn't the class that we're casting to or any of its subclasses, the cast will give us "none" to let us know.

What just happened?

In addition to letting us use functions and variables that only exist in subclasses of our variable's class, casting gives us a way to react differently to a variable depending on what class it is. As an example, take the following code. Don't write this down; trust me it's not going to compile:

```
var Pet MyPet;

function ReactToPet()
```

```
    {
        if(Cat(MyPet) != none)
            Sneeze();
        else if(Dog(MyPet) != none)
            PetTheDog();
        else
            `log("What are you, pet?");
    }
```

Next let's see if we can get a practical example of casting for our game.

Time for action – A practical example of casting for our game

Let's change the way our Pawn reacts to the weapon he's carrying. We'll make him invisible when he picks up a rocket launcher, and make him visible for a bit after he fires it. Sure why not!

1. For this example we don't need to do anything to the rocket launcher class itself, all of our work will be in our AwesomePlayerController. Let's strip out all of our AwesomeActor/UberActor experimentation and get back to our basic AwesomePlayerController:

```
class AwesomePlayerController extends UTPlayerController;

var vector PlayerViewOffset;

simulated function PostBeginPlay()
{
    super.PostBeginPlay();
    bNoCrosshair = true;
}

exec function StartFire( optional byte FireModeNum )
{
    super.StartFire(FireModeNum);
}

simulated event GetPlayerViewPoint(out vector out_Location, out
Rotator out_Rotation)
{
    super.GetPlayerViewPoint(out_Location, out_Rotation);

    if(Pawn != none)
    {
        Pawn.Mesh.SetOwnerNoSee(false);
```

```
        if(Pawn.Weapon != none)
            Pawn.Weapon.SetHidden(true);

        out_Location = Pawn.Location + PlayerViewOffset;
        out_Rotation = rotator(Pawn.Location - out_Location);
    }
}

function Rotator GetAdjustedAimFor( Weapon W, vector StartFireLoc
)
{
    return Pawn.Rotation;
}

defaultproperties
{
    PlayerViewOffset=(X=-64,Y=0,Z=1024)
}
```

Well, maybe not so basic, but as far as code goes we're just getting started!

2.   There's a function that's called on Controllers when they switch weapons, called
     `NotifyChangedWeapon`. Let's use that to find out if the player is using a rocket
     launcher and make our Pawn invisible if they are:

```
function NotifyChangedWeapon(Weapon PrevWeapon, Weapon NewWeapon)
{
    super.NotifyChangedWeapon(PrevWeapon, NewWeapon);

    if(Pawn == none)
        return;

    if(UTWeap_RocketLauncher(NewWeapon) != none)
        Pawn.SetHidden(true);
    else
        Pawn.SetHidden(false);
}
```

First thing we do is call the super. Next, if we don't have a Pawn then we can't make
it invisible, so exit out of the function if our Pawn is none (which can happen when
we're dead or in spectator mode and so on). Finally, we cast `NewWeapon`, which is a
Weapon variable, to `UTWeap_RocketLauncher`. If it is that class or a subclass, then
we make our Pawn invisible. If it isn't, we know the player has switched to another
weapon and we make them visible again.

3. Compile the code. Before we can test it out, we need to place a rocket launcher spawner in our test level. Open **AwesomeTestMap** in the editor, and in the **Actor Browser** select **NavigationPoint | PickupFactory | UDKPickupFactory | UTPickupFactory | UTWeaponPickupFactory** and place one near the player start. Double-click it to open up its properties and set its Weapon Pickup Class to `UTWeap_RocketLauncher_Content`. Remember to Build Paths in the top toolbar of the editor, then save and close the editor.

4. Run our batch file and walk to the weapon spawner to pick up the rocket launcher. We'll see our Pawn turn invisible, and we can still fire the weapon. Now use the mouse wheel to switch back to the Link Gun and we'll see the Pawn become visible again.

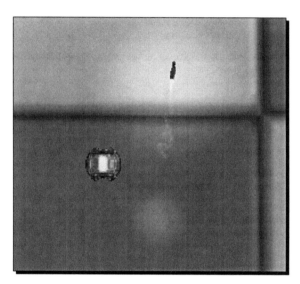

Ok, I am totally making this up as I go along and even I'll admit that's pretty awesome. Only one thing left to do, let's make the Pawn visible for a bit after we fire the rocket launcher!

5. To do that, we'll alter our `StartFire` function and use another cast:

```
exec function StartFire( optional byte FireModeNum )
{
    super.StartFire(FireModeNum);

    if(Pawn != none && UTWeap_RocketLauncher(Pawn.Weapon) != none)
    {
        Pawn.SetHidden(false);
        SetTimer(1, false, 'MakeMeInvisible');
    }
}
```

Now when we fire whatever weapon our Pawn is holding, we check if it's a `UTWeap_RocketLauncher` and if it is, show our Pawn. We also use a function called `SetTimer` to make a one second delay before calling a function we'll write next, called `MakeMeInvisible`. Don't compile yet, we need to write that function first.

6. The function we're going to write now, `MakeMeInvisible`, doesn't exist anywhere else, it's something we're making up specifically for our `AwesomePlayerController`.

```
function MakeMeInvisible()
{
    if(Pawn != none && UTWeap_RocketLauncher(Pawn.Weapon) != none)
        Pawn.SetHidden(true);
}
```

A simple function, all we do is make sure we have a Pawn and are still holding our rocket launcher (the player might have switched weapons during the delay), and if so make our Pawn invisible.

7. Now our `AwesomePlayerController` should look like this:

```
class AwesomePlayerController extends UTPlayerController;

var vector PlayerViewOffset;

simulated function PostBeginPlay()
{
    super.PostBeginPlay();
    bNoCrosshair = true;
}

function NotifyChangedWeapon(Weapon PrevWeapon, Weapon NewWeapon)
{
    super.NotifyChangedWeapon(PrevWeapon, NewWeapon);

    if(Pawn == none)
        return;

    if(UTWeap_RocketLauncher(NewWeapon) != none)
        Pawn.SetHidden(true);
    else
        Pawn.SetHidden(false);
}

exec function StartFire( optional byte FireModeNum )
{
```

```
        super.StartFire(FireModeNum);

        if(Pawn != none && UTWeap_RocketLauncher(Pawn.Weapon) != none)
        {
            Pawn.SetHidden(false);
            SetTimer(1, false, 'MakeMeInvisible');
        }
    }


function MakeMeInvisible()
{
    if(Pawn != none && UTWeap_RocketLauncher(Pawn.Weapon) != none)
        Pawn.SetHidden(true);
}
simulated event GetPlayerViewPoint(out vector out_Location, out
Rotator out_Rotation)
{
    super.GetPlayerViewPoint(out_Location, out_Rotation);

    if(Pawn != none)
    {
        Pawn.Mesh.SetOwnerNoSee(false);
        if(Pawn.Weapon != none)
            Pawn.Weapon.SetHidden(true);

        out_Location = Pawn.Location + PlayerViewOffset;
        out_Rotation = rotator(Pawn.Location - out_Location);
    }
}


function Rotator GetAdjustedAimFor( Weapon W, vector StartFireLoc
)
{
    return Pawn.Rotation;
}


defaultproperties
{
    PlayerViewOffset=(X=-64,Y=0,Z=1024)
}
```

Now we're getting somewhere! Compile the code and test it out. When we pick up the rocket launcher and switch to it, we become invisible, and when we fire it our Pawn becomes visible for a second before turning invisible again. Awesome! If we switch to the Link Gun we become visible again and stay visible even after we fire it.

What just happened?

As we can see, using casting on Actor variables lets us get really specific with our functionality, right down to reacting differently to subclasses of our variable's class.

Pop quiz – Chopping down the class tree

1. **True/False**: When we change a variable in an actor in the editor, the change applies to all actors of that class.

2. We can use casting to treat an actor variable as if it were a:
   a. Parent class
   b. Subclass
   c. Any Actor class

3. **True/False**: When a cast fails it will return 'none'.

Summary

We learned a lot in this chapter about the class tree.

Specifically, we covered:

- What classes are and how the game uses them
- What inheritance means and how to change inherited variables and functions
- Using function overriding to change a subclass' behavior
- Casting actor variables to use a subclass' functions and tell subclasses apart

Now that we've learned about how classes relate to each other in the class tree, we're ready to start learning more about classes themselves and expand our game's arsenal of classes to give us more functionality.

Making Custom Classes

Time to expand the game.

In the last chapter, we learned a lot about how classes work, how each subclass inherits the variables and functions of its parents, and how to use this to our advantage to get the functionality we want. Where do we go from here? In this chapter we're going to start creating more of our own classes to expand our custom game.

In this chapter we will:

- Discuss when and why we would want to create our own classes
- Talk about class modifiers and what they do for our classes
- Discuss the difference between Actors and Objects
- Talk about the most commonly used classes in UnrealScript

First up, we're going to talk about when and where to make custom classes for our game.

Creating a class

In my work with UnrealScript, one of the most common questions I see is "I understand how the language works, but I have no idea where to start writing my own code. What do I do?" For any project, before you start writing code it's best to have an idea of what you want your game to be. For most games this involves a design document. Let's see if we can come up with a quick one for our Awesome Game that we'll refer to when making programming decisions.

Awesome Game quicky design document

Most design documents have a detailed description of the game, from the storyline right down to the control scheme. However, we're going to keep things a little simplified for this. First of all we need to decide what type of game this will be.

◆ Awesome Game is a top-down shooter like Alien Swarm or Nation Red.

Having examples of other games in the style that you want helps define what programming needs your game will have. Let's see if we can expand this further:

◆ Enemies will spawn off screen and move toward the player. The player will have to shoot them before they get close or they will take damage.

There are a lot of programming tasks in that brief description. Let's see if we can break it down:

❑ **Enemies will spawn off screen and move toward the player**: This is actually three tasks if we think about it. First, we need them to spawn. This will involve a placeable `Actor` class we'll create that will handle spawning of enemies. The second task is getting them to spawn off screen. We don't want them randomly spawning, otherwise one could suddenly appear right next to the player which would be terribly frustrating. We'll need some code to handle this. The third task is the major one, the creation of the enemies themselves. Do we want more than one type? Maybe one type moves faster but has a weaker attack. These are things to think about when preparing a programming task list.

❑ **The player will have to shoot them before they get close...**: There are a few things to consider here. How many different types of weapons are there? How does the player get them? Maybe we'll want the player to start with a default weak weapon, and have others be picked up in the level. Some of this functionality can already be found in the UDK classes, but we'll need our own subclasses to handle some specific things we want to do. We could also have the enemies drop pickups that can upgrade our weapons. That would involve creating a group of classes for the dropped pickups as well as some code in the enemy classes that creates them when they die.

❑ **... or they will take damage**: This will involve some code in the enemy class to handle attacking. Am I close enough to the player to attack? What kind of attack do I want to use? This will also involve some interaction between our enemy class and the player to handle taking damage.

As we can see, even with short descriptions there are a lot of decisions that need to be made and programming tasks that can come out of it. It might seem overwhelming at first, but breaking the entire game down into a list of tasks makes it easier to figure out what classes will be needed as well as making it easier to keep track of our progress.

Let's see if we can go a bit further in our description of our game:

◆ Enemies will attack in waves, with each wave having more and stronger enemies.

For this we'll need some code that will keep track of the number of waves and enemies, how many enemies still need to be spawned, and how strong the current wave of enemies is.

Class breakdown

That seems like a good start for our example game, so let's see if we can figure out a few classes that we'll need for the game, and where to put them in the class tree.

Weapons

We've worked with weapons a bit in the last chapter, so this is a good place to start. Remembering our lessons on inheritance, if there is any common functionality we want out of our classes they should all have a common superclass. For instance, if we want our weapons to be upgradable through pickups, we should have some common functions in our main weapon class that any subclasses can change if we need them to. Let's set them up now.

Time for action – Creating the weapon branch

Looking in the class tree with UnCodeX, under **Actor | Inventory | Weapon | UDKWeapon | UTWeapon**, we can see the rocket launcher, shock rifle, and link gun are all subclasses. It might seem like we should subclass off of these since they're already made, but in order for us to be able to use inheritance with our classes we'll need to create a different branch here for our own weapons. Let's do that now.

1. Create a new file in our `Development/Src/AwesomeGame/Classes` folder called `AwesomeWeapon.uc`. While we're here, let's delete `AwesomeGun`, `AnotherGun`, and `UberActor` if they're still there. Now we should have `AwesomeActor`, `AwesomeGame`, `AwesomePlayerController`, and now `AwesomeWeapon`.

2. Type the following code into it:

```
class AwesomeWeapon extends UTWeapon;

var int CurrentWeaponLevel;

function UpgradeWeapon()
{
    CurrentWeaponLevel++;
}

defaultproperties
{
}
```

We're adding an int to keep track of our weapon's level, and putting a function in so we can increase the level. Now you might wonder why don't we just increase the level ourselves from our pickup class instead of having a function do it? For the most part it's best to keep all variable changes in the class that has the variables, that way it's easier to track down problems when they happen. Also, if we wanted to change the way things worked it's better to be able to find everything affecting the class inside the class itself instead of having to look in other classes to find places we changed variables. Other classes would just call `UpgradeWeapon()`, and everything else is handled in our `AwesomeWeapon` class.

3. We're not going to use the `AwesomeWeapon` class itself in our test level, it's just going to be the base for all of our other weapons. Let's create an actual weapon that we can place and test with. Create a new file in `Development/Src/AwesomeGame/Classes` called `AwesomeWeapon_RocketLauncher.uc` and type the following code into it:

```
class AwesomeWeapon_RocketLauncher extends AwesomeWeapon;

defaultproperties
{
    Begin Object Name=PickupMesh
        SkeletalMesh=SkeletalMesh'WP_RocketLauncher.Mesh.SK_WP_
RocketLauncher_3P'
    End Object

    AttachmentClass=class'UTGameContent.UTAttachment_
RocketLauncher'

    WeaponFireTypes(0)=EWFT_Projectile
    WeaponFireTypes(1)=EWFT_Projectile

    WeaponProjectiles(0)=class'UTProj_Rocket'
    WeaponProjectiles(1)=class'UTProj_Rocket'

    AmmoCount=30
    MaxAmmoCount=30
}
```

For now this is all default properties setting up the rocket launcher's visuals and functionality. We're increasing the default ammo from nine to 30 from the UDK's rocket launcher.

4. Compile the code and open up the editor. Open our `AwesomeTestMap` and change the weapon pickup's properties to add our rocket launcher.

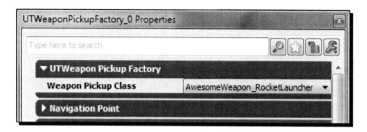

5. Save the map and close the editor, then run the game using our batch file. It works the same as before, except now we have 30 rockets instead of nine to start with.

That's good so far, but now we need a way to upgrade the weapon. Let's create a pickup class that can do this. The functionality of this class will be pretty simple, so we don't need to extend off of any UDK classes like `Inventory` or `UDKInventory`. Let's simply extend off of our `AwesomeActor`. Why `AwesomeActor` and not just Actor? To keep things organized. If we had several of these types of classes that we only needed to extend off of Actor, they'd end up all over the place in the class tree depending on their names. By using a common superclass, even if it's empty, we can keep all of our stuff in one place.

6. Let's make sure our `AwesomeActor` class is emptied out:

```
class AwesomeActor extends Actor;


defaultproperties
{
}
```

7. Now, using that as a parent class for our pickup, let's create a new class called `AwesomeWeaponUpgrade.uc` in our `Development/Src/AwesomeGame/Classes` folder and type the following code into it:

```
class AwesomeWeaponUpgrade extends AwesomeActor
    placeable;

event Touch(Actor Other, PrimitiveComponent OtherComp, vector
HitLocation, vector HitNormal)
{
    if(Pawn(Other) != none && AwesomeWeapon(Pawn(Other).Weapon) !=
none)
    {
        AwesomeWeapon(Pawn(Other).Weapon).UpgradeWeapon();
        Destroy();
```

```
        }
    }

defaultproperties
{
    bCollideActors=True

    Begin Object Class=DynamicLightEnvironmentComponent
Name=MyLightEnvironment
        bEnabled=TRUE
    End Object
    Components.Add(MyLightEnvironment)

    Begin Object Class=StaticMeshComponent Name=PickupMesh
        StaticMesh=StaticMesh'UN_SimpleMeshes.TexPropCube_Dup'
        Materials(0)=Material'EditorMaterials.WidgetMaterial_Y'
        LightEnvironment=MyLightEnvironment
        Scale3D=(X=0.125,Y=0.125,Z=0.125)
    End Object
    Components.Add(PickupMesh)

    Begin Object Class=CylinderComponent Name=CollisionCylinder
        CollisionRadius=16.0
        CollisionHeight=16.0
        BlockNonZeroExtent=true
        BlockZeroExtent=true
        BlockActors=true
        CollideActors=true
    End Object
    CollisionComponent=CollisionCylinder
    Components.Add(CollisionCylinder)
}
```

A pretty sizable chunk of code, but pretty simple. Here we're using an event called `Touch` that is called when two actors run into each other. Inside it, we check if the Actor that touched us is a Pawn and if so, check to see if it's holding an `AwesomeWeapon`. Remembering our lessons about typecasting, here we're using two of them at the same time so it might look a bit confusing at first.

The first typecast is here:

```
Pawn(Other)
```

Since the event gives us an `Actor` to work with called `Other`, we need to typecast it to see if it's a Pawn. If this typecast works, we know the Actor that touched us is a Pawn and we can continue the check:

```
Pawn(Other).Weapon
```

Since the `Weapon` variable doesn't exist in `Actor`, only in `Pawn`, we need to keep the `Pawn(Other)` typecast to be able to access the `Weapon` variable. Finally, we typecast that weapon to see if it's one of our custom classes:

```
AwesomeWeapon(Pawn(Other).Weapon)
```

This checks whether the weapon, which is of the `Weapon` class, is an `AwesomeWeapon` or subclass of `AwesomeWeapon`. If it is, then the if statement is true and we can execute some code inside it:

```
AwesomeWeapon(Pawn(Other).Weapon).UpgradeWeapon();
```

We keep the typecast here so we can call our custom `UpgradeWeapon` function. You can see why having functions instead of variables is preferred. If we wrote it like this:

```
AwesomeWeapon(Pawn(Other).Weapon).CurrentWeaponLevel++;
```

If we wanted to change how the leveling system works, for example, to add a maximum level, we would have to search through all of our code to see where we changed it, and add more code there. This could leave us with a lot of duplicated, messy code.

The `bCollideActors` in the default properties lets this actor receive `Touch` calls when something runs into it.

We then add a static mesh; in this case, a plain cube with a green material on it, with a light environment to make sure it's properly lit up.

Finally we give it some collision.

Before we test our code, let's add a log to our weapon class so we can see that it's working.

```
function UpgradeWeapon()
{
    CurrentWeaponLevel++;
    `log("Current Weapon Level:" @ CurrentWeaponLevel);
}
```

8. Compile the code, and then open up the editor. In the **Actor Browser** select our **AwesomeWeaponUpgrade**, if **Show Categories** is checked it will be under **Uncategorized | AwesomeActor**. If **Show Categories** is unchecked it will be under **Actor | AwesomeActor**. Right-click in the level and place one near our weapon spawner.

9. Click on the **Rebuild All** button to build the map, then save and exit the editor. Run the game with the batch file and walk over to the AwesomeWeaponUpgrade WITHOUT picking up the weapon first. You can see that no matter what you do, the pickup stays there and we don't get anything in the log. Why is that? Well, the default inventory we start with gives us a link gun, which isn't a subclass of our AwesomeWeapon. In the if statement on our AwesomeWeaponUpgrade, the typecasting fails and the code inside it never executes.

10. Now walk over to the weapon spawner and pick up the rocket launcher. Once we have it, run over to the weapon upgrade again. This time it disappears, and checking the log file we can see this:

```
[0009.47] ScriptLog: Current Weapon Level: 1
```

Remembering that ints start at 0, incrementing `CurrentWeaponLevel` leaves us with 1.

11. Now that we have the upgrades working, let's make them affect the weapons in some way. First we need to make a maximum level for the weapons so we don't get too crazy with them. Let's add a few things to our `AwesomeWeapon` class:

```
class AwesomeWeapon extends UTWeapon;

const MAX_LEVEL = 5;
```

```
var int CurrentWeaponLevel;

function UpgradeWeapon()
{
    if(CurrentWeaponLevel < MAX_LEVEL)
        CurrentWeaponLevel++;
    `log("Current Weapon Level:" @ CurrentWeaponLevel);
}

defaultproperties
{
}
```

A const is a special type of variable that cannot be changed (constant). They're declared slightly different from other variables because we set their value on the same line they're declared. In this case we're creating one called MAX_LEVEL and setting it to 5.

Why would we want to use a const instead of just 5? Let's say for some reason we wanted to change it. If we used the number 5 in our code, we would have to go through it line by line to find everywhere we used it and change the number. We could easily miss one, or worse change one that was only the same number by coincidence. Using a const, we would only have to change the value where it's declared and all the code that uses it would be changed.

12. Let's go into the editor and add some more AwesomeWeaponUpgrade actors so that we have at least 6 in the level.

13. Save the map and exit the editor, then run the game. Pick up our rocket launcher and run around picking up the weapon upgrades. Exit the editor and take a look at the log:

```
[0008.29] ScriptLog: Current Weapon Level: 1
[0008.60] ScriptLog: Current Weapon Level: 2
[0008.87] ScriptLog: Current Weapon Level: 3
[0010.24] ScriptLog: Current Weapon Level: 4
[0011.76] ScriptLog: Current Weapon Level: 5
[0012.55] ScriptLog: Current Weapon Level: 5
```

There we go, once we reach 5, our weapon can't be upgraded any further. Now that we have that in place, let's make it affect the gameplay in some way.

14. Let's add some more code to our `AwesomeWeapon` class. We're going to make the weapon fire faster as we upgrade it. First we'll add an array of firing rates:

```
var float FireRates[MAX_LEVEL];
```

You'll notice that we're using our `MAX_LEVEL` const here to define the array size. This is another difference between consts and regular variables. Consts can be used in other variable declarations to define array sizes while normal variables cannot. If `MAX_SIZE` were declared as an int and set in the default properties, using it here would give us a compiler error.

15. Now let's set the array in the default properties, making the max level really fast:

```
        FireRates(0)=1.5
        FireRates(1)=1.0
        FireRates(2)=0.5
        FireRates(3)=0.3
        FireRates(4)=0.1
```

That should do it. The number is the time between shots, so the lower the number the faster the weapon fires. The fastest firing rate is the same that we used before in our first experiment with weapons.

16. Now to change the firing rate in our `UpgradeWeapon` function:

```
        FireInterval[0] = FireRates[CurrentWeaponLevel - 1];
```

Remembering our arrays, when we increase `CurrentWeaponLevel` we need to access the array element that's 1 less. When the weapon is level 1 we want `FireRates[0]`, and when it's 5 we want the last element in the array, `FireRates[4]`.

17. There is another little bit of code we need to add to make sure our weapon functions properly. If we're holding down the fire button while we pick up an upgrade, we want the firing timer to reset to the new value. Let's add this bit of code to the function:

```
if(IsInState('WeaponFiring'))
{
    ClearTimer(nameof(RefireCheckTimer));
    TimeWeaponFiring(CurrentFireMode);
}
```

I know you wouldn't be able to just figure that out instantly, which is why I keep stressing the importance of reading through the source code. Using UnCodeX to track down what functions get called where, what variables are used to do what, it definitely helps to read through the source. You don't even have to memorize any of it. I forget most of it when I stand up from my computer. The important thing is knowing how to find it, by reading through the functions that get called and being able to search through the source code to trace the chain of events.

In this case, we're checking to see if the weapon is currently firing and if so we clear the refire timer and reset it to the new value.

18. Now just for some icing on the explosive tipped cake we'll refill the weapon's ammo when we pick up an upgrade.

```
AddAmmo(MaxAmmoCount);
```

With this line we don't need to worry about overfilling the weapon, if we look at the AddAmmo function in UTWeapon.uc:

```
AmmoCount = Clamp(AmmoCount + Amount,0,MaxAmmoCount);
```

We can see that it uses the Clamp function to limit the AmmoCount to between 0 and MaxAmmoCount.

19. Now our AwesomeWeapon class should look like this:

```
class AwesomeWeapon extends UTWeapon;

const MAX_LEVEL = 5;
var int CurrentWeaponLevel;
var float FireRates[MAX_LEVEL];

function UpgradeWeapon()
{
    if(CurrentWeaponLevel < MAX_LEVEL)
        CurrentWeaponLevel++;
```

```
        FireInterval[0] = FireRates[CurrentWeaponLevel - 1];

        if(IsInState('WeaponFiring'))
        {
            ClearTimer(nameof(RefireCheckTimer));
            TimeWeaponFiring(CurrentFireMode);
        }

        AddAmmo(MaxAmmoCount);
    }

defaultproperties
{
    FireRates(0)=1.5
    FireRates(1)=1.0
    FireRates(2)=0.5
    FireRates(3)=0.3
    FireRates(4)=0.1
}
```

Almost done, let's just set some defaults in our rocket launcher class.

20. Let's give our rocket launcher a default `FireInterval` that's higher than the fire rates for our upgrades.

```
    FireInterval(0)=1.75
    FireInterval(1)=1.75
```

21. Compile the code and run the test map. After picking up the rocket launcher we can pick up the upgrades and see our weapon firing faster and faster as it gains levels!

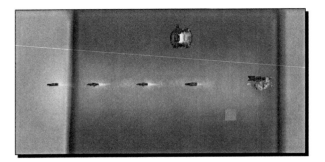

What just happened?

Now that we've created a few of our own classes, we can start to see how a design document can be turned into tasks that can be broken down into the classes we need to finish those tasks. Sometimes the functionality we need in our classes can already be found in the UDK source, as with our weapons, but sometimes we'll want to create our own branch in the class tree so we can fully control what happens, as with our upgrade pickups.

Next we'll take a look at some class modifiers we can use to control how our classes are used.

Class modifiers

Class modifiers change the way a class behaves in the editor and in the engine. Two of them we have seen before, but let's go through them to see how they're used.

Class modifiers are always specified at the top of our class in the class declaration line.

Placeable

This one we've used before, it tells the editor that this class can be placed in the editor. This is useful for most objects such as lights, player starts, weapon spawners, and so on. Some things don't need to be placed in the editor such as our `PlayerController` or Pawn, since those are spawned by the game during play. Some things wouldn't make sense to be placeable, such as a HUD. Things like that aren't level-specific, they're spawned and assigned to the player during the game. Generally, placeable classes are only those things that are level-specific and need to be put in a specific place in the level.

We can see an example right in our own code with our `AwesomeWeaponUpgrade` class:

```
class AwesomeWeaponUpgrade extends AwesomeActor
    placeable;
```

In the editor actors declared as placeable will appear bold in the Actor Browser.

Notplaceable

The opposite of placeable, this tells the editor that we don't want this actor to be able to be placed in the levels. By default, an actor class is not placeable; but say we had a subclass of our AwesomeWeaponUpgrade like this:

```
class AwesomeWeaponUpgrade_MaxAmmo extends AwesomeWeaponUpgrade;

defaultproperties
{
}
```

Even though we haven't put the placeable modifier in this class, if we compile and open the editor, this class will appear in bold and be placeable. The placeable modifier has been inherited from our parent class.

So why would we use this modifier? Say we had a group of a few different weapon upgrade classes that had a lot of common functionality and we wanted to use a common parent for them underneath our main `AwesomeWeaponUpgrade` class. If the common parent didn't have any specific functionality itself, we wouldn't want it to be placed in the editor, just its subclasses. In this case we would put the notplaceable modifier in our class.

Take the following example:

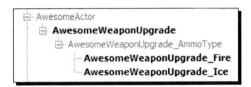

In this case we're making a group of upgrades under an `AwesomeWeaponUpgrade_ AmmoType` class. The `AmmoType` class itself wouldn't have any specific functionality, it would just have functions and variables common to all of its subclasses. We wouldn't want the generic `AmmoType` class itself to be placed, so we use the notplaceable modifier to let the editor know.

Abstract

This one's related to notplaceable, except this doesn't allow the class to be spawned or referenced at all. We would use this for similar reasons as we would use notplaceable, this class itself isn't useful, and all of the specific functionality is in its subclasses.

Let's take a look at how we can use this in our own classes.

Time for action – Using abstract

We'll use this modifier in our `AwesomeWeapon` branch to see how it's useful.

1. Before we change anything, open up our test map in the editor and take a look at the weapon spawner properties. We can change the weapon it spawns to be an `AwesomeWeapon` instead of an `AwesomeWeapon_RocketLauncher`:

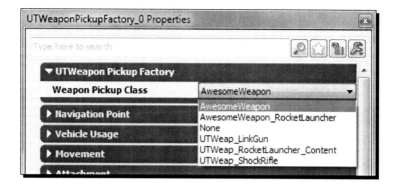

But if we look in our `AwesomeWeapon` class compared to the rocket launcher subclass, the `AwesomeWeapon` class by itself is pretty useless. It doesn't have a static mesh specified, no firing modes or projectile classes or ammo count. If we change the spawner to use `AwesomeWeapon`, in game we immediately get switched back to our default link gun.

So with this in mind, why would we want `AwesomeGun` to show up in this list or be spawned in game at all? This is where the abstract modifier comes in handy.

2. Change the top of our `AwesomeWeapon` class to the following:

```
class AwesomeWeapon extends UTWeapon
    abstract;
```

3. Now compile and take a look at the spawner properties.

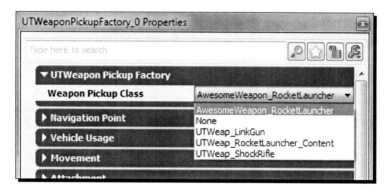

Now the class doesn't even show up in the list.

4. As a test, let's add the following code to our `AwesomePlayerController`:

```
var AwesomeWeapon AW;

simulated function PostBeginPlay()
```

```
    {
        AW = spawn(class'AwesomeWeapon');
        `log(AW);

        super.PostBeginPlay();
        bNoCrosshair = true;
    }
```

We'll try to spawn an `AwesomeWeapon` directly to see what happens.

5. Compile and test.

```
[0004.58] Warning: SpawnActor failed because class AwesomeWeapon
is abstract
[0004.58] ScriptLog: None
```

6. Remove the test code from the `AwesomePlayerController`. The
`PostBeginPlay` should look as it did before and the variable declaration should be
removed:

```
simulated function PostBeginPlay()
{
    super.PostBeginPlay();
    bNoCrosshair = true;
}
```

What just happened?

With abstract classes, we can't even spawn them through code. And for our
`AwesomeWeapon` class, this is exactly what we want. This class doesn't do anything by itself;
it's only the common parent class for all of our weapon classes. The abstract modifier is not
inherited by subclasses, which is why our rocket launcher still showed up in the weapon
spawner's list.

Native

A quick word about the native modifier. As UDK users we'll never be using this, so even
though you may see it in the source code, do NOT put this in your own classes. This keyword
tells the engine that there is C++ code behind the class, which as UDK users we don't have
access to. The engine code is only available to full licensees. We can do almost anything we
want without it though, so don't fret.

Config

We've used this one before in our experiments with variables. This one comes with parentheses after it which tells the game which configuration file in the UDKGame\Config folder to look in for this class' config variables. As a recap, with the following code:

```
class AwesomeActor extends Actor
    config(Game);

var config int Something;

defaultproperties
{
}
```

The game would look in the UDKGame.ini file for our default. Since UDKGame.ini is generated from DefaultGame.ini, we would place our default value in there:

```
[AwesomeGame.AwesomeActor]
Something=4
```

Following the standard format of:

```
[Package.Class]
VariableName=Value
```

The Package is the name of our folder in Development\Src, and Class is the .uc file inside that folder that has the config values.

The config modifier is inherited, so any subclasses can use config variables without having the config modifier or file name specified. Each subclass needs to have its own section in the INI file though:

```
[Package.Subclass]
VariableName=ADifferentValue
AnotherVariable=SomeDefault
```

Hidecategories

In our discussion of variables, we learned how we could put editable variables in certain categories by putting the name of the category in parentheses like this:

```
var(MyCategory) int MyInt;
```

And if we take a look at our `AwesomeWeaponUpgrade` actor's properties in the editor, we can see that there are a lot of categories already applied to it:

For organizational purposes, if we wanted to hide some of these categories that we're not going to need, we would use the hidecategories modifier.

Time for action – Hidecategories

Let's take a look at our `AwesomeWeaponUpgrade` actor.

1. Let's change the top line of our `AwesomeWeaponUpgrade` actor to the following:

```
class AwesomeWeaponUpgrade extends AwesomeActor
    hidecategories(Attachment,Physics,Debug,Object)
    placeable;
```

Note that the class declaration line doesn't end until the semicolon, and it's perfectly fine to spread it across a few lines to keep it readable.

2. Compile the code and take a look at the properties in the editor again.

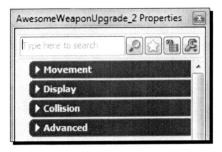

There are a lot less this time!

What just happened?

The hidecategories modifier should only be used when you're sure that a level designer isn't going to need to change any variables in that category. It doesn't get rid of any variables; it just hides them from the editor. This modifier is inherited, and if we wanted to reverse a hidecategories modifier in a subclass we would use the showcategories modifier, for example this hypothetical subclass:

```
class SomeOtherUpgrade extends AwesomeWeaponUpgrade
    showcategories(Attachment,Physics);
```

This would override the hidecategories modifier in `AwesomeWeaponUpgrade` for those two categories.

Hidedropdown

This one acts in a similar way to the abstract modifier, except this only hides the actor from drop-down lists like the one in the weapon spawner. However, using this keyword will still allow the actor to be spawned through code.

Actors versus objects

This will be a short topic, but an important one. `Object.uc` is the highest class in the class tree; all other scripts are subclasses of it. The most important subclass of Object is Actor. When working with UnrealScript, almost all of your work will be under Actor in the class tree. Actor contains code that gives classes a position in the world, lets them easily interact with each other and affect the game in some way. All of the other subclasses of Object can be thought of as more "informational" classes. For instance, if we take a look at InterpTrack and its subclasses, we can see that these classes define the tracks we can use in a Matinee such as movement or animation. The classes themselves have no useful purpose in the game world itself as, say, a projectile would.

Only `Actor` classes can be spawned, and indeed if we search through `Actor.uc` we can find the place where that function is declared:

```
native noexport final function coerce actor Spawn
(
    class<actor>      SpawnClass,
    optional actor     SpawnOwner,
    optional name      SpawnTag,
    optional vector    SpawnLocation,
    optional rotator   SpawnRotation,
    optional Actor     ActorTemplate,
    optional bool      bNoCollisionFail
);
```

There are ways of creating non-Actor object classes during gameplay, but this will rarely be needed. Nearly 100% of your time will be spent under Actor in the class tree. The only real exception to that is Kismet classes, which will be discussed in a later chapter and fall under `SequenceObject` in the class tree.

Simply put, when creating new classes, they will almost always be subclasses of Actor, not Object.

Common UnrealScript classes

Our final topic for this chapter will be a long one. We're going to go through the most commonly used classes in UnrealScript and take a look at how we can change them for our game. We'll expand their functionality and see if we can get something resembling our Awesome Game's design document. First up, let's take a look at the GameInfo class.

The GameInfo

The GameInfo class handles all of the rules for our game. It logs people in and out, tells the game when to start, keeps track of the time limit and score and decides when the game is over and who won. It also handles a few default properties like the `PlayerController` and HUD class the game uses.

Let's expand ours to see if we can make a game we can win.

Time for action – Expanding AwesomeGame

We'll start with something simple. Usually when you're working on a project you might not want to go straight toward your goal, but instead you'd use a process like the one we're about to use to slowly work your game towards your desired goal. This helps to break down tasks even further and make sure your code is working each step of the way.

Let's start by making it so we win the game by collecting all of our `AwesomeWeaponUpgrade` actors.

1. The first thing we need to do is count the number of `AwesomeWeaponUpgrade` actors and set our goal to that number. We'll use the foreach iterator to find them. Let's add a `PostBeginPlay` function to our `AwesomeGame` class:

```
simulated function PostBeginPlay()
{
    local AwesomeWeaponUpgrade AW;

    super.PostBeginPlay();
```

```
        GoalScore = 0;

        foreach DynamicActors(class'AwesomeWeaponUpgrade', AW)
            GoalScore++;
}
```

GoalScore is a variable declared in GameInfo that holds the score limit for the game. When this number is reached, the game ends. It could be number of kills for Deathmatch, number of flags captured for Capture the Flag, or in our case we're temporarily using it to hold the number of AwesomeWeaponUpgrade actors we need to collect.

2. Since we're extending from UTDeathmatch, there is a variable we need to change for the default properties. Since Deathmatch by default scores by number of kills, we need to change that so we don't get messages like "double kill" or "m-m-m-monster kill!"

```
        bScoreDeaths=false
```

bScoreDeaths is declared in UTGame.

That's it for our AwesomeGame class for now, let's see what it should look like:

```
class AwesomeGame extends UTDeathmatch;

simulated function PostBeginPlay()
{
    local AwesomeWeaponUpgrade AW;

    super.PostBeginPlay();

    GoalScore = 0;

    foreach DynamicActors(class'AwesomeWeaponUpgrade', AW)
        GoalScore++;
}

defaultproperties
{
    bScoreDeaths=false
    PlayerControllerClass=class'AwesomeGame.
AwesomePlayerController'
}
```

3. Now we need to change our `AwesomeWeaponUpgrade` class a bit. In our Touch event, let's add a bit of code so it looks like this:

```
event Touch(Actor Other, PrimitiveComponent OtherComp, vector
HitLocation, vector HitNormal)
{
    if(Pawn(Other) != none && AwesomeWeapon(Pawn(Other).Weapon) !=
none)
    {
        if(Pawn(Other).Controller != none && Pawn(Other).
Controller.PlayerReplicationInfo != none)
            WorldInfo.Game.ScoreObjective(Pawn(Other).Controller.
PlayerReplicationInfo, 1);

        AwesomeWeapon(Pawn(Other).Weapon).UpgradeWeapon();
        Destroy();
    }
}
```

Now we're checking if the Pawn that touched us has a Controller, and if so does that Controller have a `PlayerReplicationInfo`. `PlayerReplicationInfo` is a class created for every Controller that holds the number of deaths, our score, our team number, even our ping for multiplayer games. It is mainly an informational class that stores variables other players will need to know about. When we tell the `GameInfo` that a player scored, instead of telling the GameInfo which Controller or Pawn it was, we pass the `PlayerReplicationInfo` reference instead.

On the next line is where we tell the game about the score. `WorldInfo.Game` holds a reference to the `GameInfo` class, which in our case is our `AwesomeGame`. `ScoreObjective` is a function declared in `GameInfo` which handles things like figuring out if the game has ended because of this score. For this, we tell the `GameInfo` that the player that touched us receives 1 to their score. Since we set the goal to the number of `AwesomeWeaponUpgrade` actors, this makes it so that we have to collect all of them to end the game.

4. Compile the code and test. Pick up the rocket launcher and then run around collecting all of the weapon upgrades. When you pick up the last one the game should stop and you will hear "Flawless Victory!"

What just happened?

This is a small example of how to work with a class to slowly expand the game. Starting from something simple, we can work toward what we want the game to be while making sure we don't majorly break anything along the way. Next, let's make it so we have something to shoot at instead of ending the game by picking stuff up.

Time for action – SHOOT NOW!

Once again, instead of jumping right in and creating enemies with AI and attacks and health and long complicated pieces of code, let's start with something simple: A box we can shoot at and kill.

1. Create a new file in our `Development/Scr/AwesomeGame/Classes` folder and call it `TestEnemy.uc`. This way we'll know it's not a class we'll be keeping. Copy the following code into it:

```
class TestEnemy extends AwesomeActor
    placeable;

event TakeDamage(int DamageAmount, Controller EventInstigator,
vector HitLocation, vector Momentum, class<DamageType> DamageType,
optional TraceHitInfo HitInfo, optional Actor DamageCauser)
{
    Destroy();
}

defaultproperties
{
    bBlockActors=True
    bCollideActors=True

    Begin Object Class=DynamicLightEnvironmentComponent
Name=MyLightEnvironment
        bEnabled=TRUE
    End Object
    Components.Add(MyLightEnvironment)

    Begin Object Class=StaticMeshComponent Name=PickupMesh
        StaticMesh=StaticMesh'UN_SimpleMeshes.TexPropCube_Dup'
        Materials(0)=Material'EditorMaterials.WidgetMaterial_X'
        LightEnvironment=MyLightEnvironment
        Scale3D=(X=0.25,Y=0.25,Z=0.5)
    End Object
    Components.Add(PickupMesh)

    Begin Object Class=CylinderComponent Name=CollisionCylinder
        CollisionRadius=32.0
        CollisionHeight=64.0
        BlockNonZeroExtent=true
        BlockZeroExtent=true
        BlockActors=true
```

```
            CollideActors=true
        End Object
        CollisionComponent=CollisionCylinder
        Components.Add(CollisionCylinder)
}
```

The `TakeDamage` function is a biggie, there are a lot of parameters that are passed in. For now we don't need to worry about them though, we only care that it gets called.

Also notice the default properties. It may look the same as our weapon upgrades, but we've changed the collision and cube mesh sizes and added `bBlockActors=True`. This makes it so we can't run through our fake enemies.

2. Compile the code and open up the editor. Select our `TestEnemy` class in the Actor Browser and place a few around the level close to our weapon spawner and weapon upgrades.

Kinda creepy actually.

3. Run the game with our batch file and shoot at the test enemies. You'll notice that they disappear when shot, so our `TakeDamage` function is working! Time to change our `AwesomeGame` class.

4. Change the `PostBeginPlay` of our `AwesomeGame` class to this:

```
simulated function PostBeginPlay()
{
    local TestEnemy TE;

    super.PostBeginPlay();

    GoalScore = 0;

    foreach DynamicActors(class'TestEnemy', TE)
        GoalScore++;
}
```

This changes it so our goal is based on the number of enemies in the map instead of the weapon upgrades. Getting there!

5. Now let's get rid of the code in our weapon upgrades that gives us a score when they're picked up. The `Touch` function in `AwesomeWeaponUpgrade` should now look like this:

```
event Touch(Actor Other, PrimitiveComponent OtherComp, vector
HitLocation, vector HitNormal)
{
    if(Pawn(Other) != none && AwesomeWeapon(Pawn(Other).Weapon) !=
none)
    {
        AwesomeWeapon(Pawn(Other).Weapon).UpgradeWeapon();
        Destroy();
    }
}
```

6. And lastly, we need to move the goal scoring code into our `TestEnemy` class. The `TakeDamage` function there should now look like this:

```
event TakeDamage(int DamageAmount, Controller EventInstigator,
vector HitLocation, vector Momentum, class<DamageType> DamageType,
optional TraceHitInfo HitInfo, optional Actor DamageCauser)
{
    if(EventInstigator != none && EventInstigator.
PlayerReplicationInfo != none)
        WorldInfo.Game.ScoreObjective(EventInstigator.
PlayerReplicationInfo, 1);
    Destroy();
}
```

You'll notice that the if statement has changed a bit. Since `TakeDamage` already gives us a Controller in the form of the `EventInstigator` variable, we can just check that instead now.

7. Compile the code and run the game. Now when we shoot all of our TestEnemy actors, the game ends. Nice!

8. While we're here, let's make another small change to our `AwesomeGame` class. We start out with the Link Gun, but in our game we only want to use our own weapon classes. Let's start the player out with no weapon for now. We can do this with a simple change to the `AwesomeGame` default properties:

```
DefaultInventory(0)=None
```

9. Compile and test.

What just happened?

We've created a new class, `TestEnemy`, which will react to our weapon fire through its `TakeDamage` function. When destroyed they report to `AwesomeGame`, which has a tally of how many of the `TestEnemy` actors are in the map. When that number is reached, the game ends.

Now, what in the world are those two things around our player? To find out, we're going to need to investigate another class that we're soon going to need for our game, our own Pawn.

Time for action – Customizing the Pawn class

We're going to get more into the `Pawn` class in a bit, but since the `GameInfo` class tells the game which `Pawn` class to use, we'll create it now and investigate what those two things around our player are, now that we start with no weapon.

1. Create a new file in our `Development/Src/AwesomeGame/Classes` folder called `AwesomePawn.uc`. As always, we'll put some test code in `PostBeginPlay` to make sure our class is working:

```
class AwesomePawn extends UTPawn;

simulated function PostBeginPlay()
{
    super.PostBeginPlay();
    `log("AwesomePawn spawned! =====");
}

defaultproperties
{
}
```

That's it for this class for the moment; now let's tell the game to use our class.

2. In `AwesomeGame.uc`, let's set our `Pawn` class in the default properties:

```
DefaultPawnClass=class'AwesomeGame.AwesomePawn'
```

3. Compile the code and run the game, and we'll see our log show up:

```
[0006.55] ScriptLog: AwesomePawn spawned! =====
```

4. Now to get rid of the floaty thingies. As with our giant floating gun awhile back, the two floating things are supposed to be used for our first person view. They're the arms that you see holding whatever weapon you have. Since we now have no weapon by default, we need to hide these arms.

5. Let's change our AwesomePawn's `PostBeginPlay` function to look like this:

```
simulated function PostBeginPlay()
{
    super.PostBeginPlay();

    if(ArmsMesh[0] != none)
        ArmsMesh[0].SetHidden(true);
    if(ArmsMesh[1] != none)
        ArmsMesh[1].SetHidden(true);
}
```

We can see the `ArmsMesh` array declared in `UDKPawn` (don't put this anywhere):

```
var UDKSkeletalMeshComponent ArmsMesh[2];
```

Then they're set in the default properties of UDKPawn's subclass, `UTPawn` (don't write this either):

```
    Begin Object Class=UDKSkeletalMeshComponent
Name=FirstPersonArms
        PhysicsAsset=None
        FOV=55
        Animations=MeshSequenceA
        DepthPriorityGroup=SDPG_Foreground
        bUpdateSkelWhenNotRendered=false
        bIgnoreControllersWhenNotRendered=true
        bOnlyOwnerSee=true
        bOverrideAttachmentOwnerVisibility=true
        bAcceptsDynamicDecals=FALSE
        AbsoluteTranslation=false
        AbsoluteRotation=true
        AbsoluteScale=true
        bSyncActorLocationToRootRigidBody=false
```

```
        CastShadow=false
        TickGroup=TG_DuringASyncWork
        bAllowAmbientOcclusion=false
    End Object
    ArmsMesh[0]=FirstPersonArms
```

At this point I shouldn't need to say it but yep, reading through the source code definitely helps find things like this. The Pawn branch of the class tree is another one that should be added to your must-read list.

6. Compile and test. The floating arms are gone now!

What just happened?

Now we've seen a bit about how the `GameInfo` class works and what it controls. Using the functions there we can set the end game condition to whatever we want. Using a system similar to the weapon upgrades, we could make it so that the player has to reach a certain level before the game ends.

Have a go hero – A different end condition

Now that you know more about how the game comes to an end, let's see about changing it a bit. How would you rewrite the code so that you don't have to kill all of the TestEnemy actors, but instead a fixed amount, say 10 of them?

Solution: Rewrite AwesomeGame's `PostBeginPlay` function to look like this:

```
    simulated function PostBeginPlay()
    {
        super.PostBeginPlay();
        GoalScore = 10;
    }
```

The Controller

The Controller is a class we've already messed around with a bit, and is obviously very important to a custom UDK game. It's the puppet master to our Pawn, it controls the camera and processes player input, and also handles other functions such as muting players on a server. We've done some simple stuff with the camera for our `AwesomePlayerController`, but let's see if we can expand it a bit to make it work better.

Time for action – Expanding the Controller

Right now we have a pretty simple setup for our camera. It stays at a fixed position over our player and never moves from that relative position. Let's change it so that it's focusing on a point a bit ahead of our player, that way it will let them see more of what's in front of them while leaving their backs exposed to a surprise attack.

1. Let's take a look at our `GetPlayerViewPoint` function:

```
simulated event GetPlayerViewPoint(out vector out_Location, out
Rotator out_Rotation)
{
    super.GetPlayerViewPoint(out_Location, out_Rotation);

    if(Pawn != none)
    {
        Pawn.Mesh.SetOwnerNoSee(false);
        if(Pawn.Weapon != none)
            Pawn.Weapon.SetHidden(true);

        out_Location = Pawn.Location + PlayerViewOffset;
        out_Rotation = rotator(Pawn.Location - out_Location);
    }
}
```

Well some of this looks more familiar now that we have our own Pawn class. We can move the first two parts of our if statement out of this function, so let's do that real quick.

2. Delete the first two parts of our if statement:

```
simulated event GetPlayerViewPoint(out vector out_Location, out
Rotator out_Rotation)
{
    super.GetPlayerViewPoint(out_Location, out_Rotation);

    if(Pawn != none)
    {
        out_Location = Pawn.Location + PlayerViewOffset;
        out_Rotation = rotator(Pawn.Location - out_Location);
    }
}
```

3. Now let's put the first part in our AwesomePawn class instead. Add this function to our AwesomePawn:

```
simulated function SetMeshVisibility(bool bVisible)
{
    super.SetMeshVisibility(bVisible);
    Mesh.SetOwnerNoSee(false);
}
```

This will let us keep seeing our Pawn.

4. As for the weapon hiding, we can move that to our AwesomePlayerController's NotifyChangedWeapon function. Add this line after the call to the super:

```
NewWeapon.SetHidden(true);
```

Here's what the function should look like now:

```
function NotifyChangedWeapon(Weapon PrevWeapon, Weapon NewWeapon)
{
    super.NotifyChangedWeapon(PrevWeapon, NewWeapon);

    NewWeapon.SetHidden(true);

    if(Pawn == none)
        return;

    if(UTWeap_RocketLauncher(NewWeapon) != none)
        Pawn.SetHidden(true);
    else
        Pawn.SetHidden(false);
}
```

We'll leave the rocket launcher invisibility code in there for now.

5. Now we've cleaned out our GetPlayerViewPoint function, and it should look like this:

```
simulated event GetPlayerViewPoint(out vector out_Location, out
Rotator out_Rotation)
{
    super.GetPlayerViewPoint(out_Location, out_Rotation);

    if(Pawn != none)
    {
        out_Location = Pawn.Location + PlayerViewOffset;
        out_Rotation = rotator(Pawn.Location - out_Location);
    }
}
```

6. Now let's change it so it focuses on a position ahead of the player. Change our `PlayerViewOffset` in the default properties to this:

```
PlayerViewOffset=(X=384,Y=0,Z=1024)
```

We've just changed the value of X; we'll use this in a moment to keep the camera ahead of the player.

7. Change the if statement in our `GetPlayerViewPoint` function to this:

```
if(Pawn != none)
{
    out_Location = Pawn.Location + (PlayerViewOffset >> Pawn.
Rotation);
    out_Rotation = rotator((out_Location * vect(1,1,0)) - out_
Location);
}
```

There are a few changes that we should walk through so you know what the new code is doing. First we're changing the `out_Location` part by changing this:

```
+ PlayerViewOffset
```

To this:

```
+ (PlayerViewOffset >> Pawn.Rotation)
```

Using the `>>` operator effectively converts our `PlayerViewOffset` into our Pawn's local coordinates. In other words, instead of our X value of 384 always being in a certain direction in the world (say North), no matter which direction the Pawn was facing, it would make the offset change with the Pawn's rotation to always be 384 units in a certain direction according to the Pawn's viewpoint. In this case, it will always be in front of our Pawn no matter what direction it's facing.

Let's take a look at the following diagram to see how this works:

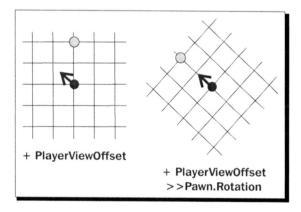

+ PlayerViewOffset

**+ PlayerViewOffset
>>Pawn.Rotation**

Without the `>>` operator, the `PlayerViewOffset` is always 384 units along the X axis of the world, no matter what direction our Pawn is facing. With the `>>` operator, `PlayerViewOffset` is 384 units along the X axis relative to the Pawn, so as the Pawn rotates the `>>` operator makes the `PlayerViewOffset` move with it.

For our `out_Rotation`, we've changed this:

```
rotator(Pawn.Location - out_Location)
```

To this:

```
rotator((out_Location * vect(1,1,0)) - out_Location)
```

Remembering our vector lessons, we subtract the start (A) from the destination (B), so B-A would give us a vector pointing from A to B. When we multiply the `out_Location` variable by `vect(1,1,0)`, all we're doing is making the Z value 0. The X and Y are unchanged since we multiplied them by 1. We do that to get a location that's directly below our camera, and then have the camera point in that direction. This makes the camera always point down.

8. Compile the code and test. It works ok, but yeesh that's some ugly twitching going on. Let's keep going with our camera code to smooth that out.

9. Let's add some smoothing to the camera so it doesn't immediately set its location. To do this we'll store the current location code as a desired position that the camera will constantly move towards. At the top of our `AwesomePlayerController` let's add two vectors:

```
var vector CurrentCameraLocation, DesiredCameraLocation;
```

We'll use `DesiredCameraLocation` to store the position we want the camera to be at, and interpolate `CurrentCameraLocation` towards that continuously.

10. Now let's change our `GetPlayerViewPoint` function.

```
simulated event GetPlayerViewPoint(out vector out_Location, out
Rotator out_Rotation)
{
    super.GetPlayerViewPoint(out_Location, out_Rotation);

    if(Pawn != none)
    {
        out_Location = CurrentCameraLocation;
        out_Rotation = rotator((out_Location * vect(1,1,0)) - out_
Location);
    }
}
```

We won't change our rotation code, but now the location will use our saved `CurrentCameraLocation` variable. Now we need to set `DesiredCameraLocation` and move `CurrentCameraLocation` towards it. To do this we'll use a function we haven't talked about yet, `PlayerTick`.

11. `PlayerTick` is a function that's run every frame during the game, so it's important to avoid putting any really slow pieces of code in it. For example, when we were learning about using actor classes as variables we used a `ForEach` iterator to find actors in the world. Using a `ForEach` here in `PlayerTick` would be really slow since it would be running every frame.

12. Add the following to our `AwesomePlayerController` class:

```
function PlayerTick(float DeltaTime)
{
    super.PlayerTick(DeltaTime);
    `log(DeltaTime);
}
```

The variable in the function, `DeltaTime`, tells us how much time has passed between frames. For example, if our game were running at 60 frames per second, `DeltaTime` would be 1 / 60 = 0.016667. We'll take a look for ourselves with the log.

13. Compile the code and run the game. Exit the game and take a look at the log:

```
[0005.34]  ScriptLog:  0.0169
[0005.36]  ScriptLog:  0.0169
[0005.37]  ScriptLog:  0.0169
[0005.39]  ScriptLog:  0.0169
```

That seems about right!

14. One of the important uses of `DeltaTime` is to make sure code we write here runs at the same speed no matter how fast our computer is or how bad our framerate gets. For instance, if we had an integer that we were adding 1 to every time `PlayerTick` ran, it would count much faster at 60 frames per second than at 30 since `PlayerTick` is run every frame. To compensate for this, we use `DeltaTime`. If we had a float that we were adding `DeltaTime` to, it would count at the same speed no matter what our framerate was, since the lower the framerate the higher `DeltaTime` would be since more time would be passing in between frames.

15. Knowing this, we'll use `DeltaTime` to make sure our camera moves at the same speed no matter what our framerate. Let's change our `PlayerTick` function:

```
function PlayerTick(float DeltaTime)
{
    super.PlayerTick(DeltaTime);
```

```
    if(Pawn != none)
    {
        DesiredCameraLocation = Pawn.Location + (PlayerViewOffset
>> Pawn.Rotation);
        CurrentCameraLocation += (DesiredCameraLocation -
CurrentCameraLocation) * DeltaTime * 3;
    }
}
```

As we can see, now we're setting our `DesiredCameraLocation` based on the old code we were using to set `out_Location` in `GetPlayerViewPoint`.

We're also moving `CurrentCameraLocation` towards `DesiredCameraLocation` in the next line. The first part gets the vector pointing from `CurrentCameraLocation` towards `DesiredCameraLocation` (remember, B – A?), then we multiply it by `DeltaTime`. If we think about it, this makes sense. If our framerate drops this function won't be called as often, so `DeltaTime` increases and this line of code makes our camera move faster to "make up for lost time". Multiplying it by 3 just speeds it up a bit more and is completely arbitrary. This can be changed if you want a slower or faster camera.

The following diagram illustrates what's happening with the camera now:

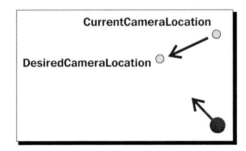

We're calculating where we want the camera to be with `DesiredCameraLocation`, and constantly moving the `CurrentCameraLocation` towards it every frame. This causes the camera movement to smooth out.

16. Compile the code and test it out. Much better, the camera lost the jerkiness it had before!

What just happened?

Now we've played around a bit more with the player's camera and learned about the `PlayerTick` function. But the `PlayerController` class can't all be about camera, camera, camera can it? The key word here is Controller, right? Earlier I mentioned that the `PlayerController` also processes the player's input, so let's see if we can change the way that works for our game.

Time for action – No, my left!

As a top down game, our control scheme is pretty terrible. When we press any of the direction keys on the keyboard, it's pretty tough to tell where the player is going to go. Right now our movement is based on our Pawn's rotation, so if we're facing the bottom of the screen, pressing left will actually make the pawn move to our right. Let's fix that.

1. To do this we're going to need a Rotator variable. We can't just pull `out_Rotation` from the `GetPlayerViewPoint` function, so we'll do the same thing we did with our `DesiredCameraRotation` and create a variable to store it.

   ```
   var rotator CurrentCameraRotation;
   ```

2. Now let's add a line to the end of our `GetPlayerViewPoint` function to store our `out_Rotation`:

   ```
   simulated event GetPlayerViewPoint(out vector out_Location, out
   Rotator out_Rotation)
   {
       super.GetPlayerViewPoint(out_Location, out_Rotation);

       if(Pawn != none)
       {
           out_Location = CurrentCameraLocation;
           out_Rotation = rotator((out_Location * vect(1,1,0)) - out_
   Location);
       }

       CurrentCameraRotation = out_Rotation;
   }
   ```

3. So why do we need that variable? We're going to use it to make our Pawn move in the direction we want it to. For this we'll use the `ProcessMove` function inside the `PlayerWalking` state. States will be covered in depth in *Chapter 6*, but for now it's enough to know that the player has many states it can be in, like walking, falling, or dead. For now we're only concerned with the `PlayerWalking` state.

4. Let's add this code to our `AwesomePlayerController`:

```
state PlayerWalking
{
    function ProcessMove( float DeltaTime, vector newAccel,
eDoubleClickDir DoubleClickMove, rotator DeltaRot)
    {
        super.ProcessMove(DeltaTime, AltAccel, DoubleClickMove,
DeltaRot);
    }
}
```

As we can see this is another function that gets called every frame, we're getting a `DeltaTime` variable here too. We don't need to worry about using it this time though. Instead, let's intercept the `newAccel` variable. This is what's making our movement completely wrong, so let's replace it with our own vector and set it to what it should be.

5. Type the following code for our `ProcessMove` function:

```
state PlayerWalking
{
    function ProcessMove( float DeltaTime, vector newAccel,
eDoubleClickDir DoubleClickMove, rotator DeltaRot)
    {
        local vector X, Y, Z, AltAccel;

        GetAxes(CurrentCameraRotation, X, Y, Z);
        AltAccel = PlayerInput.aForward * Z + PlayerInput.aStrafe
* Y;
        AltAccel.Z = 0;
        AltAccel = Pawn.AccelRate * Normal(AltAccel);
        super.ProcessMove(DeltaTime, AltAccel, DoubleClickMove,
DeltaRot);
    }
}
```

And now it's story time! In the first line we're declaring a few vectors to use in the function. `AltAccel` is the one we'll be using to replace `newAccel`.

The second line, `GetAxes`, is declared in `Object.uc`. We feed it a rotator, and it gives us three vectors pointing forward, to the right, and up from that rotator's perspective. Normally `ProcessMove` uses the Pawn's rotation for this, but here we're using our `CurrentCameraRotation` variable instead so we can base our movement on our camera.

In the next line, we're pulling `aForward` and `aStrafe` from the `PlayerInput`, which is the class that gets all of the keyboard and mouse input and sends it to the `PlayerController`. `aForward` is either positive or negative depending on whether we're pressing forward or backward on the keyboard, and the same with `aStrafe` being dependent on left/right presses.

From our camera's perspective, forward and backward are up and down, so we use the Z vector we got from `GetAxes` and multiply it by `aForward`. Left and right are left and right for our camera, so we use the Y vector and multiply it by `aStrafe`. These two added together give us the direction we want to move in.

Remembering our talk about vectors, in the next line we use `Normal` to get `AltAccel` to be one unit in length but still in the same direction. We multiply that by our Pawn's acceleration rate to get the final `AltAccel` value, the direction we want the player to move.

Finally we call ProcessMove's super, substituting `newAccel` with our own `AltAccel` value.

The following diagram illustrates what's going on:

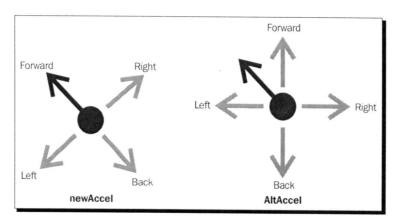

While `newAccel` is relative to the player, we've made `AltAccel` relative to the camera.

6. That was a long talk, so let's compile the code and test it out. Now the player moves like we would expect it to! The rotation and camera still work, so we're done here!

What just happened?

Now we've seen how we can change the way input is processed in the `PlayerController` classes. It seems we've done most of our work so far in this class, and looking at all of the code we have we can see how easily it can grow just from doing simple tasks.

We're done with `AwesomePlayerController` for now, so let's see what we can do with another of the UDK's common classes, the Pawn.

The Pawn

The Pawn is our physical representation in the world, with the `PlayerController` being its brain. The Pawn interacts with other objects in the world, has our health, speed, and jump height among other things. It also obviously has the visual mesh for our player, which we've experimented with when we made ourselves invisible.

For our experiment with the Pawn class, let's see if we can get our fake enemies to hurt us.

Time for action – Detecting collisions to give our Pawn damage

As the physical representation of the player, the Pawn class uses the function `TakeDamage` to subtract from our health, give us any momentum the weapon used has (such as rockets pushing us away when they explode), and tells the game what type of damage it was so it can play the appropriate effects and send the right death messages. We'll call that function from another function we're going to use, Bump.

1. While in the real world using Bump resurrects old forum threads, in the UDK it lets us know when two actors that have `bBlockActors` set to `true` run into each other. First, let's set a damage amount in our `TestEnemy` class. Add this variable to `TestEnemy`:

   ```
   var float BumpDamage;
   ```

   And give it a value in the default properties:

   ```
   BumpDamage=5.0
   ```

2. Now let's add the `Bump` function to our `AwesomePawn`:

   ```
   event Bump(Actor Other, PrimitiveComponent OtherComp, vector
   HitNormal)
   {
       `log("Bump!");
       if(TestEnemy(Other) != none)
           TakeDamage(TestEnemy(Other).BumpDamage, none, Location,
   vect(0,0,0), class'UTDmgType_LinkPlasma');
   }
   ```

   Here we test if the actor that bumped into us was a `TestEnemy`, and if so call `TakeDamage` and use its `BumpDamage` as the amount of damage we receive.

3. Compile the code and test it out. Wow, what just happened? Seems like we took a lot of damage and died pretty quick when we ran into a `TestEnemy`. Let's take a look at the log:

```
[0008.05] ScriptLog: Bump!
[0008.05] ScriptLog: Bump!
[0008.06] ScriptLog: Bump!
[0008.06] ScriptLog: Bump!
```

It seems like it gets called a lot while we're running into something. Well this is no good. Let's see if we can add an invulnerability timer to prevent constantly taking damage.

4. We'll use a `bool` and a `float` for this. Let's add these variables to the top of our AwesomePawn:

```
var bool bInvulnerable;
var float InvulnerableTime;
```

We'll set `bInvulnerable` to `true` for a bit after we take damage.

5. Let's give `InvulnerableTime` a value in our default properties:

```
InvulnerableTime=0.6
```

That should be long enough. Now for the Bump function.

1. Let's change the `Bump` function to look like this:

```
event Bump(Actor Other, PrimitiveComponent OtherComp, vector
HitNormal)
{
    if(TestEnemy(Other) != none && !bInvulnerable)
    {
        bInvulnerable = true;
        SetTimer(InvulnerableTime, false, 'EndInvulnerable');
        TakeDamage(TestEnemy(Other).BumpDamage, none, Location,
vect(0,0,0), class'UTDmgType_LinkPlasma');
    }
}
```

Now we've added a check to our `if` statement to make sure we aren't invulnerable. If we're not, we set ourselves to be invulnerable and start a timer, and then do the `TakeDamage` call.

2. Now let's write the `EndInvulnerable` function we're calling from our timer. This one's pretty simple:

```
function EndInvulnerable()
{
    bInvulnerable = false;
}
```

3. Now let's compile and test out this new code. Much better! We still take damage if we stand against a `TestEnemy`, but it isn't instantly killing us.

What just happened?

We've used the `Bump` function to identify what's running into us, and giving damage to the player if it was a `TestEnemy`. When hit we make the player invulnerable for 0.6 seconds to avoid rapid Bump calls from instantly killing the player.

This was just a simple experiment with our `Pawn` class, but now we can start to see the difference between it and the `PlayerController`. With the Pawn being our physical representation it is the thing that takes damage in the game.

Now that we're taking damage from our `TestEnemy` class let's have a little fun with `TestEnemy`. They're not much of a challenge just sitting there, so let's make them move towards us if we get too close.

Time for action – Making the TestEnemies move

Since `TestEnemy` is only a temporary class, we won't get too complex with its behavior. We'll just use some simple math and adapt some of our camera movement code to get them working.

1. The first thing we need to do in `TestEnemy.uc` is get a reference to the `AwesomePawn` that's running around shooting at us. Since the player doesn't spawn right away, we can't do this in `PostBeginPlay`. Instead, we're going to constantly check if we have a reference, and if not try to find one until we do.

2. Let's add a Pawn variable to our `TestEnemy` class:

```
var Pawn Enemy;
```

3. Now let's see if we can get a reference to the player after they've spawned. Let's use the `Tick` function for this:

```
function Tick(float DeltaTime)
{
    local AwesomePlayerController PC;

    if(Enemy == none)
    {
        foreach LocalPlayerControllers(class'AwesomePlayerControll
er', PC)
        {
            if(PC.Pawn != none)
            {
                Enemy = PC.Pawn;
                `log("My enemy is:" @ Enemy);
            }
        }
    }
}
```

For non-Controller actors the function is called `Tick` instead of `PlayerTick`, but it is still run once every frame. Now, if our `Enemy` variable isn't referencing any Pawn, we use the `LocalPlayerControllers` iterator to run through all of the `AwesomePlayerControllers` in the game and see if they have a Pawn. If so, set our Enemy variable and log it.

4. Compile the code and let's test it out. Close out the game and take a look at the log:

```
[0008.99] ScriptLog: My enemy is: AwesomePawn_0
[0008.99] ScriptLog: My enemy is: AwesomePawn_0
[0008.99] ScriptLog: My enemy is: AwesomePawn_0
[0008.99] ScriptLog: My enemy is: AwesomePawn_0
```

Four `TestEnemy` actors in our test level, four enemies set to AwesomePawn_0. It's almost as if they want to kill us or something.

5. Now we need to expand on our `Tick` function. First, let's add a `float` variable to the top to set a distance we'll check:

```
    var float FollowDistance;
```

And give it a default value:

```
    FollowDistance=512.0
```

6. Now for the movement code. Let's change our `Tick` function to the following:

```
function Tick(float DeltaTime)
{
    local AwesomePlayerController PC;
    local vector NewLocation;

    if(Enemy == none)
    {
        foreach LocalPlayerControllers(class'AwesomePlayerControll
er', PC)
        {
            if(PC.Pawn != none)
                Enemy = PC.Pawn;
        }
    }
    else if(VSize(Location - Enemy.Location) < FollowDistance)
    {
        NewLocation = Location;
        NewLocation += (Enemy.Location - Location) * DeltaTime;
        SetLocation(NewLocation);
    }
}
```

Now we've added an else if to our if statement. If our `Enemy` is `None` it will execute the code in the if statement, but if we have an enemy set it will go through the else if code. There, we check if the distance between us and our `Enemy` is less than our `FollowDistance`, and if so we use our newly declared `NewLocation` variable to move us closer to our Enemy. The second line there should look familiar; we used the same code to move our camera towards `DesiredCameraLocation` earlier.

7. Compile the code and test it out. Well that's pretty frightening. But something's wrong. If we just stand still the enemies run right through us and don't cause any more damage. The way we're moving our `TestEnemy` class seems to be causing problems, so let's make them stop and deal damage directly when they get close enough.

8. Let's add another float to our `TestEnemy` class:

```
var float AttackDistance;
```

And add a value to our default properties:

```
AttackDistance=96.0
```

Now let's change our `Tick` function:

```
function Tick(float DeltaTime)
{
    local AwesomePlayerController PC;
    local vector NewLocation;

    if(Enemy == none)
    {
        foreach LocalPlayerControllers(class'AwesomePlayerControll
er', PC)
        {
            if(PC.Pawn != none)
                Enemy = PC.Pawn;
        }
    }
    else if(VSize(Location - Enemy.Location) < FollowDistance)
    {
        if(VSize(Location - Enemy.Location) < AttackDistance)
        {
            Enemy.Bump(self, CollisionComponent, vect(0,0,0));
        }
        else
        {
            NewLocation = Location;
            NewLocation += (Enemy.Location - Location) *
DeltaTime;
            SetLocation(NewLocation);
        }
    }
}
```

9. Compile the code and test it out. Nice! Now when the TestEnemy actors get close enough they'll stop moving and start damaging us.

What just happened?

Now inside our else if statement, we check if we're close enough to attack, and if so we call the `Bump` function on our enemy ourselves. With the invulnerability code in place it will still prevent us from taking damage too fast.

If we're not close enough to attack, we go into the else statement and continue moving towards our enemy.

This is starting to look more and more like an actual game. We didn't have a whole lot to start with, but adding more and more code with each task gets us closer to where we want to be.

The next class we'll talk about is the HUD, which we can use to display information for the player.

The HUD

Although the traditional HUD has been replaced with Scaleform, we can still use the old style for prototyping. Scaleform is beyond the scope of this book, but we'll take a look at how we can use the HUD to help us in our UnrealScript programming.

Time for action – Using the HUD

We're going to use our HUD to display some useful information, such as our weapon level and the number of enemies we have left to kill. First we need to create our own HUD class.

1. Create a new file in our `Development/Src/AwesomeGame/Classes` folder called `AwesomeHUD.uc`. Type the following code into it:

```
class AwesomeHUD extends UTGFxHUDWrapper;

simulated function PostBeginPlay()
{
    super.PostBeginPlay();
    `log("AwesomeHUD spawned!");
}

defaultproperties
{
}
```

2. Now we're going to replace the default HUD with our own class. In our `AwesomePlayerController`, add the following function:

```
reliable client function ClientSetHUD(class<HUD> newHUDType)
{
    if(myHUD != none)
        myHUD.Destroy();

    myHUD = spawn(class'AwesomeHUD', self);
}
```

Now our HUD will be the only type that can be spawned for our `AwesomePlayerController`.

3. Compile the code and run the game. Nothing looks different, but close the game and check the log:

```
[0004.37] ScriptLog: AwesomeHUD spawned!
```

At least we know it's working!

1. We're not going to use `Scaleform`, but there are still some functions we can use for our prototype game. We'll use a function called `DrawText` to write our weapon's current level on the screen. Let's add the `DrawHUD` function to our `AwesomeHUD`:

```
event DrawHUD()
{
    super.DrawHUD();

    if(PlayerOwner.Pawn != none && AwesomeWeapon(PlayerOwner.Pawn.
Weapon) != none)
    {
        Canvas.DrawColor = WhiteColor;
        Canvas.Font = class'Engine'.Static.GetLargeFont();
        Canvas.SetPos(Canvas.ClipX * 0.1, Canvas.ClipY * 0.9);
        Canvas.DrawText("Weapon Level:" @
AwesomeWeapon(PlayerOwner.Pawn.Weapon).CurrentWeaponLevel);
    }
}
```

`PlayerOwner` is a variable referencing our Controller, so all we need to do is check if the Controller's Pawn is there and if it's holding an `AwesomeWeapon`. If so, we can move into the if statement.

First, we set the Canvas' `DrawColor` and `Font`. The `Canvas` is the part of the HUD we actually draw on. Next, we set the position we want to draw at. `ClipX` will give us the horizontal size of the screen in pixels, so multiplying it by 0.1 will make us draw at a location 10% from the left side of our screen. We do a similar multiplication with `ClipY`, making it 90% down from the top of the screen (or 10% up from the bottom).

2. Let's compile the code and take a look at the game. The text will only draw if we're holding an `AwesomeWeapon`, so run to our weapon spawner and pick up the rocket launcher. The text should now show up, and it will change as we pick up the weapon upgrades:

Nice!

3. What other information could we put here? Let's make it so we can tell how many enemies are left to kill. In our `AwesomeGame` class, add a new variable:

```
var int EnemiesLeft;
```

Now let's change our `PostBeginPlay` function to set its value to the initial number of TestEnemy actors:

```
simulated function PostBeginPlay()
{
    local TestEnemy TE;

    super.PostBeginPlay();

    GoalScore = 0;

    foreach DynamicActors(class'TestEnemy', TE)
        GoalScore++;

    EnemiesLeft = GoalScore;
}
```

Finally, let's add the `ScoreObjective` function and subtract from `EnemiesLeft` every time it's called:

```
function ScoreObjective(PlayerReplicationInfo Scorer, Int Score)
{
    EnemiesLeft--;
    super.ScoreObjective(Scorer, Score);
}
```

4. Now let's change our `DrawHUD` function to add the new info. We'll move the font and color lines outside our weapon level's if statement since we'll be using it for both now:

```
event DrawHUD()
{
    super.DrawHUD();

    Canvas.DrawColor = WhiteColor;
    Canvas.Font = class'Engine'.Static.GetLargeFont();

    if(PlayerOwner.Pawn != none && AwesomeWeapon(PlayerOwner.Pawn.
Weapon) != none)
    {
        Canvas.SetPos(Canvas.ClipX * 0.1, Canvas.ClipY * 0.9);
```

```
        Canvas.DrawText ("Weapon Level:" @
   AwesomeWeapon (PlayerOwner.Pawn.Weapon).CurrentWeaponLevel);
      }

   if (AwesomeGame (WorldInfo.Game) != none)
   {
       Canvas.SetPos (Canvas.ClipX * 0.1, Canvas.ClipY * 0.95);
       Canvas.DrawText ("Enemies Left:" @ AwesomeGame (WorldInfo.
   Game).EnemiesLeft);
      }
   }
```

Compile the code and run the game to check it out.

Perfect!

What just happened?

Although we wouldn't want this for our finished game, using the HUD in this way helps us quickly prototype our game and put useful information up for the player to see. We could also use this for debugging, since we can get access to pretty much any variable we want and put it up on the HUD so we can see it in real time.

Have a go hero – Kills on the HUD

Now that we've played around with the HUD a bit, see if you can get it to display the number of enemies that we've killed instead of the number that are left.

Solution - Change the last section of the DrawHUD function to look like this:

```
   if (AwesomeGame (WorldInfo.Game) != none)
   {
       Canvas.SetPos (Canvas.ClipX * 0.1, Canvas.ClipY * 0.95);
       Canvas.DrawText ("Enemies Killed:" @ AwesomeGame (WorldInfo.
   Game).GoalScore - AwesomeGame (WorldInfo.Game).EnemiesLeft);
      }
```

We've done a lot in this chapter. We've gone from messing around with weapons to having an almost fully functional game. While these are the most common classes in UnrealScript, it would still be very helpful to read through the class tree to see how everything is arranged and what classes already exist so we don't reinvent the wheel when we're working on our own project. As always, I will say that reading through the source code will give you a great insight into how the UDK's classes work and interact with each other.

Pop quiz – Figuring out Functions

1. What class is the puppet master behind our Pawn?
2. What function is called when two actors that have `bBlockActors` set collide with each other?
    1. `Touch`
    2. `PostBeginPlay`
    3. `Bump`
3. What formula do we use to get a vector pointing from actor A to actor B?

Summary

We learned a lot in this chapter about the UDK's classes and how we can use them to customize our own game.

Specifically, we covered:

- Breaking down a game's design document into programming tasks
- When and where to create custom classes for our game
- Class modifiers and what each of them does
- How to change the functionality of the UDK's classes by using our own subclasses
- The most common UDK classes and what they do

Now that we've learned about creating classes, it's time to start learning more about functions. We've been using them a lot so far, but what are they and how do they work exactly? In the next chapter, we'll take a closer look at what we can do with them.

5
Using Functions

Down to the nitty-gritty

In the last chapter we took a good look at creating our own classes for our game. We know from our talk about inheritance that we can override functions of our superclasses, and we've done a bit of that already. But what are functions exactly, and how do we know when and where to use ones that already exist or when to create our own? In this chapter we're going to expand on our Awesome Game by taking a closer look at functions.

In this chapter we will:

- ◆ Talk about what functions are and with what parameters and modifiers we can use with them
- ◆ Discuss local versus instance variables
- ◆ Take a look at commonly used functions and create our own as well
- ◆ Talk about using the super, and also when NOT to use it
- ◆ Take a look at delegates and how they are used

So with that, let's talk about functions.

What's your function?

In a nutshell, a function is a block of code written to perform a specific task that can be called as many times as we need from other parts of our program. As an example, if we had a function called EatAnApple, it would be like this:

```
var int i, NumberOfSlices;

function EatAnApple()
{
    WashApple();
    NumberOfSlices = SliceApple();
    for(i=0; i<NumberOfSlices; i++)
        ChewAppleSlice();
    ThrowAwayAppleCore();
}
```

Instead of having to write out each line every time we want to eat an apple, we just call the EatAnApple() function. As a more practical example from our own code, let's take a look at our AwesomeWeapon:

```
function UpgradeWeapon()
{
    if(CurrentWeaponLevel < MAX_LEVEL)
        CurrentWeaponLevel++;

    FireInterval[0] = FireRates[CurrentWeaponLevel - 1];

    if(IsInState('WeaponFiring'))
    {
        ClearTimer(nameof(RefireCheckTimer));
        TimeWeaponFiring(CurrentFireMode);
    }

    AddAmmo(MaxAmmoCount);
}
```

Instead of having all of these lines written out wherever we wanted to upgrade the weapon, we group them all into the UpgradeWeapon function. But we're only calling it from our upgrade pickup; why not just write it out there? Using this function as our example, let's say we wanted to make it so that the weapon could be upgraded by other means besides the upgrade pickups. Let's say we were making an RPG, and for each 50 enemies we killed with the weapon its level would go up and it would be upgraded. Having all of the code grouped into the UpgradeWeapon function makes it really easy to do this, and prevents us from having duplicate code scattered around in our classes.

For the most part, function names are completely arbitrary. We can use whatever name we like, but inside the same class no two functions can have the same name. If we do that we'll get a compiler error. Also remembering our lessons on inheritance, if a function has the same name as a function in one of our superclasses we will override that function instead of creating a new one; so when you're new to UnrealScript and are creating a function of your own, it helps to run a quick search in UnCodeX to make sure it's not already being used by your class's superclasses. As an example, say we were creating our own Pawn class and wanted to create a function called `JumpOffPawn()`. If we look at `Pawn.uc` we can see that this function has already been defined:

```
function JumpOffPawn()
{
    Velocity += (100 + CylinderComponent.CollisionRadius) * VRand();
    if ( VSize2D(Velocity) > FMax(500.0, GroundSpeed) )
    {
        Velocity = FMax(500.0, GroundSpeed) * Normal(Velocity);
    }
    Velocity.Z = 200 + CylinderComponent.CollisionHeight;
    SetPhysics(PHYS_Falling);
}
```

If we run a search in UnCodeX we can see that this function is being called from a few different places. For our custom function we might not want it to be called when Pawn's version is supposed to be called instead, so we'll rename it to avoid it being called because of inheritance.

When a function is called, the game will execute all of the code inside of that function and then return to where it left off and continue. Let's take a look at our `UpgradeWeapon` function again:

```
function UpgradeWeapon()
{
    if(CurrentWeaponLevel < MAX_LEVEL)
        CurrentWeaponLevel++;

    FireInterval[0] = FireRates[CurrentWeaponLevel - 1];

    if(IsInState('WeaponFiring'))
    {
        ClearTimer(nameof(RefireCheckTimer));
        TimeWeaponFiring(CurrentFireMode);
    }

    AddAmmo(MaxAmmoCount);
}
```

Towards the end of this function we call `TimeWeaponFiring`. That's defined in `Weapon.uc`:

```
simulated function TimeWeaponFiring( byte FireModeNum )
{
    // if weapon is not firing, then start timer. Firing state is
responsible for stopping the timer.
    if( !IsTimerActive('RefireCheckTimer') )
    {
        SetTimer( GetFireInterval(FireModeNum), true,
nameof(RefireCheckTimer) );
    }
}
```

The code in here executes to set a timer, and then execution returns to the previous position in `UpgradeWeapon()`. The next line is `AddAmmo`, which is defined in `UTWeapon`:

```
function int AddAmmo( int Amount )
{
    AmmoCount = Clamp(AmmoCount + Amount,0,MaxAmmoCount);
    // check for infinite ammo
    if (AmmoCount <= 0 && (UTInventoryManager(InvManager) == None ||
UTInventoryManager(InvManager).bInfiniteAmmo))
    {
        AmmoCount = MaxAmmoCount;
    }

    return AmmoCount;
}
```

The program then returns to the `UpgradeWeapon` function to finish.

It's a minor thing to keep in mind, but it does help figure out what's going on in the code. UnrealScript doesn't run more than one thing simultaneously. It doesn't matter how many cores your computer has, or what you've read about multithreading. Remember when we used the `Tick` function, and how it runs every frame? When `Tick` is called it isn't run on all actors at the exact same time, the game goes through the list of all of the actors in the level and calls `Tick` on each and every one of them, one at a time. This might sound slow, but with UnrealScript operating at millions of instructions per second it's not something we generally have to worry about.

With this in mind, let's take a look at these two hypothetical functions using a variable:

```
var int MyInt;

function Something()
{
```

```
    DoSomethingElse();
    `log(MyInt);
}

function DoSomethingElse()
{
    MyInt = 5;
    MyInt = 2;
    MyInt = 13;
    MyInt = 9;
}
```

Knowing that code doesn't execute simultaneously, it doesn't matter how many lines of code are in `DoSomethingElse()`, it will still execute all of it before returning to where it left off in `Something()` and the next line will log 9.

This is helpful to know when working with functions. The first three lines in the `DoSomethingElse` function above are meaningless, all that matters is the end result. When writing code we can use intermediate steps in long equations or call other functions to manipulate the variables we're working with as much as we need to, as long as the end result is what we want. We can see an example of this in our own code, in `AwesomePlayerController`:

```
    function ProcessMove( float DeltaTime, vector newAccel,
eDoubleClickDir DoubleClickMove, rotator DeltaRot)
    {
        local vector X, Y, Z, AltAccel;

        GetAxes(CurrentCameraRotation, X, Y, Z);
        AltAccel = PlayerInput.aForward * Z + PlayerInput.aStrafe * Y;
        AltAccel.Z = 0;
        AltAccel = Pawn.AccelRate * Normal(AltAccel);
        super.ProcessMove(DeltaTime, AltAccel, DoubleClickMove,
DeltaRot);
    }
```

We manipulate `AltAccel` a few times before the end of the function, but the only value that matters is the final one in this line:

```
AltAccel = Pawn.AccelRate * Normal(AltAccel);
```

Creating and calling functions

Now we know what functions are and how they work, but how do we write and call them? We've done a bit of it already, but let's take a closer look.

Time for action – Writing a function

For this we're going to need another custom class, an enemy spawner. We'll replace our current placed TestEnemy actors with this new actor, and have it spawn the enemies for us.

1. We're going to create the enemy spawner as a subclass of AwesomeActor, so let's make sure AwesomeActor looks like this:

```
class AwesomeActor extends Actor;

defaultproperties
{
}
```

2. Create a new file in our Development\Src\AwesomeGame\Classes folder called AwesomeEnemySpawner.uc.

3. Write the following code in it:

```
class AwesomeEnemySpawner extends AwesomeActor
    placeable;

defaultproperties
{
    Begin Object Class=SpriteComponent Name=Sprite
        Sprite=Texture2D'EditorResources.S_NavP'
        HiddenGame=True
    End Object
    Components.Add(Sprite)
}
```

We're adding a sprite to it so that we can see it when we place it in the editor.

4. Now, in order for this thing to spawn an enemy, we're going to need to write a function to do it. Let's make up a function called SpawnEnemy:

```
function SpawnEnemy()
{
    `log("SpawnEnemy called!");
}
```

For now we'll just have it log when it's called.

5. Now the function is created, but where do we call it from? Thinking back to our classes, the one that controls what's going on in the game is the GameInfo class, in our case our custom AwesomeGame.

6. Before we can call the function however, we need references to all of our `AwesomeEnemySpawners`. Since we don't know ahead of time how many there will be, we'll use a dynamic array and find all of them with the `foreach` iterator. First add the variable to the top of `AwesomeGame`:

```
var array<AwesomeEnemySpawner> EnemySpawners;
```

7. Now let's find them all in our `PostBeginPlay` function. Rewrite it to look like this:

```
simulated function PostBeginPlay()
{
    local AwesomeEnemySpawner ES;

    super.PostBeginPlay();

    GoalScore = EnemiesLeft;

    foreach DynamicActors(class'AwesomeEnemySpawner', ES)
        EnemySpawners[EnemySpawners.length] = ES;

    `log("Number of spawners:" @ EnemySpawners.length);
}
```

8. We've gotten rid of the old `TestEnemy` code in `PostBeginPlay` from the last chapter, but we still need to set a number for it so the game doesn't end as soon as we shoot one. Let's set a value for that in the default properties:

```
    EnemiesLeft=10
```

Our `AwesomeGame` class should now look like this:

```
class AwesomeGame extends UTDeathmatch;

var int EnemiesLeft;
var array<AwesomeEnemySpawner> EnemySpawners;

simulated function PostBeginPlay()
{
    local AwesomeEnemySpawner ES;

    super.PostBeginPlay();

    GoalScore = EnemiesLeft;

    foreach DynamicActors(class'AwesomeEnemySpawner', ES)
        EnemySpawners[EnemySpawners.length] = ES;
```

```
        `log("Number of spawners:" @ EnemySpawners.length);
}

function ScoreObjective(PlayerReplicationInfo Scorer, Int Score)
{
    EnemiesLeft--;
    super.ScoreObjective(Scorer, Score);
}

defaultproperties
{
    EnemiesLeft=10
    bScoreDeaths=false
    PlayerControllerClass=class'AwesomeGame.
AwesomePlayerController'
    DefaultPawnClass=class'AwesomeGame.AwesomePawn'
    DefaultInventory(0)=None
}
```

9. Let's test this out real quick before we continue. Compile the code, then open AwesomeTestMap in the editor and delete all of the TestEnemy actors.

10. Now add several AwesomeEnemySpawner actors to the map. Save and close, then run the game with our batch file.

11. Now let's take a look at the log:

```
[0004.46] ScriptLog: Number of spawners: 4
```

What just happened?

There's that log, but where's the log from the spawners themselves? Since we haven't called our SpawnEnemy function yet, we wouldn't expect this log to show up.

But why does our number of spawners log show? We never called PostBeginPlay! For this we have to understand something else about UnrealScript. A lot of functions are called by the engine itself, and those calls are made from native C++ code that we can't see. Things like PostBeginPlay, Tick, and the Bump function we've used before are called this way.

As a rule of thumb, functions that begin with "event" instead of "function" are called from native code, and are usually reactions to things happening in the world, like Bump which is originally declared in Actor and lets us know when two actors run into each other.

If we look at the original declarations for Tick and PostBeginPlay in Actor.uc, we can see that they use event instead of function.

Since any completely custom functions we create aren't going to be called from anywhere else, we need to call them ourselves. Let's continue working on our enemy spawners.

Time for action – Calling custom functions

We have our SpawnEnemy function, and now we have an array of AwesomeEnemySpawner actors in our AwesomeGame class. Let's call SpawnEnemy.

1. Let's add a new function to AwesomeGame called ActivateSpawners:

```
function ActivateSpawners()
{
    local int i;

    for(i=0; i<EnemySpawners.length; i++)
        EnemySpawners[i].SpawnEnemy();
}
```

2. This will iterate through the EnemySpawners array and call SpawnEnemy on each of them.

3. Let's call our ActivateSpawners function from PostBeginPlay:

```
simulated function PostBeginPlay()
{
    local AwesomeEnemySpawner ES;

    super.PostBeginPlay();

    foreach DynamicActors(class'AwesomeEnemySpawner', ES)
        EnemySpawners[EnemySpawners.length] = ES;

    ActivateSpawners();
}
```

Now, PostBeginPlay is getting an array of all of the spawners, and then calling the function that activates them.

4. Compile the code and test. Now the log in AwesomeEnemySpawner's PostBeginPlay should show up:

```
[0004.73] ScriptLog: SpawnEnemy called!
[0004.73] ScriptLog: SpawnEnemy called!
[0004.73] ScriptLog: SpawnEnemy called!
[0004.73] ScriptLog: SpawnEnemy called!
```

There we go!

5. Logs are good, but let's make this function do something useful, like... spawn an enemy. Let's change the `SpawnEnemy` function in `AwesomeEnemySpawner` to this:

```
function SpawnEnemy()
{
    spawn(class'TestEnemy',,, Location);
}
```

6. Now let's compile and test. The enemies are spawning! But wasn't this how the code worked before? This seems like a lot of work for nothing. Or is it? Now that we have spawners in place with our own `SpawnEnemy` function, we can do some interesting things. Let's see if we can get the spawners to spawn a new enemy when the old one dies. Let's change the `SpawnEnemy` function to this:

```
function SpawnEnemy()
{
    spawn(class'TestEnemy', self,, Location);
}
```

"Self" is a special variable that always refers to the object that's using it. Be sure not to miss it in the spawn call above! Let's look at the `Spawn` function in `Actor.uc`:

```
native noexport final function coerce actor Spawn
(
    class<actor>      SpawnClass,
    optional actor     SpawnOwner,
    optional name     SpawnTag,
    optional vector   SpawnLocation,
    optional rotator  SpawnRotation,
    optional Actor    ActorTemplate,
    optional bool     bNoCollisionFail
);
```

When we use `self` in our spawn call, we're setting `SpawnOwner` to be the `AwesomeEnemySpawner`. Looking at `Actor.uc`, this will show up in the `Owner` variable:

```
var const Actor    Owner;        // Owner actor.
```

Another place where this variable is used is in **Projectiles**. When spawned, projectiles have their owner set to the weapon that spawned them, that way if the projectile kills someone the game knows who caused the damage so it can award points.

In our case, we'll use the `Owner` variable to let the `AwesomeEnemySpawner` know that the enemy that it spawned has been killed so it can spawn a new one.

7. Let's add two new lines to the `TakeDamage` function in `TestEnemy`:

```
if(AwesomeEnemySpawner(Owner) != none)
    AwesomeEnemySpawner(Owner).EnemyDied();
```

Remembering our casting, since `Owner` is declared as an `Actor` we need to cast to our `AwesomeEnemyClass` so we can call the custom function we're going to create, `EnemyDied`.

`TestEnemy` class's `TakeDamage` function should look like this now:

```
event TakeDamage(int DamageAmount, Controller EventInstigator,
vector HitLocation, vector Momentum, class<DamageType> DamageType,
optional TraceHitInfo HitInfo, optional Actor DamageCauser)
{
    if(EventInstigator != none && EventInstigator.
PlayerReplicationInfo != none)
        WorldInfo.Game.ScoreObjective(EventInstigator.
PlayerReplicationInfo, 1);

    if(AwesomeEnemySpawner(Owner) != none)
        AwesomeEnemySpawner(Owner).EnemyDied();

    Destroy();
}
```

8. We're calling `EnemyDied` from there, but it's not a function that exists yet so let's create it in our `AwesomeEnemySpawner` class:

```
function EnemyDied()
{
    SpawnEnemy();
}
```

9. Compile the code and test it out. Now we see that whenever we kill an enemy, a new one spawns at the `AwesomeEnemySpawner` class's location. Nice!

What just happened?

So why did we use a separate `EnemyDied` function when all it does is call `SpawnEnemy`? For this we have to think in human terms a bit. It's the difference between letting us know something happened so we can make our own decision, and just telling us what to do. Remember when I said that variables shouldn't be manipulated from other classes? The same principle applies here. It's better to call a function that lets the class itself decide what to do than doing it ourselves from the other class. In our example, eventually we're going to add some checks to the `EnemyDied` function to see if we're able to spawn another enemy. Something like that is better done in the `AwesomeEnemySpawner` class than in the `TestEnemy` class. The `TestEnemy` just tells the `AwesomeEnemySpawner`, "Hey, I died." The `AwesomeEnemySpawner` then figures out what it should do next.

Time for action – What's your malfunction?

One bug we'll notice playing around with this new enemy spawner code is that even after the match is over, the enemies keep moving toward us. There's no "pause" button being hit so this is normal behavior, but it's not what we want. Having them vanish wouldn't look quite right either, so let's just have them stop like the player does. To do this we'll have to start in our AwesomeGame class.

1. We know the ScoreObjective function can tell us when the number of enemies reaches zero, so that's a good place to start. Let's add a bit of code to ScoreObjective:

```
function ScoreObjective(PlayerReplicationInfo Scorer, Int Score)
{
    local int i;

    EnemiesLeft--;
    super.ScoreObjective(Scorer, Score);

    if(EnemiesLeft == 0)
    {
        for(i=0; i<EnemySpawners.length; i++)
            EnemySpawners[i].FreezeEnemy();
    }
}
```

Now if EnemiesLeft is 0, it will iterate through the EnemySpawners array and tell all of them to freeze their enemies.

2. The next step is to create the FreezeEnemy function in AwesomeEnemySpawner, but first we need to get a reference to the enemy that we've spawned. We can do that through our call to Spawn. First let's add the variable to the top of our AwesomeEnemySpawner class:

```
var TestEnemy MySpawnedEnemy;
```

3. Now change the SpawnEnemy function slightly:

```
function SpawnEnemy()
{
    MySpawnedEnemy = spawn(class'TestEnemy', self,, Location);
}
```

This will give us our reference.

Now we can create the FreezeEnemy function:

```
function FreezeEnemy()
```

```
{
    if(MySpawnedEnemy != none)
        MySpawnedEnemy.Freeze();
}
```

Remember to check that it's not none first, or we may get errors in the log if we don't have a valid reference before trying to call Freeze() on it.

4. Almost done! Now we can create the Freeze function in our Test Enemy class. Add a bool variable to the top:

```
var bool bFreeze;
```

5. Now create the Freeze function:

```
function Freeze()
{
    bFreeze = true;
}
```

Simple enough.

6. Finally, let's use the bFrozen variable to stop the enemy from moving. We'll add it to the else if statement in our Tick function:

```
function Tick(float DeltaTime)
{
    local AwesomePlayerController PC;
    local vector NewLocation;

    if(Enemy == none)
    {
        foreach LocalPlayerControllers(class'AwesomePlayerControll
er', PC)
        {
            if(PC.Pawn != none)
                Enemy = PC.Pawn;
        }
    }
    else if(!bFreeze && VSize(Location - Enemy.Location) <
FollowDistance)
    {
        if(VSize(Location - Enemy.Location) < AttackDistance)
        {
            Enemy.Bump(self, CollisionComponent, vect(0,0,0));
        }
        else
        {
```

```
                          NewLocation = Location;
                          NewLocation += (Enemy.Location - Location) *
                DeltaTime;

                          SetLocation(NewLocation);
                    }
                }
          }
```

7. There, that should stop it. Compile and test, then kill the last enemy while another one is near you. It should stop in its tracks.

What just happened?

We can see from this daisy-chain of function calls that it's good to keep the function calls separate. Instead of going all the way through to the `TestEnemy` from our `AwesomeGame` class, we just call `FreezeEnemy` on the `AwesomeEnemySpawner` and let it figure out what to do. This keeps our code clean, and also makes it easier to change in the future if we want to add more functionality or change the way things work. We can see the advantage to this from our modification to the `ScoreObjective` function. If some other function somewhere just changed the score itself instead of calling `ScoreObjective`, it would be a lot harder to track down where it was happening and change it to suit our purposes.

Local versus instance variables

Most of our work so far has involved instance variables, that is, variables in a class that are accessible from any function in that class and even from other classes. Instance variables persist until that object is destroyed, so they're used for things we need to know about that object all the time, like `Health` for our `Pawn` class or the amount of ammo we have in our weapon. We've also used a few when we needed to store a variable until a different function needed to use it, like the `CurrentCameraLocation` and `CurrentCameraRotation` in our `AwesomePlayerController` class, which were processed in `PlayerTick` and used in `GetPlayerViewPoint`.

Sometimes, however, we'll want "throwaway" variables that we only need while we're in a function, and we don't need to keep them or access them from anywhere else. For this, we use local variables.

Local Variables

Let's try some experiments with local variables in our `AwesomeGame` class.

Time for action – Using local variables

1. We'll use a function we haven't used yet for this so we can keep it easily readable. In addition to PostBeginPlay, all Actor classes have a PreBeginPlay event that is called before PostBeginPlay during startup. We'll use this for our experiments.

2. Local variables are declared like instance variables, except we use local in the declaration line. Local variables can only be declared inside a function, and must be at the top of the function before any other lines of code. To see for ourselves, let's make a PreBeginPlay function in our AwesomeGame class:

```
function PreBeginPlay()
{
    super.PreBeginPlay();

    local int i;
    i = 5;
    `log("This is i:" @ i);
}
```

3. If we try to compile this, we'll get a compiler error:

```
Error, 'Local' is not allowed here
```

4. Let's try rearranging the PreBeginPlay function to move the variable declaration to the top:

```
function PreBeginPlay()
{
    local int i;

    super.PreBeginPlay();

    i = 5;
    `log("This is i:" @ i);
}
```

5. It compiles fine this time, and shows up in our log:

```
[0004.53] ScriptLog: This is i: 5
```

6. What happens if we move the variable outside of the class? At the top of AwesomeGame, create a new local variable:

```
class AwesomeGame extends UTDeathmatch;

local int MyInt;
```

7. Try to compile, and we get this error:

```
Error, Local variables are only allowed in functions
```

Well that settles that!

8. Delete the `MyInt` line. Let's try something else. What happens if we try to declare a normal variable inside a function? Let's try it in `PreBeginPlay()`:

```
function PreBeginPlay()
{
    var int MyInt;
    super.PreBeginPlay();
}
```

9. Compile and we get this error:

```
Error, Instance variables are only allowed at class scope (use
'local'?)
```

10. As we can see from these experiments, variable declaration has to happen in very specific places. Using a hypothetical class it would happen like this:

```
class MyActor extends Actor;

var int MyInstanceVariable;

function Something()
{
    local int MyLocalVariable;
    DoSomeStuff();
}
```

Instance variables are declared after the class line and before any functions, while local variables are declared inside functions before any other code.

11. Let's rewrite `PreBeginPlay` a bit. Change it to this:

```
function PreBeginPlay()
{
    local int MyInt;
    MyInt = 5;
}
```

Now let's add this line to the bottom of our `PostBeginPlay` function (not `PreBeginPlay`):

```
`log(MyInt);
```

12. Try to compile the code, and we'll get an error and a warning:

```
Error, Bad or missing expression for token: MyInt, in Call to
'LogInternal', parameter 1
Warning, 'MyInt' : unused local variable
```

13. What's going on here? First, the error. Local variables can only be used inside the class they're declared in. After the function ends, the variable is thrown away. We can't use it in any other function, so let's delete the log line from `PostBeginPlay`.

14. Now for the warning. These aren't as severe as errors. Code will still compile and work with warnings, the compiler is just letting us know that we declared `MyInt`, but we're not doing anything with it. So why have it? Deleting unused local variables helps keep code clean and frees up memory and processing power. Not much, but getting into good programming habits will help us later.

15. One thing we'll notice about local variables, and we've already done this in our `AwesomeGame` class, is that local variables in different functions can have the same name. This can get a bit confusing since you might mistake them for instance variables if you use them in a lot of functions, but for simple things like our `for` loops it's convenient to use the same variable name so you can immediately recognize what it's being used for. Let's take a look at our `ActivateSpawners` and `ScoreObjective` functions:

```
function ActivateSpawners()
{
    local int i;

    for(i=0; i<EnemySpawners.length; i++)
        EnemySpawners[i].SpawnEnemy();
}


function ScoreObjective(PlayerReplicationInfo Scorer, Int Score)
{
    local int i;

    EnemiesLeft--;
    super.ScoreObjective(Scorer, Score);

    if(EnemiesLeft == 0)
    {
        for(i=0; i<EnemySpawners.length; i++)
            EnemySpawners[i].FreezeEnemy();
    }
}
```

Both functions are declaring a local variable called `i`, and we're not getting any compiler errors. Since local variables are thrown away after a function is finished, it doesn't matter that these two have the same name. They'll never conflict with each other. And in these instances, we're using them in our `for` loops to iterate through the `EnemySpawners` array. We just need the variable to count up from 0 to the length of the array so we can call some functions on those actors, but after that we don't really need the variable anymore so declaring it as a local variable makes sense in this case. Wham bam, thank you... variable?

16. Since local variables are only used in the functions where they're declared, and they are thrown away afterward, there are a few more experiments we need to run so we know for sure how they work. Let's rewrite our `PreBeginPlay` function:

```
function PreBeginPlay()
{
    local int MyInt;

    super.PreBeginPlay();

    MyInt = 5;
    TryLoggingLocal();
}
```

Now we'll write the `TryLoggingLocal` function:

```
function TryLoggingLocal()
{
    local int MyInt;
    `log("MyInt:" @ MyInt);
}
```

17. When we compile, we'll get two warnings.

```
Warning, 'MyInt' : local variable used before assigned a value
Warning, 'MyInt' : unused local variable
```

The second one we've seen before, it's just letting us know we're not using the `MyInt` we declared in `PreBeginPlay`. The first one is new though. Local variables have the same default properties as instance variables, in an int's case it defaults to 0. This warning is just letting us know that we haven't assigned a value to the variable before trying to use it. It's not a major problem, but it's something we'll want to avoid after this experiment.

18. So now we have our two functions:

```
function PreBeginPlay()
{
    local int MyInt;

    super.PreBeginPlay();

    MyInt = 5;
    TryLoggingLocal();
}

function TryLoggingLocal()
{
    local int MyInt;
    `log("MyInt:" @ MyInt);
}
```

Knowing what we know about local variables, what would we expect the log to be? Let's find out.

19. Compile the code and ignore the warning messages for now. Run the game, then exit and check the log:

```
[0004.38] ScriptLog: MyInt: 0
```

That makes sense. The `MyInt` from `PreBeginPlay` is set to `5`, but that has no effect on the `MyInt` that's declared in `TryLoggingLocal`.

20. Let's get rid of the `TryLoggingLocal` function and rewrite our `PreBeginPlay` function:

```
function PreBeginPlay()
{
    local int MyInt;

    super.PreBeginPlay();

    MyInt = 5;
    `log("MyInt:" @ MyInt);
}
```

21. Now let's add an instance variable with the same name to the top of our class:

```
var int MyInt;
```

22. When we compile, we get the following warning:

```
Warning, Variable declaration: 'MyInt' conflicts with previously
defined field in 'AwesomeGame'
```

Even though local variables in different functions can have the same name, a local variable can't have the same name as an instance variable.

What just happened?

Knowing the difference between local and instance variables helps us figure out which type we need to use for a given situation. Local variables are helpful for calculations where we need a temporary variable to store information while we work with it, for example, if we were making more complicated calculations with our camera location we might use a local variable to store additional information while we manipulated it.

Sometimes we may need to use an actor class as a local variable. Let's take a look at an example of that using the `foreach` iterator.

Actors as local variables

We've used this in our search for all of the `AwesomeEnemySpawners` in the map, so let's see how it works.

Time for action – Using Actors as local variables

Let's take a look at the `PostBeginPlay` function from our `AwesomeGame` class:

```
simulated function PostBeginPlay()
{
    local AwesomeEnemySpawner ES;

    super.PostBeginPlay();

    GoalScore = EnemiesLeft;

    foreach DynamicActors(class'AwesomeEnemySpawner', ES)
        EnemySpawners[EnemySpawners.length] = ES;

    ActivateSpawners();
}
```

Here we're declaring a local variable of type AwesomeEnemySpawner and giving it a name of ES (short for Enemy Spawner). Near the end of the function we use the foreach iterator to find all of the AwesomeEnemySpawners in the map. The way the iterator works is that it gives us a reference to all of those actors it can find, as well as subclasses of that class, one at a time instead of in an array. To be able to sort through them we need to store the reference in a variable, so it makes sense to use a local variable here. We then take that temporary reference and assign it to the end of our more permanent array. Let's see exactly what's going on here.

1. Before we do anything, let's delete the PreBeginPlay function so it doesn't interfere with our experiments.

2. Now let's change the foreach section of our PostBeginPlay to this:

```
foreach DynamicActors(class'AwesomeEnemySpawner', ES)
{
    `log("ES:" @ ES);
    EnemySpawners[EnemySpawners.length] = ES;
}
```

We'll log our local variable each time the iterator executes and see what happens.

3. Make sure there are more than one AwesomeEnemySpawner actors placed in our test map, then run the game and check the log:

```
[0008.46] ScriptLog: ES: AwesomeEnemySpawner_1
[0008.46] ScriptLog: ES: AwesomeEnemySpawner_2
[0008.46] ScriptLog: ES: AwesomeEnemySpawner_3
[0008.46] ScriptLog: ES: AwesomeEnemySpawner_0
```

What just happened?

As we can see, each time the iterator executed, the AwesomeEnemySpawner actor it found was assigned to our local variable, which we then added to the end of our array. In this case, the local variable was just a middleman for our purposes, so the fact that it's thrown away after the function is done executing is just fine. There are other instances where using an actor as a local variable is useful; let's take a look.

Time for action – Modifying the projectile

For this experiment we're going to intercept the projectile that's being spawned from our rocket launcher and modify it before sending it on its way. We'll do this in our `AwesomeWeapon_RocketLauncher` class.

1. Open `AwesomeWeapon_RocketLauncher` and add the `ProjectileFire` function:

```
simulated function Projectile ProjectileFire()
{
    local Projectile MyProj;

    MyProj = super.ProjectileFire();
    `log(MyProj);

    return MyProj;
}
```

`ProjectileFire` is originally declared in `Weapon.uc`. Additionally, if we take a look at the `FireAmmunition` function, we can see the effect that the default property of our rocket launcher here has:

```
WeaponFireTypes(0)=EWFT_Projectile
WeaponFireTypes(1)=EWFT_Projectile
```

In the `FireAmmunition` function we can see that it uses a `Switch` statement to call `ProjectileFire` when we're using `EWFT_Projectile` for our `WeaponFireTypes`. Another piece to the puzzle!

In our `ProjectileFire` function, we're using a `Projectile` as a local variable, and getting a reference to it by calling the super. We then log it and let it continue on its way.

Let's see what happens when we compile and test it by firing the weapon a few times:

```
[0008.39] ScriptLog: UTProj_Rocket_0
[0010.09] ScriptLog: UTProj_Rocket_1
[0012.06] ScriptLog: UTProj_Rocket_2
```

Great, we're logging the references just fine! We don't really need a permanent reference to the projectiles, since they will be destroyed soon anyway and we really only need access to them while they're being spawned. Using a local variable for this is perfect.

2. Now that we have the reference, let's see if we can change something about the projectiles as they're being spawned. How about the damage and damage radius? As a goof, let's have the rockets use a crazy radius for their explosions and deal a lot of damage. The normal way to do this would be to subclass the projectile class itself and change the default properties there, but in our example game we may want them to change gradually as the weapon is upgraded so doing it here would be fine. Let's add these lines to our `ProjectileFire` function right before the return line at the end:

```
MyProj.DamageRadius = 10000;
MyProj.Damage = 1000;
```

Ooh this is going to hurt isn't it?

3. Compile the code and test. Ouch.

What just happened?

Yeah maybe that wasn't such a good idea. No matter how far we try to get from the enemies, when we hit one with a rocket we die too. Let's delete the entire `ProjectileFire` function from our rocket launcher class.

This experiment did give us some insight into ways we can use actors as local variables though! Once we've changed the damage and radius of our rocket we no longer need the reference to it, so local variables are perfect for things like this.

We've discussed instance and local variables, but there is another way to use variables that we haven't discussed yet. Since local variables can only be used inside the function they're declared in, and instance variables stick around until the actor is destroyed, what do we do when we just want to pass variables around to other functions? We COULD use instance variables for that, but that would easily become a mess. A lot of the variables wouldn't be things we cared about for long, so using instance variables wouldn't make sense anyway.

To figure this out, we need to talk about function parameters and modifiers.

Function parameters and modifiers

While writing the code in this and previous chapters we've seen plenty of functions that have more than just our plain function declaration here:

```
function Something()
{
}
```

There's bools and simulateds and a huge mess of stuff inside the parentheses sometimes, but what does it all mean? Let's take a look at what we can add to our function declarations and what they do. First up are function parameters.

Function parameters

Function parameters are variables that are given to a function so that it can use them for what it needs to do. If we're going to add ammo, we need to know how much to add. If we get shot, we want to know who shot us! To do this we add parameters to our function.

Adding parameters to our functions is pretty simple. We just need to let the game know what type of variable each is, and give it a name. The name is arbitrary; it doesn't need to match the name of the variable we're passing into the function. The only restriction is that it can't have the same name as any instance variable in our class, just like the restriction on local variables. In a sense, function parameters act as local variables, because they're only used in the function in which they're defined.

Let's take a look at them.

Time for action – Using function parameters

Time to pass some variables around! Let's start with the `PostBeginPlay` function in our `AwesomeEnemySpawner` class.

1. We haven't defined the `PostBeginPlay` function for our `AwesomeEnemySpawner` class, so let's do it now, and let's add an `int` to the function parameters:

```
function PostBeginPlay(int MyInt)
{
}
```

Compile the code. Uh oh, an error right out of the gate:

```
Error, Redefinition of 'function PostBeginPlay' differs from
original; different number of parameters
```

This is the most important thing to remember about function parameters. Once a function is defined, if it's ever used in a subclass, then it must have the exact same number and type of parameters as the original. The names of the variables don't have to be the same, but if the original function has a `bool` and an `int`, any subclasses must have a `bool` and an `int` in their parameters.

2. Let's take a look at an example of this. We've been using the `Tick` function a lot. If we look in `Actor.uc` where it's declared, we can see the parameter it uses is a `float`:

```
event Tick( float DeltaTime );
```

For our subclasses the only thing that matters is the variable type.

3. To prove this, let's overrride the `Tick` function in `AwesomeEnemySpawner`:

```
function Tick(float RandomName)
{
}
```

This compiles fine.

4. Also, since we changed the name of the parameter, we wouldn't be able to use its original name. We have to use the name we gave it. If we tried a log inside `Tick` like this:

```
function Tick(float RandomName)
{
    `log(DeltaTime);
}
```

We would get a compiler error.

5. For multiple parameters, simply separate them with a comma. Let's delete the `Tick` function and make up a function in our `AwesomeEnemySpawner` class.

```
function DoSomething(float MyFloat, bool MyBool)
{
}
```

That's compiling fine.

6. So how do we call `DoSomething`? With a plain function with no parameters we would simply do this:

```
DoSomething();
```

But since our function has parameters, we need to supply it with values for those parameters. Let's call `DoSomething` from a `PostBeginPlay` function:

```
function PostBeginPlay()
{
    super.PostBeginPlay();
    DoSomething(4.0, true);
}
```

Let's also add a log to DoSomething:

```
function DoSomething(float MyFloat, bool MyBool)
{
    `log(MyFloat @ MyBool);
}
```

7. Compile the code and run the game. Now let's look at the log:

```
[0005.96] ScriptLog: 4.0000 True
```

8. We can also pass variables' values to functions. Let's try this in PostBeginPlay:

```
function PostBeginPlay()
{
    local float SomeFloat;

    super.PostBeginPlay();

    SomeFloat = 34.0;
    DoSomething(SomeFloat, true);
}
```

9. Compile and test:

```
[0004.38] ScriptLog: 34.0000 True
```

Note that in this case we're simply passing the VALUE of the variable, not the variable itself. We can't use SomeFloat in DoSomething(), since it's a local variable only of use to PostBeginPlay. We're simply passing the value of 34.0 along, which is then assigned to the MyFloat parameter of DoSomething.

What just happened?

Any variable can be used as a parameter in a function. For example, let's take a look at the TakeDamage function we've used in our TestEnemy class:

```
event TakeDamage(int DamageAmount, Controller EventInstigator, vector
HitLocation, vector Momentum, class<DamageType> DamageType, optional
TraceHitInfo HitInfo, optional Actor DamageCauser)
```

This function has a lot of parameters, including an int, two vectors, even an actor variable of the Controller class. All of these are things the TakeDamage event needs to know before it can do anything.

We'll also notice two parameters at the end that have optional written before them. These are exactly what they mean, parameters that we don't need to pass if we don't want to use them. If we changed our DoSomething function to this:

```
function DoSomething(float MyFloat, optional bool MyBool)
{
}
```

We could call DoSomething a few different ways:

```
        DoSomething(5.0, true);
        DoSomething(5.0, false);
        DoSomething(5.0);
```

The last line works, and it's because of the optional declaration. When DoSomething executes it will simply use the default value for that type of variable, in this case false. Why have optional parameters? Sometimes we don't have all the information a function would need, or sometimes it doesn't need all of the information. As an example we can take a look at the massive Spawn function again:

```
native noexport final function coerce actor Spawn
(
    class<actor>        SpawnClass,
    optional actor       SpawnOwner,
    optional name       SpawnTag,
    optional vector     SpawnLocation,
    optional rotator    SpawnRotation,
    optional Actor      ActorTemplate,
    optional bool       bNoCollisionFail
);
```

There are a LOT of parameters for this function, but we're not going to need all of them every time we call Spawn. Sometimes as in the case of our enemy class we'll need to give it a SpawnLocation, but for some actors, say, informational actors such as PlayerReplicationInfo or even the GameInfo, we really don't care where they're spawned so specifying the parameters makes it quicker and cleaner to spawn them. If they weren't optional, this:

```
spawn(class'GameInfo');
```

Would turn into this:

```
spawn(class'GameInfo', none, '', vect(0,0,0), rot(0,0,0), none,
false);
```

That's just unnecessary and harder to read.

One thing we'll notice if we take a look at the spawn call we used in
AwesomeEnemySpawner:

```
MySpawnedEnemy = spawn(class'TestEnemy', self,, Location);
```

For optional parameters, you can skip over them by simply adding a comma. In this case we
skipped over the SpawnTag parameter since we don't need to use it, but we did need to give
it a SpawnLocation, which was the next parameter.

In addition to optional parameters, we can also specify "out" parameters. Let's take a look at
those now.

Time for action – Out parameters

Passing parameters to functions lets us do things with the values that are passed, but what
if we need to modify the variables themselves and pass them back? For this we would use
out parameters.

1. Let's change the DoSomething function in our AwesomeEnemySpawner class:

```
function DoSomething(out float MyFloat, out int MyInt)
{
    MyFloat = 5.0;
    MyInt = 18;
}
```

We've declared two out parameters, one int, and one float. In the function we
change their values, and that's it.

2. Now let's rewrite our PostBeginPlay function to call it:

```
function PostBeginPlay()
{
    local float MyF;
    local int MyI;

    super.PostBeginPlay();

    DoSomething(MyF, MyI);
    `log(MyF @ MyI);
}
```

We'll use two local variables, and then call DoSomething using them. Afterward
we'll log their values.

3. Compile the code and test. Now let's look at the log:

```
[0004.54] ScriptLog: 5.0000 18
```

4. It's important to remember that the values aren't passed back to the function that called us unless our parameters use the `out` modifier. To test this, let's remove the `out` modifiers like this:

```
function DoSomething(float MyFloat, int MyInt)
{
    MyFloat = 5.0;
    MyInt = 18;
}
```

Now let's try it.

5. Compile the code. We'll get warnings about using the local variables in `PostBeginPlay` without giving them values first, but let's ignore that for a second. Run the game and then check the log:

```
[0004.73] ScriptLog: 0.0000 0
```

This time the values weren't changed, because `DoSomething` wasn't able to pass them back to `PostBeginPlay` without the `out` modifiers.

What just happened?

Function parameters are obviously extremely important concepts in UnrealScript and any other programming language. The vast majority of functions you'll see in the source code will use parameters. It's the essential way functions communicate information to each other.

Out variables are useful for functions that need to pass more than one variable back to the function that called them. As an example of two out variables that we've been using for awhile, let's take a look at our `GetPlayerViewPoint` function in `AwesomePlayerController`:

```
simulated event GetPlayerViewPoint(out vector out_Location, out
Rotator out_Rotation)
{
    super.GetPlayerViewPoint(out_Location, out_Rotation);

    if(Pawn != none)
    {
        out_Location = CurrentCameraLocation;
        out_Rotation = rotator((out_Location * vect(1,1,0)) - out_
Location);
    }

    CurrentCameraRotation = out_Rotation;
}
```

Functions that call `GetPlayerViewPoint` need to know our current location and rotation, and to do that they hand us a vector and rotator for us to fill in, and in this case we've named them `out_Location` and `out_Rotation`. We give those variables values, and they're passed back to the function that called us. `GetPlayerViewPoint` is called from a few different places in UnrealScript. It's called in `Actor.uc` to figure out if we'll be able to see an effect being spawned so it can avoid spawning ones we won't see anyway. It's called from `UTVehicle.uc` to get the aim for the vehicle's weapon. It's even used in a single player cheat command to teleport the player to the location they're looking at.

There's another way for functions to pass information, and that is by returning a value to the function that called them. Let's take a look at that next.

Return values

Return values are a simpler, more commonly used method of passing information back to a function than using out parameters. A function can only return one value, which most of the time is all we need anyway. Let's try some experiments.

Time for action – I'd like to return this please

To have a function that uses a return value, first we need to tell the code what type of variable it's going to return.

1. If we still have `DoSomething` in our `AwesomeEnemySpawner` class, delete that function. We'll make a new one called `CanHasCheeseburger` with a Boolean for a return value:

    ```
    function bool CanHasCheeseburger()
    {
        return true;
    }
    ```

    The return type is declared after `function` and before the function name.

2. Now let's call our function from `PostBeginPlay`. There are two different ways we can use the function. The first would be to create a variable and let the function assign a value to it:

    ```
    function PostBeginPlay()
    {
        local bool bCheeseburger;

        super.PostBeginPlay();

        bCheeseburger = CanHasCheeseburger();
        `log(bCheeseburger);
    }
    ```

This will give `bCheeseburger` whatever value the function returns us.

3. Compile the code and test:

```
[0004.86] ScriptLog: True
```

4. The second way to use it would be to use the function itself as the variable. Since it returns a Boolean, we can use `CanHasCheeseburger()` itself as a Boolean without needing a variable to assign it to:

```
function PostBeginPlay()
{
    super.PostBeginPlay();

    `log(CanHasCheeseburger());
}
```

This gives us the same result.

5. Using functions as variables this way is useful when we're dealing with complex statements where we need clean code to keep it readable. Take the following hypothetical code:

```
if(CanHasCheeseburger() && AmHungry())
    EatCheeseburger();
```

Instead of using Boolean variables in the `if` statement, we simply use the function calls themselves as the variables. We'll see this used a lot in the UnrealScript source code. It keeps us from having to create a bunch of local variables and assign their values with function calls and THEN use those variables in other statements. If we had to write the preceding code without using the function calls as variables, it would look like this:

```
local bool bCheeseburger, bHungry;

bCheeseburger = CanHasCheeseburger();
bHungry = AmHungry();

if(bCheeseburger && bHungry)
    EatCheeseburger();
```

That's a lot more complex than what we had before.

6. Since we're returning a `bool`, we can use comparison statements as our return value as well. Let's add an `int` to our class:

```
var int NumberOfCheeseburgers;
```

And give it a default value:

```
NumberOfCheeseburgers=4
```

Now let's rewrite our function:

```
function bool CanHasCheeseburger()
{
    return NumberOfCheeseburgers > 0;
}
```

7. Compile the code and test it out:

```
[0004.70] ScriptLog: True
```

We could use even more complex statements using and (&&), or (||), and so on if we wanted.

8. Any type of variable can be used as a return value. Let's write a new function to return an `int` data type:

```
function int HowManyCheeseburgers()
{
    return NumberOfCheeseburgers;
}
```

And add this line to `PostBeginPlay`:

```
`log(HowManyCheeseburgers());
```

9. Now compile and test:

```
[0004.54] ScriptLog: 4
```

What just happened?

When we only need to pass one variable, using a return value is the way to do it. Using values in this way fits right in with the good programming practice of not accessing variables directly, but letting the class itself do it. As a crazy real-world example, it would be like me asking how much money you have with you as opposed to just opening your wallet and looking for it myself. If we wanted to change the way things worked in the class, changing one function would be a lot easier than trying to track down all the places we've accessed the variables.

Actors themselves can also be used as return values. We've used it a few times already with the Spawn function:

```
native noexport final function coerce actor Spawn
(
    class<actor>      SpawnClass,
    optional actor     SpawnOwner,
    optional name      SpawnTag,
    optional vector    SpawnLocation,
    optional rotator   SpawnRotation,
    optional Actor     ActorTemplate,
    optional bool      bNoCollisionFail
);
```

As we can see, right before the word Spawn we have actor, which is this function's return type (we'll get to all the other gobbledegook in the next topic). When we've used Spawn here:

```
MySpawnedEnemy = Spawn(class'TestEnemy', self,, Location);
```

We were assigning the actor returned by Spawn to our MySpawnedEnemy variable.

We also used an actor as a return value in our earlier experiment with Projectiles:

```
simulated function Projectile ProjectileFire()
{
    local Projectile MyProj;

    MyProj = super.ProjectileFire();
    `log(MyProj);

    return MyProj;
}
```

Our local MyProj had the actor returned by the superclass assigned to it, and we were manipulating it before passing it on in our own return value.

Similar to parameters, functions with a return value must always be written with that type of variable as the return value, and the function must always have a return statement in it. However, we can have more than one return statement when we're using flow control statements. As an example, let's take a look at a section of UTBot.uc's GetOrders function:

```
if ( UTHoldSpot(DefensePoint) != None )
{
    return 'Hold';
}
else if (UTSquad == None)
{
    return 'Attack';
}
```

`GetOrders` is declared with a name as the return type. Using flow control statements like this lets us return different values based on certain conditions in our class.

Now, that crazy wall of text in the `Spawn` function's declaration? Let's take a look at that now.

Function modifiers

Just as variables have modifiers that can make them configurable, editable, and so on, functions also have modifiers that we can use to change the way they work. Let's take a look at them. First we'll cover the ones that we're not likely to use ourselves but will still see often enough in the source code that we'll want to know what they do.

Native

The Native modifier means that an UnrealScript function has C++ running under the hood. Many of Epic's classes use this, and a lot of them won't have any UnrealScript code inside them. Unless you're working with a full Unreal Engine license as opposed to just the Unreal Development Kit, you will never use this modifier in either class or function declarations. Don't use it even if the superclass's version of the function uses it. To go along with Native…

Const, NoExport, latent, and iterator

These are all modifiers that only apply to native functions, so we will never use these either. The first two control how the function behaves in C++. Latent has some small meaning to us as UnrealScript programmers; it tells us that the function can only be used in state code, which will be covered in the next chapter. Iterator is one we've seen and used before when we were searching for all of the `AwesomeEnemySpawner` actors in the map. These functions are executed as loops.

None of those four are modifiers that we can declare ourselves.

Event

Functions declared as events have C++ code behind them that calls the function. This is usually for engine-related notifications such as two actors colliding with each other through Bump or Touch or startup events like Pre and PostBeginPlay. We'll never use Event ourselves, but when we're overriding an Event we will write it as a normal function instead. We've been doing that with PostBeginPlay.

Simulated, server, client, reliable, and unreliable

These ones we actually will use, but not yet. All of these are network-related modifiers used for multiplayer games. That's a huge topic that we'll devote an entire chapter to. If we were making a single player game we wouldn't have to worry about these modifiers at all, except for the occasional complaint by the compiler that one of our overridden functions needs to be simulated. For now it's enough to recognize these as network-related modifiers.

Singular

The singular modifier prevents infinite loops by keeping the functions it's calling from calling the singular function. Take the following hypothetical code:

```
function DoSomething()
{
    DoWhatever();
}

function DoWhatever()
{
    DoSomeOtherStuff();
    DoSomething();
}
```

That last line is what would get us into trouble. It would cause an infinite loop of DoSomething and DoWhatever function calls. If, however, we wrote it like this:

```
singular function DoSomething()
{
    DoWhatever();
}

function DoWhatever()
{
    DoSomeOtherStuff();
    DoSomething();
}
```

When the code is run, it would ignore the DoSomething call at the end since it's running as part of the original DoSomething's DoWhatever call. An example of where this would happen would be two actors running into each other and calling Touch on each other in an infinite loop. The Touch event uses the singular modifier to prevent this. It's extremely rare that you'd have to use this, in my time with UnrealScript I've never used it, but it's always good to know what it does when you see it in the source or need to use it for yourself.

That leaves us with two other modifiers that we'll see occasionally, ones which we can use on our own functions if we want to. Let's use them now!

Exec

Exec functions are ones we can interact with as players. They're used for player input like jumping, crouching, or firing a weapon, and they can also be used through the console that shows up when we press the tilde key (~) in game. Exec functions can only be used in a few classes, most notably the `PlayerController` and `CheatManager`. Let's see if we can make one in our own `AwesomePlayerController` class.

Time for action – Filthy cheater

Declaring an exec function is easy enough; using it is almost as easy. Let's make a function that will make it easier to test our game by upgrading our weapon when we call it. Exec functions can only be used in a few places, mostly `Controller`, `Pawn`, `GameInfo`, and `CheatManager` (which can be subclassed and put in the default properties of a `PlayerController`). For this experiment we'll put ours in `AwesomePlayerController`.

1. First, let's delete all of the cheeseburger functions and related variables and default properties from `AwesomeEnemySpawner` so we don't get logs from that class anymore.

2. Now for the function declaration. Add the following function to `AwesomePlayerController`:

    ```
    exec function Upgrade()
    {
        if(Pawn != none && AwesomeWeapon(Pawn.Weapon) != none)
            AwesomeWeapon(Pawn.Weapon).UpgradeWeapon();
    }
    ```

    This will test if we have a `Pawn` and it's holding an `AwesomeWeapon`, and if so upgrade it. Easy!

3. That's all we need to do in the classes, so let's compile the code.

4. Now for the first test. Run the game and pick up the weapon. Now open the console by pressing the tilde (~) key. Type `upgrade` without quotes into it (you should see it try and auto-complete as you're typing) and press *Enter*. On our HUD we'll see the weapon's level increase!

5. Now we'll see if we can make that a keybind. This is really pretty simple, but opening the `config` file can be confusing at first. Open `UDKGame\Config\DefaultInput.ini` and search for the section with this label:

```
[Engine.PlayerInput]
```

It should be the third section down. Right below that, add a line so it looks like this:

```
[Engine.PlayerInput]
Bindings=(Name="U",Command="Upgrade")
```

If we scroll down further in the file we can see that this is where all of the keyboard and mouse inputs are defined. With the line that we've added, pressing *U* will call our `Upgrade` exec function. Let's test it out.

6. Save `DefaultInput.ini` and run the game. Now when we press *U* we can see the weapon's level increase on the HUD!

What just happened?

Exec functions are useful when we want to add custom functionality to the player's input, or when we want to add easy-to-use debug functions for our game as in the case of us typing it in the console. Searching the UnrealScript source for "exec" will show you the commands that are defined this way such as the standard "god" and "fly", as well as non-cheat execs like "jump" and "throwweapon".

Static

Static functions are a bit of an oddity. The difference between a static function and other functions is that we don't need a reference to an object to be able to call a static function. For instance, when we're calling `UpgradeWeapon` on our `AwesomeWeapon` class, we have a valid reference to that actor in the world when we call it. That makes sense; otherwise there would be no object in the world to change. With a static function we wouldn't need the reference. They're used mostly for informational purposes. Static functions can access the default properties of instance variables, but since there is no instance of the object none of the variables will have changed. Additionally, static functions can only call other static functions, not normal ones.

Let's see if we can use a static function of our own.

Time for action – Using static functions

For this experiment let's use our AwesomeWeapon class.

1. The first thing we need to do is delete the weapon spawner from our test level. We don't want any instances of an AwesomeWeapon class in the game. This will help us better understand what the static function is doing.

2. Now let's write a static function in our AwesomeWeapon class:

```
static function float GetDefaultFireRate()
{
    return default.FireRates[0];
}
```

We're also giving this function a return value, which will tell us what the default firing rate of the weapon class is.

3. Now let's call the function from our Upgrade exec function in AwesomePlayerController:

```
exec function Upgrade()
{
    local float f;
    f = class'AwesomeWeapon_RocketLauncher'.static.
GetDefaultFireRate();
    `log(f);

    if(Pawn != none && AwesomeWeapon(Pawn.Weapon) != none)
        AwesomeWeapon(Pawn.Weapon).UpgradeWeapon();
}
```

Remembering inheritance, our rocket launcher inherits the static function so we can call it on that class as well.

4. Compile the code and run the game. Press *U* to call the Upgrade function and take a look at the log:

```
[0009.07] ScriptLog: 1.5000
```

What just happened?

Now we can see, even without any instances of the actor in the game, we can still call static functions on that class. As an example of how static functions can be useful, let's take a look at one from Actor.uc:

```
static function ReplaceText(out string Text, string Replace, string
With)
```

Replacing text is a function we may want to use, but would it really make sense to have to have a reference to an actor to be able to do it? We could call it on whatever class is making the call, but what if it's not a subclass of actor? Most of the UI stuff isn't, which is mainly where this function would come in handy. Having static functions lets us execute code that really doesn't need a valid object reference to be able to do so.

The super

From our lessons on inheritance, we know that when we override a function we completely change the functionality of it. But what if we still want the functionality of the superclass, we just want to add to it? We've used it before, so let's talk about the super real quick.

Calling the super executes the function in the superclass. When we used `PostBeginPlay` in `AwesomeGame` for instance, we started by writing it like this:

```
simulated function PostBeginPlay()
{
    super.PostBeginPlay();
}
```

Instead of completely overriding it and emptying it out, this has the same effect of not having `PostBeginPlay` in our class at all since all we're doing is calling the superclass's version. With that in place we started to add more functionality.

There are instances where we wouldn't want the superclass's version of the function to run at all, so we wouldn't use the call to the super. If, for example, we had a `Projectile` class, the event called `HitWall` calls the `Explode` function. But what if this particular Projectile were a listening device we were shooting at a wall? We wouldn't want it to call the `Explode` function, so in our overriding of `HitWall` we wouldn't call the super.

Very rarely it will happen where we want a class higher up in the hierarchy to run its version of the function, but not our immediate superclass. In cases like this we can skip up the class tree by specifying a superclass in parentheses when we call the super, like this:

```
super(WhateverClass).SomeFunction();
```

If there were any classes in between us and `WhateverClass` in the hierarchy, their versions of `SomeFunction` wouldn't be executed, but `WhateverClass` class's `SomeFunction` would.

Using timers

Another short but important lesson, timers! Sometimes we don't want functions to run right away, rather we want them to run after a certain amount of time has passed. For this we would use a timer. Let's see how they work.

Time for action – Just five more minutes mom

Let's say instead of spawning enemies straight away when the game started, we wanted them to spawn after say, 10 seconds. That should give us enough time to start running.

1. Let's create a new function in `AwesomeEnemySpawner` called `TimedEnemySpawn`. We'll create the timer here:

```
function TimedEnemySpawn()
{
    SetTimer(10, false, 'SpawnEnemy');
}
```

The parameters for the `SetTimer` function are pretty easy. The first one is the amount of time for the timer. The second is an optional `bool` that controls whether or not we want the timer to run in a loop, in this case it would run every 10 seconds if we set it to true. The third parameter is the name of the function we want the timer to call when the time runs out. In this case, it will call the function that actually spawns the enemy.

2. With this new functionality, we're going to need to keep a closer eye on the enemies we're spawning. If the spawner has already spawned an enemy, we don't want it to spawn another one until the current one is killed. Let's change the `SpawnEnemy` function a bit:

```
function SpawnEnemy()
{
    if(MySpawnedEnemy == none)
        MySpawnedEnemy = spawn(class'TestEnemy', self,, Location);
}
```

Now a `TestEnemy` will only be created if we don't already have one.

3. Now to call the function with the timer. In `AwesomeGame`, let's change our `ActivateSpawners` function to call the new function:

```
function ActivateSpawners()
{
    local int i;

    for(i=0; i<EnemySpawners.length; i++)
        EnemySpawners[i].TimedEnemySpawn();
}
```

4. Now compile the code and test. We'll notice right away that the enemies don't spawn immediately, but if we wait for 10 seconds they'll all spawn. That's great, but let's see if we can randomize it a bit.

5. Let's use `FRand` to get a random float and make it so the enemies spawn between 5 and 10 seconds after the game starts:

```
function TimedEnemySpawn()
{
    SetTimer(5.0 + FRand() * 5.0, false, 'SpawnEnemy');
}
```

Since `FRand()` gives us a value between 0.0 and 1.0, using it in this equation will give us a time between 5.0 and 10.0.

6. Compile and test. Now, instead of all of them spawning at once, they'll spawn randomly. Nice!

7. Let's change the `EnemyDied` function to call this timed version now. This way when we kill an enemy its replacement will take a bit before spawning:

```
function EnemyDied()
{
    TimedEnemySpawn();
}
```

8. One thing we may notice with this new timed functionality is that even after a game ends, if a timer was started, it will still spawn an enemy after the time runs out. Let's see if we can stop it from doing that. For this we'll add a line to our `FreezeEnemy` function:

```
function FreezeEnemy()
{
    if(MySpawnedEnemy != none)
        MySpawnedEnemy.Freeze();

    ClearTimer('SpawnEnemy');
}
```

9. Compile and test. Now enemies won't spawn after the game has finished!

What just happened?

As we can see, timers are very useful. Running a search for `SetTimer` in UnCodeX will reveal hundreds of instances of it. There are a few more timer-related functions in `Actor.uc`; finding the original declaration of `SetTimer` there will lead you to the right section of code. Some of the more useful ones are `ClearAllTimers`, `PauseTimer`, and `GetRemainingTimeForTimer`.

Putting it all together

Let's use some of the knowledge we've gained about functions to expand our Awesome Game a bit. The spawners are working well right now, but let's see if we can refine their behavior.

Time for action – Expanding Awesome Game

We're going to change the way the spawners work so that enemies will only spawn off screen. That way they won't suddenly appear in our view. This experiment is a bit long, so you may want to read through it real quick before diving in, and go slow so you don't miss any of the steps!

1. First thing's first! Let's get rid of the restriction on the `TestEnemy` class that makes them wait until we're in range before they start moving toward us. When they spawn, we want them to immediately start moving toward us. Change this line:

   ```
   else if (!bFreeze && VSize(Location - Enemy.Location) <
   FollowDistance)
   ```

   To this:

   ```
   else if (!bFreeze)
   ```

   Now the enemies will move toward us no matter how far away from us they are. Since we don't need the `FollowDistance` variable anymore, let's change its name and refine our movement behavior a bit. At the top of `TestEnemy`, rename the `FollowDistance` variable like this:

   ```
   var float MovementSpeed;
   ```

   And rename and change the default property:

   ```
   MovementSpeed=256.0
   ```

2. Now let's change the movement equations a bit. We'll notice that right now, as the enemies get closer to us they slow down, and this is because they're only moving a percentage of their current distance towards us, so as that distance gets shorter they move less and less until they're in range to attack us. Let's rewrite that section of our code to look like this:

   ```
   {
       NewLocation = Location;
       NewLocation += normal(Enemy.Location - Location) *
   MovementSpeed * DeltaTime;
       SetLocation(NewLocation);
   }
   ```

Now we're using our new `MovementSpeed` variable. We get a one unit long vector pointing towards the player, then multiply it by the `MovementSpeed` and `DeltaTime` to compensate for the framerate.

Our `TestEnemy`'s `Tick` function should look like this now:

```
function Tick(float DeltaTime)
{
    local AwesomePlayerController PC;
    local vector NewLocation;

    if(Enemy == none)
    {
        foreach LocalPlayerControllers(class'AwesomePlayerControll
er', PC)
        {
            if(PC.Pawn != none)
                Enemy = PC.Pawn;
        }
    }
    else if(!bFreeze)
    {
        if(VSize(Location - Enemy.Location) < AttackDistance)
        {
            Enemy.Bump(self, CollisionComponent, vect(0,0,0));
        }
        else
        {
            NewLocation = Location;
            NewLocation += normal(Enemy.Location - Location) *
MovementSpeed * DeltaTime;
            SetLocation(NewLocation);
        }
    }
}
```

3. Compile the code and test. Now we'll see that the enemies move at a constant speed toward us when they spawn, so now it's actually possible to outrun them!

4. This next functionality is a bit of a doozy, so let's take it one step at a time. We're going to make it so enemies always spawn off screen. First off, we need to move the timer functionality from the `AwesomeEnemySpawner` into the `AwesomeGame` class. Let's rewrite the `AwesomeEnemySpawner` class to get rid of the timer:

```
class AwesomeEnemySpawner extends AwesomeActor
    placeable;

var TestEnemy MySpawnedEnemy;

function SpawnEnemy()
{
    if(MySpawnedEnemy == none)
        MySpawnedEnemy = spawn(class'TestEnemy', self,, Location);
}

function EnemyDied()
{
    SpawnEnemy();
}

function FreezeEnemy()
{
    if(MySpawnedEnemy != none)
        MySpawnedEnemy.Freeze();
}

defaultproperties
{
    Begin Object Class=SpriteComponent Name=Sprite
        Sprite=Texture2D'EditorResources.S_NavP'
        HiddenGame=True
    End Object
    Components.Add(Sprite)
}
```

Let's also change the `ActivateSpawners` function in `AwesomeGame` to get rid of the timer call:

```
function ActivateSpawners()
{
    local int i;

    for(i=0; i<EnemySpawners.length; i++)
        EnemySpawners[i].SpawnEnemy();
}
```

5. Compile the code we have now and open the editor. Place
`AwesomeEnemySpawners` around the map until there are dozens of them. It
doesn't matter if any are close to the player start, we'll make sure no enemies spawn
too close to us. Just make sure there are spawners far enough away from the player
so that there will always be some off screen. If you just feel like getting to the code,
I've provided a map with spawners scattered everywhere that works great for me.
Check the files that came with the book for it.

6. Now for some code. In my tests with logging distances, I found that with the
camera values we're using the enemy spawners will be off screen at a distance of
about 1700 units. We also don't want them to be too far out of range, so let's set a
maximum distance of about 3000 units. That gives us a 1300 unit range to look for
spawners. First, let's define these variables in AwesomeGame:

```
var float MinSpawnerDistance, MaxSpawnerDistance;
```

As well as defining default values for them:

```
MinSpawnerDistance=1700.0
MaxSpawnerDistance=3000.0
```

These distances may need to be adjusted depending on the size of your test map.
These values work for the test map included with the book though. To help you find
the right distance, you can click and hold the middle mouse button in any of the
editor's 2D viewports to measure.

7. Now for some real fun. We already have a dynamic array of all of the spawners
on the map, so let's create a local one in our `ActivateSpawners` function in
`AwesomeGame` where we'll put the ones that are in the right range. Empty out the
`ActivateSpawners` function and add the local variable:

```
function ActivateSpawners()
{
    local array<AwesomeEnemySpawner> InRangeSpawners;
}
```

8. Next, we need to make sure the player has a Pawn that we can measure the distance
against. If not we'll just set a timer and exit out of the function:

```
function ActivateSpawners()
{
    local int i;
    local array<AwesomeEnemySpawner> InRangeSpawners;
    local AwesomePlayerController PC;

    foreach LocalPlayerControllers(class'AwesomePlayerController',
PC)
        break;
```

```
if(PC.Pawn == none)
{
    SetTimer(1.0, false, 'ActivateSpawners');
    return;
}
}
```

A bit complicated looking but easy to figure out. First we declare a local variable for the AwesomePlayerController that we can use in the foreach iterator. Then we look for all of the AwesomePlayerControllers in the level. If we find one, we break out of the iterator. Then we check to see if it has a Pawn. If not, set a 1 second timer and exit out of the function. The timer will call this same function again in 1 second so we can recheck until we find a Pawn. The player won't have a Pawn until a little bit into the game's startup as well as after they die, so we need to make sure.

9. Now let's add the code that will populate the local AwesomeEnemySpawner array:

```
for(i=0; i<EnemySpawners.length; i++)
{
    if(VSize(PC.Pawn.Location - EnemySpawners[i].Location) >
MinSpawnerDistance && VSize(PC.Pawn.Location - EnemySpawners[i].
Location) < MaxSpawnerDistance)
    {
        if(EnemySpawners[i].CanSpawnEnemy())
            InRangeSpawners[InRangeSpawners.length] =
EnemySpawners[i];
    }
}
```

Here we're using a for loop to go through all of the spawners. We test the distance between them and the PC's Pawn to make sure it's within range. Then we check if it can spawn an enemy with the CanSpawnEnemy function in AwesomeEnemySpawner, which we're going to write right now.

10. Switch over to the AwesomeEnemySpawner class and write our CanSpawnEnemy function:

```
function bool CanSpawnEnemy()
{
    return MySpawnedEnemy == none;
}
```

This will make it so we return true if we don't already have a spawned enemy.

11. Now, if we've done all of these checks and the `InRangeSpawners` array turned up empty, let's log it so we know, then set a timer and exit the function:

```
if(InRangeSpawners.length == 0)
{
    `log("No enemy spawners within range!");
    SetTimer(1.0, false, 'ActivateSpawners');
    return;
}
```

12. If there are spawners in the array, randomly pick one and spawn an enemy:

```
InRangeSpawners[Rand(InRangeSpawners.length)].SpawnEnemy();
```

13. Finally, set a timer so that we can spawn a new one between 1 and 4 seconds later:

```
SetTimer(1.0 + FRand() * 3.0, false, 'ActivateSpawners');
```

Our `ActivateSpawners` function should look like this now:

```
function ActivateSpawners()
{
    local int i;
    local array<AwesomeEnemySpawner> InRangeSpawners;
    local AwesomePlayerController PC;

    foreach LocalPlayerControllers
      (class'AwesomePlayerController', PC)
        break;
    if(PC.Pawn == none)
    {
        SetTimer(1.0, false, 'ActivateSpawners');
        return;
    }

    for(i=0; i<EnemySpawners.length; i++)
    {
        if(VSize(PC.Pawn.Location - EnemySpawners[i].Location) >
          MinSpawnerDistance && VSize(PC.Pawn.Location -
          EnemySpawners[i].Location) < MaxSpawnerDistance)
        {
            if(EnemySpawners[i].CanSpawnEnemy())
                InRangeSpawners[InRangeSpawners.length] =
EnemySpawners[i];
        }
    }
```

```
        if(InRangeSpawners.length == 0)
        {
            `log("No enemy spawners within range!");
            SetTimer(1.0, false, 'ActivateSpawners');
            return;
        }

        InRangeSpawners[Rand(InRangeSpawners.length)].SpawnEnemy();

        SetTimer(1.0 + FRand() * 3.0, false, 'ActivateSpawners');
    }
```

14. Just a few minor things and we'll be done. Instead of spawning the first enemy right away, let's give the player 5 seconds before the first one spawns. Change the line at the end of `PostBeginPlay` that calls `ActivateSpawners` to this:

```
        SetTimer(5.0, false, 'ActivateSpawners');
```

15. One more thing left. Once the game ends we don't want any more enemies spawning, so let's change our `ScoreObjective` function:

```
    function ScoreObjective(PlayerReplicationInfo Scorer, Int Score)
    {
        local int i;

        EnemiesLeft--;
        super.ScoreObjective(Scorer, Score);

        if(EnemiesLeft == 0)
        {
            for(i=0; i<EnemySpawners.length; i++)
                EnemySpawners[i].FreezeEnemy();
            ClearTimer('ActivateSpawners');
        }
    }
```

All we've done here is add the `ClearTimer` call to prevent any more enemies from spawning.

16. Finally! Compile the code and run the map to test it. It's working great! None of the enemies are spawning on screen, and it seems to be pretty random as far as the direction they come from. And when the game ends, the enemies freeze in place and no more are spawned. Awesome!

What just happened?

In this expansion of AwesomeGame we've reinforced some of the concepts we've learned in this chapter, including function creation, return values, and timers. We've also used local variables where instance variables wouldn't have made sense, specifically for the array of enemy spawners that are in the right range.

Have a go hero – Displaying a timer

In our discussion on timers, I mentioned a function called GetRemainingTimeForTimer. With the code we've made the player has 5 seconds until the first enemy is spawned. See if you can use that function to show the time the player has left on the HUD. Don't worry if you can't figure this one out, we'll be adding this functionality soon!

Hint – Add a new instance variable called bFirstEnemySpawned to AwesomeGame:

```
var bool bFirstEnemySpawned;
```

Set it to true at the beginning of ActivateSpawners in AwesomeGame:

```
function ActivateSpawners()
{
    local int i;
    local array<AwesomeEnemySpawner> InRangeSpawners;
    local AwesomePlayerController PC;

    bFirstEnemySpawned = true;
... (the rest of the ActivateSpawners code) ...
}
```

Then in AwesomeHUD, check the timer if bFirstEnemySpawned is false:

```
    if(AwesomeGame(WorldInfo.Game) != none && !AwesomeGame(WorldInfo.
Game).bFirstEnemySpawned && AwesomeGame(WorldInfo.Game).IsTimerActive(
'ActivateSpawners'))
    {
        Canvas.SetPos(Canvas.ClipX * 0.1, Canvas.ClipY * 0.85);
        Canvas.DrawText("Time Left To First Spawn:" @
AwesomeGame(WorldInfo.Game).GetRemainingTimeForTimer('ActivateSpawne
rs'));
    }
```

Pop quiz – All about functions

1. What does the function modifier `static` do?

2. Which of these functions would return a Boolean?

    a. `function bool Something()`

    b. `function Something(out bool bMyBool)`

3. How would you skip over an optional function parameter if you wanted to use a later one?

Summary

Well this was a pretty major chapter. We learned a lot about how functions work, how to write them and how to use them. We've also expanded our Awesome Game a bit using the knowledge we've gained here.

Specifically, we covered:

◆ What functions are and how to write them

◆ When to use local variables as opposed to instance ones

◆ How to use parameters when creating functions

◆ The different types of function modifiers we can use

◆ When to call the super and when not to

◆ The use of timers

Now that we've learned about functions, it's time to learn about how to use state code to define sets of functions to be used at different times. On to the next chapter!

6

Using States to Control Behavior

When Functions aren't enough

Functions can get a lot of what we want done, but what if our classes need more complex behavior? We could use a lot of Booleans and flow control statements to get the functionality we need, but for something as complex as say, Artificial Intelligence (AI), it would start to get messy in a hurry. To really take advantage of UnrealScript, we'll need to learn how to use states.

In this chapter, we will:

- ◆ Learn what a state is and how to create them
- ◆ Learn how functions behave inside and outside of states
- ◆ Switch between states to change the way our classes operate
- ◆ Use a few functions and statements that are unique to states

So with that, let's take a look at what we can do with state code.

It's a state of mind

We can think of a state as a collection of functions that are only used when an actor is in that state. If we have an NPC in our game, then having it be "Wandering" would create very different behavior than if it were "Attacking". It's perfectly possible to have an NPC do all of this without using states, but using them makes the code a lot easier to write and change.

Creating a state

The syntax for writing a state looks a lot like a function, so it isn't much work to create them. Let's write our first state now.

Time for action – Writing a state

The best place to learn about writing states is in our enemy class. Up until now we've been using `TestEnemy.uc` for our enemy code, but now it's time to develop this class more.

1. Rename `TestEnemy.uc` to `AwesomeEnemy.uc`.

2. At the top of the renamed class, change the class declaration line to this:

    ```
    class AwesomeEnemy extends AwesomeActor;
    ```

    Notice that we're also removing the `placeable` keyword. Our enemies are handled entirely by the `AwesomeEnemySpawner` class now.

3. Speaking of the `spawner` class, we need to change the class reference in our spawn function there. Open up `AwesomeEnemySpawner` and change the `SpawnEnemy` function and variable declaration to look like the following code snippet:

    ```
    var AwesomeEnemy MySpawnedEnemy;

    function SpawnEnemy()
    {
      if(MySpawnedEnemy == none)
        MySpawnedEnemy = spawn(class'AwesomeEnemy', self,,
          Location);
    }
    ```

4. We'll also need to change the references in our `AwesomePawn` class's `Bump` function:

    ```
    event Bump(Actor Other, PrimitiveComponent OtherComp, vector
      HitNormal)
    {
      if(AwesomeEnemy(Other) != none && !bInvulnerable)
      {
        bInvulnerable = true;
        SetTimer(InvulnerableTime, false, 'EndInvulnerable');
        TakeDamage(AwesomeEnemy(Other).BumpDamage, none, Location,
          vect(0,0,0), class'UTDmgType_LinkPlasma');
      }
    }
    ```

Why didn't we just name it `AwesomeEnemy` in the first place? Another one of my sneaky lessons. As we can see, changing a class's name can involve a lot of tracking down code, or running an **UnCodeX** search, or trying to compile to see what classes and lines give us errors. Before creating a class it's really important to think about its name, if a group of actors will need a common custom superclass, and where in the class tree it needs to be before creating it. Renaming a class is easy enough, but rearranging classes after creation can turn ugly quickly if functions we're calling in its old superclass aren't available in the new one. It's something to think about when planning your game.

1. Now that that's out of the way, we can start writing our states. Right now our enemy is always moving toward the player and attacking. Let's see if we can split those two behaviors up into separate states. Let's start by creating a `Seeking` state where the enemy will chase down the player.

```
state Seeking
{
}
```

Well that's easy enough. Now let's see what we can add to it.

1. If we take a look at the functions in our `AwesomeEnemy` class, we can see `TakeDamage`, `Freeze` and `Tick`. Thinking about what the `Seeking` state should be, `TakeDamage` and `Freeze` don't seem specific to a `Seeking` state. Those functions' behaviors won't change while this class is `Seeking`, so we'll leave those out of it. The only one we're concerned about right now is `Tick`.

2. Let's start by copying the entire `Tick` function into the `Seeking` state. It should look like the following code snippet:

```
state Seeking
{
  function Tick(float DeltaTime)
  {
    local AwesomePlayerController PC;
    local vector NewLocation;

    if(Enemy == none)
    {
      foreach LocalPlayerControllers(
        class'AwesomePlayerController', PC)
      {
        if(PC.Pawn != none)
          Enemy = PC.Pawn;
      }
    }
    else if(!bFreeze)
```

```
    {
      if(VSize(Location - Enemy.Location) < AttackDistance)
      {
        Enemy.Bump(self, CollisionComponent, vect(0,0,0));
      }
      else
      {
        NewLocation = Location;
        NewLocation += normal(Enemy.Location - Location) *
          MovementSpeed * DeltaTime;
        SetLocation(NewLocation);
      }
    }
  }
}
```

For readability's sake, functions inside states are usually indented.

1. Now, let's take a look at the `Tick` function. Thinking about it from the perspective of something that's `Seeking`, we don't want any attack code in here, we'll handle that in another state. We also don't care if we're frozen, that will be handled in another state as well. Let's trim it down a bit so it looks like the following code snippet:

```
state Seeking
{
  function Tick(float DeltaTime)
  {
    local AwesomePlayerController PC;
    local vector NewLocation;

    if(Enemy == none)
    {
      foreach LocalPlayerControllers
        (class'AwesomePlayerController', PC)
      {
        if(PC.Pawn != none)
          Enemy = PC.Pawn;
      }
    }

    NewLocation = Location;
    NewLocation += normal(Enemy.Location - Location) *
      MovementSpeed * DeltaTime;
    SetLocation(NewLocation);
  }
}
```

Already we've gotten rid of an `else if`, `if`, and an `else`. It's starting to get cleaner already! Let's see if there's anything else we can do here.

1. The `foreach` iterator we're using here seems like it would be a handy function to have, separate from any state code. We might want to use it somewhere else, so let's move it out of the `Seeking` state. We'll name it something like `GetEnemy`. First, let's write the function outside of the `Seeking` state:

```
function GetEnemy()
{
  local AwesomePlayerController PC;

  foreach LocalPlayerControllers(class'AwesomePlayerController',
    PC)
  {
    if(PC.Pawn != none)
      Enemy = PC.Pawn;
  }
}
```

2. Now let's further rewrite our `Seeking` state's `Tick` function:

```
state Seeking
{
  function Tick(float DeltaTime)
  {
    local vector NewLocation;

    if(Enemy == none)
      GetEnemy();

    if(Enemy != none)
    {
      NewLocation = Location;
      NewLocation += normal(Enemy.Location - Location) *
        MovementSpeed * DeltaTime;
      SetLocation(NewLocation);
    }
  }
}
```

Comparing this to our original `Tick` function, it's a lot more compact and easier to read. This `Tick` function has one purpose and one purpose only: to find our enemy and move towards it. We're done with the `Seeking` state for now, so let's move on to `Attacking`.

1. We'll start the `Attacking` state the same way as `Seeking`:

```
state Attacking
{
}
```

2. This time, instead of copying the original `Tick` function into our state, we're going to move it there. Our original `Tick` function was only concerned with seeking and attacking, so we don't need it outside of these two states for now. The `Tick` function for `Attacking` is going to be really small. Let's prune it down to the following code snippet:

```
state Attacking
{
  function Tick(float DeltaTime)
  {
    if(Enemy == none)
      GetEnemy();

    if(Enemy != none)
      Enemy.Bump(self, CollisionComponent, vect(0,0,0));
  }
}
```

One thing we'll notice is that we're not using an `else` statement here. It may seem odd as it would seem like we should use it here; either `Enemy` is none or it has a value. If we think about it though, then it makes sense to write it like this in this instance. If we come into this function and `Enemy` doesn't have a value, then we'll call `GetEnemy` to give it a chance to find one. After that we check if `Enemy` has a value and if so call `Bump` on it. If we were using an `else` statement here, then the `Bump` call would get skipped over after `GetEnemy` was called. It might not seem like it matters with a function such as `Tick` that's going to be called the next frame anyway, but this is one of those cases where we have to think about what we want to have happen very carefully. If our enemy class only had once chance to attack before moving to another state, then `Bump` might never be called if we had it behind an `else` statement.

1. We're almost done splitting up our `Tick` function. The only thing we haven't taken into account is the `bFreeze` variable that stops it from moving or attacking. Instead of using `bFreeze` in the `Attacking` and `Seeking` states, we'll get rid of it completely and make a `Frozen` state instead. First, let's create the state:

```
state Frozen
{
}
```

2. As we still don't want the enemy moving or attacking while frozen, let's empty out the `Tick` function in our new state:

```
state Frozen
{
  function Tick(float DeltaTime)
  {
  }
}
```

3. Before we delete the `bFreeze` variable, let's remove the reference to it in our `Freeze` function:

```
function Freeze()
{
}
```

4. Now delete this line from the top of our class:

```
var bool bFreeze;
```

What just happened?

Now we've separated out the functionality of our enemy class into specific states. We can see how compact and clean the code becomes without the extra `if/else` statements. If we wanted to expand the way this class worked, it would be a lot easier as the code in the states is pretty self contained now.

If we compiled the code now, then we'd find that the enemies would still spawn, but they won't do anything other than sit there. Even though we've created the states, none of the code inside them will execute until we tell the actor to use those states. Let's do that next.

Switching between states

An actor can only be in one state at a time. In order for us to use the new functionality we've created, we need to tell our actor which state to go to and when. Let's take a look at how to do that.

Time for action – Switching states

Three states, `Seeking`, `Attacking`, and `Frozen`. The first thing we need to do is tell our actor which state to start in.

1. To do that, we'll simply add the `auto` keyword to the beginning of our `Seeking` state:

```
auto state Seeking
```

Only one state can be declared with the `auto` keyword, and this state is the default state for that actor. We want ours to do the same thing it did before, automatically start moving toward the player when it spawns.

1. Now that we're in the `Seeking` state, we need to tell the actor when to move into the `Attacking` state. We'll do this in the `Tick` function by comparing the distance between the actor and its enemy:

```
function Tick(float DeltaTime)
{
  local vector NewLocation;

  if(Enemy == none)
    GetEnemy();

  if(Enemy != none)
  {
    NewLocation = Location;
    NewLocation += normal(Enemy.Location - Location) *
      MovementSpeed * DeltaTime;
    SetLocation(NewLocation);

    if(VSize(NewLocation - Enemy.Location) < AttackDistance)
      GoToState('Attacking');
  }
}
```

Moving from one state to another is as simple as using the `GoToState` function with the name of the new state.

1. Now we're attacking! We don't want to get stuck in this state though, so let's reverse the less than sign in our `Attacking` state's `Tick` function to get us back out of it:

```
function Tick(float DeltaTime)
{
  if(Enemy == none)
```

```
    GetEnemy();

  if(Enemy != none)
  {
    Enemy.Bump(self, CollisionComponent, vect(0,0,0));

    if(VSize(Location - Enemy.Location) > AttackDistance)
      GoToState('Seeking');
  }
}
```

2. Almost done! We still have to use the `Frozen` state at the end of the game, so let's put a new line of code in our `Freeze` function:

```
function Freeze()
{
  GoToState('Frozen');
}
```

3. Now let's compile the code and test it. The enemies still act the same way they normally do, so we haven't broken anything!

4. Let's see if we can change the functionality a bit. What if, instead of freezing at the end, the enemies ran away like the red boxed cowards they are? First, let's rename a few things, starting with the `Frozen` state. Change it to the following:

```
state Fleeing
```

5. Now let's rename the `Freeze` function and change the line inside it:

```
function RunAway()
{
  GoToState('Fleeing');
}
```

6. The only place we were calling the `Freeze` function was from the `AwesomeEnemySpawner` class, so let's change its `FreezeEnemy` function:

```
function FreezeEnemy()
{
  if(MySpawnedEnemy != none)
    MySpawnedEnemy.RunAway();
}
```

7. Having this function named `FreezeEnemy` doesn't quite fit anymore, so let's change that as well:

```
function MakeEnemyRunAway()
{
  if(MySpawnedEnemy != none)
    MySpawnedEnemy.RunAway();
}
```

8. We were calling the `FreezeEnemy` function from our `AwesomeGame` class, so let's change that line:

```
function ScoreObjective(PlayerReplicationInfo Scorer, Int Score)
{
  local int i;

  EnemiesLeft--;
  super.ScoreObjective(Scorer, Score);

  if(EnemiesLeft == 0)
  {
    for(i=0; i<EnemySpawners.length; i++)
      EnemySpawners[i].MakeEnemyRunAway();
      ClearTimer('ActivateSpawners');
  }
}
```

9. Now that we've cleaned up the code, let's change the `Tick` function inside the `AwesomeEnemy`'s `Fleeing` state:

```
function Tick(float DeltaTime)
{
  local vector NewLocation;

  if(Enemy == none)
    GetEnemy();

  if(Enemy != none)
  {
    NewLocation = Location;
    NewLocation -= normal(Enemy.Location - Location) *
      MovementSpeed * DeltaTime;
    SetLocation(NewLocation);
  }
}
```

10. Compile the code and test. Shoot your way down to 1 enemy left, then let a few gather around you before shooting the last one. We'll see the other ones start moving away once you have won!

What just happened?

Moving between states is easy, and we can see how easy it would be to change the functionality of a single one without affecting the others or worrying about breaking any of the other functionality with complicated `if`/`else` statements. With the state code all self contained, it makes it a lot easier to manage.

Function overriding in states

One question we might ask at this point is how can we have more than one `Tick` function in our class? Don't they interfere with each other? With states, each one can have functions operate differently, as with our use of `Tick` and how it changes depending on what state we're in. Functions can be changed in each state or ignored completely. We left `TakeDamage` alone, for instance, although we could have made an empty version inside the `Fleeing` state to keep the enemies from taking damage as they fled.

Taking a look at our updated `AwesomeEnemy` class, we can also see that functions don't even need to be in a state. With our `TakeDamage` function, as it's not in a state and not overridden in any state, it will operate the same way no matter what state the actor is in.

Red state, blue state, no state, new state?

Let's take a look at function overriding in states so we can understand how it works.

Time for action – Multiple personalities

Let's add a bit of code to our various `Tick` functions so we can see exactly what happens as we change states. Normally, we wouldn't want to put logs in the `Tick` function as it's called at every frame, but sometimes it's good for testing purposes.

1. First, we'll add a `Tick` function outside of the states so we can get a complete picture of what's going on.

```
function Tick(float DeltaTime)
{
  log("Non-State Tick");
}
```

2. Now let's add logs to our other `Tick` functions. First, the `Seeking Tick`:

```
function Tick(float DeltaTime)
{
  local vector NewLocation;

  `log("Seeking Tick");

  if(Enemy == none)
    GetEnemy();

  if(Enemy != none)
  {
    NewLocation = Location;
    NewLocation += normal(Enemy.Location - Location) *
      MovementSpeed * DeltaTime;
    SetLocation(NewLocation);

    if(VSize(NewLocation - Enemy.Location) < AttackDistance)
      GoToState('Attacking');
  }
}
```

3. Next, the `Attacking Tick`:

```
function Tick(float DeltaTime)
{
  ``log("Attacking Tick");

  if(Enemy == none)
    GetEnemy();

  if(Enemy != none)
  {
    Enemy.Bump(self, CollisionComponent, vect(0,0,0));

    if(VSize(Location - Enemy.Location) > AttackDistance)
      GoToState('Seeking');
  }
}
```

4. Finally, the `Fleeing Tick`:

```
function Tick(float DeltaTime)
{
  local vector NewLocation;

  `log("Fleeing Tick");

    if(Enemy == none)
        GetEnemy();

    if(Enemy != none)
    {
        NewLocation = Location;
        NewLocation -= normal(Enemy.Location - Location) *
MovementSpeed * DeltaTime;
        SetLocation(NewLocation);
    }
}
```

5. To test this we're going to need the game to only have one enemy, so the log that we'll get will only be one actor. To do this, let's first make the `AwesomeEnemy` class placeable:

```
class AwesomeEnemy extends AwesomeActor
  placeable;
```

6. Instead of deleting the spawners, we'll simply disable them by removing the timer from our `AwesomeGame`'s `PostBeginPlay` function:

```
simulated function PostBeginPlay()
{
  local AwesomeEnemySpawner ES;

  super.PostBeginPlay();

  GoalScore = EnemiesLeft;

  foreach DynamicActors(class'AwesomeEnemySpawner', ES)
    EnemySpawners[EnemySpawners.length] = ES;
}
```

7. Now for a little trick. To test the fleeing code, we'll need to do a few things. First, let's change the `EnemiesLeft` default property in `AwesomeGame` to 1:

```
EnemiesLeft=1
```

8. Then, change the `TakeDamage` function inside our `AwesomeEnemy` so that it won't destroy itself when we kill it:

```
event TakeDamage(int DamageAmount, Controller EventInstigator,
  vector HitLocation, vector Momentum, class<DamageType>
  DamageType, optional TraceHitInfo HitInfo, optional Actor
  DamageCauser)
{
  if(EventInstigator != none &&
    EventInstigator.PlayerReplicationInfo != none)
    WorldInfo.Game.ScoreObjective
      (EventInstigator.PlayerReplicationInfo, 1);

  if(AwesomeEnemySpawner(Owner) != none)
    AwesomeEnemySpawner(Owner).EnemyDied();
}
```

9. With this change, the enemy will still report to `AwesomeGame` that it was killed, but it will stay on the map so we can see the `Fleeing` state working.

10. One last thing we need to do. This placed enemy doesn't have a spawner, so the normal code we're using to make it run away isn't going to be called. Instead, as we know there's only one enemy on the map, let's call `RunAway` ourselves from our `TakeDamage` function:

```
event TakeDamage(int DamageAmount, Controller EventInstigator,
  vector HitLocation, vector Momentum, class<DamageType>
  DamageType, optional TraceHitInfo HitInfo, optional Actor
  DamageCauser)
{
  if(EventInstigator != none &&
    EventInstigator.PlayerReplicationInfo != none)
    WorldInfo.Game.ScoreObjective
      (EventInstigator.PlayerReplicationInfo, 1);

  if(AwesomeEnemySpawner(Owner) != none)
    AwesomeEnemySpawner(Owner).EnemyDied();

  RunAway();
}
```

Sometimes while testing out new code, we'll need to bypass the normal operation of the game. It can get a bit tricky to keep track of all of the changes, but it's necessary to make sure we can track down any problems with the code without having other things interfering with what we're testing. In this case, if we were having trouble getting our AwesomeEnemy class working, what we're doing would be a good way to single out one enemy so that we can figure out what's going wrong without having logs from all of the other AwesomeEnemies getting mixed up with it.

1. Now let's compile the code. Then, open the editor and place an AwesomeEnemy actor a little away from the weapon so we have time to pick it up.

2. Save the map and close the editor, then run the game.

3. Let's take a look at the log:

    ```
    [0008.45] ScriptLog: Seeking Tick

    [0010.24] ScriptLog: Attacking Tick

    [0012.08] ScriptLog: Fleeing Tick
    ```

We can see that the three state ticks being logged are fine, and that only one of them is being logged at any one time. The actor automatically starts in the Seeking state as we specified. However, what about the non-state Tick? We know how to switch between states, but can we tell the actor to go into no state?

1. Well, of course we can. Let's do that now! We'll give the AwesomeEnemy a few seconds to flee, then we'll tell it not to use any of the states. First, let's add a timer to the RunAway function:

    ```
    function RunAway()
    {
      GoToState('Fleeing');
      SetTimer(2.0, false, 'NoState');
    }
    ```

2. Now let's make the NoState function:

    ```
    function NoState()
    {
      GoToState('');
    }
    ```

That's all there is to it, an empty name in our `GoToState` call.

1. Now let's run the game, kill the enemy, and wait for it to stop. Exit the game and take a look at the log:

```
[0011.03]  ScriptLog:  Non-State Tick
[0011.05]  ScriptLog:  Non-State Tick
```

What just happened?

There we go, now our non-state `Tick` function is being called! If we wanted the `AwesomeEnemy` to start like this, we would simply remove the `auto` keyword from our `Seeking` state. If no state is declared as `auto`, then none of the states and none of the functions in those states will be used until we tell the actor to go into one of the states.

We can see from this that even though the non-state `Tick` function seems like it would be called all the time, being in a state tells the actor to use the state's functions instead. If a function isn't declared in the state we're in, then the code will look for the non-state version of that function. There's a better word for those functions though, which we'll take a look at next.

Non-state functions

Non-state functions are kind of similar to calling `Super`, except that calling `Global` will make sure that the non-state version of a function is called. Let's take a look.

Time for action – Calling non-state functions

Before we get into this experiment, there's a small cleanup job we have to do. We'll leave the single-enemy code intact; we'll just take out our `Tick` logging stuff.

1. Delete the non-state `Tick` function as well as the `NoState` function.

2. Take the `NoState` timer out of the `RunAway` function:

```
function RunAway()
{
  GoToState('Fleeing');
}
```

3. Delete the log lines from the `Seeking`, `Attacking`, and Fleeing states' `Tick` functions.

4. There we go, now we're ready to start our next experiment. First, let's set up a repeating timer by adding a `PostBeginPlay` function:

```
function PostBeginPlay()
{
   SetTimer(1.0, true, 'LogTimer');
}
```

Every second we'll be calling this new function.

1. Now let's create the `LogTimer` function:

```
function LogTimer()
{
   `log("=======================");
   `log("Global call:");
   Global.LogMe();
   `log("Non-Global call:");
   LogMe();
}
```

A lot of stuff here, but it's simple. First, we call `Global.LogMe`, then a normal `LogMe`. We'll see the difference soon.

1. Let's first make the `LogMe` function outside of the states:

```
function LogMe()
{
   `log("Non-state LogMe");
}
```

2. Now let's add one to the `Seeking` state:

```
function LogMe()
{
   `log("Seeking LogMe");
}
```

3. Now, the `Attacking` state:

```
function LogMe()
{
   `log("Attacking LogMe");
}
```

4. And finally, the `Fleeing` state:

```
function LogMe()
{
    `log("Fleeing LogMe");
}
```

5. Now let's compile the code and run the game. Exit and take a look at the log:

```
[0008.90] ScriptLog: =========================
[0008.90] ScriptLog: Global call:
[0008.90] ScriptLog: Non-state LogMe
[0008.90] ScriptLog: Regular call:
[0008.90] ScriptLog: Seeking LogMe
[0009.85] ScriptLog: =========================
[0009.85] ScriptLog: Global call:
[0009.85] ScriptLog: Non-state LogMe
[0009.85] ScriptLog: Regular call:
[0009.85] ScriptLog: Attacking LogMe
```

What just happened?

We can see that no matter what state we're in, calling `Global.LogMe` always calls the non-state version of the function. This applies even when we're using it inside a state's function. Let's take a look at that now.

Time for action – Non-state functions from inside a state

Before we start this experiment, another cleanup job.

1. Delete the `LogMe`, `LogTimer`, and `PostBeginPlay` functions.

2. Make sure the `LogMe` functions in all three states are deleted as well.

3. We're going to write a new version of `TakeDamage` inside the `Seeking` function. This will stop the non-state function from being called:

```
event TakeDamage(int DamageAmount, Controller EventInstigator,
    vector HitLocation, vector Momentum, class<DamageType>
    DamageType, optional TraceHitInfo HitInfo, optional Actor
    DamageCauser)
{
    `log("Seeking TakeDamage");
}
```

4. Let's also add a log to the non-state `TakeDamage` function:

```
event TakeDamage(int DamageAmount, Controller EventInstigator,
  vector HitLocation, vector Momentum, class<DamageType>
  DamageType, optional TraceHitInfo HitInfo, optional Actor
  DamageCauser)
{
  `log("Global TakeDamage");

  if(EventInstigator != none &&
    EventInstigator.PlayerReplicationInfo != none)
  WorldInfo.Game.ScoreObjective
    (EventInstigator.PlayerReplicationInfo, 1);

  if(AwesomeEnemySpawner(Owner) != none)
    AwesomeEnemySpawner(Owner).EnemyDied();

  RunAway();
}
```

5. Now let's compile and test.

6. Oh God, the `AwesomeEnemy` doesn't feel pain, it can't be reasoned with! Let's take a look at the log to find out why:

```
[0008.64] ScriptLog: Seeking TakeDamage
[0010.49] ScriptLog: Seeking TakeDamage
```

7. Now that we've declared `TakeDamage` inside the `Seeking` state, the non-state one isn't being called anymore. However, what if we wanted to? Calling Super here would just call the superclass's version of the function, which isn't what we need. Time to use `Global`. Let's add a line to the `Seeking` state's `TakeDamage` function:

```
event TakeDamage(int DamageAmount, Controller EventInstigator,
  vector HitLocation, vector Momentum, class<DamageType>
  DamageType, optional TraceHitInfo HitInfo, optional Actor
  DamageCauser)
{
  `log("Seeking TakeDamage");
  Global.TakeDamage(DamageAmount, EventInstigator, HitLocation,
    Momentum, DamageType, HitInfo, DamageCauser);
}
```

8. Now let's compile and test.

9. Shoot the enemy, then shut down the game and take a look at the log:

```
[0008.21] ScriptLog: Seeking TakeDamage
[0008.21] ScriptLog: Global TakeDamage
```

Much better.

What just happened?

Using non-state functions can come in handy. If you had some functionality that needed to be used in quite a few states, then it might be better to move it to the non-state version of the function and call Global from the states' versions. Conversely, if you had a state that needed to add a bit of functionality to the non-state version, then you could easily do it without duplicating all of the non-state version's code.

Before we move on, let's clean up the code a bit.

1. Delete the TakeDamage function from the Seeking state.

2. Remove the log from the non-state TakeDamage function.

Now to take a closer look at what happens and what we can do when we change states.

State changes and detection

We know how to change states now. However, what if we need a bit of setup when an actor enters a state, or we need to do a few things before it leaves that state? There are two functions we can use for this that we'll take a look at now, BeginState and EndState.

BeginState

First, let's take a look at BeginState.

Time for action – BeginState

BeginState and EndState are both declared in Object.uc, and like other functions, they don't necessarily have to be used inside a state, although that's where they are most useful. BeginState is called when an actor enters any state, before any of that state's code is run. This makes it useful for running any set-up code that the state needs. EndState is run right before an actor leaves a state and lets us do any cleanup or other changes we need to at that point. Both of these functions are called during the chain of events when GoToState is called. EndState is called on the state that's being left and BeginState on the state that the actor is going into.

Let's see how we can use these functions in our `AwesomeEnemy` class.

1. The easiest thing we could do to try out these functions is change the enemy's appearance based on what state it's in, so let's try that. First, let's declare a few materials to use for the various states:

```
var Material SeekingMat, AttackingMat, FleeingMat;
```

2. Now let's set some values in the default properties:

```
SeekingMat=Material'EditorMaterials.WidgetMaterial_X'
AttackingMat=Material'EditorMaterials.WidgetMaterial_Z'
FleeingMat=Material'EditorMaterials.WidgetMaterial_Y'
```

These are simple red, blue, and green materials normally used by the movement/rotation widget in the editor, but I like to use them for testing.

1. Now, we'll need to give the `AwesomeEnemy`'s mesh a variable so we can edit it. Let's add this to the top of our class:

```
var StaticMeshComponent MyMesh;
```

2. Now let's change the section of the default properties to set `MyMesh` variable's value:

```
Begin Object Class=StaticMeshComponent Name=EnemyMesh
  StaticMesh=StaticMesh'UN_SimpleMeshes.TexPropCube_Dup'
  Materials(0)=Material'EditorMaterials.WidgetMaterial_X'
  LightEnvironment=MyLightEnvironment
  Scale3D=(X=0.25,Y=0.25,Z=0.5)
End Object
Components.Add(EnemyMesh)
MyMesh=EnemyMesh
```

The last line is the important one, it assigns the mesh to the `MyMesh` variable.

1. Now that we have everything set up, let's write our `BeginState` functions. First, we'll write one in the `Seeking` state:

```
function BeginState(Name PreviousStateName)
{
  MyMesh.SetMaterial(0, SeekingMat);
}
```

The `SetMaterial` function is declared in `MeshComponent`; it allows us to change the materials a mesh uses. The first parameter is an `int` corresponding to the material index (if you double-click a mesh in the content browser in the editor, you can see a list of the materials and indices under the `LODInfo` property). The second parameter is the material we want it to use. In this case, when the `AwesomeEnemy` enters the `Seeking` state we want it to use its normal red material, which we've set as `SeekingMat`.

1. Now let's write a `BeginState` function for the `Attacking` state:

   ```
   function BeginState(Name PreviousStateName)
   {
       MyMesh.SetMaterial(0, AttackingMat);
   }
   ```

2. And finally, one for the `Fleeing` state:

   ```
   function BeginState(Name PreviousStateName)
   {
       MyMesh.SetMaterial(0, FleeingMat);
   }
   ```

3. Now let's compile the code and test it out. The enemy starts out at its normal red color, turns blue while it's attacking us, and turns green when we shoot it to win the match and make it flee. Nice!

What just happened?

We can see how `BeginState` can be useful to us. If it didn't exist, then we'd have to use some trickery with `Tick` to figure out when we've changed states.

EndState

Now let's see what we can do with `EndState`.

Time for action – EndState

Let's use `EndState` to stop the enemies from moving for a second after they've attacked us. That will give us a little bit of time to get away from them, so they're not constantly swarming around us.

1. First, let's add a `bool` to the top of our class:

   ```
   var bool bAttacking;
   ```

We'll use this variable to keep the enemy from moving during an attack.

2. This will only really apply to the `Seeking` state, we don't want to stop the enemy from fleeing just because they were attacking us. Let's change the `Tick` function in the `Seeking` state:

```
function Tick(float DeltaTime)
{
  local vector NewLocation;

  if(bAttacking)
    return;

  if(Enemy == none)
    GetEnemy();

  if(Enemy != none)
  {
    NewLocation = Location;
    NewLocation += normal(Enemy.Location - Location) *
      MovementSpeed * DeltaTime;
    SetLocation(NewLocation);

    if(VSize(NewLocation - Enemy.Location) < AttackDistance)
      GoToState('Attacking');
  }
}
```

Now if `bAttacking` is `true`, then none of the movement code will run.

3. Now to figure out where to set `bAttacking` to `true`. We'll do this in `Attacking`'s `Tick` function:

```
function Tick(float DeltaTime)
{
  bAttacking = true;

  if(Enemy == none)
    GetEnemy();

  if(Enemy != none)
  {
    Enemy.Bump(self, CollisionComponent, vect(0,0,0));

    if(VSize(Location - Enemy.Location) > AttackDistance)
      GoToState('Seeking');
  }
}
```

4. That takes care of setting it to `true`, but where do we set it to `false`? To do this, we'll create a timer in the `Attacking` state's `EndState` function:

```
function EndState(name NextStateName)
{
    SetTimer(1, false, 'EndAttack');
}
```

Now when the enemy leaves the `Attacking` state, a one-second timer will start to call `EndAttack`. If during this time the enemy re-enters the `Attacking` state, then `bAttacking` will be kept `true` by that state's `Tick` function, and the timer will be reset to one second after the attack ends again.

1. Now to create the `EndAttack` function. This one contains a single line and should be created outside of all of the states:

```
function EndAttack()
{
    bAttacking = false;
}
```

2. Now let's compile and test. When the enemies attack us they freeze for a second before continuing. Nice!

What just happened?

`BeginState` and `EndState` are extremely useful when dealing with states. They provide convenient places to do some setup or cleanup when entering and leaving different states. As an example, in `PlayerController` `BeginState` is used to set the `Pawn`'s physics when necessary, like entering water or flying while spectating a match.

State detection

There is one more thing we need to discuss while talking about entering and leaving various states. How do we know what state we're in at any given time? Sometimes we'll want to know. For an example of this, one of the states in `UTPawn` is `FeigningDeath`, where you pretend to be dead to confuse the enemy. We don't want the player to be able to use objects while in this state, so in `UTPlayerController`'s `PerformedUseAction` function we check that they're not in that state. Let's see if we can use the state detection functions to help us with `AwesomeEnemy`.

Time for action – Using state detection functions

The first thing that would be handy to know is: what state are we in? We can use a function called GetStateName to find this out.

1. Let's put a PostBeginPlay function back in our AwesomeEnemy class, and use it to start a repeating timer:

```
function PostBeginPlay()
{
   SetTimer(0.5, true, 'WhatState');
}
```

2. Now, let's create the WhatState function:

```
function WhatState()
{
   `log(GetStateName());
}
```

3. Now we're ready to test. Compile the code and run the game, then exit and check the log:

```
[0009.81] ScriptLog: Seeking
[0010.30] ScriptLog: Seeking
[0010.76] ScriptLog: Attacking
[0011.25] ScriptLog: Attacking
```

Working great!

1. Now how can we use this to our advantage? Well, let's take a look at the material-changing functionality we're using in AwesomeEnemy. It seems a bit inconsistent with what's going on with that actor's movement. It turns blue when attacking, then back to red for seeking. However, as we added that one-second delay before it starts moving again, it's frozen but still red. Let's see if we can change that.

2. First, let's delete the PostBeginPlay and WhatState functions that we've created.

3. Now what we need to do is stop the actor from automatically turning red when it enters the Attacking state. If bAttacking is still true, then we don't want to change the material. Let's rewrite the Attacking state's BeginState function:

```
function BeginState(Name PreviousStateName)
{
   if(!bAttacking)
      MyMesh.SetMaterial(0, SeekingMat);
}
```

4. We don't want to do the same thing in `Fleeing`, we want it to keep turning green and running away no matter what else is going on, so we'll leave that state alone.

5. Now in the `EndAttack` function, we'll check what state we're in. If we're `Seeking`, then we'll change our material to the `SeekingMat`:

```
function EndAttack()
{
  bAttacking = false;

  if(GetStateName() == 'Seeking')
    MyMesh.SetMaterial(0, SeekingMat);
}
```

6. Now let's compile the code and test. We can see that when the enemy attacks, it will stay blue until it begins to move again. Perfect!

What just happened?

Another function that serves the same purpose is `IsInState`. We could rewrite our `EndAttack` function like the following code snippet and it would behave the same:

```
function EndAttack()
{
  bAttacking = false;

  if(IsInState('Seeking'))
    MyMesh.SetMaterial(0, SeekingMat);
}
```

Have a go hero – Rewriting the SetMaterial calls

We seem to be using `MyMesh.SetMaterial` a lot. See if you can move it into a non-state function that the states and other functions pass a material parameter to instead.

 Hint – Think about how we're calling the `SetMaterial` function and if a material could be used as a function parameter.

One other state detection function we can use is called `IsChildState`. Much like classes, states themselves can be subclassed. It's rare that you'd ever need to use it, but we'll discuss it a bit now.

Subclassing states

Subclassing a state is pretty easy to do; it's just a matter of figuring out when you need to use it. Say we had a state called `Moving`. We could create states that extend `Moving` and call them `Running`, `Walking`, and so on. These would all have functionality in common with `Moving`, but would have slight alterations. It wouldn't make sense to duplicate all of the functions that would be in the `Moving` state just to slightly change them, so subclassing the `Moving` state would make sense in this instance. Let's try it out with a simple experiment.

Time for action – Subclassing the Seeking state

We'll use an extension of the `Seeking` state to make our enemy move faster.

1. First, delete the `auto` keyword from our `Seeking` state. We'll make our new state the `auto` state.

2. Now let's create our new state and call it `FastSeeking`:

```
auto state FastSeeking extends Seeking
{
}
```

Don't let the name throw you, the new state's name doesn't have to contain the old state's name or be related to it at all, we could call it Fiddlesticks if we wanted to.

Be sure to place this state AFTER the `Seeking` state, otherwise the compiler will give you an error telling you that it cannot find the state we're extending from.

1. Now let's create a `BeginState` function inside our new state and change it slightly from the regular `Seeking` state's version:

```
function BeginState(Name PreviousStateName)
{
  MovementSpeed = default.MovementSpeed * 2.0;

  if(!bAttacking)
    MyMesh.SetMaterial(0, SeekingMat);
}
```

We're using `default.MovementSpeed` here instead of just `MovementSpeed`, otherwise every time we entered this state our speed would double. We just want it to stay at twice the default speed.

1. Compile the code and test. We can't even run away from it now.

What just happened?

Even without a `Tick` function in our new state, it inherits all of the functions declared in the state we're extending from. Now we can see how helpful this can be if we have a lot of states with similar functionality. As I said it's rare that you'd ever need to use this, but it can save a lot of unnecessary code when it can be used.

Before we continue, let's delete the `FastSeeking` state and put the `auto` keyword back in our `Seeking` state.

Keywords, labels, and latent functions

Just a few other things we need to discuss about states, keywords, labels, and latent functions. Let's start by going over the keywords we can use in states.

Keywords

One keyword that we've already been using is `auto`; it designates the state as the one the actor will start in when it is created. Only one state can have the `auto` keyword, but if we wanted to we could have no states with it. In that case, the actor will only use the non-state functions until it enters one of the states.

The other keyword we can use with states is `ignores`. Unlike `auto`, `ignores` goes inside the state at the top, before any functions are declared. Using `ignores` tells the state not to use the functions we tell it to while it's in this state. It has the same effect as declaring the function and leaving it empty, but it's a lot cleaner to use `ignores`. Let's see if we can use it in our `AwesomeEnemy` class.

Time for action – Using ignores

This will be a simple experiment; we're just going to have `AwesomeEnemy` not take any damage while it's fleeing.

1. At the top of `AwesomeEnemy`'s `Fleeing` state, add the following line:

   ```
   ignores TakeDamage;
   ```

2. This one's pretty hard to test, but adding this line will make `AwesomeEnemy` ignore calls to `TakeDamage` while it is in the `Fleeing` state.

What just happened?

If we had more than one function that we wanted to ignore, then we would separate them with commas. For example, if we wanted it to ignore the `EndAttack` function as well, we would write it like this:

```
ignores TakeDamage, EndAttack;
```

Labels and latent functions

States can have special functions that can only be executed from within that state, code that can't be called from normal functions. These are called latent functions. In addition, states can use labels to control the flow of state code. Let's take a look.

Time for action – Do we really need to give labels to everything?

One label is special and indicates where state code should start executing; this one is called `Begin`. Let's take a look at a few things we can do with state code, labels, and latent functions.

1. At the bottom of our `Seeking` state, underneath all of the functions, but before the closing } symbol, let's write the following code:

```
Begin:
   `log("Man I'm tired, I'm going to sleep.");
   Sleep(3.0);
   `log("French toast please!");
SomeOtherLabel:
   `log("You ever have a deja vu Joel?");
   Sleep(3.0);
   GoTo('SomeOtherLabel');
```

When state code starts, it starts at the `Begin` label. First we log something, then we use a latent function called `Sleep`. Usually when code is running, it will prevent any other code from running until it's finished. This doesn't apply to latent functions, which won't stop other code from running while it's waiting on whatever function it's performing to finish.

After it's done sleeping, we log something else, then the code automatically moves down past the `SomeOtherLabel` label into the code down there. We set this up to loop by calling `GoTo('SomeOtherLabel')`.

1. We can also specify which label a state should start at during our call to `GoToState`. Let's change the `Attacking` state's `Tick` function:

```
function Tick(float DeltaTime)
{
  bAttacking = true;

  if(Enemy == none)
    GetEnemy();

  if(Enemy != none)
  {
    Enemy.Bump(self, CollisionComponent, vect(0,0,0));

    if(VSize(Location - Enemy.Location) > AttackDistance)
      GoToState('Seeking', 'SomeOtherLabel');
  }
}
```

2. Compile the code and test. When the `AwesomeEnemy` leaves the `Attacking` state and returns to `Seeking`, it will start at the `SomeOtherLabel` instead of the default `Begin` now.

3. Let's change the `Attacking` state's `Tick` function to what it was before:

```
function Tick(float DeltaTime)
{
  bAttacking = true;

  if(Enemy == none)
    GetEnemy();

  if(Enemy != none)
  {
    Enemy.Bump(self, CollisionComponent, vect(0,0,0));

    if(VSize(Location - Enemy.Location) > AttackDistance)
      GoToState('Seeking');
  }
}
```

4. Finally, let's remove the labels and latent functions at the bottom of our `Seeking` state.

What just happened?

This only briefly touched on labels and latent functions. It can get pretty advanced and complicated quickly. The most important place these are used is in the `Controller` classes, specifically for the AI. Two latent functions, `MoveTo` and `MoveToward`, are used a lot there to cause the bots to move towards a specific location while still allowing other code to run in the meantime. I'd recommend searching through `UTBot` to see how labels and latent functions are used there.

Like a boss

Oh man, what a mess. Must have been some party. Let's clean up our code so we can get our game working right again.

The cleanup job

Before we get into some fun stuff, we need to get our game back in shape by removing the test code that let us have only one enemy.

Time for action – Reverting our code

Now let's get the test code out of here!

1. The first thing we need to do is open the `AwesomeTestMap` and delete the placed `AwesomeEnemy` there. Save the map and exit the editor.

2. Next, let's take out the `placeable` keyword from the top of `AwesomeEnemy`:

   ```
   class AwesomeEnemy extends AwesomeActor;
   ```

3. Now let's change `AwesomeEnemy`'s `TakeDamage` function back to what it was before we started these experiments:

   ```
   event TakeDamage(int DamageAmount, Controller EventInstigator,
     vector HitLocation, vector Momentum, class<DamageType>
     DamageType, optional TraceHitInfo HitInfo, optional Actor
     DamageCauser)
   {
     if(EventInstigator != none &&
       EventInstigator.PlayerReplicationInfo != none)
       WorldInfo.Game.ScoreObjective
         (EventInstigator.PlayerReplicationInfo, 1);

     if(AwesomeEnemySpawner(Owner) != none)
       AwesomeEnemySpawner(Owner).EnemyDied();

     Destroy();
   }
   ```

4. Now in `AwesomeGame`, let's change the `EnemiesLeft` default property back to 10:

```
EnemiesLeft=10
```

5. Finally, let's add the timer back to `AwesomeGame`'s `PostBeginPlay`:

```
simulated function PostBeginPlay()
{
  local AwesomeEnemySpawner ES;

  super.PostBeginPlay();

  GoalScore = EnemiesLeft;

  foreach DynamicActors(class'AwesomeEnemySpawner', ES)
    EnemySpawners[EnemySpawners.length] = ES;

  SetTimer(5.0, false, 'ActivateSpawners');
}
```

6. Compile the code and test. The game should be working as before, with our improvements from the `AwesomeEnemy` states still intact.

What just happened?

We've cleaned up the code to get the game working again so we can further expand on it. Our experiment with states is completed, and now it's time to put that knowledge to use! We'll also be using the concepts we've learned in previous chapters to keep that knowledge fresh too.

Let's get started!

Attack of Schellenberg

The next step in expanding our game is making a boss at the end of the enemy wave. He will be a giant version of the normal enemies, and we will call him...Schellenberg.

Time for action – Creating the abstract base class

This boss class will have a few things in common with `AwesomeEnemy`, so there are a few things we'll want to separate out into a common parent class.

1. Create a copy of `AwesomeEnemy.uc` and name it `AwesomeEnemy_Minion.uc`. `AwesomeEnemy` will now be the parent class for all of our enemies, and `AwesomeEnemy_Minion` will take on the functionality of the enemies we've seen so far in our game.

2. We're going to change a lot in `AwesomeEnemy` and `AwesomeEnemy_Minion` to get the functionality separated, so let's start with `AwesomeEnemy`. As the boss and minion will both be subclassed of `AwesomeEnemy`, but we won't want `AwesomeEnemy` spawned directly anymore, let's declare it as `abstract`. Change the declaration in `AwesomeEnemy` to this:

```
class AwesomeEnemy extends AwesomeActor
  abstract;
```

3. The variables in this class are fine, so now let's examine the non-state functions. `TakeDamage` is going to have different functionality for both subclasses, so let's delete `TakeDamage` from `AwesomeEnemy`.

4. `RunAway` really only applies to the minions, but to make sure we don't need to do any unnecessary typecasting let's leave the function in `AwesomeEnemy`, but empty it out:

```
function RunAway()
{
}
```

5. The states and default properties for `AwesomeEnemy` are fine, we'll change those for the boss, but if we decide to make different minion classes it will be convenient for all of them to have the same functionality available by default.

6. Our new `AwesomeEnemy` class should look like this huge wall of text, and I apologize in advance, but we need to make sure we're both on the same page:

```
class AwesomeEnemy extends AwesomeActor
    abstract;

var float BumpDamage;
var Pawn Enemy;
var float MovementSpeed;
var float AttackDistance;
var Material SeekingMat, AttackingMat, FleeingMat;
var StaticMeshComponent MyMesh;
var bool bAttacking;

function GetEnemy()
{
  local AwesomePlayerController PC;

  foreach LocalPlayerControllers(class'AwesomePlayerController',
    PC)
  {
```

```
      if(PC.Pawn != none)
        Enemy = PC.Pawn;
  }
}

function EndAttack()
{
  bAttacking = false;

  if(GetStateName() == 'Seeking')
    MyMesh.SetMaterial(0, SeekingMat);
}

function RunAway()
{
}

auto state Seeking
{
  function BeginState(Name PreviousStateName)
  {
    if(!bAttacking)
      MyMesh.SetMaterial(0, SeekingMat);
  }

  function Tick(float DeltaTime)
  {
    local vector NewLocation;

    if(bAttacking)
      return;

    if(Enemy == none)
      GetEnemy();

    if(Enemy != none)
    {
      NewLocation = Location;
      NewLocation += normal(Enemy.Location - Location) *
        MovementSpeed * DeltaTime;
      SetLocation(NewLocation);

      if(VSize(NewLocation - Enemy.Location) < AttackDistance)
        GoToState('Attacking');
```

```
      }
    }
  }

  state Attacking
  {
    function BeginState(Name PreviousStateName)
    {
      MyMesh.SetMaterial(0, AttackingMat);
    }

    function Tick(float DeltaTime)
    {
      bAttacking = true;

      if(Enemy == none)
        GetEnemy();

      if(Enemy != none)
      {
        Enemy.Bump(self, CollisionComponent, vect(0,0,0));

        if(VSize(Location - Enemy.Location) > AttackDistance)
          GoToState('Seeking');
      }
    }

    function EndState(name NextStateName)
    {
      SetTimer(1, false, 'EndAttack');
    }
  }

  state Fleeing
  {
    ignores TakeDamage;

    function BeginState(Name PreviousStateName)
    {
      MyMesh.SetMaterial(0, FleeingMat);
    }

    function Tick(float DeltaTime)
    {
```

```
        local vector NewLocation;

      if(Enemy == none)
        GetEnemy();

      if(Enemy != none)
      {
        NewLocation = Location;
        NewLocation -= normal(Enemy.Location - Location) *
          MovementSpeed * DeltaTime;
        SetLocation(NewLocation);
      }
    }
  }
}


defaultproperties
{
  SeekingMat=Material'EditorMaterials.WidgetMaterial_X'
  AttackingMat=Material'EditorMaterials.WidgetMaterial_Z'
  FleeingMat=Material'EditorMaterials.WidgetMaterial_Y'
  AttackDistance=96.0
  MovementSpeed=256.0
  BumpDamage=5.0
  bBlockActors=True
  bCollideActors=True

  Begin Object Class=DynamicLightEnvironmentComponent
    Name=MyLightEnvironment
  bEnabled=TRUE
  End Object
  Components.Add(MyLightEnvironment)

  Begin Object Class=StaticMeshComponent Name=EnemyMesh
    StaticMesh=StaticMesh'UN_SimpleMeshes.TexPropCube_Dup'
    Materials(0)=Material'EditorMaterials.WidgetMaterial_X'
    LightEnvironment=MyLightEnvironment
    Scale3D=(X=0.25,Y=0.25,Z=0.5)
  End Object
  Components.Add(EnemyMesh)
  MyMesh=EnemyMesh

  Begin Object Class=CylinderComponent Name=CollisionCylinder
    CollisionRadius=32.0
    CollisionHeight=64.0
```

```
        BlockNonZeroExtent=true
        BlockZeroExtent=true
        BlockActors=true
        CollideActors=true
    End Object
    CollisionComponent=CollisionCylinder
    Components.Add(CollisionCylinder)
}
```

7. Now to deal with AwesomeEnemy_Minion. As most of the functionality has been kept in the AwesomeEnemy superclass, this one will be small. Let's start with the class declaration:

```
class AwesomeEnemy_Minion extends AwesomeEnemy;
```

8. All of the variables have been kept in the superclass, so make sure there are no variables declared in AwesomeEnemy_Minion.

9. For non-state functions, the only two we need to keep are TakeDamage and RunAway:

```
event TakeDamage(int DamageAmount, Controller EventInstigator,
    vector HitLocation, vector Momentum, class<DamageType>
    DamageType, optional TraceHitInfo HitInfo, optional Actor
    DamageCauser)
{
    if(EventInstigator != none &&
        EventInstigator.PlayerReplicationInfo != none)
        WorldInfo.Game.ScoreObjective
            (EventInstigator.PlayerReplicationInfo, 1);

        if(AwesomeEnemySpawner(Owner) != none)
            AwesomeEnemySpawner(Owner).EnemyDied();

    Destroy();
}

function RunAway()
{
    GoToState('Fleeing');
}
```

10. The state code and default properties are handled by the AwesomeEnemy superclass now, so the default property block should be empty and there shouldn't be any other code. The AwesomeEnemy_Minion class should look like the following code snippet:

```
class AwesomeEnemy_Minion extends AwesomeEnemy;

event TakeDamage(int DamageAmount, Controller EventInstigator,
   vector HitLocation, vector Momentum, class<DamageType>
   DamageType, optional TraceHitInfo HitInfo, optional Actor
   DamageCauser)
{
   if(EventInstigator != none &&
     EventInstigator.PlayerReplicationInfo != none)
     WorldInfo.Game.ScoreObjective
       (EventInstigator.PlayerReplicationInfo, 1);

     if(AwesomeEnemySpawner(Owner) != none)
       AwesomeEnemySpawner(Owner).EnemyDied();

     Destroy();
}

function RunAway()
{
   GoToState('Fleeing');
}

defaultproperties
{
}
```

11. **IMPORTANT**: As we're reordering our classes, we need to change the reference in the AwesomeEnemySpawner. Otherwise, it will try to spawn our abstract class, which will fail. Change the SpawnEnemy function to the following:

```
function SpawnEnemy()
{
   if(MySpawnedEnemy == none)
     MySpawnedEnemy = spawn(class'AwesomeEnemy_Minion', self,,
       Location);
}
```

12. Compile the code.

What just happened?

We're going to take a small break here to talk about what we've done. We've used our lessons on inheritance, function overriding, and class modifiers to set up a new structure for our enemy classes. AwesomeEnemy is now an abstract base class for all of our game's enemies, and contains common functionality that all of our enemies will use.

As AwesomeEnemy is now abstract, we've created a subclass, AwesomeEnemy_Minion, which has the same functionality as the enemies we've been using throughout this book.

Next, we're going to create the boss class. It will have simple functionality at first, but creating it will let us alter AwesomeGame to get the boss to spawn after the enemies have been defeated.

Let's get started on that.

Time for action – Creating and spawning the boss

Let's start by creating the boss class:

1. Create a new file in `Development\Src\AwesomeGame\Classes` called `AwesomeBoss.uc`.

2. Let's write the class declaration:

   ```
   class AwesomeBoss extends AwesomeEnemy;
   ```

3. We'll change two default properties to make him bigger and slower than the minions:

   ```
   defaultproperties
   {
     MovementSpeed=128.0

     Begin Object Name=EnemyMesh
       Scale3D=(X=1.0,Y=1.0,Z=2.0)
     End Object

     Begin Object Name=CollisionCylinder
       CollisionRadius=128.0
       CollisionHeight=256.0
     End Object
   }
   ```

This will make him pretty huge.

1. Now that we have the basic boss class created, let's integrate him into the game. As we don't want the game to end when the minions are defeated, let's change the way their deaths are reported. First, delete the `EnemyDied` function from `AwesomeEnemySpawner`.

2. Now, let's rewrite the `TakeDamage` function in our `AwesomeEnemy_Minion` class:

```
event TakeDamage(int DamageAmount, Controller EventInstigator,
  vector HitLocation, vector Momentum, class<DamageType>
  DamageType, optional TraceHitInfo HitInfo, optional Actor
  DamageCauser)
{
  if(AwesomeGame(WorldInfo.Game) != none)
    AwesomeGame(WorldInfo.Game).EnemyKilled();

  Destroy();
}
```

Instead of calling `ScoreObjective`, we'll call `EnemyKilled` in our `AwesomeGame`.

1. Now let's write that function in `AwesomeGame`:

```
function EnemyKilled()
{
  local int i;

  if(bSpawnBoss)
    return;

  EnemiesLeft--;
  if(EnemiesLeft <= 0)
  {
    for(i=0; i<EnemySpawners.length; i++)
      EnemySpawners[i].MakeEnemyRunAway();
      ClearTimer('ActivateSpawners');
      bSpawnBoss = true;
      ActivateSpawners();
  }
}
```

Now the enemies will run away as usual, and we'll use `bSpawnBoss` to make the boss spawn in `ActivateSpawners`.

1. Now as we're using it, let's declare `bSpawnBoss` at the top of `AwesomeGame`:

```
var bool bSpawnBoss;
```

2. This variable will be used by `ActivateSpawners` to spawn the boss, so let's rewrite that function:

```
function ActivateSpawners()
{
  local int i;
  local array<AwesomeEnemySpawner> InRangeSpawners;
  local AwesomePlayerController PC;

  foreach LocalPlayerControllers(class'AwesomePlayerController',
    PC)
    break;
    if(PC.Pawn == none)
    {
      SetTimer(1.0, false, 'ActivateSpawners');
      return;
    }

  for(i=0; i<EnemySpawners.length; i++)
  {
    if(VSize(PC.Pawn.Location - EnemySpawners[i].Location) >
      MinSpawnerDistance && VSize(PC.Pawn.Location -
      EnemySpawners[i].Location) < MaxSpawnerDistance)
    {
      if(EnemySpawners[i].CanSpawnEnemy())
        InRangeSpawners[InRangeSpawners.length] =
        EnemySpawners[i];
    }
  }

  if(InRangeSpawners.length == 0)
  {
    `log("No enemy spawners within range!");
    SetTimer(1.0, false, 'ActivateSpawners');
    return;
  }

  if(bSpawnBoss)
    InRangeSpawners[Rand(InRangeSpawners.length)].SpawnBoss();
```

```
else
{
  InRangeSpawners[Rand(InRangeSpawners.length)].SpawnEnemy();
    SetTimer(1.0 + FRand() * 3.0, false, 'ActivateSpawners');
}
}
```

3. Before we leave AwesomeGame, let's fix the scoring system. First, we'll change PostBeginPlay:

```
simulated function PostBeginPlay()
{
  local AwesomeEnemySpawner ES;

  super.PostBeginPlay();

  GoalScore = 1;

  foreach DynamicActors(class'AwesomeEnemySpawner', ES)
    EnemySpawners[EnemySpawners.length] = ES;

  SetTimer(5.0, false, 'ActivateSpawners');
}
```

4. Finally, let's empty out ScoreObjective and just leave a call to the super. We may want to use this function later:

```
function ScoreObjective(PlayerReplicationInfo Scorer, Int Score)
{
  super.ScoreObjective(Scorer, Score);
}
```

5. Now for the AwesomeEnemySpawner class. We're calling SpawnBoss on it, so let's create that function now:

```
function SpawnBoss()
{
  spawn(class'AwesomeBoss', self,, Location);
}
```

6. Now let's compile the code and test the game out.

What just happened?

Now when the enemies have been defeated, Schellenberg spawns. Right now, we can't defeat him because we haven't written the `TakeDamage` function there, and he only has simple `Seeking` behavior and the normal attack. Now that we have the game rules set up, we can work on the boss's behavior.

Time for action – I like you, I kill you last

First, let's start by writing the boss's version of the `Seeking` state. This will be a bit different than the minions, as the boss won't move into a separate `Attacking` state.

1. First, the state declaration:

```
auto state Seeking
{
}
```

2. Now the `Tick` function. We're altering this slightly from the minions; the boss won't stop while attacking and we're adding a line to make him strafe around the player a bit:

```
function Tick(float DeltaTime)
{
  local vector NewLocation;

  if(Enemy == none)
    GetEnemy();

  if(Enemy != none)
  {
    NewLocation = Location;
    NewLocation += normal(Enemy.Location - Location) *
      MovementSpeed * DeltaTime;
    NewLocation += normal((Enemy.Location - Location) cross
      vect(0, 0, 1)) * MovementSpeed * DeltaTime;
    SetLocation(NewLocation);
  }
}
```

3. Now let's add a timer in the `BeginState` function to make him attack every four seconds:

```
function BeginState(Name PreviousStateName)
{
  SetTimer(4.0, true, 'Attack');
}
```

4. For the boss' attack, we'll just have him spawn minions:

```
function Attack()
{
  spawn(class'AwesomeEnemy_Minion',,, Location);
  MyMesh.SetMaterial(0, AttackingMat);
  SetTimer(1, false, 'EndAttack');
}
```

5. Now we just need a way to kill him. Let's make him stronger than the minions. Let's add a health `int` to `AwesomeEnemy` so we can use it in the other classes as well later:

```
var int Health;
```

6. Now back in `AwesomeBoss`, let's set it in the default properties:

```
Health=30
```

7. Now for the `TakeDamage` function:

```
event TakeDamage(int DamageAmount, Controller EventInstigator,
  vector HitLocation, vector Momentum, class<DamageType>
  DamageType, optional TraceHitInfo HitInfo, optional Actor
  DamageCauser)
{
  Health--;
  if(Health == 0 && EventInstigator != none &&
    EventInstigator.PlayerReplicationInfo != none)
    WorldInfo.Game.ScoreObjective
      (EventInstigator.PlayerReplicationInfo, 1);
}
```

8. Almost done! If we compiled and tested the code now, then we'd notice that the boss and any enemies it spawned would keep moving after the match was over. Let's fix that in the `TakeDamage` function of `AwesomeBoss`:

```
event TakeDamage(int DamageAmount, Controller EventInstigator,
  vector HitLocation, vector Momentum, class<DamageType>
  DamageType, optional TraceHitInfo HitInfo, optional Actor
  DamageCauser)
{
  local AwesomeEnemy AE;

  Health--;

  if(Health == 0 && EventInstigator != none &&
    EventInstigator.PlayerReplicationInfo != none)
```

```
    {
      WorldInfo.Game.ScoreObjective
        (EventInstigator.PlayerReplicationInfo, 1);
      foreach DynamicActors(class'AwesomeEnemy', AE)
      {
        if(AE != self)
          AE.RunAway();
      }

      Destroy();
    }
  }
```

Now, when defeated, the smaller minions will run away and the boss will be destroyed.

1. There's one last thing we need to do for now. Games usually have the boss's health displayed on the HUD, so let's go ahead and do that. We'll start by making a variable to reference the boss actor in AwesomeGame:

```
var AwesomeEnemy TheBoss;
```

2. Now we'll rewrite the section of ActivateSpawners that calls the SpawnBoss function:

```
if(bSpawnBoss)
  TheBoss = InRangeSpawners[Rand
    (InRangeSpawners.length)].SpawnBoss();
else
{
  InRangeSpawners[Rand(InRangeSpawners.length)].SpawnEnemy();
  SetTimer(1.0 + FRand() * 3.0, false, 'ActivateSpawners');
}
```

We'll use a return value to assign the actor to the variable.

1. Now let's rewrite the SpawnBoss function in AwesomeEnemySpawner to return the actor spawned:

```
function AwesomeEnemy SpawnBoss()
{
  return spawn(class'AwesomeBoss', self,, Location);
}
```

We're using `AwesomeEnemy` here, so we don't have to do any typecasting.

1. Now for the HUD. Let's rewrite the last section of the `DrawHUD` function in our `AwesomeHUD` class:

```
event DrawHUD()
{
  super.DrawHUD();

  Canvas.DrawColor = WhiteColor;
  Canvas.Font = class'Engine'.Static.GetLargeFont();

  if(PlayerOwner.Pawn != none &&
    AwesomeWeapon(PlayerOwner.Pawn.Weapon) != none)
  {
    Canvas.SetPos(Canvas.ClipX * 0.1, Canvas.ClipY * 0.9);
    Canvas.DrawText("Weapon Level:" @
      AwesomeWeapon(PlayerOwner.Pawn.Weapon).CurrentWeaponLevel);
  }

  if(AwesomeGame(WorldInfo.Game) != none)
  {
    Canvas.SetPos(Canvas.ClipX * 0.1, Canvas.ClipY * 0.95);
    if(!AwesomeGame(WorldInfo.Game).bSpawnBoss)
      Canvas.DrawText("Enemies Left:" @
        AwesomeGame(WorldInfo.Game).EnemiesLeft);
    else if(AwesomeGame(WorldInfo.Game).TheBoss != none)
      Canvas.DrawText("Boss Health:" @
        AwesomeGame(WorldInfo.Game).TheBoss.Health);
  }
}
```

2. Now let's compile the code and test it out. Now when the boss spawns, we can see his health on the HUD!

What just happened?

Now we've used our lessons about states to create the boss and abstract base class for the enemies. Is there any way we can use state subclassing in our game? I think there is! Let's power up the boss a bit.

Time for action – Rage mode activate

A lot of games have the boss change into a different form as it gets weaker, or use stronger attacks. Let's do the same thing with our boss by having him switch from spawning minions to shooting rockets right at your face. That'll teach you.

1. To do this, we'll create a subclass of the `Seeking` state in `AwesomeBoss` and call it `StageTwo`:

```
state StageTwo extends Seeking
{
}
```

2. Now let's rewrite the `Attack` function here:

```
function Attack()
{
  local UTProj_Rocket MyRocket;
  MyRocket = spawn(class'UTProj_Rocket', self,, Location);
  MyRocket.Init(normal(Enemy.Location - Location));
  MyMesh.SetMaterial(0, AttackingMat);
  SetTimer(1, false, 'EndAttack');
}
```

The `Init` function for the projectile tells it which direction to travel.

1. Now to tell it when to move into this state. We'll do this in `TakeDamage`:

```
event TakeDamage(int DamageAmount, Controller EventInstigator,
  vector HitLocation, vector Momentum, class<DamageType>
  DamageType, optional TraceHitInfo HitInfo, optional Actor
  DamageCauser)
{
  local AwesomeEnemy AE;

  Health--;

  if(Health == 0 && EventInstigator != none &&
    EventInstigator.PlayerReplicationInfo != none)
  {
    WorldInfo.Game.ScoreObjective
      (EventInstigator.PlayerReplicationInfo, 1);
    foreach DynamicActors(class'AwesomeEnemy', AE)
    {
      if(AE != self)
        AE.RunAway();
```

```
    }

    Destroy();
  }

  if(Health == 10)
    GoToState('StageTwo');
}
```

2. We'll also add an indicator to the HUD to let us know we're about to get a rocket to the face:

```
if(AwesomeGame(WorldInfo.Game) != none)
{
  Canvas.SetPos(Canvas.ClipX * 0.1, Canvas.ClipY * 0.95);
  if(!AwesomeGame(WorldInfo.Game).bSpawnBoss)
    Canvas.DrawText("Enemies Left:" @
      AwesomeGame(WorldInfo.Game).EnemiesLeft);
  else if(AwesomeGame(WorldInfo.Game).TheBoss != none)
  {
    Canvas.DrawText("Boss Health:" @
      AwesomeGame(WorldInfo.Game).TheBoss.Health);
    if(AwesomeGame(WorldInfo.Game).TheBoss.Health <= 10)
    {
      Canvas.SetPos(Canvas.ClipX * 0.4, Canvas.ClipY * 0.7);
      Canvas.DrawText("BOSS SUPER RAGE MODE");
    }
  }
}
```

3. Only one minor issue remains to be fixed, and then we're done! As we're now in a subclass of `Seeking`, the `EndAttack` code doesn't reset the boss' material to red after it attacks while in `StageTwo`. We can fix this by adding another check to our `if` statement in `EndAttack` in the `AwesomeEnemy` class:

```
function EndAttack()
{
  bAttacking = false;

  if(GetStateName() == 'Seeking' || IsChildState(GetStateName(),
    'Seeking'))
    MyMesh.SetMaterial(0, SeekingMat);
}
```

4. Compile the code and we're done!

What just happened?

Don't stand still when you get the boss's health down or you'll get rockets to the face.

Now our game is really starting to shape up!

Have a go hero – Subclassing

This one will challenge you, but if you've been paying attention to all of the chapters so far it should be easy. See if you can create another subclass of AwesomeEnemy that's smaller and faster than the normal minion, and rewrite the SpawnEnemy function in AwesomeEnemySpawner to have a random chance of spawning one.

 Hint – Think about how the Minion class was created and how another subclass of AwesomeEnemy could be created. Furthermore, think about where we spawn them from and how it could be altered to work with a random chance.

Pop quiz – Using states

1. When calling a function, what is the order of priority that UnrealScript uses when looking for it?

    a. Non-state, Super, State

    b. State, Non-state, Super

    c. Super, Non-state, State

2. What is the function used to switch between states?

3. What types of functions can only be used in state code?

Summary

We learned a lot in this chapter about states. We learned how to use them to create different behavior in our actors without needlessly complicated if/else statements and Booleans. In our game, we used states to change the way the enemies work.

Specifically, we covered:

- ◆ What a state is, how to create them, and how to switch between them
- ◆ How functions behave when used with states and the use of non-state functions
- ◆ Functions specific to states and how to find out what state we're in
- • How to subclass states
- ◆ The keywords, labels, and latent functions associated with states

Now that we've learned about states, we're ready to start working with Kismet to get some level-specific functionality out of our game!

7
Working with Kismet

Dual-classing as a programmer/designer.

As a programmer working within a team, or even as a lone wolf creating a game by yourself, knowing how to use Kismet can be an essential tool when working with the UDK. Instead of relying solely on the Kismet events and actions that come with the UDK, we can expand on them by creating and using our own.

In this chapter we will do the following:

- Take a look at what Kismet is and what it is used for
- Create our own Kismet events and actions
- Learn how to use latent Kismet actions

So with that, let's take a look at Kismet!

Overview of Kismet

While UnrealScript can cover fundamental game mechanics, Kismet works with level-specific functionality such as opening doors or reacting to game events, such as the death of the player, in ways specific to that level.

As an example, in our game, if we wanted to have the weapon upgrades spawn in specific locations when we killed a boss, we would use UnrealScript to create generic Kismet actions and events. Some of the events and actions we would need for this purpose already exist, so in the end we would have a mix of stock and custom Kismet in our game.

A simple introduction

Before we start getting into the UnrealScript side of things, let's take a look at some things we can do with the Kismet that's already present.

Time for action – Using Kismet

This section is mostly going to take place in the editor, so let's fire it up and get to work!

1. Start up the editor, then open `AwesomeTestMap`.

2. We'll start with some simple Kismet at first, so let's open up the Kismet window by pressing the green K button in the top toolbar:

3. The Kismet window will open. Let's see what's going on here:

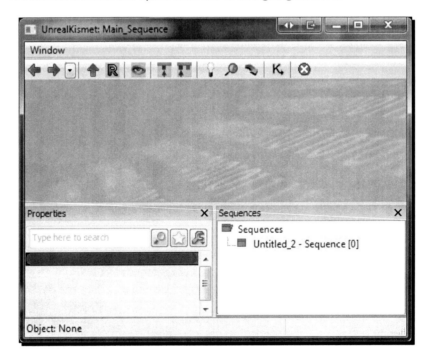

The main gray area with the binary on the right side is the workspace where the Kismet actions and events are placed and linked together. At the bottom left, we have the **Properties** panel where the editable variables of the actions and events can be changed, exactly the same way we've done with Actor classes. Finally to the bottom right is the **Sequences** panel. If we had multiple streamed levels or groups of Kismet actions combined into sub-sequences, we would select the different Kismet sequences here.

1. Let's start with something simple. We can create the Kismet version of the Hello World program pretty easily, so let's do that. Right-click in the main workspace and select **New Event | Player | Player Spawned**. You should see the event show up where you clicked:

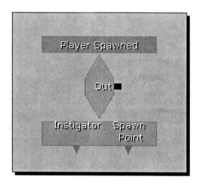

In Kismet, events have the diamond shape and are triggered by UnrealScript classes. In this case, the GameInfo class triggers this event when a player spawns. We could have more than one of these events in our Kismet sequence, if we wanted; all of them would be triggered when a player spawns. That decision is mainly up to aesthetics and organization within the Kismet window.

1. The pink spikes at the bottom of this event let us get variable references from that event if we need them. In this case, we have the option to get the **PlayerController** in the form of the **Instigator**, and the **PlayerStart** in the form of the **Spawn Point** variable. We could use these if, for example, we only wanted certain things to happen to a specific player, or any player that spawns at a particular spawn point.

2. The black node labeled Out is used to connect to other Kismet actions, and these connections define the flow of this Kismet sequence. To see this, let's add an action to our sequence. Right-click off to the right of the Player Spawned event and select **New Action | Misc | Log**:

3. The **Log** action works the same as the log command that we've been using in UnrealScript, which makes Log actions a convenient tool for debugging Kismet sequences. These also have the option of displaying the log on the screen, which makes them even more helpful. If we click on the **Log** action and take a look at the **SeqAct_Log** section of the **Properties** in the lower-left window, we can see the following:

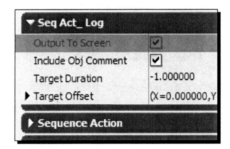

The **Properties** panel might look more familiar now. In our work with variables in *Chapter 2, Storing and Manipulating Data*, we created editable variables that showed up in an Actor's properties in a similar way. Kismet is no different; when actions and events are created in UnrealScript, we can define editable variables and their default properties, just like the Actor classes.

1. For anything to show up, we need to tell it what to log. Let's open up the **Sequence Object** section and type **Player has spawned!** into the **Obj Comment** property:

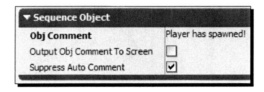

The **Obj Comment** property is available to all Kismet actions and events, and is normally used to write notes to ourselves so we know what the sequence is doing. In the **Log** action's case, this is what is written to the log and shown on screen.

1. Before we test, we need to link the Event to the Action, so let's do that now. Click and hold on the black **Out** node of the **Player Spawned** event, then drag the line over to the **In** node of the **Log** action. When you release the mouse, the connection should be made:

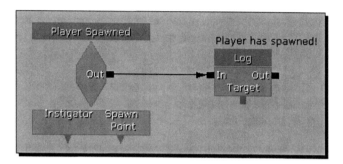

Now we can see how the flow works in Kismet. When the **Player Spawned** event is activated, it in turns activates the **Log** action. We could connect the **Out** node of the **Log** action to more actions. We could also connect the Out node of the **Player Spawned** event to more than one action. By adding more events and actions, we could create some complex Kismet sequences.

1. Save the map, but we can keep the editor open for this. Let's fire up the game with our batch file and see what happens. We'll notice the log show up on the screen right as the game starts:

2. Exit the game and take a look at the log. We can see it show up there as well:

        [0005.71] Log: Kismet: Player has spawned!

What just happened?

This was a pretty simple introduction to Kismet, but it's enough to get us started. Next, let's see if we can use it to do something useful.

Building complexity

I've never liked the way our weapon upgrades worked. They're just sitting there, waiting for the player to pick them up. Even trained birds have to poke a button to get some food. Actually, that sounds like a good idea. Let's make the player do a bit of work to get a weapon upgrade, the lazy robot.

Time for action – A more complex Kismet sequence

The idea sounds simple in theory: the player walks over a trigger, and a weapon upgrade appears. In reality, we'll see that simple ideas can get complicated pretty quickly, even in Kismet:

1. We should still have the editor open, if not, open it and open our AwesomeTestMap. Delete the Kismet from the last experiment by clicking on each action and event and hitting *Delete* on the keyboard.

2. Delete all of the AwesomeWeaponUpgrade actors, we'll be placing them in the map through Kismet.

3. The first thing we'll need is the trigger. Open up the **Content Browser** and select the **Actor Classes** tab. Make sure **Show Categories** is unchecked, and select **Actor | Trigger** (Not the subclasses, just **Trigger**). In the level, right-click somewhere near the start player and hit **Add Trigger Here**.

4. The trigger we've added won't be visible in game by default, so let's fix that real quick. Double-click on the trigger to open its properties, and under **Display**, uncheck **Hidden**. Close the trigger's properties.

5. We don't want the upgrade weapon to spawn in the same place as the trigger, so we need to add an actor that we'll use in Kismet to set the spawn location. I like to use **TargetPoints** for this, although any placeable actor will work. Select **Actor | Keypoint | TargetPoint**, and right-click near the trigger and hit **Place TargetPoint Here**. Use the blue arrow of the movement widget to raise it up off of the ground a bit.

6. OK, we're ready for some Kismet. We know from the **Player Spawned** event that UnrealScript triggers Events. That one was triggered by the `GameInfo` class, but actors placed in the level can also trigger Events in reaction to things happening in the game. In this case, the **Trigger** actor can fire an Event whenever it is touched.

7. To use Kismet events this way, we need to select the **Trigger** in the level by clicking on it. Now open the Kismet window and right-click in the main workspace. This time instead of going under **New Event**, below this we should see an option for **New Event Using Trigger_0**. If not, make sure the **Trigger** is selected in the level. Under **New Event Using Trigger_0**, select **Touch**:

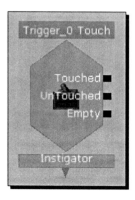

We can see this Event has three outputs, **Touched**, **UnTouched** and **Empty**. The first two are self-explanatory. The third one acts the same as the **UnTouched** output, except that **UnTouched** fires whenever any actor that was touching this trigger moves away from it, and **Empty** only fires when ALL actors that were touching it aren't touching it anymore.

1. By default this Trigger event is only set up to fire once. To get it to work an infinite number of times, we need to change one property. Select the Event, and in the **Properties** panel open up the **Sequence Event** section. Set **Max Trigger Count** to **0**. This will let this event fire an unlimited number of times.

2. Now we have the Trigger's event set up, so we need the Action that's going to spawn the AwesomeWeaponUpgrade. For this, right-click to the right of the Trigger event and select **New Action | Actor | Actor Factory**:

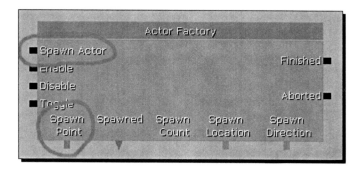

Right now, we're only concerned about two of the nodes, the **Spawn Actor** input and the **Spawn Point** property. Let's take care of the **Spawn Point** property first.

3. Select the **TargetPoint** in the level, and in the Kismet window, right-click under the **Actor Factory** action and hit **New Object Var Using TargetPoint_0**. We'll see a circle show up with the **TargetPoint** inside it:

In Kismet, variables are represented as circles and act the same way they do in UnrealScript. We can change their value or read their value to do what we need to do. In this case, we're going to use the target point's location as the spawn point for our weapon upgrades.

4. Click and hold on the **Spawn Point** node on the **Actor Factory** action, and drag the line to the **TargetPoint** variable. When you let go, the connection should be made.

5. Now click and hold on the **Touched** output of the **Trigger** event, and drag the line over to the **Spawn Actor** input on the **Actor Factory** action.

6. One last thing we need to do: tell the **Actor Factory** what to spawn. Select the action in the main workspace, and in the **Properties** panel open up the **SeqAct_ ActorFactory** section. In the **Factory** property, there should be a blue arrow pointing down. Click it, and in the pop-up list select **ActorFactoryActor** at the top. Once that's selected, a new property should show up under **Factory** called **Actor Class**. Set **Actor Class** to **AwesomeWeaponUpgrade**.

7. For debug purposes, while we're in the **Actor Factory** action's properties, under the **Sequence Object** section let's check **Output Obj Comment To Screen**, and set **ObjComment** to **Upgrade Spawned!**

8. That's it! Our Kismet sequence should now look like this:

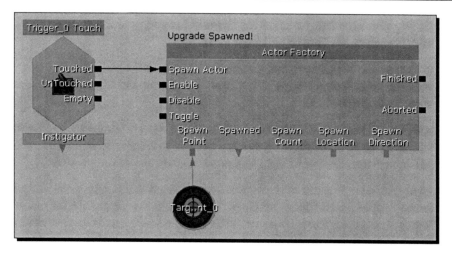

6. Save the map and start up the game. We can see that the Kismet is working fine, whenever we run over the trigger, a weapon upgrade spawns! Remember that to pick the upgrade up, we have to hold a weapon.

What just happened?

One thing we'll notice is that if we just run back and forth over the trigger, it will keep spawning weapon upgrades. What if we only wanted it to be able to spawn one at a time? This is where the complex part comes in, but thinking like a programmer it should be easy to figure out. Let's give it a shot.

Time for action – Bug fixing time!

If we were writing this Kismet sequence as code, we might use a Boolean to keep track of whether a weapon upgrade has been spawned or not. If we hit the trigger and bUpgradeSpawned was false, we'd set it to true and spawn one. Once it was picked up, we'd set the Boolean back to false. We already know how to do that in code, but how about Kismet?

There are a few different ways we could do this, but to keep it relatively simple we'll just use another trigger:

1. Open AwesomeTestMap and delete the **TargetPoint** that we're using as the upgrade spawn location. Since it's referenced by Kismet, the editor will ask you if you're sure. Click on **Continue**. Now if we open our Kismet editor, we'll see that the variable that held our **TargetPoint** now has **???** written on it. This lets us know that the variable doesn't have an actor associated with it. If this were UnrealScript, it would be the same as a variable being none. Don't delete this Kismet variable, we'll use it in a second.

2. Go into the **Actor Classes** tab of the **Content Browser** and select **Actor | Trigger**, and add one where the **TargetPoint** used to be.

3. With the new **Trigger** selected, go into the Kismet editor and right-click on the **???** variable. Press **Assign Trigger_1 To Object Variable(s)** and the trigger should now show up in the variable.

4. Now for the Boolean. Right-click underneath the current sequence and hit **New Variable | Bool**. It will show up as a red circle with **False** written inside it. We'll use this to indicate whether or not a weapon upgrade has been spawned.

5. Right-click on either end of the connection between the **Trigger** event and the **Actor Factory** action and hit **Break All Links**. The link should be broken. Now move the **Trigger** event away from the **Actor Factory** action so we can add more actions in between them. To move it, select it, then hold *Ctrl*, then click and drag it.

6. If we were writing this as code, this part might look like:

```
if(!bUpgradeSpawned)
{
    bUpgradeSpawned = true;
    SpawnUpgrade();
}
```

7. The `SpawnUpgrade()` function would be the **Actor Factory** action, so that leaves us with two lines of code. Each one can be represented by a Kismet action, so there are two that we need to add. Let's do the bool comparison first.

8. Right-click between the **Trigger** event and the **Actor Factory** action and hit **New Condition | Comparison | Compare Bool**. This will show up as a blue box.

9. The variable we want to check needs to be hooked up to the **Bool** node at the bottom of this action, so click on the **Bool** node and drag the line to our **Bool** variable.

10. Now connect the **Touched** node of our **Trigger** event to the **In** node of the **Compare Bool** action.

11. That takes care if the `if` statement in our hypothetical code, so let's do the second line where we set the bool to **True**. Right-click next to the **Compare Bool** action and hit **New Action | Set Variable | Bool**.

12. For this new Action to work, we need to connect it to our **Bool** variable. Connect the **Target** node at the bottom of the **Bool** action to the **Bool** variable.

13. With the new action selected, open up the **SeqAct_SetBool** section of its properties and check **Default Value** so that it will set the bool to **True**.

14. Now connect the **False** node of the **Compare Bool** action to the **In** node of the **Bool** action, and the **Out** node of the **Bool** action to the **Spawn Actor** node of the **Actor Factory** action. Our Kismet sequence should look like this:

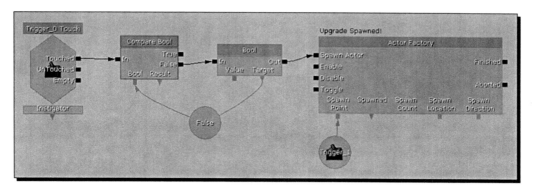

15. Almost there. Now we need to set that **Bool** back to **False** when the upgrade is picked up. Since we're spawning it on a Trigger, we can simply use its **Touch** event as a quick way to do this.

16. Select **Trigger_1** in the editor, and go back into the Kismet window. Right-click below the first triggered event and hit **New Event Using Trigger_1 | Touch**.

17. In the new **Touch** event's properties set **Max Trigger Count** to 0.

18. Next to the **Touch** event, right-click and add a **New Action | Set Variable | Bool**. We don't need to change its properties, so next let's connect everything.

19. Connect the **Touched** node of the new **Trigger** event to the **In** node of the new **Bool** action.

20. Connect the **Target** node of the new **Bool** action to the **Bool** variable.

21. That's it! The sequence should now look like this:

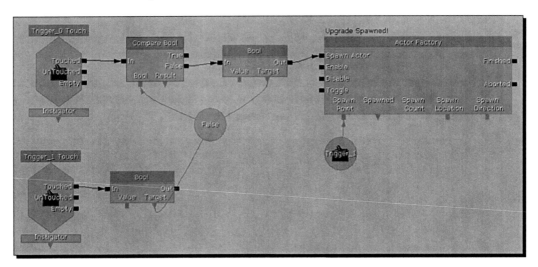

22. Save the map and run the game. Now when we run over the first trigger, it will only spawn one upgrade until we pick it up!

What just happened?

We can easily see how complicated Kismet can get. This was only a simple sequence and it took eight Kismet objects to create it. Creating more complex sequences would require even more Kismet actions and events, and a lot of time and testing to make sure they functioned properly.

We can also see a brief glimpse at Kismet's power. Looking at the list, there are a lot of actions and events at our disposal, and with clever use of them it's entirely possible to create a game with nothing but Kismet.

It does have limitations though. Since the sequences only exist in levels, any changes need to be copied to all levels or used in a persistent level with other levels streamed in. Since it's running as a layer on top of UnrealScript, it's not as fast. Dealing with arrays or structs is extremely complicated, and Kismet can be incredibly hard to debug with any sort of complexity. Core gameplay mechanics should be left to UnrealScript, and Kismet should only be used for level-specific functionality of your game.

With that said, it is incredibly useful. Long sequences of events, such as a tutorial level would be tedious to create with UnrealScript, but easy to make and tweak with Kismet. Simple sequences like doors opening and closing, spawning actors at specific locations, and triggering effects and sounds would require entire `Actor` classes dedicated for those purposes without Kismet, and would clutter up a project's class folder. For teams with separate programmers and designers, it would also be difficult for designers to make changes without programmer support. Kismet makes a level designer's life easier while freeing up programming time for more important core gameplay tasks.

Next, we're going to look behind the scenes at the UnrealScript in the Kismet actions and events, and learn how to create and use our own, or simply modify our classes to work with existing Kismet.

Kismet actions

As far as the class tree goes, Kismet classes are not created under Actor. In UnCodeX, if we take a look way down under **Object** we'll see a class called **SequenceObject**. This is where all of the Kismet classes are created. Underneath **SequenceObject**, we can see **SequenceOp** where **Actions**, **Events**, and **Conditions** are, and **SequenceVariable** where the Bools, Floats, and other data types are located.

Creating Kismet actions

For this section of the chapter, we're going to look at the **SequenceAction**, how it works, and how to create our own.

Time for action – Creating Kismet actions

As far as creating a custom class goes, Kismet should be pretty easy for us by now. For our first experiment, let's disable the default spawning of enemies in our game and create a Kismet action to do it instead. That will give us more control over when the enemies spawn in our Awesome Game.

1. Make sure the editor is closed.

2. Open **AwesomeGame.uc** in ConTEXT. At the bottom of our `PostBeginPlay` function, let's take out the timer that activates the spawners. The function should now look like this:

    ```
    simulated function PostBeginPlay()
    {
        local AwesomeEnemySpawner ES;
    ```

```
      super.PostBeginPlay();

      GoalScore = 1;

      foreach DynamicActors(class'AwesomeEnemySpawner', ES)
          EnemySpawners[EnemySpawners.length] = ES;
}
```

3. Now we're ready to create the Kismet action that will handle the spawning. In our `Development\Src\AwesomeGame\Classes` folder, create a new file called `AwesomeSeqAct_SpawnerActivation.uc`.

4. Write the following code in this new file:

```
class AwesomeSeqAct_SpawnerActivation extends SequenceAction;

defaultproperties
{
    ObjName="Spawner Activation"
    ObjCategory="Awesome Game"
}
```

5. This will do for a moment; let's take a look. Compile the code, then open up the editor. Open the Kismet editor. When we right-click in the main workspace and look under **New Action**, we can see our new category, **Awesome Game**, and underneath it is our **Spawner Activation** action. Place one and let's see what it looks like:

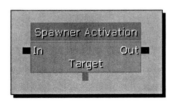

6. Nice! What's that **Target** variable node though? Kismet actions use this node to call functions on the object or objects connected to the node. For example, connecting an object variable to the **Target** node of a **SeqAct_Destroy** would destroy that actor when the **SeqAct_Destroy** action is activated. We don't need this node for this action though, since we'll be calling a function in our **AwesomeGame** class and we can't make a Kismet variable for it. To get rid of it, we'll add a line to our default properties:

```
defaultproperties
{
    ObjName="Spawner Activation"
    ObjCategory="Awesome Game"
    VariableLinks.Empty
}
```

This will clear out the variable nodes at the bottom of our action, in this case just the **Target** node.

7. Now for the heart of our Kismet action. When a Kismet action is activated, an event called, oddly enough, `Activated` is called. Let's add it to our custom action:

```
event Activated()
{
}
```

8. For this event, there isn't any code in our parent class, so we don't need to worry about calling the super. We only need two more lines of code to finish this part of the experiment:

```
event Activated()
{
    if(AwesomeGame(GetWorldInfo().Game) != none)
        AwesomeGame(GetWorldInfo().Game).ActivateSpawners();
}
```

In other classes, we've simply used `WorldInfo.Game`, but since Kismet classes aren't subclasses of `Actor` we need to use the special `GetWorldInfo()` function. We cast our `AwesomeGame` class, then call ActivateSpawners on it.

9. We're done! Well that was easy. Our class should look like this now:

```
class AwesomeSeqAct_SpawnerActivation extends SequenceAction;

event Activated()
{
    if(AwesomeGame(GetWorldInfo().Game) != none)
        AwesomeGame(GetWorldInfo().Game).ActivateSpawners();
}

defaultproperties
{
    ObjName="Spawner Activation"
    ObjCategory="Awesome Game"
    VariableLinks.Empty
}
```

As far as our custom classes go, this one's tiny.

10. Compile the code and open up AwesomeTestMap in the editor. If the previous **Spawner Activation** action is still there, delete it. Keep the weapon upgrade Kismet though, we'll use that later.

11. Now, since we've broken the default behavior of our game to move the spawner activation into Kismet, let's set it up so our game works again. Open the Kismet editor, right-click in the main workspace and add a **New Event | Player | Player Spawned** event. Next to it, add our **New Action | Awesome Game | Spawner Activation** action. Connect the **Out** node of the **Player Spawned** event to the **In** node of our **Spawner Activation** action.

12. We had a five seconds delay earlier, so let's put that back in. Right-click on the **Out** node of the **Player Spawned** event, and click **Set Activate Delay**. Set it to **5** and click on **OK**.

13. As a bonus, let's select our **Spawner Activation** action and check **Output Obj Comment To Screen** in its properties, and set the **Obj Comment** to **Enemies Incoming!**

14. Our Kismet sequence should now look like the following:

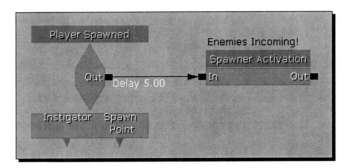

15. Save the map and run the game. After five seconds, the message should pop up on the screen, and then enemies should start spawning and heading toward you. Awesome!

What just happened?

We can see how much flexibility Kismet has already added to our game. By giving the level designer control over the spawner activation, we can keep the core gameplay mechanic of the enemies spawning while easily changing when it happens. If we wanted to change the amount of time before they started spawning, or wait until the player walked through a door and hit a trigger, we could easily do that in Kismet now instead of having it always be five seconds after the game starts. Doing something like that in UnrealScript would get messy.

Using variables in Kismet actions

For our next experiment, we're going to take a look at variables in Kismet and see how we can use them.

Time for action – Using variables in Kismet

One thing we might want to know from Kismet is the current level of the weapon the player is holding. We could use this information to control the spawning of weapon upgrades, for instance. Let's see if we can do that:

1. To do this, we'll create a new file in our `Development\Src\AwesomeGame\Classes` folder called `AwesomeSeqAct_GetWeaponLevel.uc`.

2. Write the following code in the new file:

```
class AwesomeSeqAct_GetWeaponLevel extends SequenceAction;

event Activated()
{
}

defaultproperties
{
    ObjName="Get Weapon Level"
    ObjCategory="Awesome Game"
    VariableLinks.Empty
}
```

3. Now we'll need an UnrealScript variable to store the weapon level as well as a node that we can use in Kismet for it. First let's add the variable:

```
var int WeaponLevel;
```

4. Now let's add the variable link node. If we look in **SequenceOp** in UnCodeX, we can see that `VariableLinks` is an array of the `SeqVarLink` struct. Inside that struct are a lot of variables, but we're only concerned about a few of them. Let's use them to define a new variable link in our default properties:

```
VariableLinks(0)=(ExpectedType=class'SeqVar_Int',LinkDesc="Weapon
Level",PropertyName=WeaponLevel,bWriteable=true)
```

Here we're setting the `ExpectedType` to use an Int variable, giving it a description, and then setting the `PropertyName` to the name of our UnrealScript variable we added in the last step. Finally we set it to `bWriteable` so this action can change the linked Kismet variable (otherwise, it would only be able to read it, which isn't what we need).

5. Now we need to get the player's weapon level and set our `WeaponLevel` variable to it in our `Activated` event.

```
event Activated()
{
    local PlayerController PC;

    PC = GetWorldInfo().GetALocalPlayerController();

    if(PC != none && PC.Pawn != none && AwesomeWeapon(PC.Pawn.
Weapon) != none)
        WeaponLevel = AwesomeWeapon(PC.Pawn.Weapon).
CurrentWeaponLevel;
}
```

We're doing a lot of checking here to get all the way down to the `AwesomeWeapon`, we need to make sure it actually exists before trying to access the `CurrentWeaponLevel` variable.

6. That does it for the UnrealScript side of things. Here's what the class should look like now:

```
class AwesomeSeqAct_GetWeaponLevel extends SequenceAction;

var int WeaponLevel;

event Activated()
{
    local PlayerController PC;

    PC = GetWorldInfo().GetALocalPlayerController();

    if(PC != none && PC.Pawn != none && AwesomeWeapon(PC.Pawn.
Weapon) != none)
        WeaponLevel = AwesomeWeapon(PC.Pawn.Weapon).
CurrentWeaponLevel;
}

defaultproperties
{
    ObjName="Get Weapon Level"
```

```
    ObjCategory="Awesome Game"
    VariableLinks.Empty
    VariableLinks(0)=(ExpectedType=class'SeqVar_
Int',LinkDesc="Weapon Level",PropertyName=WeaponLevel,bWriteable=t
rue)
}
```

7. Compile the code, then open up AwesomeTestMap in the editor. Time to add our new Action.

8. Open the Kismet editor. Our big mess of Kismet from our weapon upgrade experiments should still be there. Right-click on the **Spawn Actor** input of the **Actor Factory** action and hit **Break Link | Compare Bool**. We're going to put our custom action in between.

9. Move the **Actor Factory** action off to the right, then right-click in between it and the rest of this sequence and hit **New Action | Awesome Game | Get Weapon Level**:

10. To the right of that, right-click and hit **New Condition | Comparison | Compare Int**.

11. We're going to need an **Int** Kismet variable, so let's add it. Right-click below the actions we've just added and hit **New Variable | Int | Int**. We don't need to change the value, that will be done by our **Get Weapon Level** action.

12. Connect the **Int** variable to the **Weapon Level** node of our **Get Weapon Level** action, and to the **A** node of the **Compare Int** action.

13. Select the **Compare Int** action, and in its properties open the **SeqCond_CompareInt** section and change **Value B** to **5**. If we're less than this, we still want to spawn upgrades.

14. Now for the connection between actions. Connect the **Out** node of the **Bool** action to the **In** node of our **Get Weapon Level** action.

15. Now connect the **Out** node of our **Get Weapon Level** action to the **In** node of the **Compare Int** action.

16. Finally, connect the **A < B** output node of the **Compare Int** to the **Spawn Actor** input of the **Actor Factory** action.

17. Our Kismet sequence should now look something like the following (I'm breaking it into two parts so it's clearer):

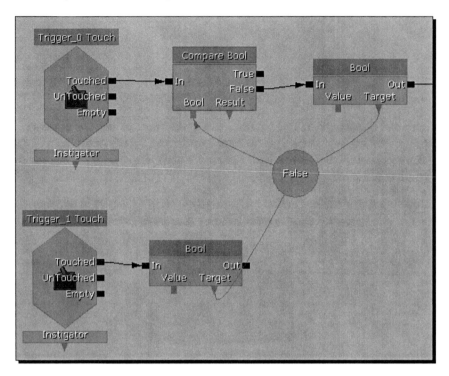

That section should connect to this:

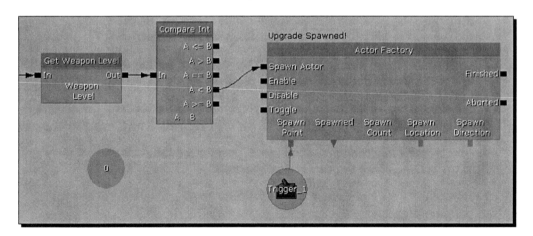

18. We're done with the Kismet, unless you want to temporarily break the link to the **Spawner Activation** action to make it easier to test without being attacked—another advantage to moving that to Kismet!

19. Save the level and run the game. Now when the player's weapon reaches level 5, the upgrades stop spawning when the player runs over the trigger. It's working perfectly!

What just happened?

We can see that variables in Kismet are really just an outer layer for variables in UnrealScript. They're easy to work with in Kismet, but require a bit of setting up in UnrealScript to make them useful. We could use any type of Kismet variable with these links, all we would have to do is change the variable type in our Kismet class and its associated VariableLinks default property.

Kismet handler functions

For our last experiment with Kismet actions, we're going to talk about how to use handler functions in our non-Kismet classes. Handlers let us create specific functionality if an Actor class is acted upon by a Kismet action. Let's take a look.

Time for action – Using handler functions

We're going to take a rocket ship to goofy town on this one. The easiest way to learn about handler functions is to use an already existing Kismet action, so we're going to use the **Toggle** action on our **AwesomeWeaponUpgrade** actors to see how they work. To let us know that it's working, we're going to make the weapon upgrade actors change the size and color when the toggle's handler function is called on them:

1. Open `AwesomeWeaponUpgrade.uc` in ConTEXT.

2. The first thing we need to do is give ourselves access to the static mesh so we can change its size and color. Let's add a variable to reference it:

```
var StaticMeshComponent MyMesh;
```

3. Now let's change the static mesh part of the default properties to add a line:

```
Begin Object Class=StaticMeshComponent Name=PickupMesh
    StaticMesh=StaticMesh'UN_SimpleMeshes.TexPropCube_Dup'
    Materials(0)=Material'EditorMaterials.WidgetMaterial_Y'
    LightEnvironment=MyLightEnvironment
    Scale3D=(X=0.125,Y=0.125,Z=0.125)
End Object
Components.Add(PickupMesh)
MyMesh=PickupMesh
```

4. Now some setup for the color change. Add a new material variable at the top:

    ```
    var Material BigMaterial;
    ```

5. And set its default property to the blue material:

    ```
    BigMaterial=Material'EditorMaterials.WidgetMaterial_Z'
    ```

6. Now we're ready for the handler function. These have a specific naming convention, and it explains the underscore used in the action name. For example, if we had a Kismet action called **SeqAct_Whatever**, the handler function for it would be called OnWhatever. The Kismet action itself is passed into the function as its only parameter. So for the Kismet action **SeqAct_Toggle**, the handler function for it would be written like this:

    ```
    function OnToggle(SeqAct_Toggle Action)
    {
    }
    ```

As a hypothetical example with one of our own Kismet actions, if we wanted to use the **Target** variable link with our **AwesomeSeqAct_SpawnerActivation** action, the handler function for any of our Actor classes would look like this:

```
function OnSpawnerActivation(AwesomeSeqAct_SpawnerActivation Action)
{
}
```

That's just hypothetical code though, for this experiment we're going to use the OnToggle function.

1. Now for the code inside the OnToggle function:

    ```
    function OnToggle(SeqAct_Toggle Action)
    {
        MyMesh.SetScale(2.0);
        MyMesh.SetMaterial(0, BigMaterial);
    }
    ```

2. Compile the code, then open up the editor.

3. Away from all of our other experiments, place a few **AwesomeWeaponUpgrade** actors near a new **Trigger**. In the **Trigger** properties, change **Display | Hidden** to false (uncheck it).

4. Now for the Kismet. Hold *Ctrl* and click on the **AwesomeWeaponUpgrade** actors to select all of them. In the Kismet editor, right-click and hit New **Object Vars Using AwesomeWeaponUpgrade_0...** This will create multiple Kismet variables, one for each **AwesomeWeaponUpgrade** actor selected.

5. Back in the level, select the **Trigger** near the **AwesomeWeaponUpgrade** actors. In the Kismet editor, right-click to the left of the new object variables and hit **New Event Using Trigger_2 | Touch** (the number may be different for you, it doesn't matter).

6. Now right-click above the object vars and hit **New Action | Toggle | Toggle**.

7. Connect the **Touched** output of the **Trigger** event to the **Turn On** input of the **Toggle** action.

8. Connect the **Targets** variable link of the **Toggle** action to each of the **AwesomeWeaponUpgrade** object variables.

9. The Kismet sequence should now look like the following:

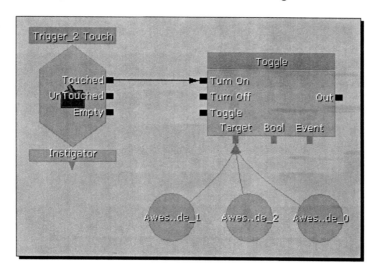

10. Save the level and run the game. When we hit the trigger the **AwesomeWeaponUpgrade** actors should get bigger and turn blue. It's working!

What just happened?

Using Kismet actions on object variables will only work if the Actor we're using it on has a handler function defined. As an experiment, delete the OnToggle function from our **AwesomeWeaponUpgrade** class, compile, and run the game again. This time hitting the trigger will give us log warnings that will also show up on screen:

```
[0006.77] Warning: Obj AwesomeWeaponUpgrade_0 has no handler for
SeqAct_Toggle_0
[0006.77] Log: Obj AwesomeWeaponUpgrade_0 has no handler for SeqAct_
Toggle_0
```

This is a useful warning to let you know that you need to add a handler function, or that you're using the wrong Kismet action on the object variable.

One thing we'll notice with our current setup is that, it doesn't matter what **Toggle** input node we connect the **Trigger** event to, the **AwesomeWeaponUpgrade** actors will do the same thing, regardless. What if we wanted them to act differently depending on the input activated?

Time for action – Differentiating Kismet inputs

That's pretty easy to do actually, so let's do it! We'll have the **Turn On** input do what it's doing now, and the **Turn Off** input return the **AwesomeWeaponUpgrade** actors to their normal size and color.

1. We only need to change our `OnToggle` function to make this work, using the `InputLinks` array:

```
function OnToggle(SeqAct_Toggle Action)
{
    if(Action.InputLinks[0].bHasImpulse)
    {
        MyMesh.SetScale(2.0);
        MyMesh.SetMaterial(0, BigMaterial);
    }
    else if(Action.InputLinks[1].bHasImpulse)
    {

        MyMesh.SetScale(MyMesh.default.Scale);
        MyMesh.SetMaterial(0, MyMesh.default.Materials[0]);
    }
}
```

2. That's easy enough, but where do we get the numbers from for the `InputLinks` array index? If we look at the `SeqAct_Toggle` class, we can see the answer:

```
InputLinks(0)=(LinkDesc="Turn On")
InputLinks(1)=(LinkDesc="Turn Off")
InputLinks(2)=(LinkDesc="Toggle")
```

3. Compile the code with our new `OnToggle` function, then open the editor.

4. Time for the Kismet. Add another **Trigger** near the first one that we added for this experiment, and uncheck its **Hidden** property so we can see it.

5. Select the **Trigger**, then add a **Touch** event for it in the Kismet editor.

6. Hook the **Touched** output of this new event to the **Turn Off** input of the **Toggle** action.

7. In both of the **Touched** events, make sure their **Max Trigger Count** properties are set to **0**.

8. The Kismet sequence should now look like the following:

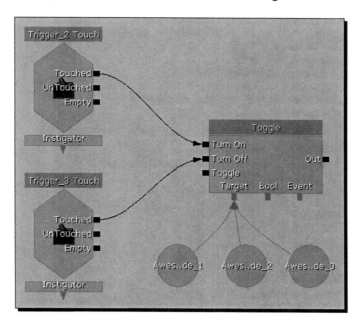

9. Save the map and run the game. Now running back and forth between the two triggers will cause the **AwesomeWeaponUpgrade** actors to switch between large blue and green and normal size.

What just happened?

Working with multiple inputs is easy, and as we can see from the default properties of SeqAct_Toggle, creating them for our own classes is easy as well. We can also check the bHasImpulse variable on them in the Action's own Activate function to do different things within the Action class itself.

Have a go hero – The toggle input

Using a Boolean in the **AwesomeWeaponUpgrade** class, see if you can have it store the status of the actor so that the `OnToggle` function could be rewritten to work with the **Toggle** input on the **SeqAct_Toggle** action. Make the actor switch back and forth when this input is repeatedly activated.

Hint: A new variable would be added to the `AwesomeWeaponUpgrade` class:

```
var bool bLargeBlue;
```

And the `OnToggle` function would look like this:

```
function OnToggle(SeqAct_Toggle Action)
{
    if(Action.InputLinks[0].bHasImpulse)
        bLargeBlue = true;
    else if(Action.InputLinks[1].bHasImpulse)
        bLargeBlue = true;
    else
        bLargeBlue = !bLargeBlue;

    if(bLargeBlue)
    {
        MyMesh.SetScale(2.0);
        MyMesh.SetMaterial(0, BigMaterial);
    }
    else
    {
        MyMesh.SetScale(default.MyMesh.Scale);
        MyMesh.SetMaterial(0, default.MyMesh.Materials[0]);
    }
}
```

Kismet conditions

For the most part **Actions** and **Events** will cover everything you need to do with custom Kismet, but sometimes you'll want to create your own **Condition** to check for various things. To see how we can use these, we'll create one that has multiple outputs and activate a single one based on the condition we're checking.

Time for action – What condition my condition was in

We already have a Kismet action to check the level of the player's weapon, but what if we had a custom **Condition** to check whether the player's weapon was at max level or not? Let's do it!

Create a new file in our `Development\Src\AwesomeGame\Classes` folder called `AwesomeSeqCond_IsWeaponMaxLevel.uc`.

Now open the new file in ConTEXT. First we'll declare the class and write up a few default properties:

```
class AwesomeSeqCond_IsWeaponMaxLevel extends SequenceCondition;

defaultproperties
{
    ObjName="Is Weapon Max Level"
    ObjCategory="Awesome Game"

    OutputLinks(0)=(LinkDesc="True")
    OutputLinks(1)=(LinkDesc="False")
}
```

By default **SequenceCondition** classes don't have any variable links, so we don't need to empty out that array or add any of our own.

You will notice though that we're adding two `OutputLinks`. Normally all **SequenceOp** classes have the first one defined by that class's default properties:

```
OutputLinks(0)=(LinkDesc="Out")
```

Here we're overriding the default description in our own `OutputLinks(0)` and setting it to `True`. We're also adding another output and setting that to `False`. We could add more outputs if we wanted to, but in this case we only need two. We could also rename and add inputs for our Kismet actions by using the `InputLinks` array in the same way.

By default Kismet **SequenceOp** classes activate their output links automatically once any `Activated` function is finished executing. This is done through a `bool` called `bAutoActivateOutputLinks` in **SequenceOp**, which is set to `True` in the default properties of that class. **SequenceConditions** however set this to `False`. Since **SequenceConditions** have more than one output, we want to decide for ourselves which one(s) to activate. We can do that in our `Activated` function.

1. We use a variable called `bHasImpulse` to activate an output link. Let's check the player's weapon level and set it to `True` for the output we want to activate:

```
event Activated()
{
    local PlayerController PC;

    PC = GetWorldInfo().GetALocalPlayerController();

    if(PC != none && PC.Pawn != none && AwesomeWeapon(PC.
Pawn.Weapon) != none && AwesomeWeapon(PC.Pawn.Weapon).
CurrentWeaponLevel == class'AwesomeWeapon'.const.MAX_LEVEL)
        OutputLinks[0].bHasImpulse = true;
    else
        OutputLinks[1].bHasImpulse = true;
}
```

   If the weapon is at max level, activate the **True** output, otherwise activate the **False** output. Note that we're setting the bool to true both times, don't let the names of the outputs confuse you.

2. Now let's compile the code and open our map in the editor.

3. In the Kismet editor, delete the **Get Weapon Level**, **Compare Int**, and the **Int** variable. We're going to add our new condition here instead. Right-click where the deleted actions were and hit **New Condition | Awesome Game | Is Weapon Max Level**.

4. Connect the output of the **Bool** action from our old Kismet to the **In** node of our condition. Now connect the **False** output of our condition to the **Spawn Actor** input of the **Actor Factory** action.

5. Right-click above the **Actor Factory** action and hit **New Action | Misc | Log**.

6. Give the **Log** action an **Obj Comment** of **Weapon At Max Level!** The **Log** action has its own **Output To Screen** property, so we don't need to worry about checking **Output Obj Comment To Screen** unless we want two messages to show up. And I'm not just saying that because I forgot about that while I was writing this.

7. Connect the **True** output of our **Is Weapon Max Level** condition to the input of the **Log** action.

8. Save the map, then run the game. Pick up the weapon, then run over the trigger and collect the upgrades a few times until the weapon reaches level 5. Now run over the trigger again and we should see our log message. After that the Boolean checks before our condition prevent it from activating again, so we don't get any more messages or pickups.

What just happened?

Conditions aren't the only classes that can have multiple outputs, if we look at **SeqAct_CameraFade** we can see that actions can also use multiple outputs if we set its `bAutoActivateOutputLinks` to `False`. And from our use of the **Trigger** event we can see that **Events** can have them as well. And although it's not generally used in **Conditions**, **Actions** can have multiple inputs. We can see an example of how to do that in **UTSeqAct_ToggleAnnouncements**.

Kismet events

The last main topic we'll discuss is the use of **Events**. As we've seen from our use of the **Trigger** event, something has to start the chain of activations that make up a Kismet sequence, and **Events** are it. They have no input nodes, only outputs, and are called directly from within UnrealScript. To discuss how to create and use events, we'll be expanding on our AwesomeGame instead of running random experiments, so let's get to it!

Time for action – The cleanup job

We've made a bit of a mess in our map file again, so let's clean it up in preparation for this section of the chapter.

1. Open AwesomeTestMap in the editor.

2. We'll be starting fresh with our Kismet, so open the Kismet editor and delete all of it.

3. In the level, delete all of the **Trigger** actors and **AwesomeWeaponUpgrades** but leave the weapon spawner, enemy spawners, and player start.

What just happened?

Now we're ready to start working with Kismet events.

Creating and triggering a Kismet event

For our game there are a few things we might want to know about in Kismet. One thing that comes to mind is when all of the enemies have been killed. We could use this event to do certain things in Kismet, for example, if we wanted to spawn a weapon upgrade as a reward for the player before the boss showed up. Let's see if we can do it!

Time for action – Our first Kismet event

We're going to make it so that we can spawn as many waves of enemies as we want, so instead of calling this event something like `EnemiesDefeated`, we'll use something like `WaveComplete`.

1. Create a new file in our `Development\Src\AwesomeGame\Classes` folder called `AwesomeSeqEvent_WaveComplete.uc`.

2. The code for this one is going to be really simple:

```
class AwesomeSeqEvent_WaveComplete extends SequenceEvent;

defaultproperties
{
    ObjName="Wave Complete"
    ObjCategory="Awesome Game"
    VariableLinks.Empty
    bPlayerOnly=false
}
```

Yep, that's it. We don't have an instigator so we don't need to have any variable links. The `bPlayersOnly` variable lets classes other than `PlayerControllers` trigger the event.

3. The event is created, so now we need to trigger it. Open up AwesomeGame in ConTEXT and add a line to our `EnemyKilled` function:

```
function EnemyKilled()
{
    local int i;

    if(bSpawnBoss)
        return;

    EnemiesLeft--;
    if(EnemiesLeft <= 0)
    {
        for(i=0; i<EnemySpawners.length; i++)
            EnemySpawners[i].MakeEnemyRunAway();
```

```
        ClearTimer('ActivateSpawners');
        bSpawnBoss = true;
        ActivateSpawners();

        TriggerGlobalEventClass(class'AwesomeSeqEvent_
WaveComplete', self);
    }
}
```

Calling this function will make the game find all of the **Wave Complete** actions in Kismet and trigger them.

4. Now we need to add the Kismet to our level, so open it up in the editor.

5. First we need the enemies to spawn, so add a **New Event | Player | Player Spawned** and hook its output to the input of a **New Action | AwesomeGame | Spawner Activation**. You can add a delay if you want (right-click on either node of the connection and hit **Set Activate Delay**).

6. Below that, right-click and add a **New Event | Awesome Game | Wave Complete**. Connect the output to a **New Action | Misc | Log**.

7. In the **Log**'s properties, give it an **Obj Comment** of **Wave Complete!**

8. Save the map and run the game.

What just happened?

Now when the enemies have been defeated and the boss is spawned, we get our **Log**'s comment, letting us know our custom **Event** is working!

Giving the event some meaning

Having a custom event is good, but right now it seems too passive. It's letting us know the wave is complete, but then the boss immediately spawns. What if we moved that functionality into Kismet to give the level designers some control over when the boss spawns after a wave is complete?

Time for action – Moving functionality into Kismet

To do this we're going to create a new action that will spawn the boss, and also alter an existing action to give us more control over the waves of enemies:

1. Create a new file in `Development\Src\AwesomeGame\Classes` called `AwesomeSeqAct_SpawnBoss.uc`.

2. Let's write the following code in it:

```
class AwesomeSeqAct_SpawnBoss extends SequenceAction;

event Activated()
{
    if(AwesomeGame(GetWorldInfo().Game) != none)
        AwesomeGame(GetWorldInfo().Game).SpawnBoss();
}

defaultproperties
{
    ObjName="Spawn Boss"
    ObjCategory="Awesome Game"
    VariableLinks.Empty
}
```

3. The `SpawnBoss` function doesn't exist in AwesomeGame yet, so let's create it. Open up **AwesomeGame.uc** and add this function:

```
function SpawnBoss()
{
    bSpawnBoss = true;
    ActivateSpawners();
}
```

4. Now to keep the game from automatically spawning the boss, let's delete those two lines from `EnemyKilled` so it looks like this:

```
function EnemyKilled()
{
    local int i;

    if(bSpawnBoss)
        return;

    EnemiesLeft--;
    if(EnemiesLeft <= 0)
    {
        for(i=0; i<EnemySpawners.length; i++)
            EnemySpawners[i].MakeEnemyRunAway();
        ClearTimer('ActivateSpawners');
        TriggerGlobalEventClass(class'AwesomeSeqEvent_
WaveComplete', self);
    }
}
```

5. Ok, we're done code side, so compile the code and open our map in the editor.

6. Now let's give the player a weapon upgrade and a bit of time before the boss spawns. Open up the Kismet editor and add a **New Action | Actor | Actor Factory**. Connect the **Wave Complete!** log's output to the **Spawn Actor** input of the **Actor Factory**.

7. In the **Actor Factory's** properties, select **ActorFactoryActor** from the list that pops up when you click the blue arrow for the **Factory** property.

8. In the **Actor Class** property that shows up, select **AwesomeWeaponUpgrade**.

9. Now we need a place for it to spawn. To keep it easy we'll use the player start, so select it in the level and go back to the Kismet editor.

10. Right-click under the **Actor Factory** action and hit **New Object Var Using PlayerStart_0**. Hook the **Spawn Point** variable link under the **Actor Factory** action to it.

11. Ok that's done! Now to spawn the boss. Right-click above the **Actor Factory** action and hit **New Action | Awesome Game | Spawn Boss**.

12. Instead of hooking it to the output of the **Actor Factory**, hook the output of the **Log** action to the input of **Spawn Boss**. We want the boss to spawn even if something goes wrong with the **Actor Factory** and the **Finished** output never activates.

13. Now to give us some delay, right-click the input of the **Spawn Boss** action and hit **Set Activate Delay**, and give it a delay of **5**.

14. Finally, add another **New Action | Misc | Log** and hook it to the output of **Spawn Boss**. Give the new **Log** action an **Obj Comment** of **Boss Incoming!**

15. Our Kismet sequence should now look like the following:

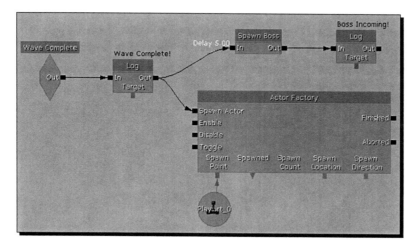

16. Save the map and run the game. Now when we defeat the enemies, a weapon upgrade spawns at the player start, and five seconds later the boss spawns and the log message shows. Nice!

What just happened?

Now we can see how moving parts of our gameplay into Kismet actions and events can help make our game more flexible. We can take this even further, however.

Further expanding our Kismet

There are some more things we could do to really expand the possibilities of our game's Kismet. One thing we could do is give the level designer control over the size of the wave that's spawned.

Time for action – Setting the wave size

For this we'll need to modify our **Spawner Activation** action as well as our AwesomeGame. Let's get to it!

1. Let's start with the Kismet action. We'll need to add an `int` that the level designer can change to set the size of the wave, and then pass that on to the AwesomeGame. Open up **AwesomeSeqAct_SpawnerActivation** in ConTEXT.

2. Let's add an editable `int` variable to the top of the class:

```
var() int WaveSize;
```

Then give it a default property:

```
WaveSize=10
```

3. To give some added flexibility, let's hook it up to a variable link so we can set it that way as well if we wanted to. Add this line to the default properties:

```
VariableLinks(0)=(ExpectedType=class'SeqVar_Int',LinkDesc="Wave
Size",PropertyName=WaveSize)
```

Note that this variable link is optional, we don't have to hook an **Int** Kismet variable to it, the action will still work fine with the editable property.

4. Now to pass this along to the game. Let's call a new function that we'll create in AwesomeGame. Change the **Spawner Activation's** `Activated` function to this:

```
event Activated()
{
    if(AwesomeGame(GetWorldInfo().Game) != none)
        AwesomeGame(GetWorldInfo().Game).StartWave(WaveSize);
}
```

The **AwesomeSeqAct_SpawnerActivation** class should look like the following:

```
class AwesomeSeqAct_SpawnerActivation extends SequenceAction;

var() int WaveSize;

event Activated()
{
    if(AwesomeGame(GetWorldInfo().Game) != none)
        AwesomeGame(GetWorldInfo().Game).StartWave(WaveSize);
}

defaultproperties
{
    WaveSize=10
    ObjName="Spawner Activation"
    ObjCategory="Awesome Game"
    VariableLinks.Empty
    VariableLinks(0)=(ExpectedType=class'SeqVar_
Int',LinkDesc="Wave Size",PropertyName=WaveSize)
}
```

The `VariableLinks.Empty` line might be confusing, but we're using it to clear out the **Targets** link that was there before adding our own.

5. We're done with the Kismet action, so let's open up AwesomeGame and create the `StartWave` function that we're calling from Kismet:

```
function StartWave(int WaveSize)
{
    local AwesomeEnemy AE;

    foreach DynamicActors(class'AwesomeEnemy', AE)
        AE.Destroy();

    EnemiesLeft = WaveSize;
    bSpawnBoss = false;
    ActivateSpawners();
}
```

This might seem a bit more complicated than we were expecting, but we need to make sure that any fleeing enemy left behind from a previous wave is properly destroyed before we start a new one. We also need to set `bSpawnBoss` to `false` to make sure we spawn normal minions for the wave.

6. That's it for the UnrealScript side! Compile the code and open AwesomeTestMap in the editor.

7. We'll notice in the Kismet editor that our **Wave Size** variable link shows up on our **Spawner Activation** action now, and if we look at its properties we can change it there too.

8. Now let's change our level's Kismet so we have two waves and then a boss. First set our **Spawner Activation's Wave Size** to **5**. Also right-click on its input and set the activation delay to **5**.

9. Hook an **Enemies Incoming!** log action to the output of our **Spawner Activation**.

10. Open up our **Wave Complete** event's properties and set **Max Trigger Count** to **0**. We want it to be able to trigger more than once this time.

11. Now right-click on the input of our **Spawn Boss** action and hit **Break All Links**. We're going to put some stuff in between.

12. Add a **New Action | Misc | Gate**. We use **Gates** to control the flow of Kismet. If the **Gate** is closed the output won't activate until we send a signal to its **Open** input.

13. In the **Gate's** properties, set **Auto Close Count** to **1**. This way the **Gate** will close after it has been activated once.

14. Hook the output of the **Wave Complete** log action to the **In** input of the **Gate**. Right-click on the gate's **In** input and set the activation delay to **one** second. This will become important in a bit.

15. Hook the output of the **Gate** up to the input of our **Spawner Activation**. Now when the first wave is complete, a second wave will start after another five seconds. The **Gate** will close to prevent any more waves from spawning.

16. Add another **New Action | Misc | Gate**. In its properties, set **SeqAct_Gate | Open** to unchecked. This will close it.

17. Hook the output of the first **Gate** to the **Open** input of this new one. Now when the second wave spawns, it will open the **Gate** so the next **Wave Complete** call can pass through it. The one-second delay we added earlier is to prevent both signals from hitting it at the same time and activating the output before we want it to.

18. Hook the output of the **Wave Complete** log action to the **In** input of the new **Gate**.

19. Hook the output of the new **Gate** to the input of the **Spawn Boss** action.

20. The Kismet sequences should now look like the following. Here is the first wave:

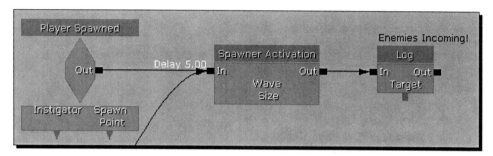

The line coming from the bottom is from the second wave and boss Kismet here:

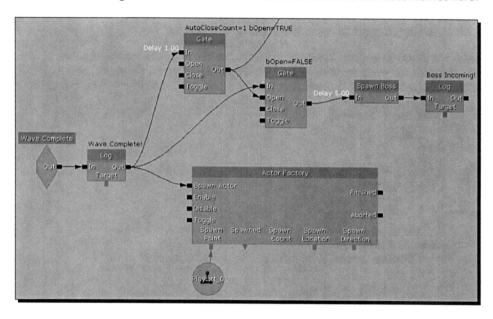

21. That's it! Save the map and run the game.

What just happened?

Now we can definitely see the effect that moving functionality into Kismet has had. We can really customize each level of our game, add more waves, change the size of the waves, and do things in between the waves.

Have a go hero – Expanding the Kismet

Now that we've separated the minion spawning into Kismet actions and events, see if you can do the same thing with the boss spawning. Create a **Boss Defeated** event and **Game Complete** action so that you can have more than one boss per level.

Hint:The Boss Defeated event would look like this:

```
class AwesomeSeqEvent_BossDefeated extends SequenceEvent;

defaultproperties
{
    ObjName="Boss Defeated"
    ObjCategory="Awesome Game"
    VariableLinks.Empty
    bPlayerOnly=false
}
```

With the following changes to AwesomeBoss:

```
event TakeDamage(int DamageAmount, Controller EventInstigator, vector
HitLocation, vector Momentum, class<DamageType> DamageType, optional
TraceHitInfo HitInfo, optional Actor DamageCauser)
{
    local AwesomeEnemy AE;

    Health--;

    if(Health == 0 && EventInstigator != none && EventInstigator.
PlayerReplicationInfo != none)
    {
        // Delete this line:
        WorldInfo.Game.ScoreObjective(EventInstigator.
PlayerReplicationInfo, 1);
        foreach DynamicActors(class'AwesomeEnemy', AE)
        {
            if(AE != self)
                AE.RunAway();
        }

        TriggerGlobalEventClass(class'AwesomeSeqEvent_BossDefeated',
self);
        Destroy();
    }

    if(Health == 10)
        GoToState('StageTwo');
}
```

The Game Complete action would look like this:

```
class AwesomeSeqAct_GameComplete extends SequenceAction;

event Activated()
{
    if(AwesomeGame(GetWorldInfo().Game) != none)
        AwesomeGame(GetWorldInfo().Game).ScoreObjective(GetALocalPlaye
rController().PlayerReplicationInfo, 1);
}

defaultproperties
{
    ObjName="Game Complete"
    ObjCategory="Awesome Game"
    VariableLinks.Empty
}
```

Supported events

In addition to general events that can be triggered globally from any class, Actors have an array of **Event** classes called `SupportedEvents`. We've used this before with **Triggers**. When you have an Actor selected in the level, right-clicking in the Kismet editor will reveal the `SupportedEvents` of that class under **New Event Using (Actor's Name)**. If we look at **Actor**'s default properties, we can see the list:

```
SupportedEvents(0)=class'SeqEvent_Touch'
SupportedEvents(1)=class'SeqEvent_Destroyed'
SupportedEvents(2)=class'SeqEvent_TakeDamage'
SupportedEvents(3)=class'SeqEvent_HitWall'
SupportedEvents(4)=class'SeqEvent_AnimNotify'
```

And under **Trigger**, a new one is added:

```
SupportedEvents.Add(class'SeqEvent_Used')
```

If we had any custom events that we wanted to be used in this way, that's how we would add them. We can also empty out the `SupportedEvents` array the same way we did with the variable links of our Kismet actions. Taking a look at the **TriggerVolume** class we can see an example of that:

```
SupportedEvents.Empty
SupportedEvents(0)=class'SeqEvent_Touch'
SupportedEvents(1)=class'SeqEvent_TakeDamage'
```

Here, the array is emptied, and then the two desired events are added back in.

Let's see if we can take advantage of these in our game.

Time for action – Using SupportedEvents

Let's see if we can change the beginning of our game. Instead of automatically triggering the first wave when the player spawns, let's make it so they have to pick up the weapon and a weapon upgrade first as a kind of tutorial:

1. Open AwesomeTestMap in the editor.

2. Place an **AwesomeWeaponUpgrade** in the level near the weapon.

3. With the **AwesomeWeaponUpgrade** selected, open the Kismet editor.

4. Right-click above the **Player Spawned** event and hit **New Event Using AwesomeWeaponUpgrade_0 | Touch**.

5. Hook the **Touched** output of the event to the input of the **Spawner Activation** action.

6. Delete the **Player Spawned** event.

7. Save the map and run the game.

What just happened?

We can see the problem with this setup pretty quickly. Even if we don't actually pick it up, simply running over it triggers the first wave. The problem is that the **AwesomeWeaponUpgrade** receives touches and triggers its **Touch** events regardless of what we're doing inside the UnrealScript class's **Touch** function. We'll need to create our own event for this.

Time for action – Creating a custom SupportedEvent

We'll create a custom event called **Picked Up**.

1. Create a new file in Development\Src\AwesomeGame\Classes called AwesomeSeqEvent_PickedUp.uc.

2. Write the following code in the new file:

```
class AwesomeSeqEvent_PickedUp extends SequenceEvent;

defaultproperties
{
    ObjName="Picked Up"
    ObjCategory="Awesome Game"
    bPlayerOnly=false
}
```

3. Simple enough. Now we need to add this to the `SupportedEvents` of our **AwesomeWeaponUpgrade** class's default properties. In **AwesomeWeaponUpgrade** add this to the defaults:

```
SupportedEvents.Add(class'AwesomeSeqEvent_PickedUp')
```

4. Now we can use it in the editor, but we need to trigger it. Let's rewrite our `Touch` function to add a new line. Change **AwesomeWeaponUpgrade**'s `Touch` function to look like the following:

```
event Touch(Actor Other, PrimitiveComponent OtherComp, vector
HitLocation, vector HitNormal)
{
    if(Pawn(Other) != none && AwesomeWeapon(Pawn(Other).Weapon) !=
none)
    {
        AwesomeWeapon(Pawn(Other).Weapon).UpgradeWeapon();
        TriggerEventClass(class'AwesomeSeqEvent_PickedUp', self);
        Destroy();
    }
}
```

The function `TriggerEventClass` is defined in **Actor**, and triggers all of the events that are linked to this Actor. Those events are automatically added to that actor's `GeneratedEvents` array when we create them in the Kismet editor.

5. Compile the code and open up the editor.

6. In the Kismet editor, delete the **Touch** event we were using before.

7. Select the **AwesomeWeaponUpgrade** in the level, then right-click in the Kismet editor and hit **New Event Using AwesomeWeaponUpgrade_0 | Picked Up**.

8. Hook the output of this event to the input of the Spawner Activation action. That takes care of the functionality, but let's see if we can spice it up a bit with instructions for the player.

9. Right-click above this sequence and hit **New Event | Player | Player Spawned**.

10. Next to it, add a **New Action | Misc | Log**. Give it an **Obj Comment** of **Pick up the weapon**.

11. Connect the **Player Spawned** event to the **Log**.

12. Now select the weapon spawner in the level, and right-click in the Kismet Editor and hit **New Event Using UTWeaponPickupFactory_0 | Pickup Status Change**. This is a `SupportedEvent` added to weapon factories to let us know when it changes.

13. Next to that, add another **Log** action with an **Obj Comment** of **Now pick up the weapon upgrade**.

14. Connect the **Pickup Status Change** event's **Taken** output to this new **Log** action.

15. Now add a new **Log** next to the **Picked Up** event for the **AwesomeWeaponUpgrade**, and give it an **Obj Comment** of **Prepare yourself!**

16. Hook up the **Picked Up** event to the **Log**.

17. This is what the Kismet sequence should look like now:

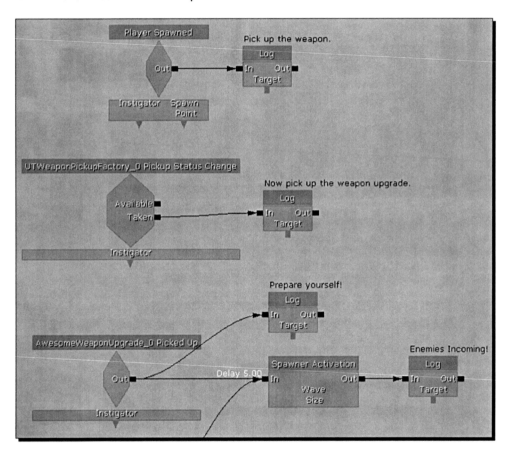

18. Save the map and run the game. Now we have a small tutorial for the game before the enemies start spawning. Nice!

What just happened?

Using `SupportedEvents` we can have Kismet events that are specific to an actor placed in the level as opposed to a global event that could be triggered by any actor. Each has its use, and as we can see they're incredibly helpful when trying to create Kismet with flexibility in mind.

Latent actions

The last topic of this chapter is dealing with latent Kismet actions. Normally Kismet actions are activated, some code is run, and their outputs are sent out immediately, but sometimes we'll want to delay an output until some condition has been met. For example, if we take a look at **SeqAct_PlaySound**, we can see this in the default properties:

```
OutputLinks(1)=(LinkDesc="Finished")
```

This obviously isn't an output that activates immediately; it waits until the sound is finished playing and then activates this output. But how do we do that for our own actions? Let's find out!

Time for action – Creating a latent action

Latent actions have their own section under the **SequenceAction** tree, under **SeqAct_Latent**. Instead of creating an entirely new action, we'll move our **Spawner Activation** action here. We'll do this so we can create a timer instead of having to use delays on the inputs and outputs. Let's get started!

1. First we need to create the timer. Let's do this in **AwesomeGame**. We'll start with the `int` variable at the top:

```
var int NextWaveTimer;
```

2. Now let's change the `StartWave` function:

```
function StartWave(int WaveSize, int WaveTimer)
{
    local AwesomeEnemy AE;

    foreach DynamicActors(class'AwesomeEnemy', AE)
        AE.Destroy();

    EnemiesLeft = WaveSize;
    NextWaveTime = WaveTimer;

    Broadcast(self, NextWaveTime);
    SetTimer(1, true, 'WaveCountdown');
}
```

We've added a new parameter to take the desired countdown time, then set it to our new variable and called a repeating timer for `WaveCountdown`, which we'll write next. We also broadcast the time left, similar to how the **Log** action shows its **Obj Comment** on screen.

3. Now we'll write the `WaveCountdown` function:

```
function WaveCountdown()
{
    NextWaveTime--;

    if(NextWaveTime <= 0)
    {
        ClearTimer('WaveCountdown');
        bSpawnBoss = false;
        ActivateSpawners();
    }
    else
        Broadcast(self, NextWaveTime);
}
```

In this function, if the time has reached **0,** we'll clear the repeating timer and start the spawning. If not, we'll broadcast the time left.

4. Now let's give `NextWaveTime` a default property.

```
NextWaveTime=5
```

This will get overridden the first time the wave is called, but it's good to have a default for it.

5. Before we get to the **Spawner Activation** action, let's fix a small bug we've been getting with our HUD. We don't want the number of enemies left to display until the wave starts, so let's change the `DrawHUD` function of **AwesomeHUD**. Find this line:

```
if(!AwesomeGame(WorldInfo.Game).bSpawnBoss)
```

And change it to this:

```
if(!AwesomeGame(WorldInfo.Game).bSpawnBoss &&
AwesomeGame(WorldInfo.Game).NextWaveTime == 0)
```

Now the number of enemies will only show once the wave has spawned. To get the number to stop showing after the wave has ended, let's add a line to our `EnemiesKilled` function in **AwesomeGame**:

```
function EnemyKilled()
{
    local int i;
```

```
    if(bSpawnBoss)
        return;

    EnemiesLeft--;
    if(EnemiesLeft <= 0)
    {
        for(i=0; i<EnemySpawners.length; i++)
            EnemySpawners[i].MakeEnemyRunAway();
        ClearTimer('ActivateSpawners');
        TriggerGlobalEventClass(class'AwesomeSeqEvent_
WaveComplete', self);
        NextWaveTime = -1;
    }
}
```

Since we're checking if `NextWaveTime` is equal to zero in the HUD, setting it to **-1** here will make sure it doesn't display after the wave is over, while still letting us set it to an appropriate number whenever we call the next wave.

6. Now for the **Spawner Activation** action. First we need to change the class we're extending from:

```
class AwesomeSeqAct_SpawnerActivation extends SeqAct_Latent;
```

7. Now we need to add the wave time variable here:

```
var() int WaveSize, WaveTimer;
```

And give it a default property:

```
WaveTimer=5
```

8. We'll also add a variable link for it:

```
VariableLinks(1)=(ExpectedType=class'SeqVar_Int',LinkDesc="Wave
Timer",PropertyName=WaveTimer)
```

9. Now let's change our outputs and make sure they don't automatically activate:

```
OutputLinks(0)=(LinkDesc="Out")
OutputLinks(1)=(LinkDesc="Finished")
bAutoActivateOutputLinks=false
```

10. We want the **Out** output to activate immediately, so let's change our `Activated` function:

```
event Activated()
{
    if(AwesomeGame(GetWorldInfo().Game) != none)
        AwesomeGame(GetWorldInfo().Game).StartWave(WaveSize,
WaveTimer);
    OutputLinks[0].bHasImpulse = true;
}
```

11. And now for the `Update` function. This is what keeps the Kismet action going until we're ready to deactivate it. Returning `true` from this function tells the game that we're not done, that we want to keep calling `Update` on this action until we return `false`. Here, we'll check the time in the **AwesomeGame** and keep updating until it reaches **0**:

```
event bool Update(float DT)
{
    if(AwesomeGame(GetWorldInfo().Game) != none &&
AwesomeGame(GetWorldInfo().Game).NextWaveTime > 0)
        return true;

    OutputLinks[1].bHasImpulse = true;
    return false;
}
```

12. That's it for the UnrealScript, so compile the code and open the editor.

13. We're going to delete the old **Spawner Activation** action, but before we do, right-click on its input link and hit **Copy Connections**. That will make the next step easier.

14. Delete the **Spawner Activation** action and add a new one. Right-click on its input link and hit **Paste Connections**. This saves us a bit of time.

15. Connect the **Finished** output link to the **Enemies Incoming** in the **Log** action.

16. Delete the **Prepare yourself!** in the **Log** action. The countdown timer will replace that.

17. Save the map and run the game. Now we have a nice countdown before the enemy spawn, and the number of enemies doesn't show on the HUD until the wave starts. Nice!

What just happened?

Latent actions are useful when you need to wait for something beyond Kismet's control to happen before you end the execution of an action. It's used for camera fades to wait until the fade is complete before activating an output. Matinee is a huge example of latent actions since it's used to create in-game movies and object movement. Knowing how to use latent actions will help you create Kismet that's specifically tailored to your needs.

Pop quiz – Kismet craziness!

1.   What are the four types of Kismet objects?

2.   What type of Kismet does not have input links?

3.   What does `TriggerEventClass` do?

Summary

We learned a lot in this chapter about using and creating Kismet in our game.

Specifically, we covered the following:

◆   How to use existing Kismet

◆   How to create our own Kismet actions and use them to interact with other UnrealScript classes

◆   How to create and use conditions to control the flow of Kismet

◆   How to create and trigger Kismet events

◆   How to use latent Kismet actions to delay activation of outputs

Now that we've learned about Kismet, we're ready to start playing our game on a server, which can run on our own computer!

8

Creating Multiplayer Games

What you see is just a Simulation.

Working with networking code is probably the most difficult part of creating a game with the Unreal Development Kit. It requires you to think about the code that's running not as a single set of actors, functions, and variables, but rather as a master set with the clients trying to simulate it as best they can. It's not an easy skill to master and it takes longer to create and debug functional multiplayer code, but as an UnrealScript programmer it will be an essential tool in your arsenal.

In this chapter we will:

- ◆ Discuss the server-client relationship and how each of them views the game world
- ◆ Set up for testing in a network environment using a single computer
- ◆ Learn about the different variables and functions associated with networking
- ◆ Replicate our own variables and functions from the server to the client and vice versa

So with that, let's start working in multiplayer!

The server-client relationship

When talking about multiplayer games, people will talk about the server. "*I'm going to join the server.*" But what does that mean exactly? How do the different computers involved in the game connect to one another?

One state to bind us all

In the world of Unreal, the server is king. It holds the one true game state, while the clients connected to it simulate it as best they can. The clients run the same code and predict where objects in the game world are by using their last known location and velocity, until the server updates the client with their actual positions. If you've ever experienced heavy lag while playing online and had the characters seemingly teleport around, then you know what happens when this prediction model goes too far out of sync.

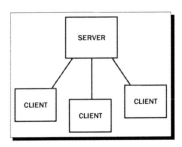

In the client-server model each player (client) connects to the server and is unaware of other clients connected to that server. That might not make sense at first, but if you think about it each player in the game is represented by an actor class, a Pawn, whose short term movements can be predicted as with all other actors in the game by using their current location and velocity. The client doesn't care what other clients are doing, what keys they're pressing, whether or not they're firing their weapon. The server has control over the state of the game, so the client doesn't need to communicate with other clients to get that information. It only needs to communicate with the server. When we move, we send that information to the server, which in turn sends that information to each of the clients connected to it. When we fire our rocket launcher, the server tells the other clients that a projectile has been spawned at this location and heading in this direction.

In an ideal world the server would send the exact state of all objects in the game world to each client after every tick. Unfortunately modems just aren't fast enough to do that. Instead, the server only sends information when something changes. If our character were holding a flashlight and we had a Boolean `bFlashlightOn` variable to keep track of it, we wouldn't want the server sending its state to other clients all the time, only when it changes. The same is true for all actors and variables in the game world.

Additionally, there is some information we don't need to send to other clients at all. Our Pawn's health, for instance, is really only useful to the server and the client who owns that Pawn. When other clients shoot us, the server calculates our new health value and tells us what it is so we can display it on our HUD. Other clients don't use our Pawn's health value at all. If they do enough damage to kill our Pawn, the server will let all of the clients know that we have died as well as the killing client's new score. Their knowing our actual health value would be an unnecessary waste of bandwidth.

The process that the server goes through to determine what information to send to clients is called replication. The goal of replication is for the clients to have as close a representation of the server's game state as possible given bandwidth limitations. Sometimes we don't care if the information arrives at the client at all. For instance, particle effects are pretty and are an important part of a game's visuals, but for network games if we had the choice between replicating a particle effect or another player's location, we would choose the player position every time. To that end there are ways to prioritize network traffic within UnrealScript and we'll take a look at them.

Alright, enough yammering, time to start networking!

Testing network code

Even though we've been talking about a server and a client, it is possible for both of those entities to exist on the same computer. We'll be using a different method for running our game to do this. Let's set it up now!

Setting up the server

Since we're already using a batch file to run our game, this part will be easy. All we need to do is change the batch file a bit.

Time for action – The server batch file

We may still want to run our game in a single player environment, so instead of editing our existing batch file we'll duplicate it.

1. Make a copy of the batch file we use to run the game. Name it `Awesome Test Server.bat`.

2. Right-click on the new batch file and click on **Edit**.

3. We only need to add one word to the batch file, here:

   ```
   C:\UDK\UDK-AwesomeGame\Binaries\Win32\UDK.exe server AwesomeTestMap?TimeLimit=0?Game=AwesomeGame.AwesomeGame -log
   ```

   The `server` keyword tells the game to run as a server.

4. Save and close the file.

What just happened?

That was easy, but what does this mysterious "server" thing look like? Double-click on the file and we'll find out. After starting up, the DOS window will just kind of... sit there. Yep, this is a running server:

Where's the game window? Well, if we think about it, a server doesn't really need one. It's running code and keeping track of the actors, functions, and variables in our game, but all that's done in code. There isn't a need to render anything. In all likelihood a server running our game would be in a box in a room with dozens of other servers, none of which would even have a monitor connected. The game window is a human need; the server can run the game just fine without one.

Shut down the server by closing the DOS window.

Setting up the client

Now that we have the server set up, we need to connect to our server. To do this we'll be running another instance of the game as a client.

Time for action – The client batch file

When we run a game and connect to a server, we give the game an IP address to connect to. When it's the same computer there's only one number we need to know.

1. Create a new batch file called `Awesome Test Client.bat`.

2. Write the following in it:

```
R:\UDK\UDK-AwesomeGame\Binaries\Win32\UDK.exe 127.0.0.1 -log
```

When connecting to the same computer, the IP address will be 127.0.0.1. This is the IP we'll use to connect to our server.

3. Save the file and close it.

What just happened?

We're about to learn a very tough lesson here, so get ready. Double-click on the server batch file to start the server up, then once you see it say "Initializing Game Engine Complete", double-click on the client batch file to start up the client. If everything goes well, you should see some more lines being logged by the server as the client connects, starting with this:

```
[0009.17] NetComeGo: Open TheWorld 08/15/11 19:43:35 127.0.0.1
```

But now what's happening? Instead of starting into our game, we get a first person view with the message "Waiting for other players". If we wait a few seconds the game will start, and the server window will start being spammed with error messages:

```
[0029.44] ScriptWarning: Accessed None 'PlayerInput'
    AwesomePlayerController AwesomeTestMap.TheWorld:PersistentLevel.
AwesomePlayerController_0
    Function AwesomeGame.AwesomePlayerController:PlayerWalking.
ProcessMove:003C
```

Also, we can't move! Well then, this is a pretty frustrating foray into multiplayer game making. This also brings us to the most important lesson in this book:

If you are going to make a multiplayer game, test it on a server from the beginning.

I can't stress this enough. Seeing how broken our game is on the server should be enough of a reason for that. It can be extremely difficult to rewrite a game's code to work in multiplayer if it wasn't written that way in the first place. It requires a lot of planning ahead of time and different ways of thinking about the variables and functions in a game to get it to work properly on a server. If our game were more complicated it would take awhile to get it functioning; luckily it's relatively simple.

Fixing Awesome Game

Let's see if we can get it working on the server.

Time for action – Unbreaking the player

We'll start with the most game-breaking problem first, the fact that we can't move. If we take a look in the `PlayerController` class in UnCodeX, we can see a huge comment starting with this line:

```
Here's how player movement prediction, replication and correction
works in network games:
```

Reading this section we can see that we've put our code too far down the chain of events. The `ProcessMove` function isn't used for network games. We need to move it up to `PlayerMove` instead. Let's do that now.

1. Create the `PlayerMove` function in our `AwesomePlayerController`'s `PlayerWalking` state:

   ```
   function PlayerMove(float DeltaTime)
   {
       local vector X, Y, Z, AltAccel;
       local rotator OldRotation;

       GetAxes(CurrentCameraRotation, X, Y, Z);
       AltAccel = PlayerInput.aForward * Z + PlayerInput.aStrafe
   * Y;
       AltAccel.Z = 0;
       AltAccel = Pawn.AccelRate * Normal(AltAccel);

       OldRotation = Rotation;
       UpdateRotation(DeltaTime);

       if(Role < ROLE_Authority)
           ReplicateMove(DeltaTime, AltAccel, DCLICK_None,
   OldRotation - Rotation);
       else
           ProcessMove(DeltaTime, AltAccel, DCLICK_None,
   OldRotation - Rotation);
   }
   ```

   Now the code should work correctly.

2. Delete the `ProcessMove` function from our `PlayerWalking` state.

3. Compile and test the game.

What just happened?

When the player couldn't move and the server's logs were being spammed with errors, it was due to the fact that the server doesn't have a `PlayerInput` actor. They're only spawned on the clients. The clients use the `PlayerInput` and functions like `ReplicatedMove` to send information to the server about where we want to move, but the server doesn't have our keyboard attached to it so it doesn't need a `PlayerInput` actor of its own.

With this new function, we're processing our own `PlayerInput` data into acceleration, and sending that along with our rotation data to the server through `ReplicateMove`.

That fixes our movement problem, but now in addition to the "Waiting for other players" message we can see a few more problems. We can pick up the weapon, but when the game tells us to pick up the weapon upgrade we can't see it. We can run over to where it should be and the timer will start counting down though. After the timer runs out and we get the "Enemies incoming!" message, errors start showing up in the log:

```
[0019.51] ScriptWarning: Accessed None 'PC'
    AwesomeGame AwesomeTestMap.TheWorld:PersistentLevel.AwesomeGame_0
    Function AwesomeGame.AwesomeGame:ActivateSpawners:0040
```

Plus, no enemies spawn, looks like we have a bit more work to do.

Time for action – Unbreaking the game

The delayed start is easy enough to take care of, so let's start with that. We simply need to add a line to AwesomeGame's default properties to tell it not to wait for other players.

1. Add the following line to AwesomeGame's default properties:

   ```
   bDelayedStart=false
   ```

   That's it! If we compiled now and tested, the game would start up like we're used to, with the player immediately spawning.

2. Now for the next step. We're missing the "Pick up the weapon" message. This is due to the `Log Kismet` action being called directly from the `Player Spawned` event. There are a lot of things happening all at once when the player is spawned, so we need to give the game a few ticks before everything is ready for the player to receive messages on their HUD. For simplicity's sake we'll just wait a second, so open `AwesomeTestMap`'s `Kismet` and add a one second delay to the output of the `Player Spawned` event.

3. Now that's working, but the weapon upgrade doesn't appear! We can walk over it and continue the sequence though. Right now, the `AwesomeWeaponUpgrade` is only being spawned on the server. We need to tell the game that we want the client to spawn it too. We'll add two default properties for this:

```
RemoteRole=ROLE_SimulatedProxy
bAlwaysRelevant=true
```

The first property, `RemoteRole`, tells the game what control the clients have over the actor. In this case we're using `SimulatedProxy`, essentially saying "the client has a local copy of the actor that represents what the server has". The second variable makes sure that the `AwesomeWeaponUpgrade` stays relevant to the player.

4. Now if we compile our code and test, the `AwesomeWeaponUpgrade` spawns, but when we pick it up our weapon's level stays at 0. To fix this we're going to have to let the game know that we want the server to tell the client when the variable has changed. To do this we'll add it to the replication block. We'll discuss the replication block in more detail in the next section of this chapter, but for now let's open up `AwesomeWeapon.uc` and add this code in between the variables and the functions:

```
replication
{
    if(bNetDirty)
        CurrentWeaponLevel;
}
```

`bNetDirty` is set to `true` whenever any variable changes, and we add the weapon level variable to tell the game: "If any variable changes, make sure the clients have the right value for `CurrentWeaponLevel`."

5. Now when we compile and test the weapon upgrade functions properly, of course, we can't see the enemies. They're obviously there since after we run over the weapon upgrade and sit still for a bit we'll start taking damage. Looks like we're having the same problem we were having with the `AwesomeWeaponUpgrade` not being there, so let's add those same two variables to the default properties of `AwesomeEnemy`:

```
RemoteRole=ROLE_SimulatedProxy
bAlwaysRelevant=true
```

6. In addition, our enemy spawning function is broken, but this is an easy fix. If we take a look at the `ActivateSpawners` function in `AwesomeGame`, we can see these two lines:

```
foreach LocalPlayerControllers(class'AwesomePlayerController',
PC)
    break;
```

A server does not have any local player controllers, but it does have access to the player controllers through the dynamic actor iterator. Let's change the lines as follows:

```
foreach DynamicActors(class'AwesomePlayerController', PC)
        break;
```

This isn't the only place we're doing this though. We also need to open `AwesomeEnemy.uc` and look in the `GetEnemy` function. Let's change this:

```
    foreach LocalPlayerControllers(class'AwesomePlayerController',
PC)
    {
        if(PC.Pawn != none)
            Enemy = PC.Pawn;
    }
```

To this:

```
    foreach DynamicActors(class'AwesomePlayerController', PC)
    {
        if(PC.Pawn != none)
            Enemy = PC.Pawn;
    }
```

7. If we compile and test, it seems like they're still not spawning, but if we run around a bit we'll see that they're there, they're just not moving on the client. Normally, when we write functions they only run on the server, but if we use the `simulated` keyword on them they'll also be able to run on clients. Let's take a look at our AwesomeEnemy's `Tick` function inside the `Seeking` state. All of the movement code is in there, so let's rewrite the function declaration:

```
        simulated function Tick(float DeltaTime)
```

8. If we compile now we'll get a warning:

```
[0003.78] Warning: R:\UDK\UDK-AwesomeGame\Development\Src\
AwesomeGame\Classes\AwesomeBoss.uc(35) : Warning, Superclass
version is simulated so 'Tick' should be!
```

Since we've changed the function declaration in `AwesomeEnemy`, we'll also have to change it in `AwesomeBoss` to make sure the boss class works too. So let's add the `simulated` keyword to the `AwesomeBoss`'s `Tick` function in its `Seeking` state.

9. Still not working! What could be going wrong now? Let's add a line to the top of the AwesomeEnemy's `Seeking` state's `Tick` function, right below the local variable:

```
`log(Enemy);
```

10. We'll get a lot of log spam with this, but it will let us know what's going on. Compile and test, and we'll see this on the server:

```
[0023.02] ScriptLog: AwesomePawn_0
```

But if we take a look at the client, we'll see this:

```
[0015.80] ScriptLog: None
```

Looks like the Enemy variable isn't being replicated.

11. We've dealt with this problem with the weapons being upgraded, so we know what to do here. Let's add a replication block to the top of AwesomeEnemy between the variables and functions:

```
replication
{
    if(bNetDirty)
        Enemy;
}
```

12. Compile and test. Yes, they're finally moving! But we'll see another problem with them; when they attack they never go back to the seeking state on the client. To fix this we'll also need to let the client know about changes in the bAttacking variable, so let's add that to our replication block:

```
replication
{
    if(bNetDirty)
        Enemy, bAttacking;
}
```

In addition, the client will also need to run the Attacking state's Tick function, so let's add the simulated keyword there:

```
        simulated function Tick(float DeltaTime)
```

13. Now let's compile and run. OK, we're getting there! Another problem we'll see is the enemies don't change colors when they're attacking us. To fix that the client will need to run the BeginState functions for our states, so let's add the simulated keyword to BeginState in the Seeking, Attacking, and Fleeing states. Since the Attacking state runs a timer to call EndAttack, we'll also need to set EndAttack to simulated as well so that function will run to change the color.

14. To make sure the Fleeing state works properly, let's also add the simulated keyword to its Tick function. We want to make sure the enemies get the call to enter the Fleeing state as well, so add the simulated keyword to the RunAway function in both AwesomeEnemy and AwesomeEnemy_Minion (and any other subclasses of AwesomeEnemy that you may have made).

15. Now let's see what we have left. We'll notice that no wave information is being displayed on the HUD. If we take a look at our code there:

```
if(AwesomeGame(WorldInfo.Game) != none)
```

All of the wave information is dependent on the GameInfo being there. But if we look at GameInfo's superclass, Info, we'll see this in the default properties:

```
RemoteRole=ROLE_None
```

This means that the GameInfo class doesn't exist on the client at all. We're going to have to come up with a new way to get that information.

What just happened?

We've fixed a lot of our code to work on a server. It's a hard lesson, but when you're going to make a game for multiplayer you need to write your code to work online from the very beginning. We've almost got our game working, so let's see if we can finish that.

The GameReplicationInfo class

For online games, since the GameInfo itself doesn't exist on the clients, it uses the GameReplicationInfo class to let the players know any game relevant information such as the score and time limit. In our case, we need to let the player know about the waves of enemies as well as information about the boss when it spawns. Let's do that now.

Time for action – Making the GameReplicationInfo

One of the things a GameInfo does when it spawns is create its GameReplicationInfo, so it can send information to the players. The class to use is specified in its default properties, so let's create our own and set it there.

1. Create a new file in our Development\Src\AwesomeGame\Classes folder called AwesomeGameReplicationInfo.uc. Type the following code into it:

```
class AwesomeGameReplicationInfo extends UTGameReplicationInfo;

var bool bSpawnBoss;
var float NextWaveTime;
var int EnemiesLeft;
var AwesomeEnemy TheBoss;

replication
{
    if(bNetDirty)
        bSpawnBoss, NextWaveTime, EnemiesLeft, TheBoss;
```

```
}

defaultproperties
{
}
```

This will be all the information we need to pass to the player.

2. Now we need the `GameInfo` to use this class as its `GameReplicationInfo`, so let's add a line to `AwesomeGame`'s default properties:

```
GameReplicationInfoClass=class'AwesomeGame.
AwesomeGameReplicationInfo'
```

3. Now we need to pass the information from `AwesomeGame` to `AwesomeGameReplicationInfo`. Let's start with the `EnemiesLeft` property. First we need to set its initial value; let's do this in `PostBeginPlay`:

```
simulated function PostBeginPlay()
{
    local AwesomeEnemySpawner ES;

    super.PostBeginPlay();

    GoalScore = 1;

    foreach DynamicActors(class'AwesomeEnemySpawner', ES)
        EnemySpawners[EnemySpawners.length] = ES;

    if(AwesomeGameReplicationInfo(GameReplicationInfo) != none)
        AwesomeGameReplicationInfo(GameReplicationInfo).
EnemiesLeft = EnemiesLeft;
}
```

4. Now we need to let it know when it changes; we do that in `EnemyKilled`:

```
function EnemyKilled()
{
    local int i;

    if(bSpawnBoss)
        return;

    EnemiesLeft--;

    if(EnemiesLeft <= 0)
    {
```

```
        for(i=0; i<EnemySpawners.length; i++)
            EnemySpawners[i].MakeEnemyRunAway();
        ClearTimer('ActivateSpawners');
        TriggerGlobalEventClass(class'AwesomeSeqEvent_
WaveComplete', self);
        NextWaveTime = -1;
    }

    if(AwesomeGameReplicationInfo(GameReplicationInfo) != none)
        AwesomeGameReplicationInfo(GameReplicationInfo).
EnemiesLeft = EnemiesLeft;
}
```

5. Since we've also added a function for the wave size to be set through Kismet, we need to set it there too:

```
function StartWave(int WaveSize, int WaveTimer)
{
    local AwesomeEnemy AE;

    foreach DynamicActors(class'AwesomeEnemy', AE)
        AE.Destroy();

    EnemiesLeft = WaveSize;
    NextWaveTime = WaveTimer;

    if(AwesomeGameReplicationInfo(GameReplicationInfo) != none)
        AwesomeGameReplicationInfo(GameReplicationInfo).
EnemiesLeft = EnemiesLeft;

    Broadcast(self, NextWaveTime);
    SetTimer(1, true, 'WaveCountdown');
}
```

6. Now for the `NextWaveTime`. The player uses this information to know whether it should display the information on the HUD, so it's not displaying when there isn't a wave of enemies attacking. First up, `PostBeginPlay`. Since we already have the if statement for the `EnemiesLeft` we'll just alter it a bit there:

```
    if(AwesomeGameReplicationInfo(GameReplicationInfo) != none)
    {
        AwesomeGameReplicationInfo(GameReplicationInfo).
EnemiesLeft = EnemiesLeft;
        AwesomeGameReplicationInfo(GameReplicationInfo).
NextWaveTime = NextWaveTime;
    }
```

Let's make the same alteration to the one at the bottom of the `EnemyKilled` function.

7. Let's make the same changes as in step 6 to the `StartWave` function.

8. Now we just need to add it to the bottom of `WaveCountdown`:

```
function WaveCountdown()
{
    NextWaveTime--;

    if(NextWaveTime <= 0)
    {
        ClearTimer('WaveCountdown');
        bSpawnBoss = false;
        ActivateSpawners();
    }
    else
        Broadcast(self, NextWaveTime);

    if(AwesomeGameReplicationInfo(GameReplicationInfo) != none)
        AwesomeGameReplicationInfo(GameReplicationInfo).
NextWaveTime = NextWaveTime;
}
```

9. Now for `bSpawnBoss`. The first place we'll set it is in the `SpawnBoss` function:

```
function SpawnBoss()
{
    bSpawnBoss = true;
    if(AwesomeGameReplicationInfo(GameReplicationInfo) != none)
        AwesomeGameReplicationInfo(GameReplicationInfo).bSpawnBoss
= bSpawnBoss;
    ActivateSpawners();
}
```

10. Next, we'll alter the `if` statement in WaveCountdown to set it back to `false`:

```
if(AwesomeGameReplicationInfo(GameReplicationInfo) != none)
{
    AwesomeGameReplicationInfo(GameReplicationInfo).NextWaveTime =
NextWaveTime;
    AwesomeGameReplicationInfo(GameReplicationInfo).bSpawnBoss =
bSpawnBoss;
}
```

11. Now for `TheBoss`. We only need to change this at the bottom of the `ActivateSpawners` function:

```
if(bSpawnBoss)
{
    TheBoss = InRangeSpawners[Rand(InRangeSpawners.length)].
SpawnBoss();
    if(AwesomeGameReplicationInfo(GameReplicationInfo) !=
none)
        AwesomeGameReplicationInfo(GameReplicationInfo).
TheBoss = TheBoss;
}
else
{
    InRangeSpawners[Rand(InRangeSpawners.length)].
SpawnEnemy();
    SetTimer(1.0 + FRand() * 3.0, false, 'ActivateSpawners');
}
```

12. To get the boss's health displaying correctly, we'll need to make sure that variable gets replicated. Add that to `AwesomeEnemy`'s replication block:

```
replication
{
    if(bNetDirty)
        Enemy, bAttacking, Health;
}
```

13. Now that we have it out of the way, we need to change the `AwesomeHUD` class to get the variables from the `AwesomeGameReplicationInfo` instead of the `GameInfo`. Let's rewrite that section of `AwesomeHUD`'s `DrawHUD` function:

```
if(AwesomeGameReplicationInfo(WorldInfo.GRI) != none)
{
    Canvas.SetPos(Canvas.ClipX * 0.1, Canvas.ClipY * 0.95);
    if(!AwesomeGameReplicationInfo(WorldInfo.GRI).bSpawnBoss
&& AwesomeGameReplicationInfo(WorldInfo.GRI).NextWaveTime == 0)
        Canvas.DrawText("Enemies Left:" @ AwesomeGameReplicati
onInfo(WorldInfo.GRI).EnemiesLeft);
    else if(AwesomeGameReplicationInfo(WorldInfo.GRI).TheBoss
!= none)
    {
        Canvas.DrawText("Boss Health:" @ AwesomeGameReplicatio
nInfo(WorldInfo.GRI).TheBoss.Health);
        if(AwesomeGameReplicationInfo(WorldInfo.GRI).TheBoss.
Health <= 10)
        {
```

```
                              Canvas.SetPos(Canvas.ClipX * 0.4, Canvas.ClipY *
            0.7);

                              Canvas.DrawText("BOSS SUPER RAGE MODE");
                      }
                }
          }
```

14. Now let's compile and test the game. Alright, looks like the HUD's working again!

What just happened?

The GameReplicationInfo class is helpful when you need clients to know certain information that the GameInfo has control of, since the GameInfo only exists on the server. There's a lot of information that's irrelevant to the player. They don't need the array of enemy spawners or the min and max spawner distances, they only care about when an enemy is spawned, and that's taken care of by the enemy itself through its replication properties.

There is a similar Info class that players have access to, so they know relevant information about other players such as their team numbers, names, and scores called the PlayerReplicationInfo. An array of PlayerReplicationInfo actors can be accessed through the GameReplicationInfo in the PRIArray variable. For our own player, we would access it through the PlayerController's PlayerReplicationInfo variable.

Fixing enemy fleeing

Our game is almost working again, but one thing still seems to be broken: The enemy Fleeing state. Let's see if we can figure out what's going wrong and fix it.

Time for action – RUN AWAY!

The first thing we need to do is figure out if the enemies are running away at all. Is what we're seeing happening on both the server AND the client?

1. Let's change the RunAway function of AwesomeEnemy_Minion:

```
simulated function RunAway()
{
    `log("Run away!");
    GoToState('Fleeing');
}
```

This will let us know if this function is getting called.

2. Let's also change the `AwesomeEnemy` class's `Fleeing` state:

```
simulated function BeginState(Name PreviousStateName)
{
    `log("Begin fleeing state!");
    MyMesh.SetMaterial(0, FleeingMat);
}
```

3. We should have our bases covered for debugging this, so let's see what happens. Compile the code and run it. Looks like we're getting the logs, but only on the server:

```
[0050.61] ScriptLog: Run away!
[0050.61] ScriptLog: Begin fleeing state!
```

4. So the client is never receiving the `RunAway` function call, even though we changed it to simulated. The reason for this is that the `RunAway` function call is coming from the enemy spawner, which we haven't made relevant to the client. Since the spawner doesn't exist on the client, none of its functions are being called, including function calls to other classes. We don't want to make the enemy spawners relevant to the client since it's not really necessary, so instead let's change the way our fleeing state works. First let's add a Boolean to the top of `AwesomeEnemy`:

```
var bool bFleeing;
```

5. Let's also add it to our replication block so we can let the client know when it has changed:

```
replication
{
    if(bNetDirty)
        Enemy, bAttacking, Health, bFleeing;
}
```

6. Now in our subclass `AwesomeEnemy_Minion`, let's change the `RunAway` function:

```
simulated function RunAway()
{
    `log("Run away!");
    bFleeing = true;
}
```

7. Now we need to use this variable to enter the `Fleeing` state. We can do this in the `Tick` functions of the other two states. First the `Seeking` state:

```
simulated function Tick(float DeltaTime)
{
    local vector NewLocation;

    if(bAttacking)
        return;

    if(bFleeing)
    {
        GoToState('Fleeing');
        return;
    }

    if(Enemy == none)
        GetEnemy();

    if(Enemy != none)
    {
        NewLocation = Location;
        NewLocation += normal(Enemy.Location - Location) *
MovementSpeed * DeltaTime;
        SetLocation(NewLocation);

        if(VSize(NewLocation - Enemy.Location) <
AttackDistance)
            GoToState('Attacking');
    }
}
```

8. Now for the `Attacking` state:

```
simulated function Tick(float DeltaTime)
{
    if(bFleeing)
    {
        GoToState('Fleeing');
        return;
    }

    bAttacking = true;
```

```
    if(Enemy == none)
        GetEnemy();

    if(Enemy != none)
    {
        Enemy.Bump(self, CollisionComponent, vect(0,0,0));

        if(VSize(Location - Enemy.Location) > AttackDistance)
            GoToState('Seeking');
    }
}
```

9. Compile the code and test. They're fleeing now!

What just happened?

We'll notice something interesting when we check the logs now. This is what we'll see on the server:

```
[0049.25] ScriptLog: Run away!
[0049.27] ScriptLog: Begin fleeing state!
```

And this is what we'll see on the client:

```
[0041.00] ScriptLog: Begin fleeing state!
```

Even though the client never receives the RunAway function call, using the variable and making sure it's replicated makes sure that the client enters the Fleeing state anyway. Rewriting the classes to get the RunAway function called would have been more than necessary.

Now, just one more thing! Our boss needs a bit of work to get him fully functional, and then we're done!

Time for action – Bossing around

Alright, let's get this going! We'll be working in AwesomeBoss.uc for this.

1. The first thing we'll need to do is make sure the states are working properly, so make sure we have the simulated keyword on all of the functions in the Seeking and StageTwo states.

2. The Attack functions in those two states both call EndAttack, but if we look in AwesomeEnemy that function isn't simulated. Let's add the simulated keyword to it.

3. As it is now, the boss won't enter the `StageTwo` state on the client because the call to do that is in the `TakeDamage` function, which isn't simulated. We don't want the client running that function since it's the server's job to keep track of that, so instead let's add a variable we can use in a similar way to what we did with the minions to get them to flee. Add this variable to `AwesomeBoss`:

```
var bool bStageTwo;
```

4. Now let's add that to a replication block for `AwesomeBoss`:

```
replication
{
    if(bNetDirty)
        bStageTwo;
}
```

5. Now let's alter the `TakeDamage` function. Change this:

```
if(Health == 10)
    GoToState('StageTwo');
```

to this:

```
if(Health == 10)
    bStageTwo = true;
```

6. Now we'll use that variable to change states. Let's add this to the bottom of the `Seeking` state's `Tick` function:

```
if(bStageTwo && GetStateName() != 'StageTwo')
    GoToState('StageTwo');
```

Normally, we'd only need the variable check, but since `StageTwo` extends off of the `Seeking` state we don't want the actor getting caught in an infinite loop of entering the `StageTwo` state every `Tick`.

7. Compile and test. Now the boss is working properly!

What just happened?

Now we're starting to see the relationship between the server and the client a bit better. Certain things the client needs to know about, such as our boss's health for our HUD or the color changes of the enemies. Some things the client isn't concerned with, such as the enemy spawners. Stuff like that is taken care of by the server, with the end result of the enemy being replicated to the client.

Now that we've played around with replication in our game, let's take a look at how we can use functions to communicate between the server and the client.

Replicating function calls

We've been using variables and functions a bit with our replication experiments, but we haven't quite talked about how to use functions to their fullest extent with replication. First up we're going to talk about the function modifiers we can use and how they affect when and where the functions are called.

Replication function modifiers

We talked briefly about these back in *Chapter 5*, *insert Using Functions*, and now it's time to take a closer look. These function modifiers only apply when we're working in an online environment; if we were making a single-player game these wouldn't matter.

Reliable versus Unreliable

The meaning of these is pretty self explanatory. Functions designated as reliable will always be sent across the network. Even if bandwidth is saturated these function calls will eventually be replicated. On the other hand, unreliable function calls aren't guaranteed to make it to their destination. In a lot of cases we're not worried about this as the function calls serve no gameplay purpose, for example `ReceiveBotVoiceMessage` or the `ClientPlaySound` function. In other cases they're sent so often that we're not worried about them getting lost, rather we're worried that by making them reliable they will saturate the server's bandwidth and it will encounter severe lag. These can be seen in functions like `ServerMove`, which contains information about movement the client is trying to send to the server, and `ClientAdjustPosition` where the server is trying to send information to the client.

Overall, you want to keep the number of reliable function calls to a minimum unless they're absolutely necessary to gameplay. However, in this chapter we'll be using reliable functions so we can be sure our experiments work.

Client functions

When the server needs to call a function on a client, it will do it through a client function. Client functions are ONLY run on the clients, never on the server. As an example, in `PlayerController` there is a function called `GivePawn`, which is declared as a client function, and has a Pawn as a parameter. On the server, when a client requests a Pawn (on game start, or when going from spectator to player for example), the server will spawn the Pawn at a `PlayerStart` it chooses, and then set any initial information it needs to. It then calls the client function `GivePawn` to tell the client "here is your Pawn". The client will then do what it needs to do with it, such as setting its view to that Pawn.

We're going to run some experiments using our own `AwesomeActor` on a new map to see for ourselves how this type of function replication works.

Time for action – Setting up for the client function

The first thing we need to do is create a new map we can test with. The one we have is fine enough, but we need to change it a bit.

1. Open `AwesomeTestMap` in the editor.

2. Delete the entire Kismet.

3. Optionally, delete all of the `AwesomeEnemySpawners`, `TargetPoints`, and other actors on the map. Be sure to leave the player start, the ground, and the lights.

4. Save the map as `AwesomeReplicationMap.udk` and close the editor.

5. Now we can start programming. Open `AwesomePawn.uc` in ConTEXT.

6. We'll be using a Toggle Kismet action on our `AwesomePawn`, so we need to add the `OnToggle` function. For this experiment we don't need to worry about which input is being activated. For now, let's just put a log in the function:

```
function OnToggle(SeqAct_Toggle InAction)
{
    `log("I have been toggled!");
}
```

7. Compile the code and open `AwesomeReplicationMap` in the editor.

8. Add a trigger near the player start.

9. Double-click on the **Trigger** to open up its properties, and uncheck **Display | Hidden**.

10. With the **Trigger** still selected, open up the Kismet editor. Right-click and hit **New Event Using Trigger_0 | Touch**.

11. In the **Touch** event's properties, set **Sequence Event | Max Trigger Count to 0**.

12. Next to the **Touch** event, add a **New Action | Toggle | Toggle**.

13. Right-click below the event and action and click on **New Variable | Object | Object**. It will have question marks to indicate it's blank.

14. Connect the **Touched** output of the **Touch** event to any input on the **Toggle** action.

15. Connect the **Instigator** variable link on the **Touch** event to the blank variable. When the **Trigger** is touched, it will set the blank variable to the instigator, which in our case will be our **AwesomePawn**.

16. Now connect the **Target** variable link of the **Toggle** action to the blank variable.

The Kismet sequence should now look like this:

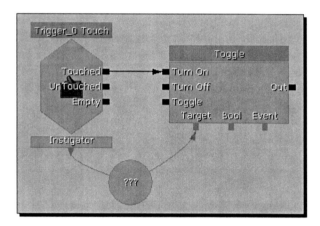

17. Save the map and close the editor.

18. Now we need to rewrite our server batch file a bit. Change the Awesome Test Server.bat file to reference the new map:

```
C:\UDK\UDK-AwesomeGame\Binaries\Win32\UDK.exe server AwesomeReplic
ationMap?GoalScore=0?TimeLimit=0?Game=AwesomeGame.AwesomeGame -log
```

19. The client batch file doesn't need to be changed, so it's fine.

20. Double-click to start up the server, and then start the client.

21. Walk over and hit the trigger and we'll see our log show up on the server:

```
[0013.86] ScriptLog: I have been toggled!
```

22. We'll see that this log does not show up on the client.

What just happened?

Now we have a setup that you might encounter when making your own game. The server would like to pass some information to the client from a function that's only running on the server. Now we can use a client function to do this.

One important thing to know about client functions is that they only work when a client owns the actor where they're being called. We can figure out who owns an actor through its `Owner` variable. Some things like the `PlayerController`, Pawn, and weapons are owned by the client who's using them. Most actors are not owned by any client, such as objects placed in the level. As an example, if we tried using a client function on our `AwesomeEnemySpawner` it wouldn't work, as no client owns those actors. They're running on the server and are not even relevant to the clients.

Time for action – Using the client function

Now we're ready to write the client function and call it from the server.

1. Make sure that the game and the server are shut down.

2. Open `AwesomePawn` in ConTEXT.

3. We're going to write our client function now:

    ```
    reliable client function CallTheClient()
    {
        `log("Reliable client function called!");
    }
    ```

    One thing to note is that these modifiers go together; you can't have a client function without specifying whether it's reliable or unreliable. If you try, the compiler will give you an error.

4. Now that we have that function written, we need to call it from our `OnToggle` function:

    ```
    function OnToggle(SeqAct_Toggle InAction)
    {
        `log("I have been toggled!");
        CallTheClient();
    }
    ```

5. Now let's see what happens. Compile the code, then run the server and the game. Run over to the trigger.

6. We'll see this log show up on the server:

    ```
    [0015.35] ScriptLog: I have been toggled!
    ```

7. And we'll see this log show up on the client:

```
[0009.81] ScriptLog: Reliable client function called!
```

We'll notice that the client function was not called on the server.

8. We can also pass parameters to the client inside client functions. Let's rewrite our `Toggle` function a bit:

```
function OnToggle(SeqAct_Toggle InAction)
{
    `log("I have been toggled!");
    CallTheClient(4.0);
}
```

9. And the `CallTheClient` function:

```
reliable client function CallTheClient(float MyFloat)
{
    `log("Reliable client function called:" @ MyFloat);
}
```

10. Compile the code and run the server and game. We'll see the parameter show up in the client's log:

```
[0012.21] ScriptLog: Reliable client function called: 4.0000
```

What just happened?

This is of course different than the modifications we made to our own game to get it to work on the server. We'll talk about simulated functions in a bit, but first we need to figure out how to send function calls in the other direction using server functions.

Server functions

Just like client functions, server functions are used to send function calls across the network. The difference is that server functions are called from the client when it needs to send a call to the server. As an example, when you press the Use key it calls an exec function, which is only executed on the client. Since the server controls the game state, we need to send that function call across the network so the server can figure out what if anything will change because of that. Let's take a look.

Time for action – Using a server function

With the `Use` functionality we already have a function we can test this with, so let's try it out. Since exec functions aren't called on `Pawn` classes, we'll need to use `AwesomePlayerController`.

1. Open `AwesomePlayerController` in ConTEXT.

2. First let's write the `Use` function:

```
exec function Use()
{
    `log("I have been used!");
}
```

3. Compile the code, and then run the server and the client.

4. Press the Use key (default: *E*). We should see the log show up on the client:

```
[0011.44] ScriptLog: I have been used!
```

5. Close the client and the server.

6. Now that we can see the `Use` function is only called on the client, let's send a function call to the server. Let's change our `Use` function a bit:

```
exec function Use()
{
    `log("I have been used!");
    CallTheServer();
}
```

7. Now let's write our server function:

```
reliable server function CallTheServer()
{
    `log("Reliable server function called!");
}
```

8. Compile the code and run the server and the client.

9. Press the Use key and we should see the logs. On the client we get the same one, and now on the server we see this:

```
[0014.17] ScriptLog: Reliable server function called!
```

10. And as with client functions, we can also use these to send information to the server. For example, if we were making a class-based multiplayer game, we might want to send our desired class as an `int` to the server. Let's send an `int` now. We'll start by changing our `Use` function:

```
exec function Use()
{
    `log("I have been used!");
    CallTheServer(3);
}
```

11. Now we'll change our `CallTheServer` function:

```
reliable server function CallTheServer(int MyInt)
{
    `log("Reliable server function called:" @ MyInt);
}
```

12. Compile the code.

13. Run the server and the client. Press the Use key and now we should see this on the server:

```
[0014.43] ScriptLog: Reliable server function called: 3
```

What just happened?

Client and server functions aren't used all of the time. Most of the information that needs to be passed between them doesn't apply to just one client. For example, when a vehicle in the map spawns, the server would need to let everyone know. But if you wanted to enter that vehicle, a server function would be sent to let the server know, and if the server's game logic said that you could enter it, the server would send a client function back to you so your client could run any code it needed to for that (changing camera view, changing control from your Pawn to the vehicle, and so on).

Next we're going to take a look at the final function modifier that applies for replication.

Simulated functions

Let's face it, the server can't do everything. We don't have fiber optic connections of bridge cables' size, so the server isn't going to be able to send us the exact state of the game every tick. The client is going to have to do some of the work itself. To do this, we use simulated functions. Since the client and the server have the exact same code in their files, it stands to reason that the client could do a pretty good job of predicting what's going on on the server. Simulated functions are what let the client predict what's going on on the server. Let's take a look.

Time for action – Setting up the map

We're going to use our old friend `AwesomeWeaponUpgrade` to help us here. First we need to set up a little Kismet.

1. Open `AwesomeReplicationMap` in the editor.

2. In the Kismet editor, delete the `Toggle` action and the blank object variable linked to it.

3. Next to the Trigger's `Touch` event, right-click and click on **New Action | Actor | Actor Factory**.

4. In the **Actor Factory** action's properties, click on the blue down arrow at the end of **Seq Act Actor Factory | Factory** and select **ActorFactoryActor**.

5. In the **Actor Class** property that appears, select **AwesomeWeaponUpgrade**.

6. In the level, select the player start.

7. Right-click in the Kismet editor and click on **New Object Var Using PlayerStart_0**.

8. Connect the **Touched** output of the `Touch` event to the Spawn Actor input of the **Actor Factory** action.

9. Connect the **Spawn Point** variable link of the **Actor Factory** action to the Player Start object variable. The Kismet should now look like this:

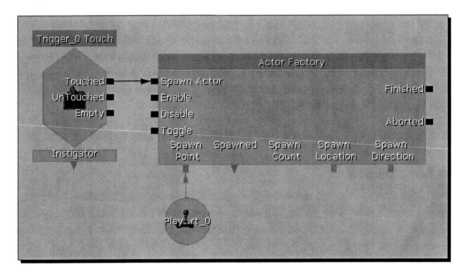

10. Save and close the editor.

What just happened?

Now we're set up for some coding. We're going to spawn an `AwesomeWeaponUpgrade` while the game is running so we can see what happens when we experiment with the `simulated` function modifier.

Time for action – Using simulated functions

We'll be using `PostBeginPlay` for this, which is why we're spawning the `AwesomeWeaponUpgrade` with Kismet instead of just placing one directly in the editor. `PostBeginPlay` is called when an actor is first created, but our client won't connect to the server until that's already happened. This is an important thing to note when dealing with replication for editor-placed actors.

1. Open `AwesomeWeaponUpgrade` in ConTEXT.

2. To start, we're going to write a non-simulated version of `PostBeginPlay`.

   ```
   function PostBeginPlay()
   {
       `log("PostBeginPlay====================");
   }
   ```

   We'll add some equal signs to the end of our log to make it easier to spot.

3. Compile the code.

4. Run the server and the client, and then run over to the trigger. We'll see the log show up on the server:

   ```
   [0013.84] ScriptLog: PostBeginPlay====================
   ```

   We won't see this on the client.

5. Now let's see what happens when we add the `simulated` function modifier:

   ```
   simulated function PostBeginPlay()
   {
       `log("PostBeginPlay====================");
   }
   ```

6. Compile the code.

7. Run the server and the client again, and then run over to the trigger. This time we'll see the log show up on the client as well:

   ```
   [0017.31] ScriptLog: PostBeginPlay====================
   ```

What just happened?

In a network environment, only exec functions, client functions, and simulated functions are called on the client. If a function doesn't have any of those modifiers, it will only run on the server. Additionally, for a simulated function to be called on the client, it must either be called from another simulated function or from native C++ code. We'll know it's one of those if it uses the word "event" instead of "function" in its initial declaration. As an example, PostBeginPlay is initially declared in Actor.uc like this:

```
event PostBeginPlay();
```

It's called from native code right after gameplay begins.

For our next experiment we're going to see this for ourselves.

Time for action – COMBO BREAKER!

We're going to chain a few events together and see what happens on the server and on the client. We'll start with PostBeginPlay.

1. Let's add a line to our PostBeginPlay function:

```
simulated function PostBeginPlay()
{
    `log("PostBeginPlay====================");
    NumberOne();
}
```

2. Now let's write the NumberOne function. We'll use the simulated modifier on it and have it call the next function in the chain:

```
simulated function NumberOne()
{
    `log("NumberOne========================");
    NumberTwo();
}
```

3. Now for NumberTwo, we'll leave out the simulated modifier:

```
function NumberTwo()
{
    `log("NumberTwo========================");
    NumberThree();
}
```

4. And finally, that non-simulated function will call a simulated `NumberThree`:

```
simulated function NumberThree()
{
    `log("NumberThree=======================");
}
```

5. Compile the code.

6. Now, before we run it, what is your guess as to what will show on the client and what will show on the server? We know that simulated functions will only run on the client if they're called from other simulated functions, and that non-simulated functions won't run on the client at all. Let's see if you're right.

7. Run the server and the client.

8. Hit the trigger and take a look at the logs. On the server we'll see this:

```
[0015.22] ScriptLog: PostBeginPlay====================
[0015.22] ScriptLog: NumberOne=======================
[0015.22] ScriptLog: NumberTwo=======================
[0015.22] ScriptLog: NumberThree=====================
```

That's what we were expecting; knowing that all but client functions will run on the server.

9. Now take a look at the client log:

```
[0009.92] ScriptLog: PostBeginPlay====================
[0009.92] ScriptLog: NumberOne=======================
```

What just happened?

It looks like our combo breaker was after `NumberOne` was called. We didn't expect `NumberTwo` to get called since it wasn't simulated, and knowing that simulated functions only run on the client when called from other simulated functions, it makes sense that `NumberThree` wouldn't get called since it was called from the non-simulated `NumberTwo`.

The use of simulated functions is a bit tricky. We want the client to stay as much in sync with the server as possible, and using simulated functions helps us to do that. Running a function on both the server and the client saves bandwidth that would have had to have been used sending client functions or variables.

We don't want all functions to be simulated though. The client doesn't have access to all of the actors in the level all of the time, so there are a lot of functions it just wouldn't be able to run. Looking at our own game, we never changed the functionality of the enemy spawners, and indeed they don't exist on the client (you can put a log in a simulated `PostBeginPlay` to test that if you'd like). Any functions that deal with them wouldn't work on the client, so we wouldn't make them simulated.

Even when running simulated functions, there may be parts of them that we don't want to run on the client, or parts that we don't want the server to execute. Next up we're going to take a look at roles and their effect on actors.

Role and authority

We know that non-simulated functions don't run on clients. But when we're in a simulated function, how do we tell the server and the client apart? For that matter, how do we know we're running the game in a network environment at all? There are a few variables we can use to help us out. The first, and most important, are Role and RemoteRole.

Role and RemoteRole

These two variables are declared in Actor as an enum and tell the game how the server and client should treat this actor. Let's take a look at the list:

```
enum ENetRole
{
    ROLE_None,                // No role at all.
    ROLE_SimulatedProxy,      // Locally simulated proxy of this actor.
    ROLE_AutonomousProxy,     // Locally autonomous proxy of this actor.
    ROLE_Authority,           // Authoritative control over the actor.
};
var ENetRole RemoteRole, Role;
```

By default, Role will always be ROLE_Authority on the server. This makes sense, since the server needs to have the last word on the state of all actors in the game. While writing actors, RemoteRole tells us how we want the client to treat them:

- ROLE_None: This actor has no role on the clients and is never replicated to them. The GameInfo class is an example of this, as it only exists on the server. In our own game, the AwesomeEnemySpawner had a RemoteRole of ROLE_None, since all of its logic was handled by the server.

- ROLE_SimulatedProxy: Almost all replicated actors use this role. Projectiles, Vehicles, anything that the client will need to predict physics and other behavior on.

- ROLE_AutonomousProxy: Used only in two places, for the client's own Pawn and DemoRecSpectators. Actors with this role behave similarly to ROLE_SimulatedProxy, except that they're not limited to simulated functions and states.

- ROLE_Authority: Not used for RemoteRole. ROLE_Authority means the actor is running on the server or in a single player environment.

And you probably saw this coming, so let's take a look for ourselves!

Time for action – Examining Role and RemoteRole

We'll use `AwesomeWeaponUpgrade` for this.

1. Let's delete the combo breaker functions, but leave `PostBeginPlay`.

2. Let's rewrite `PostBeginPlay` a bit so we can take a look at `Role` and `RemoteRole`:

```
simulated function PostBeginPlay()
{
    `log("PostBeginPlay===================");
    `log("Role =" @ Role);
    `log("RemoteRole =" @ RemoteRole);
}
```

3. Compile the code.

4. Run the server and the client, and then run over to the trigger to spawn the `AwesomeWeaponUpgrade`.

5. Let's take a look at what we see on the server:

```
[0020.03] ScriptLog: PostBeginPlay====================
[0020.03] ScriptLog: Role = ROLE_Authority
[0020.03] ScriptLog: RemoteRole = ROLE_SimulatedProxy
```

This is what we'd expect.

6. Now let's take a look at the client:

```
[0011.66] ScriptLog: PostBeginPlay====================
[0011.66] ScriptLog: Role = ROLE_SimulatedProxy
[0011.66] ScriptLog: RemoteRole = ROLE_Authority
```

What's going on there?

What just happened?

If you think about it, it makes sense that the variables are switched on the client. As a client, code running on us wouldn't have a `Role` of `ROLE_Authority`, and the `RemoteRole` wouldn't be `ROLE_SimulatedProxy`, they'd be the opposite of what they are on the server.

Knowing this, we now have a way to differentiate them while running functions!

Time for action – Respect my authority!

Once again, back to `AwesomeWeaponUpgrade`.

1. Let's change the `PostBeginPlay` function a bit:

```
simulated function PostBeginPlay()
{
    `log("PostBeginPlay====================");

    if(Role == ROLE_Authority)
        `log("I am running on the server!");
    else
        `log("I am running on the client!");
}
```

2. Compile the code.

3. Run the server and the client. Now let's take a look at what happens.

4. Run to the trigger, then take a look at the server's log:

```
[0014.57] ScriptLog: PostBeginPlay====================
[0014.57] ScriptLog: I am running on the server!
```

5. Now let's take a look at the client:

```
[0010.53] ScriptLog: PostBeginPlay====================
[0010.53] ScriptLog: I am running on the client!
```

What just happened?

This is useful when we want both the client and the server to run a function, but we want them to have different responses to that function. As an example, since particle effects don't need to be spawned on the server since they'd just waste processing power, we'd check `Role` and only spawn them on clients. We might also have some gameplay-related code that we only want the server to run, so we would differentiate it the same way.

Knowing that enums can be treated as ints in `if` statements, we can also find out if we're not running on a server by checking:

```
if(Role < ROLE_Authority)
```

Sometimes, we need to know if the game is being run in a network environment, but using Role to do this wouldn't help because it would still be `ROLE_Authority` offline. For this, we would use a different variable.

NetMode

The other variable that we can use to check our network environment is called NetMode. It's declared in the WorldInfo class:

```
var enum ENetMode
{
    NM_Standalone,          // Standalone game.
    NM_DedicatedServer,     // Dedicated server, no local client.
    NM_ListenServer,        // Listen server.
    NM_Client               // Client only, no local server.
} NetMode;
```

Let's see what each one means:

- NM_Standalone: A non-server game. All of the previous chapters of this book ran the game this way.

- NM_DedicatedServer: Running on a server where clients connect to it separately.

- NM_ListenServer: The local client is also acting as the server for other clients. Think "Host Game" where other players connect to you, instead of everyone connecting to a remote machine.

- NM_Client: Running as a client connected to a server.

Time to test!

Time for action – Checking the level's NetMode.

Let's change our AwesomeWeaponUpgrade actor to check for our level's NetMode.

1. Let's rewrite the PostBeginPlay function:

    ```
    simulated function PostBeginPlay()
    {
        `log("PostBeginPlay====================");
        `log("NetMode:" @ WorldInfo.NetMode);
    }
    ```

2. Compile the code.

3. Now run the server and client. Let's see what shows up in the server's log:

    ```
    [0019.97] ScriptLog: PostBeginPlay====================
    [0019.97] ScriptLog: NetMode: NM_DedicatedServer
    ```

4. And now for the client:

```
[0013.26] ScriptLog: PostBeginPlay=====================
[0013.26] ScriptLog: NetMode: NM_Client
```

What just happened?

So why don't we just use `NetMode` instead of `Role` and `RemoteRole`? As a server, `NetMode` can either be `NM_DedicatedServer` or `NM_ListenServer`, but `Role` will always be `ROLE_Authority`.

So when WOULD we use this? In the discussion of Role, one example we used was not spawning effects on the server. However, with `NM_ListenServer` we WOULD want the effect to spawn, since the server is also a local client.

Next up we're going to discuss our last topic, replication of variables.

Replicating variables

Variable replication is probably the most important part of working in a network environment. From variables like an actor's `Location` and `Rotation` to the amount of ammo a weapon has, the server has a lot of variables to keep track of and keep the clients in sync with. Unlike functions, variables are always reliable and will always reach the clients regardless of bandwidth saturation or packet loss. It may just take a bit of time, as replicated function calls take priority.

When dealing with replication, it's important to realize that all types of variables can be replicated EXCEPT dynamic arrays. Static arrays work just fine, but if you need to replicate a dynamic array the only way you'll be able to do that is by passing the individual elements of the array through a replicated function one at a time, which can get messy. If possible it's best to avoid having dynamic arrays that the client needs to know about. For our game, if we wanted to replicate the GameInfo's array of enemy spawners to a client's `PlayerController`, for example, it would take some work to do that.

First up we're going to talk about the place where we determine what variables get replicated and when, the replication block.

The replication block

We've used this a bit while we were fixing our game to work online, so we know what it looks like at least. Let's take a closer look.

Time for action – Replicating a variable

Let's keep working with `AwesomeWeaponUpgrade`, and add in some variable replication.

1. First let's add a new variable to the class:

```
var int TestInt;
```

2. Now let's write the replication block. We've already discussed `bNetDirty`, which we'll be using here. If any replicated property is changed, `bNetDirty` will be set to true. We need to let the game know that our variable needs to be replicated in that case.

```
replication
{
    if(bNetDirty)
        TestInt;
}
```

3. Now for `PostBeginPlay`. We'll leave it as simulated, but we'll call different functions for the client and the server.

```
simulated function PostBeginPlay()
{
    if(Role == ROLE_Authority)
        SetTimer(1.0, true, 'ServerTest');
    else
        SetTimer(1.0, true, 'ClientTest');
}
```

4. Now for `ServerTest`:

```
function ServerTest()
{
    TestInt++;
    `log("ServerTest:" @ TestInt);
}
```

5. And `ClientTest`:

```
simulated function ClientTest()
{
    `log("ClientTest:" @ TestInt);
}
```

6. Now compile the code.

7. `ServerTest` will only be called on the server, and will increment the variable and log the new value. On the client, we use `ClientTest` to log the value so we can see if it gets replicated properly. Let's take a look.

8. Run the server and the client, and hit the trigger. Now let's take a look at the server's log:

```
[0017.29] ScriptLog: ServerTest: 1
[0018.26] ScriptLog: ServerTest: 2
[0019.19] ScriptLog: ServerTest: 3
[0020.16] ScriptLog: ServerTest: 4
```

9. Ok, looking good there. Now let's take a look at the client:

```
[0011.37] ScriptLog: ClientTest: 1
[0012.33] ScriptLog: ClientTest: 2
[0013.28] ScriptLog: ClientTest: 3
[0014.23] ScriptLog: ClientTest: 4
```

What just happened?

And there we go! Variable replication is a lot easier to deal with than functions. If you keep an eye on the log for a bit you might notice the numbers don't match up every once in awhile. This is mostly due to the fact that the timers we start aren't running perfectly in synch, so the server may change and replicate the variable after the client has already logged the old value again. In reality it wouldn't take that long for the variable to replicate. If you wanted, you could keep track of the changes using `Tick` instead, to get a more real-time view of it.

That's pretty much all there is to variable replication, but there are some conditional variables we need to take a look at that we can use to specify when and where variables get replicated.

Replication variables

Let's take a look at some of the variables that affect how replication is handled.

- `NetPriority`: Giving this a higher value will make sure that this actor gets higher priority than others when figuring out what to replicate. Note that this is relative to other actors' `NetPriority` values, so giving it a value of one billion won't make it replicate any faster.

- `bNetDirty`: As discussed, this gets set to true whenever any replicated variable's value changes.

- ◆ bNetInitial: True until the initial replication of all values has been completed.

- ◆ bNetOwner: This is true if the local client's PlayerController owns this actor.

- ◆ bAlwaysRelevant: If this is set to true, this actor is always relevant to all clients on the network. This shouldn't be overused, as you don't necessarily want actors that the client can't even see to have their properties updated all the time.

- ◆ bReplicateInstigator: If this actor has an Instigator (Pawn responsible for damage caused by this actor), replicate that to clients.

- ◆ bReplicateMovement: Replicate location and movement variables (like velocity).

- ◆ bSkipActorPropertyReplication: Don't replicate properties for this actor.

- ◆ NetUpdateFrequency: How often to consider this actor for replication. Use lower values for low priority actors.

Some of these are set in the default properties of the actor; some are set at run time and can be used to control replication conditions. If we take a look at Actor.uc's replication block we can see a lot of examples of the usage of these variables. For instance, the Instigator:

```
    if ( (!bSkipActorPropertyReplication || bNetInitial) &&
(Role==ROLE_Authority)
                && bNetDirty && bReplicateInstigator )
        Instigator;
```

Reading it, this tells us that if we're not skipping property replication or we're still initializing, and we're the server, and a replicated property has changed, and we want to replicate the instigator, then replicate the Instigator variable. These replication statements can seem confusing at first, but examining what each variable does and taking a look at other examples in the source code will give you an understanding of when they should be used.

Lastly we're going to take a look at ReplicatedEvent, which tells us when a property has been replicated so we can execute any specific code we need to when that happens.

ReplicatedEvent

There is one last variable modifier that we haven't discussed, repnotify. Using this on a variable causes ReplicatedEvent to be called on the actor when that variable is replicated. Let's take a look at how we can use it.

Time for action – Using ReplicatedEvent

We need to make some changes to AwesomeWeaponUpgrade for this to work.

1. Delete ClientTest, but we're still going to use ServerTest so leave that for now.

2. Let's rewrite the PostBeginPlay function:

```
simulated function PostBeginPlay()
{
    if(Role == ROLE_Authority)
        SetTimer(3.0, false, 'ServerTest');
}
```

This time we're using a non-repeating timer with a longer delay.

3. ServerTest doesn't need to be changed for this, so let's leave it as it is.

4. Now we need to let the game know that we want ReplicatedEvent called when TestInt is replicated, so let's put the variable modifier in:

```
var repnotify int TestInt;
```

5. Now let's write the ReplicatedEvent function:

```
simulated event ReplicatedEvent(name VarName)
{
    if(VarName == 'TestInt')
        `log("TestInt was replicated!");
}
```

6. Compile the code.

7. Run the server and the client, and hit the trigger.

8. Now let's take a look at what happened on the server:

```
[0016.42] ScriptLog: ServerTest: 1
```

We'll notice that ReplicatedEvent wasn't called here.

9. Now let's look at the client:

```
[0011.39] ScriptLog: TestInt was replicated!
```

What just happened?

Now, if there were any specific code we needed to run whenever this variable was replicated, we could do that. If, for example, that `int` were used as an index to an array of materials for an object, if that `int` changed we could use `ReplicatedEvent` to change the object's material in response.

Have a go hero – The Replication, The!

Take replication and throw it in a fire please.

Personally, I hate it. It is the most frustrating part of working with UnrealScript, but with enough practice and experience it gets easier to deal with. Just remember that if you're going to be working on a multiplayer project, you ABSOLUTELY MUST incorporate replication from the very beginning. If not you may end up rewriting vast sections of your code and even rearranging entire classes to get it to work. You will save yourself a lot of time and effort if you constantly test your code in a network environment to detect and fix replication issues early on. Getting in the mindset of thinking about the server and the client separately will help you make sure your game works properly online.

Pop quiz – Replication

1. What function modifier is used to let a client execute code inside that function?

    a. `replicated`

    b. `simulated`

    c. `server`

2. What two function modifiers are used to let the game know whether or not we care if the function call is ever replicated?

3. What variable modifier is used to call `ReplicatedEvent` whenever that variable is replicated?

Summary

We learned a lot in this chapter about replication and working with UnrealScript in a network environment.

Specifically, we covered:

◆ How to run the game with a server and a client on a single machine

◆ The differences in how the server and client interact with the game world

◆ Using function modifiers to change the way functions are called on the server and the client

◆ How to use `Role`, `RemoteRole`, and `Netmode` to differentiate the server from clients and network games from single-player games

◆ How to replicate variables and use `ReplicatedEvent`

Now that we've learned about replication, we're ready to start learning about some of the common pitfalls of UnrealScript, and how to fix compiler and log errors so our game runs smoothly.

9
Debugging and Optimization

PC Load Letter? What does that mean?

The problem with computers is that they're not psychics. They have no idea what you're trying to accomplish. With any programming language, my mantra has always been this: Computers will never do what you want them to do. They will do exactly what you tell them to do. A lot of the time what you're telling them to do isn't what you want them to do, which causes unexpected bugs, errors, even crashes. Knowing a programming language is one thing, but the most important skill in programming is having the critical thinking skills to figure out why a program is broken and being able to fix it. Most of the code you write will not work correctly the first time. Things will break. A lot!

In this chapter we will:

- Cover some of the most common errors that you'll encounter while compiling UnrealScript
- Take a look at some broken code to see if we can fix it
- Use the log to debug and further clean up our code
- Use the profiler to minimize performance hits from our code

So with that, let's break stuff!

Compiler errors

While getting used to any programming language, you will inevitably encounter a lot of errors trying to compile or run your code, most often from syntax errors. Write the code slightly wrong and nothing will work, even if it compiles. In this section, we'll take a look at some of the most common errors you'll encounter working with UnrealScript, what they mean, and how to fix them. Let's get started!

Time for action – Preparing for brokenness

Before we break anything, we need to set up a new map and a new script folder specifically for these experiments. We're not going to use AwesomeGame because we want to focus specifically on the errors we create, and we don't want any interference from other code:

1. Create a copy of `AwesomeTestMap.udk` in the `UDKGame\Content\Maps\AwesomeGame` folder and call it `BrokenMap.udk`.

2. Open `BrokenMap.udk` in the editor.

3. Delete all of the Kismet, plus all of the `AwesomeEnemySpawners` and other actors on the map apart from `PlayerStart`, the ground, and the lights.

4. Save and close the map.

What just happened?

Now we have the map set up for testing. Next we're going to create a new script folder specifically for these tests.

Time for action – A new script package

It's been awhile since we set up a script folder, so let's go through the steps again:

1. Create a new folder in the `Development\Src` folder called `BrokenGame`.

2. Create a folder inside `BrokenGame` called `Classes`.

3. In the `BrokenGame\Classes` folder, create a new file called `BrokenActor.uc`.

4. In `BrokenActor.uc`, write the following code:

    ```
    class BrokenActor extends Actor
        placeable;

    defaultproperties
    {
    ```

```
Begin Object Class=SpriteComponent Name=Sprite
    Sprite=Texture2D'EditorMaterials.TargetIcon'
    Scale=0.35
    HiddenGame=true
End Object
Components.Add(Sprite)
}
```

5. Before we can compile, we need to add our new package to `DefaultEngine.ini`. Open `UDKGame\Config\DefaultEngine.ini`, and at the end of the `[Engine.ScriptPackages]` section add our new package:

```
[Engine.ScriptPackages]
+NonNativePackages=UTGame
+NonNativePackages=UTGameContent
+NonNativePackages=AwesomeGame
+NonNativePackages=BrokenGame
```

6. Also at the end of the `[UnrealEd.EditorEngine]` section:

```
[UnrealEd.EditorEngine]
+EditPackages=UTGame
+EditPackages=UTGameContent
+EditPackages=AwesomeGame
+EditPackages=BrokenGame
```

7. Save and close `DefaultEngine.ini`.

8. Back in ConTEXT, compile our code.

9. Once it compiles successfully, open `BrokenMap` in the editor.

10. Select `BrokenActor` in the **Actor Classes** tab of the **Content Browser** (it will be in the **Uncategorized** section if you have **Show Categories** checked), and place one in the map near the player start.

11. Save the map, but don't close the editor yet.

12. Let's add a `PostBeginPlay` function to our class:

```
simulated function PostBeginPlay()
{
    `log("BrokenActor PostBeginPlay!");
}
```

13. Compile the code.

What just happened?

Wow that's ugly. Here we have our first compiler error, but luckily it's also the easiest to fix.

```
[0005.15] Log: Warning/Error Summary
[0005.15] Log: ---------------------
[0005.15] Log: Error, Error deleting file 'R:\UDK\UDK-AwesomeGame\
Binaries\Win32\..\..\UDKGame\Script\BrokenGame.u' (GetLastError:
32)
[0005.15] Log: Error, Error saving '..\..\UDKGame\Script\
BrokenGame.u'
[0005.15] Log: Warning, Failed to delete ..\..\UDKGame\Script\
BrokenGame.u
[0005.15] Log: Warning, DeleteFile was unable to delete 'R:\UDK\
UDK-AwesomeGame\Binaries\Win32\..\..\UDKGame\Script\BrokenGame.u',
retrying... (GetLastE-r-r-o-r: 32)
[0005.16] Log:
[0005.16] Log: Failure - 3 error(s), 3 warning(s)
```

A lot of references to being unable to delete `BrokenGame.u`. If you ever get an error like this, make sure the editor is closed and no instances of the game are running before you compile. With any of those running, `BrokenGame.u` will be in use and the compiler won't be able to delete the old `.u` file so it can replace it with the new one. With that in mind, close the editor and compile the code again.

```
[0004.11] Log: Success - 0 error(s), 0 warning(s)
```

Much better. It's a bit of a pain, but while you're working on your game you will have to close the editor before you compile. Luckily for us this is the scariest looking error to encounter while working with UnrealScript. Most of them will be simple and pretty self-explanatory.

Time for action – Breaking the class itself

Another common mistake is a class name mismatch. Let's take a look.

1. At the top of our class, let's change the class declaration:

```
class Borked extends Actor
    placeable;
```

2. Now try to compile the code. We'll get this in the log:

```
[0004.13] Log: R:\UDK\UDK-AwesomeGame\Binaries\..\Development\Src\
BrokenGame\Classes\BrokenActor.uc : Error, Script vs. class name
mismatch (BrokenActor/Borked)
```

What just happened?

The names of the classes in each file must match the file name. In our case, since the file is called `BrokenActor.uc`, the class must be declared as `BrokenActor`. Let's change it back:

```
class BrokenActor extends Actor
    placeable;
```

It's a minor error, but you may encounter it from time to time. It's easy to forget to rename a class if you've copied it from another of your projects, for example.

Another common error that breaks the class file itself is saving the text file in the wrong format. If you ever encounter an error such as this:

```
[0004.03] Log: R:\UDK\UDK-AwesomeGame\Development\Src\BrokenGame\
Classes\BrokenActor.uc(1) : Error, Unexpected 'ï'
```

The ï with the umlaut is part of the UTF-8 file encoding, so if you get an error like this make sure your `.uc` files are saved with ANSI encoding. You can double-check this by opening the file in Notepad and looking at the Encoding drop-down list in the **Save As** dialogue.

Now that we've broken the class, let's break some code!

Time for action – Breaking some more code

Let's take a look at two more common errors when working with UnrealScript. We'll add a bit more to our `BrokenActor`.

1. Let's change our `BrokenActor` to look like this:

```
class BrokenActor extends Actor
    placeable;

var int MyInt;

simulated function PostBeginPlay()
{
    if(MyInt > 5)
    {
        `log("MyInt is greater than 5!  MyInt is:" @ MyInt);
    }
    else
    {
        `log("MyInt is less than or equal to 5!  MyInt is:" @
MyInt);
    }
```

```
defaultproperties {
    MyInt=13

    Begin Object Class=SpriteComponent Name=Sprite
        Sprite=Texture2D'EditorMaterials.TargetIcon'
        Scale=0.35
        HiddenGame=true
    End Object
    Components.Add(Sprite)
}
```

2. Compile the code. We'll see this error pop up:

```
[0003.94] Log: R:\UDK\UDK-AwesomeGame\Development\Src\BrokenGame\
Classes\BrokenActor.uc(13) : Error, Unexpected end of file at end
of Class
```

3. Whenever this error shows up, it means we've missed a closing } bracket somewhere. In this case, we haven't properly ended our PostBeginPlay function with one, so let's add it:

```
simulated function PostBeginPlay()
{
    if(MyInt > 5)
    {
        `log("MyInt is greater than 5!  MyInt is:" @ MyInt);
    }
    else
    {
        `log("MyInt is less than or equal to 5!  MyInt is:" @
MyInt);
    }
}
```

Now let's compile the code. It works this time!

4. Since we already have BrokenActor placed in our map, we don't need to open the editor for this next step. Instead let's create a copy of our Awesome Test Map.bat batch file and name it Broken Map.bat.

5. Open Broken Map.bat and change it to look like this:

```
C:\UDK\UDK-AwesomeGame\Binaries\Win32\UDK.exe BrokenMap?GoalScore=
0?TimeLimit=0 -log
```

The map name has changed, but also note that we're not running it with AwesomeGame anymore. Goodbye AwesomeGame! You have served us well.

6. Save and close `Broken Map.bat`.

7. Double-click the batch file to run the game. While it's loading think about what we should see in the log. We've set `MyInt` to `13` in the default properties, so we should see the first log in our script show up. We'll see this isn't the case though:

```
[0005.20] ScriptLog: MyInt is less than or equal to 5!  MyInt is:
0
```

8. Well what happened there? Let's change our default properties block. Right now it looks like this:

```
defaultproperties {
    MyInt=13

    Begin Object Class=SpriteComponent Name=Sprite
        Sprite=Texture2D'EditorMaterials.TargetIcon'
        Scale=0.35
        HiddenGame=true
    End Object
    Components.Add(Sprite)
}
```

Let's move the first bracket down to the next line, so it looks like this instead:

```
defaultproperties
{
    MyInt=13

    Begin Object Class=SpriteComponent Name=Sprite
        Sprite=Texture2D'EditorMaterials.TargetIcon'
        Scale=0.35
        HiddenGame=true
    End Object
    Components.Add(Sprite)
}
```

9. Now let's compile the code and run the game again:

```
[0005.40] ScriptLog: MyInt is greater than 5!  MyInt is: 13
```

Much better!

What just happened?

Misplacing or missing brackets, that is. { } are fairly common for new programmers. To avoid this problem, it's best to create both of them at the same time, before you start writing code inside them.

The second problem with the default properties is more common among programmers who are used to other languages and who format their code differently. The rest of an UnrealScript class can be written with the opening bracket on the same line as the function declaration:

```
function Something() {
    SomeCode();
}
```

The default properties block is the only place where you can't do this, the opening bracket has to be on a new line, like this:

```
defaultproperties
{
    SomeVariable=2
}
```

Time for action – Misleading errors

Sometimes error messages might seem a little misleading, as we'll see in this next experiment:

1. Let's rewrite our `PostBeginPlay` function. We'll leave in our `MyInt` variable and use it for this experiment:

    ```
    simulated function PostBeginPlay()
    {
        if(UTGame(WorldInfo.Game != none)
            MyInt = UTGame(WorldInfo.Game).DefaultMaxLives;
    }
    ```

2. Seems fine, but when we try to compile we get this error:

    ```
    [0004.84] Log: R:\UDK\UDK-AwesomeGame\Development\Src\BrokenGame\
    Classes\BrokenActor.uc(8) : Error, Bad or missing expression for
    token: UTGame, in 'If'
    ```

    What could this mean? It seems to be telling us that it doesn't know what `UTGame` is, even though it's a valid class. If we take a closer look at our if statement, we can see the problem:

    ```
        if(UTGame(WorldInfo.Game != none)
    ```

I'm counting two open parentheses, but only one closed one. If we take the `if` part out of this line and examine it separately:

```
UTGame(WorldInfo.Game != none)
```

To the compiler, it looks like we're trying to call a function called UTGame and that we're trying to send this function a bool (WorldInfo.Game != none). Since it can't find a function called UTGame, it gives us this error:

```
[0004.84] Log: R:\UDK\UDK-AwesomeGame\Development\Src\BrokenGame\
Classes\BrokenActor.uc(8) : Error, Bad or missing expression for
token: UTGame, in 'If'
```

So the error message might seem misleading, but to the compiler it makes perfect sense.

3. Let's fix the error by adding the closing parenthesis:

```
simulated function PostBeginPlay()
{
    if(UTGame(WorldInfo.Game) != none)
        MyInt = UTGame(WorldInfo.Game).DefaultMaxLives;
}
```

4. Now it compiles just fine.

What just happened?

It would be nice if the compiler just said *You're missing a closing parenthesis here*, but remember the mantra: The computer is just doing exactly what you told it to do. You're trying to typecast to UTGame, but without the parenthesis you've told the code to try to call a function.

As with brackets, when working with parentheses it's best to write both of them at the same time, and then fill them in afterward. This can be especially important when working with complicated math equations.

Sometimes the errors are easy to figure out, as we'll see in our next experiment.

Time for action – Captain obvious to the rescue!

Sometimes we'll get lucky and the compiler error message will trigger an *Oh, durhey* moment the second we see it.

1. Let's rewrite `PostBeginPlay` function again:

```
simulated function PostBeginPlay()
{
    MyInt = class'UTGame'.default.CountDown
}
```

2. Now let's try to compile.

```
[0003.91] Log: R:\UDK\UDK-AwesomeGame\Development\Src\BrokenGame\
Classes\BrokenActor.uc(9) : Error, Missing ';' before '}'
```

3. Oh, duh, we forgot the semicolon at the end of the line.

```
simulated function PostBeginPlay()
{
    MyInt = class'UTGame'.default.CountDown;
}
```

4. Now it compiles!

What just happened?

Sometimes compiler errors are really self explanatory. Let's take a look at another one.

Time for action – Setting up a twofer

Another obvious error, with a twist!

1. Let's rewrite our `PostBeginPlay` function:

```
simulated function PostBeginPlay()
{
    var int AnotherInt;

    AnotherInt = class'UTGame'.default.CountDown;
}
```

2. Looks fine this time, we have our brackets, parentheses, and semicolons in place. What could go wrong?

```
[0003.93] Log: R:\UDK\UDK-AwesomeGame\Development\Src\BrokenGame\
Classes\BrokenActor.uc(8) : Error, Instance variables are only
allowed at class scope (use 'local'?)
```

3. Oh, right. Inside functions we're only allowed to use local variables. Let's fix that real quick:

```
simulated function PostBeginPlay()
{
    local int AnotherInt;

    AnotherInt = class'UTGame'.default.CountDown;
}
```

4. Now it should work, so let's compile it:

```
[0004.08] Log: R:\UDK\UDK-AwesomeGame\Development\Src\BrokenGame\
Classes\BrokenActor.uc(10) : Warning, 'AnotherInt' : unused local
variable
```

5. Well this is new, a warning this time instead of an error! *Unused local variable.* We're assigning a value to it, but we're never actually using it anywhere. Warnings aren't game breaking and they won't prevent the code from compiling, they're more helpful hints. In this case it's saying *hey, if you're not doing anything with this variable do you really need it at all?* We can delete it and the line assigning it a value, but instead let's just use it in a log:

```
simulated function PostBeginPlay()
{
    local int AnotherInt;

    AnotherInt = class'UTGame'.default.CountDown;
    `log("AnotherInt is:" @ AnotherInt);
}
```

6. This time it compiles fine, no errors, and no warnings.

What just happened?

Missing semicolons is another easy error to fix. You also have to watch out for extra semicolons. Take a look at the following code:

```
var int MyInt;

simulated function PostBeginPlay()
{
    if(MyInt < 5);
        MyInt = class'UTGame'.default.CountDown;

    `log("MyInt is:" @ MyInt);
}

defaultproperties
{
    MyInt=13
}
```

It seems like it should be logging 13 since `MyInt` is greater than 5 and the assignment inside the `if` statement shouldn't execute, but running it gives us this:

```
[0009.32] ScriptLog: MyInt is: 4
```

The default value for CountDown in UTGame is 4, so that part is being executed. But why? The problem is in our if statement:

```
if(MyInt < 5);
```

The semicolon at the end completes the if statement, essentially making it do nothing. The code treats the next line as separate from the if statement, so it will always execute with this code. Written correctly it should look like this:

```
if(MyInt < 5)
    MyInt = class'UTGame'.default.CountDown;
```

Next we'll take a look at some things that can go wrong when working with functions.

Time for action – Mal-function

First, we'll take a look at what can go wrong in function declarations.

1. Let's add a new function to our class:

```
simulated function HitWall()
{
}
```

2. Compile the code and we'll get this error:

```
[0003.93] Log: R:\UDK\UDK-AwesomeGame\Development\Src\BrokenGame\
Classes\BrokenActor.uc(4) : Error, Redefinition of 'function
HitWall' differs from original; different number of parameters
```

3. If we look at Actor.uc we can see the original declaration of this function:

```
event HitWall( vector HitNormal, actor Wall, PrimitiveComponent
WallComp )
```

4. When overriding a function, you must use the same parameters as the original. You can change the names if you want, for instance this would work:

```
simulated function HitWall( vector Norm, actor HitActor,
PrimitiveComponent Prim )
{
}
```

The number and type of parameters must stay the same though.

This type of error usually results from misreading the parameters when overriding a function, or accidentally making up a function that already exists in a superclass.

5. The same thing can happen with return values. Let's rewrite our `HitWall` function to look like this:

```
simulated function bool HitWall( vector Norm, actor HitActor,
PrimitiveComponent Prim )
{
}
```

6. Compile the code and we'll get this error:

```
[0003.84] Log: R:\UDK\UDK-AwesomeGame\Development\Src\BrokenGame\
Classes\BrokenActor.uc(4) : Error, Redefinition of 'function
HitWall' differs from original: return value mismatch
```

This is most commonly caused by not including the return value when you write your function.

7. Along the same lines, we can accidentally leave out the return value for a function. Let's delete `HitWall` and add this made up function:

```
function bool AmIAwesome()
{
    return;
}
```

8. If we try to compile the preceding code we'll get this error:

```
[0003.82] Log: R:\UDK\UDK-AwesomeGame\Development\Src\BrokenGame\
Classes\BrokenActor.uc(6) : Error, Bad or missing expression in
'Return'
```

 When working with functions that have a return value, always make sure you're returning the right type of variable.

9. Let's change the function to look like this:

```
function bool AmIAwesome()
{
    return 5;
}
```

10. Trying to compile this code would give us a different error stemming from the same problem of the wrong type of return value:

```
[0003.84] Log: R:\UDK\UDK-AwesomeGame\Development\Src\BrokenGame\
Classes\BrokenActor.uc(6) : Error, Type mismatch in 'Return'
```

What just happened?

These types of errors are pretty obvious, and easy to fix. Just make sure to take careful note of any parameters and the return type of functions you're using.

We also need to be careful when we're calling other functions, to make sure that we're passing the correct number and type of variables. If we had this code:

```
simulated function PostBeginPlay()
{
    TakeDamage(5.0);
}
```

we would get this error when we compiled:

```
[0003.89] Log: R:\UDK\UDK-AwesomeGame\Development\Src\BrokenGame\
Classes\BrokenActor.uc(6) : Error, Call to 'TakeDamage': missing or
bad parameter 2
```

Taking a look at the original declaration of `TakeDamage` in Actor, we can see the correct number and type of variables that we need to pass to this function:

```
event TakeDamage(int DamageAmount, Controller EventInstigator, vector
HitLocation, vector Momentum, class<DamageType> DamageType, optional
TraceHitInfo HitInfo, optional Actor DamageCauser)
```

The last two are optional, but the first five need to be included in our call to this function.

There are a few other errors that we need to watch out for when dealing with functions.

Time for action – Taking care of other function errors.

Let's take a look at some more function errors:

1. Say we had the following code:

```
simulated function PostBeginPlay()
{
    `log("PostBeginPlay!");
}

simulated function PostBeginPlay()
{
    local int SomeInt;
    SomeInt = 5;
    `log("SomeInt is:" @ SomeInt);
}
```

2. The code seems fine, but if we compile it we get:

```
[0003.86] Log: R:\UDK\UDK-AwesomeGame\Development\Src\BrokenGame\
Classes\BrokenActor.uc(9) : Error, 'PostBeginPlay' conflicts with
'Function BrokenGame.BrokenActor:PostBeginPlay'
```

3. This one's easy to avoid. Classes can only have one function with any one name; trying to have more than one with the same name will give us an error.

4. This next one's a bit obscure, since `static` functions aren't used that much. Suppose we had this code:

```
static function float GetRadius()
{
    local float Radius, Height;

    GetBoundingCylinder(Radius, Height);
    return Radius;
}
```

5. Trying to compile that would give us this error:

```
[0003.87] Log: R:\UDK\UDK-AwesomeGame\Development\Src\BrokenGame\
Classes\BrokenActor.uc(7) : Error, Can't call instance functions
from within static functions
```

What just happened?

Remembering that `static` functions are called on the class without the need for the actor to exist in the world, it makes sense that we wouldn't be able to call normal functions in them. Static functions are only able to call other static functions, but normal functions can call static functions.

Now let's take a look at some errors that can result when typecasting Actor variables.

Time for action – Actor variable errors

Errors of this type are common when you're getting used to UnrealScript. Knowing when and how to use typecasting and dealing with Actor variables takes some time to get used to. Let's see some of the errors we can come across when doing this:

1. Let's say this Actor killed anyone who touched it while holding a weapon. We might have a function that looked something like this:

```
event Bump( Actor Other, PrimitiveComponent OtherComp, Vector
HitNormal )
{
```

```
    if(Other.Weapon != none)
        Other.Suicide();
}
```

2. Compiling this code gives us an error:

```
[0003.90] Log: R:\UDK\UDK-AwesomeGame\Development\Src\BrokenGame\
Classes\BrokenActor.uc(6) : Error, Unrecognized member 'Weapon' in
class 'Actor'
```

3. What's causing this error? If we search `Actor.uc` we won't find a `Weapon` variable; what we meant to do is check if the actor bumping us is a Pawn, and check if that Pawn has a weapon. Let's rewrite the function a bit:

```
event Bump( Actor Other, PrimitiveComponent OtherComp, Vector
HitNormal )
{
    if(Pawn(Other) != none && Pawn(Other).Weapon != none)
        Other.Suicide();
}
```

Now we're checking if `Other` is `Pawn` and if it is, if it has `Weapon`.

4. If we try to compile now we'll receive another error message:

```
[0003.87] Log: R:\UDK\UDK-AwesomeGame\Development\Src\BrokenGame\
Classes\BrokenActor.uc(7) : Error, Unrecognized member 'Suicide'
in class 'Actor'
```

5. We're running into the same problem here, Actor doesn't have a function called `Suicide`, but `Pawn` does. Let's change the function again:

```
event Bump( Actor Other, PrimitiveComponent OtherComp, Vector
HitNormal )
{
    if(Pawn(Other) != none && Pawn(Other).Weapon != none)
        Pawn(Other).Suicide();
}
```

6. Compiling this time works fine.

7. Of course, the opposite problem is also true. Let's take a look at this function:

```
function KilledBy( Pawn EventInstigator )
{
    if(Pawn(EventInstigator) != none)
        Pawn(EventInstigator).Suicide();
}
```

8. If we compile that, we get this error:

```
[0003.88] Log: R:\UDK\UDK-AwesomeGame\Development\Src\BrokenGame\
Classes\BrokenActor.uc(6) : Error, Cast from 'Pawn' to 'Pawn' is
unnecessary
```

9. We don't need to typecast if the variable is already the type of variable we need. If we rewrote it like this:

```
function KilledBy( Pawn EventInstigator )
{
    if(Actor(EventInstigator) != none)
        Actor(EventInstigator).Suicide();
}
```

We would get the same error:

```
[0003.89] Log: R:\UDK\UDK-AwesomeGame\Development\Src\BrokenGame\
Classes\BrokenActor.uc(6) : Error, Cast from 'Pawn' to 'Actor' is
unnecessary
```

10. The correct way to write this particular function would be:

```
function KilledBy( Pawn EventInstigator )
{
    if(EventInstigator != none)
        EventInstigator.Suicide();
}
```

What just happened?

Typecasting is only necessary when you need to access variables and functions of a subclass of an Actor variable, otherwise you already have access to them because of inheritance, so typecasting is unnecessary.

Another thing to look out for when typecasting is that the class you're casting to is a subclass of the one you have. If it's somewhere else in the class tree you'll get another error. Let's look at this code:,

```
function KilledBy( Pawn EventInstigator )
{
    if(UTGame(EventInstigator) != none)
        EventInstigator.Suicide();
}
```

Since UTGame is not a subclass of Pawn, and is nowhere near it on the class tree, we'll get this error when we compile:

```
[0003.84] Log: R:\UDK\UDK-AwesomeGame\Development\Src\BrokenGame\
Classes\BrokenActor.uc(6) : Error, Cast from 'Pawn' to 'UTGame' will
always fail
```

What this is telling us is that since the class we're trying to cast to isn't a subclass of Pawn, the cast will always return none.

Time for action – Other variable errors

There are a few more errors we need to take a look at before we move on. These ones have to do with the declaration and use of variables.

1. Let's take a look at this PostBeginPlay function:

```
simulated function PostBeginPlay()
{
    local int Int1, Int2;

    Int1 = 3;
    Int2 = 5;
    Int1 + Int2;
}
```

2. If we try to compile that, we'll get this error message:

```
[0003.77] Error: R:\UDK\UDK-AwesomeGame\Development\Src\
BrokenGame\Classes\BrokenActor.uc(11) : Error, ';': Expression has
no effect
```

3. The source of that error is in this line:

```
    Int1 + Int2;
```

We're not assigning the result of that to any variable, and we're not using it as a comparison or anything like that. If we wrote it like the following we wouldn't get the error:

```
Int1 = Int1 + Int2;
```

Not something you'd come across often, but it's good to know what the error message means.

4. You would also get the same error message if a function parameter had the same name as another function, and you tried calling that function as in the following code:

```
function bool UsedBy(Pawn Bump)
{
    Bump(none, none, vect(0,0,0));
}
```

In this case we're naming the parameter `Bump`, which is the same name as a function that already exists for Actor classes. When we try calling `Bump` the function, it thinks we're trying to typecast the variable, giving us an error.

5. Variable declarations themselves are pretty simple as long as we remember when to use `var` and when to use `local`. There is one special case that you may come across. If we wanted to make an array of class variables, we would want to write it like the following:

```
var array<class<Projectile>> ProjectileClasses;
```

This is different than having an array of actual Projectile actors, here we're just specifying class names.

6. If we compiled that code, we would get this error:

```
[0003.87] Log: R:\UDK\UDK-AwesomeGame\Development\Src\BrokenGame\
Classes\BrokenActor.uc(4) : Error, Missing '>' in 'class limitor'
```

7. The reason that error comes up is that the compiler thinks that the two greater-than signs (>>) are bitwise or vector rotating operator. To fix this, we would put a space in between them:

```
var array<class<Projectile> > ProjectileClasses;
```

What just happened?

There aren't many instances where variable declaration and its use would give you compiler errors, as long as you're careful with the names and typecasting.

This is by no means is an exhaustive list of compiler errors you may encounter when working with UnrealScript. Most of them will be self-explanatory, and the error will always have a line number associated with it:

```
[0003.77] Error: R:\UDK\UDK-AwesomeGame\Development\Src\BrokenGame\
Classes\BrokenActor.uc(11) : Error, ';': Expression has no effect
```

The number in parentheses tells us what line to look at in the class, in this case 11. Keep in mind that although the compiler encountered the error on that line, the actual error may not be on that line. Missing brackets or parentheses often cause the compiler to give a line number that is after the actual error.

Just remember, when you get a compiler error, don't panic! Read what the compiler is telling you, and carefully examine your code. Most compiler errors are very simple to fix. *Are you trying to use a variable or function that hasn't been declared or doesn't exist for the class you're working in? Are all your brackets, parentheses, and semicolons in place?* With experience you will quickly be able to find and fix any errors that the compiler is giving you.

Debugging

Just because code compiles, however, doesn't mean it's going to work. There are a lot of things that can go wrong that the compiler won't complain about, but will break your game nonetheless. In this section of the chapter, we're going to talk about some debugging techniques you can use to figure out why the code isn't doing what you want it to do. We'll also keep an eye on the log to catch and fix any errors that happen while the game is running.

Accessed none

By far the most common problem you will run into while debugging your code is the **Accessed None**. It is also the easiest to avoid, as long as you make no assumptions about Actor variables in your code. Let's take a look.

Time for action – Dealing with Accessed None

To test this we need to purposely create an Accessed None, so let's do that now. We'll add a `PostBeginPlay` function to our `BrokenActor`.

1. Let's say we wanted to know the speed of a Projectile. We could add a variable and write a function like this in our `PostBeginPlay`:

```
var Projectile MyProjectile;

simulated function PostBeginPlay()
{
    local float ProjectileSpeed;

    ProjectileSpeed = MyProjectile.Speed;
    `log("ProjectileSpeed:" @ ProjectileSpeed);
}
```

2. Compile the code and run the game.

3. Exit the game and check the log:

```
[0004.99] ScriptWarning: Accessed None 'P'
    BrokenActor BrokenMap.TheWorld:PersistentLevel.BrokenActor_0
    Function BrokenGame.BrokenActor:PostBeginPlay:004F
[0004.99] ScriptLog: ProjectileSpeed: 0.0000
```

4. We're getting an Accessed None warning and the speed is logging as 0. That doesn't seem right, especially when the default for the `Projectile` class is 2000. Let's add another log to see what's going on:

```
var Projectile MyProjectile;

simulated function PostBeginPlay()
{
    local float ProjectileSpeed;

    `log("Projectile:" @ P);
    ProjectileSpeed = P.Speed;
    `log("ProjectileSpeed:" @ ProjectileSpeed);
}
```

5. Compile the code and run the game.

6. Exit the game and check the log again:

```
[0005.03] ScriptLog: Projectile: None
[0005.03] ScriptWarning: Accessed None 'P'
    BrokenActor BrokenMap.TheWorld:PersistentLevel.BrokenActor_0
    Function BrokenGame.BrokenActor:PostBeginPlay:004F
[0005.03] ScriptLog: ProjectileSpeed: 0.0000
```

What just happened?

Accessed None warnings happen when you try to access variables or functions in an Actor variable that isn't referencing an actor, in other words:

```
SomeActorVariable = none
```

This could happen if you never assign a reference to an Actor variable, as happened here. We declared a variable of the type `Projectile`, but we never assigned it a value. By default Actor variables are `None`, so we're trying to access a variable in an actor that doesn't exist, which gives us the error.

Let's see if we can fix this by assigning a value to it.

Time for action – Fixing an Accessed None

Our Projectile variable doesn't have anything assigned to it, so let's try to fix that. We'll use the `foreach` iterator to find one and assign it to our `MyProjectile` variable.

1. Let's add the lines to our `PostBeginPlay` function:

    ```
    var Projectile MyProjectile;

    simulated function PostBeginPlay()
    {
        local float ProjectileSpeed;

        foreach DynamicActors(class'Projectile', MyProjectile)
            break;

        `log("Projectile:" @ MyProjectile);
        ProjectileSpeed = MyProjectile.Speed;
        `log("ProjectileSpeed:" @ ProjectileSpeed);
    }
    ```

2. Now the code will search for a `Projectile` and assign it to our `MyProjectile` variable.

3. Compile the code and run the game.

4. Exit the game and take a look at the log:

    ```
    [0005.14] ScriptLog: Projectile: None
    [0005.14] ScriptWarning: Accessed None 'MyProjectile'
            BrokenActor BrokenMap.TheWorld:PersistentLevel.BrokenActor_0
            Function BrokenGame.BrokenActor:PostBeginPlay:004F
    [0005.14] ScriptLog: ProjectileSpeed: 0.0000
    ```

5. Well that didn't work, and if we think about it it's obvious why. `PostBeginPlay` is run as soon as the game starts, so there aren't going to be any Projectile actors on the map.

6. In addition to the warning, when we try to access any variables or functions, we can also get another error if we try to assign any values to variables in a non-existent actor. If we changed our function to this, for instance:

    ```
    var Projectile MyProjectile;

    simulated function PostBeginPlay()
    {
        foreach DynamicActors(class'Projectile', MyProjectile)
    ```

```
        break;

    MyProjectile.Speed = 1000.0;
}
```

7. Instead of just accessing the `Speed` variable, we're trying to assign a value here. Let's compile the code and run the game.

8. Exit the game and take a look at the log:

```
[0005.15] ScriptWarning: Accessed None 'MyProjectile'
        BrokenActor BrokenMap.TheWorld:PersistentLevel.BrokenActor_0
        Function BrokenGame.BrokenActor:PostBeginPlay:0029
[0005.16] ScriptWarning: Attempt to assign variable through None
        BrokenActor BrokenMap.TheWorld:PersistentLevel.BrokenActor_0
        Function BrokenGame.BrokenActor:PostBeginPlay:003D
```

9. That second line is new, and is caused by the following line:

```
    MyProjectile.Speed = 1000.0;
```

The game is letting us know that we're trying to assign a value to a variable in an actor that doesn't exist.

10. These warnings are helpful, but how do we avoid Accessed None warnings? Let's use a conditional statement to check if our actor variable has anything assigned to it before we try to use it:

```
var Projectile MyProjectile;

simulated function PostBeginPlay()
{
    foreach DynamicActors(class'Projectile', MyProjectile)
        break;

    if(MyProjectile != none)
        MyProjectile.Speed = 1000.0;
    else
        `log("MyProjectile == none, not doing anything.");
}
```

11. Compile the code and run the game.

12. Exit and take a look at the log:

```
[0005.06] ScriptLog: MyProjectile == none, not doing anything.
```

What just happened?

Using conditional statements to check if an actor has a variable will prevent you from getting an Accessed None warning, and can help you do different actions based on whether or not it has a value. For instance, if we wanted to have the player do a different action based on whether they were holding a weapon or not, we might use the `StartFire` function in our `PlayerController` like this:

```
exec function StartFire( optional byte FireModeNum )
{
    if(Pawn.Weapon != none)
        FireWeapon();
    else
        DoSomeOtherAction();
}
```

The important thing is, before you try to access any variables or functions in an actor, ALWAYS check to see if it exists before you do. This also applies to function parameters, as we'll see next.

Time for action – Accessed None in function parameters

Even when we're using functions, we have to be careful about Accessed None warnings. Just because a function is passing an actor in doesn't mean it's a valid reference.

1. Let's remove our `MyProjectile` variable and rewrite the `PostBeginPlay` function:

    ```
    simulated function PostBeginPlay()
    {
        AdjustProjectile(none);
    }
    ```

2. Now let's write the custom `AdjustProjectile` function:

    ```
    function AdjustProjectile(Projectile MyProj)
    {
        `log("MyProj:" @ MyProj);
        MyProj.Speed = 1000.0;
    }
    ```

3. Compile the code and run the game.

4. Exit and take a look at the log. We're getting the same warnings as before:

    ```
    [0005.09] ScriptWarning: Accessed None 'MyProj'
            BrokenActor BrokenMap.TheWorld:PersistentLevel.BrokenActor_0
            Function BrokenGame.BrokenActor:AdjustProjectile:0024
    ```

```
[0005.09] ScriptWarning: Attempt to assign variable through None
        BrokenActor BrokenMap.TheWorld:PersistentLevel.BrokenActor_0
        Function BrokenGame.BrokenActor:AdjustProjectile:0038
```

What just happened?

In `PostBeginPlay` we're calling `AdjustProjectile` with `none`. It may not seem logical but it's perfectly valid. To see how something like this could happen with actual code, let's take a look at the `Died` function in `Pawn`:

```
function bool Died(Controller Killer, class<DamageType> DamageType,
vector HitLocation)
```

Useful information is used in the preceding function, like `Killer`. That variable is passed along to the `GameInfo` so it can give our killer a score for killing us, among other things. But what if there was no `Killer`? It can happen sometimes, for instance when we change teams our `Pawn` is killed, but no one was the `Killer`:

```
function PlayerChangedTeam()
{
    Died( None, class'DamageType', Location );
}
```

When writing and using variables, even as function parameters, we have to write our code knowing that they might not always have a value. ALWAYS check that your actor variables are not None before trying to use them.

Using the log

More than anything else, the **log** is your main tool to figure out why your code isn't working. Using it to log values of variables, or at the beginning of functions to let you know they're being called, even just throwing one in `PostBeginPlay` to make sure your actor classes are being used at all, the log is an incredibly useful debugging tool. Let's take a look at a problem and see if we can figure out what's going wrong using the log.

Time for action – Setting up a scenario

Before we start debugging, we need something that's broken that we can use to test our skills. The first thing we need to do is get our own `PlayerController` class working.

1. Remembering that our `PlayerController` class is specified in the `GameInfo`, that is where we need to start. Let's add a new file to our `Development\Src\ BrokenGame\Classes` folder called `BrokenGame.uc`.

2. Write the following code into `BrokenGame.uc`:

```
class BrokenGame extends UTDeathmatch;

defaultproperties
{
    PlayerControllerClass=class'BrokenGame.BrokenPlayerController'
    bDelayedStart=false
    bUseClassicHUD=true
}
```

3. Now we need to create the `BrokenPlayerController` class. Start by creating a new file in `Development\Src\BrokenGame\Classes` called `BrokenPlayerController.uc`.

4. Write the following code in `BrokenPlayerController.uc`:

```
class BrokenPlayerController extends UTPlayerController;

defaultproperties
{
}
```

5. Now we're going to change `BrokenActor` a bit. We'll borrow some code from the `AwesomeEnemy` class to turn it into a kind of *pet* that will follow us around. Open `BrokenActor.uc` and type the following code into it:

```
class BrokenActor extends Actor
    placeable;

var Pawn Master;
var float MovementSpeed;
var float StopDistance;

simulated function PostBeginPlay()
{
    foreach DynamicActors(class'Pawn', Master)
        break;
}

auto state Following
{
    simulated function Tick(float DeltaTime)
    {
        local vector NewLocation;
```

```
        if(Master != none && VSize(Location - Master.Location) >
StopDistance)
        {
            NewLocation = Location;
            NewLocation += normal(Master.Location - Location) *
MovementSpeed * DeltaTime;
            SetLocation(NewLocation);
        }
    }
}


defaultproperties
{
    MovementSpeed=256.0
    StopDistance=128.0
    bBlockActors=true
    bCollideActors=true

    Begin Object Class=DynamicLightEnvironmentComponent
Name=MyLightEnvironment
        bEnabled=true
    End Object
    Components.Add(MyLightEnvironment)

    Begin Object Class=StaticMeshComponent Name=PetMesh
        StaticMesh=StaticMesh'UN_SimpleMeshes.TexPropCube_Dup'
        Materials(0)=Material'EditorMaterials.WidgetMaterial_Y'
        LightEnvironment=MyLightEnvironment
        Scale3D=(X=0.125,Y=0.125,Z=0.25)
    End Object
    Components.Add(PetMesh)

    Begin Object Class=CylinderComponent Name=CollisionCylinder
        CollisionRadius=32.0
        CollisionHeight=64.0
        BlockNonZeroExtent=true
        BlockZeroExtent=true
        BlockActors=true
        CollideActors=true
    End Object
    CollisionComponent=CollisionCylinder
    Components.Add(CollisionCylinder)
}
```

6. Compile the code.

7. Before we test the code, let's open `BrokenMap` in the editor and make sure a `BrokenActor` is still placed somewhere near the player start. Once that's done save the map and close the editor.

8. For the final step, we have to change our batch file to use our `BrokenGame` so our `BrokenPlayerController` will be used. Change `Broken Map.bat` to this:

```
C:\UDK\UDK-AwesomeGame\Binaries\Win32\UDK.exe BrokenMap?GoalScore=
0?TimeLimit=0?Game=BrokenGame.BrokenGame -log
```

9. Save and close the batch file.

10. Run the game with the changed batch file.

What just happened?

Our pet doesn't seem to be following us. What's going on? Let's see if we can use the log to find out why it's not working and fix the problem.

Time for action – Debugging using the log

The first question we need to ask is: are our classes being used in the first place? Let's put a few logs in to find out.

1. We'll start with `BrokenActor`. Even though we see it in the map when we run the game, we shouldn't make any assumptions about what's going on. We'll add a log in `PostBeginPlay`:

```
simulated function PostBeginPlay()
{
    `log("BrokenActor PostBeginPlay!");

    foreach DynamicActors(class'Pawn', Master)
        break;
}
```

2. We'll also add one in `BrokenGame`:

```
function PostBeginPlay()
{
    `log("BrokenGame PostBeginPlay!");
}
```

3. And finally one in `BrokenPlayerController`:

```
simulated function PostBeginPlay()
{
    `log("BrokenPlayerController PostBeginPlay!");
}
```

4. Compile the code and run the game.

5. Exit and take a look at the log. We'll see that all three actors are logging their `PostBeginPlay` functions:

```
[0005.44] ScriptLog: BrokenActor PostBeginPlay!
[0005.44] ScriptLog: BrokenGame PostBeginPlay!
[0005.44] Log: Bringing up level for play took: 0.032277
[0005.44] ScriptLog: BrokenPlayerController PostBeginPlay!
```

5. Now that we know our actors are indeed being used, we need to debug further. We know the movement code for our `BrokenActor` takes place in its `Following` state's `Tick` function, so let's add some logs there:

```
simulated function Tick(float DeltaTime)
{
    local vector NewLocation;

    `log("BrokenActor Tick!");

    if(Master != none && VSize(Location - Master.Location) >
StopDistance)
    {
        `log("BrokenActor Calculating new location!");
        NewLocation = Location;
        NewLocation += normal(Master.Location - Location) *
MovementSpeed * DeltaTime;
        SetLocation(NewLocation);
    }
}
```

6. Let's compile the code and see what happens when we run the game.

7. Exit the game and take a look at the log:

```
[0005.88] ScriptLog: BrokenActor Tick!
[0005.92] ScriptLog: BrokenActor Tick!
[0005.94] ScriptLog: BrokenActor Tick!
[0005.95] ScriptLog: BrokenActor Tick!
```

8. The code doesn't seem to be getting into our `if` statement. Let's see if we can figure out why. Let's log the conditions to see which one is failing. We'll start with `Master`:

```
simulated function Tick(float DeltaTime)
{
    local vector NewLocation;

    `log(Master);

    if(Master != none && VSize(Location - Master.Location) >
StopDistance)
        {
            `log("BrokenActor Calculating new location!");
            NewLocation = Location;
            NewLocation += normal(Master.Location - Location) *
MovementSpeed * DeltaTime;
            SetLocation(NewLocation);
        }
}
```

9. Compile the code and run the game.

10. Exit and take a look at the log:

```
[0005.68] ScriptLog: None
[0005.73] ScriptLog: None
[0005.75] ScriptLog: None
```

11. Well that would explain it. `Master` is never getting set. Let's see why. If we take a look a bit earlier in the log we'll see our `PostBeginPlays`:

```
[0005.35] ScriptLog: BrokenActor PostBeginPlay!
[0005.35] ScriptLog: BrokenGame PostBeginPlay!
[0005.36] Log: Bringing up level for play took: 0.035747
[0005.36] ScriptLog: BrokenPlayerController PostBeginPlay!
```

12. It looks like the `BrokenActor` is being initialized first, so we're not going to be able to get our `Master` there. Let's try checking it in `Tick` and assigning it if it doesn't exist. First we'll rename `PostBeginPlay` to `GetMaster`:

```
function GetMaster()
{
    `log("BrokenActor GetMaster!");

    foreach DynamicActors(class'Pawn', Master)
        break;
}
```

13. Now we'll add the function call in `Tick`:

```
simulated function Tick(float DeltaTime)
{
    local vector NewLocation;

    if(Master == none)
        GetMaster();

    if(Master != none && VSize(Master.Location - Location) >
StopDistance)
    {
        `log("BrokenActor Calculating new location!");
        NewLocation = Location;
        NewLocation += normal(Master.Location - Location) *
MovementSpeed * DeltaTime;
        SetLocation(NewLocation);
    }
}
```

14. Now let's compile the code and check if it works.

15. Run the game and we'll see that the `BrokenActor` is now following us around! And if we check the log we'll see we're finally getting into the `if` statement:

```
[0007.66] ScriptLog: BrokenActor Calculating new location!
[0007.67] ScriptLog: BrokenActor Calculating new location!
[0007.69] ScriptLog: BrokenActor Calculating new location!
```

16. Close the game and remove all of the log lines from our classes.

What just happened?

This was a simple example of debugging, but we can see how using the log can help us figure out where our code is going wrong and give us clues to what we need to do to fix it. Knowing how we think the code should act, we can put logs in places where it's breaking and follow the chain of events written to the log file. This helps us narrow it down to the specific line, function, or variable that's causing the issue.

Sometimes we'll want to debug a class that has several instances running at the same time. With all of them logging it can be difficult to figure out what's going on. Ideally we would only want one of the Actors in the level, but if that's not feasible there are ways around it. One method we can use to filter down the log is to use the Actor's name variable in an `if` statement. That way only one of the Actors will write to the log. If the Actors are placed in the level, selecting one will show the Actor's name at the bottom of the editor:

Persistent Level.BrokenActor_0 Selected (12 Tris, 24 Verts, 0 Sections)

We can use that in an `if` statement like this:

```
if(Name == 'BrokenActor_0')
    `log(Master);
```

This also works for Actors that are spawned during gameplay. The first instance will start with 0 as its suffix, and increase by 1 with every instance spawned, so **BrokenActor_0**, **BrokenActor_1**, **BrokenActor_2**, and so on. This would be helpful if we were trying to debug the `AwesomeEnemy` class from the previous chapters, for instance.

Next we're going to discuss a few ways we can optimize our code for performance, and a few things to avoid when writing code to keep it running fast.

Optimization

We've gotten through the compiler errors. We've fixed all of the Accessed None warnings. We've used the log to debug our broken code. What else can go wrong? Well, if we're using inefficient code we can start to take hits to our game's frame rate as well. There are a few things we need to avoid doing, as well as a few tools to help us keep our code running quickly. The most important of these is the profiler.

The profiler

Something we might not think about when we start programming is how fast our code is running, and which classes or functions are taking the most time to run. So how do we find out? This is where the profiler comes in handy. It can give us an organized view of exactly where UnrealScript is spending its time. Let's take a look at it.

Time for action – Using the profiler

To use the profiler we don't need to do anything in UnrealScript itself; we'll use a built-in function of the Unreal engine for it.

1. Double-click on the batch file to run `BrokenMap`.

2. Hit the tilde key (~) to bring up the console.

3. Type `profilegame start` into the console and hit *Enter*. We'll see this message on screen:

PROFILING WITH AI LOGGING ON!

As well as this message in the log:

`[0009.46] Log: GameplayProfiler STARTING capture.`

4. Run around for a little bit to give the profiler time to collect information. Around ten seconds is good.

5. When you're ready, hit tilde (~) to bring up the console again, and type `profilegame stop` and hit *Enter*. The message on screen will go away and we'll see this message in the log:

`[0036.62] Log: GameplayProfiler STOPPING capture.`

6. Exit the game.

7. If we look in the `UDKGame` folder, we'll see a new folder has appeared called `Profiling`. If we look in that folder, we'll see a file with the time that we ran the profiler in its file name: `UDK-2011.09.22-14.46.15.gprof`

8. To open this file, go into the `UDK-AwesomeGame\Binaries` folder and run `GameplayProfiler.exe`. We'll see the program start up looking like this:

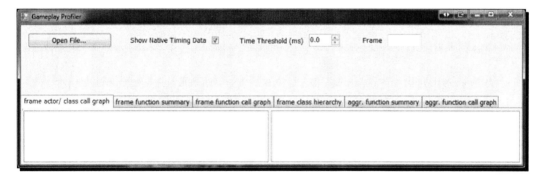

9. Press **Open File**, and navigate to the `UDKGame\Profiling` folder and select the `.gprof` file:

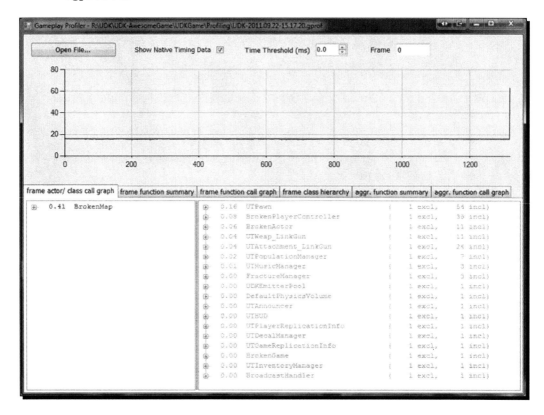

10. The top panel of the profiler shows us the frame by frame performance of our game. If there are any spikes you know that those are the areas to focus on. Clicking anywhere on this graph will set the profiler to that frame. If your graph extends out that far, click somewhere near **200** so we can take a look at the performance a little bit into the game.

11. The bottom-left panel of the profiler will show us the time taken for scripts to run, broken down by actor. If we expand our `BrokenActor` we can see the performance of it:

```
0.20   BrokenActor_1
   0.14   DynamicLightEnvironmentComponent_1
   0.06   Script Time
      0.05   Function BrokenGame.Following.Tick
         0.05   Farmove Actor Time
            0.02   Encroach Check Time
               0.01   SM Point Check
            0.01   Update Components Time
               0.00   Add Time
               0.00   Remove Time
            0.01   Encroach Check Time
   0.00 CylinderComponent_1
   0.00 StaticMeshComponent_1 (TexPropCube_Dup)
```

12. For our `BrokenActor`, calculating the dynamic lighting on it is taking the most time, followed by our `Tick` function with the movement calculations. Overall not a lot of time. What would we see if we really screwed things up?

13. Close the profiler for now and open `BrokenActor` in ConTEXT.

14. What if we rewrote our `Tick` function to run the search for `Master` every time?

```
simulated function Tick(float DeltaTime)
{
    local vector NewLocation;

    foreach AllActors(class'Pawn', Master)
        break;

    if(Master != none && VSize(Location - Master.Location) >
StopDistance)
    {
        NewLocation = Location;
        NewLocation += normal(Master.Location - Location) *
MovementSpeed * DeltaTime;
        SetLocation(NewLocation);
    }
}
```

15. If we compiled that code and ran the game, then recorded with the profiler for a few seconds, we might see something like this when we took a look at the .gprof file:

```
⊟   0.23  BrokenActor_1
  ⊞    0.15  DynamicLightEnvironmentComponent_1
  ⊟    0.08  Script Time
    ⊞    0.08  Function BrokenGame.Following.Tick
        0.00  CylinderComponent_1
```

16. We can see that our **Script Time** has increased. It might seem like a small increase, but with enough BrokenActors on the map a small increase like this could really impact performance.

What just happened?

With our relatively simple game the profiler might seem useless. There isn't a whole lot going on, obviously. But as an example, take a look at a typical profile from a normal UDK Deathmatch with a few bots running around:

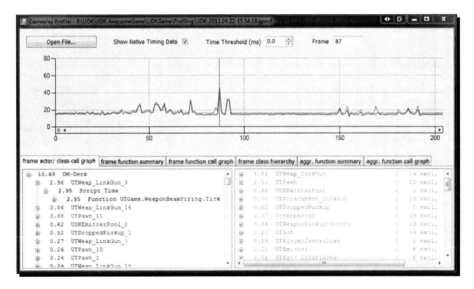

With a profile like this we can see how it can become useful. Spikes like that in the graph can easily start to impact performance, making the game stutter in places. As you're developing a game it's a good idea to run the profiler every once in a while even if your performance seems fine. It will help you catch problems before they start hurting your game's performance.

Clock / UnClock

The profiler is useful for seeing the overall picture of your game's performance, but what if you just want to know how fast a certain piece of code is executing? You might want to see if a certain way of writing an iterator is faster than another, for instance, or you might just want to go further than the profiler and figure out which part of a slow running function is impacting your game's performance. An easy way to do this is to use the `Clock` and `UnClock` functions defined in `Actor.uc`.

Time for action – Using Clock and UnClock

Let's run a little test with `BrokenActor` to see how to use these two functions.

1. Open `BrokenActor.uc` in ConTEXT.

2. We'll use `PostBeginPlay` for this. Let's write it like this:

```
function PostBeginPlay()
{
    local int i;
    local float StopWatch, Size;
    local vector A, B;

    Clock(StopWatch);

    for(i=0; i<1000; i++)
    {
        A = VRand() * 1000;
        B = VRand() * 1000;
        Size = VSize(A - B);
    }

    UnClock(StopWatch);
    `log("Time taken to execute:" @ StopWatch);
}
```

3. What we're doing here is running a loop 1000 times. Each time we take two vectors, `A` and `B`, and randomize them. Then we calculate the distance between them with `VSize`. We use a float called `StopWatch` in the `Clock` and `UnClock` functions, then log the value so we can see how long it took to run the loop.

4. Compile the code. We'll get a warning about `Size`, but we'll ignore it for this test.

5. Run the game, then exit and take a look at the log:

```
[0005.32] ScriptLog: Time taken to execute: 0.6553
```

What just happened?

The value used by `Clock` and `UnClock` is given in milliseconds, so running that loop took a little over half a millisecond. It might not seem like a lot of time, but if we remember that for a game running 60 frames per second, each frame is taking 16.667 milliseconds, it can add up quick especially if there are a lot of these actors on the map.

Best practices

When creating a game you absolutely must keep performance in mind when writing your scripts. Even though most of your game's performance will be focused on the art side of things with polygon counts and texture usage, unoptimized scripts can have a bad effect on your game. Here are a few things to look out for:

◆ Avoid using too much code in `Tick`:

Since `Tick` is run every frame, any code inside it must be carefully considered. Avoid iterators like `foreach` and other slow functions like `Trace` unless they're absolutely necessary. When possible, store the results of a `foreach` in an array, which can be iterated through faster. Also consider using a repeating `Timer` instead of `Tick` if your code needs to run often but doesn't necessarily need to run every frame.

◆ Let the engine handle it:

Collision, movement, physics... some things are best left to the engine to handle. Native engine code runs faster than UnrealScript, so when possible use functions that are already provided, instead of writing your own. For example, it would be easy to calculate gravity for an actor and set its velocity yourself, but letting the engine deal with the physics lets you avoid unnecessary performance hits from it.

◆ Create and destroy actors only when necessary:

This is doubly important for online games, where replication of new actors takes up valuable bandwidth. As an example, it would be horribly inefficient to create a gun that ejected shell casings in the form of actual actors when a particle effect would suffice.

◆ Optimize your variable usage:

In addition to making your code easier to read, keeping variable usage to a minimum saves memory and calculations. If you're constantly calculating a local variable's value for use in equations or as an actor reference, consider if it should be moved to an instance variable for that class. For example, the `EyeHeight` variable in the `Pawn` class is used in a few different functions, but only one function changes its value.

♦ Optimize your conditional statements:

When writing conditional statements such as `if`, write them in a way that will exit the statement as soon as possible. For example, if you wanted to check if a Pawn's health was less than 25/100 and it had a weapon, which would be the least likely? For the most part you're always going to have a weapon, so writing it like the follwoing would exit the if statement sooner:

```
if(Health < 25 && Weapon != none)
        DoSomething();
```

Most of the time your Pawn's Health will be greater than 25, so the `if` statement will read the first part of your statement and exit immediately. If it were written the other way around, most of the time the `if` statement would check the `Weapon`, see that it exists, and then continue to the second part where it would exit. Writing it as above will save the execution of one of the statements.

The opposite is true when using OR instead of AND. You would want to examine the most likely thing first.

The exception to this is when you need to write the conditional statement to avoid Accessed None warnings. Speaking of which...

♦ Fix log errors as you find them:

Don't let Accessed None warnings and other errors accumulate in your log. The log is there to help you, so fix any errors that show up from your code! Also, don't forget to remove any debugging code you have added. Writing to the log creates a small but noticeable performance hit, especially when used in a function like `Tick`.

Pop quiz – Errors and conditions

1. What does this compiler error mean?

   ```
   Error, Unexpected end of file at end of Class
   ```

2. If this line were giving us an Accessed None, how would we fix it?

   ```
   if(SomeActor.SomeVariable > 8)
   ```

3. When writing an AND conditional statement, which check should go first?

   Most likely to return true.

   Most likely to return false.

Summary

We learned a lot in this chapter about debugging and optimizing our code.

Specifically, we covered:

◆ Common compiler errors, what they mean, and how to fix them

◆ How to avoid Accessed None warnings

◆ How to use the log to debug code

◆ How to use the Profiler and Clock/UnClock

Now that we've learned about code optimization, we can cover a few other random topics to finish our course in UnrealScript!

10
Odds and Ends

Random knick knacks

We're pretty much done with our lessons in UnrealScript. By now you should have enough confidence to start poking around in the scripts on your own to learn how things work. There are a few other random topics I wanted to discuss though, ones that didn't really fit with any of the other chapters.

In this chapter we will:

- Discuss the use of **Components** in our Actor classes
- Interact with code outside the **UDK (Unreal Development Kit)** with DLLBind
- Discuss other resources for UnrealScript

So with that, let's take a look at Components!

Using Components

Components let us add objects to our Actors through its default properties. We can think of it like a weapon-upgrade system in a game: You can add a silencer, laser sight, a bigger clip to a weapon. With an Actor, we could add a static mesh, a directional light, or an ambient sound using Components. Let's take a look.

Creating Components

Time for action – Adding a Component to an Actor

For these experiments, we'll go back to our `AwesomeGame` classes, specifically our
`AwesomeActor`. We'll take a look at how to add and remove Components and how to
manipulate them through our functions.

1. We'll need a blank map for our experiments, so open `AwesomeTestMap` in the
   editor and delete all of the Kismet, `AwesomeEnemySpawners`, the look target, and
   the weapon spawner. All that should be left is the ground, the player start, and the
   lights.

2. Save the map and close the editor.

3. Open `AwesomeActor.uc` in ConTEXT.

4. Components are found under `Object` in the class tree. The one we're most
   concerned with for this is `ActorComponents`, which is the one that will be used
   most when working with UnrealScript. We'll start by adding a **SpriteComponent** to
   a new class we'll create, `AwesomeComponentActor`. SpriteComponents are most
   commonly used to give the Actor a physical representation in the editor. First let's
   create a new file called `AwesomeComponentActor.uc` in `Development/Src/`
   `AwesomeGame/Classes` and write the following code in it:

   ```
   class AwesomeComponentActor extends Actor;

   defaultproperties
   {
   }
   ```

5. Let's add a `SpriteComponent` to the default properties and also make this class
   placeable:

   ```
   class AwesomeComponentActor extends Actor
     placeable;

   defaultproperties
   {
     Begin Object Class=SpriteComponent Name=MySprite
       Sprite=Texture2D'EditorResources.S_Keypoint'
     End Object
     Components.Add(MySprite)
   }
   ```

6. Anything can be used as the `Name` of the Component, just make sure the name is the same in the `Components.Add()` line.

7. Compile the code and open up `AwesomeTestMap` in the editor.

8. Select `AwesomeComponentActor` in the Actor tab of the content browser and place one in the map. We'll see the sprite on it:

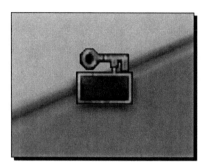

9. Save and close the map. If you deleted the batch file to run the game or don't have one, then create a new file called `Awesome Test Map.bat` and write the following in it:

```
C:\UDK\UDK-AwesomeGame\Binaries\Win32\UDK.exe AwesomeTestMap?GoalS
core=0?TimeLimit=0?Game=AwesomeGame.AwesomeGame -log
```

10. Run the game and we'll also see the sprite in game.

11. Good so far, but we usually don't see the sprites of Actor classes in game. If we take a look at `SpriteComponent`'s parent class, `PrimitiveComponent`, then we can see a few properties we may find useful:

```
var(Rendering) const bool       HiddenGame;
var(Rendering) const bool       HiddenEditor;

/** If this is True, this component won't be visible when the view
   actor is the component's owner, directly or indirectly. */
var(Rendering) const bool bOwnerNoSee;

/** If this is True, this component will only be visible when the
   view actor is the component's owner, directly or indirectly. */
var(Rendering) const bool bOnlyOwnerSee;

/** If true, bHidden on the Owner of this component will be
   ignored. */
var(Rendering) const bool bIgnoreOwnerHidden;
```

12. These options control when the Component is visible. For this Actor, we want it to be visible in the editor, but not in game, so let's add that to the Component's properties:

```
defaultproperties
{
  Begin Object Class=SpriteComponent Name=MySprite
  Sprite=Texture2D'EditorResources.S_Keypoint'
  HiddenGame=true
  End Object
  Components.Add(MySprite)
}
```

13. Now when we compile the code, we can see the Component in the editor, but not in game.

14. Sprites are nice, but let's see if we can find something more useful. We'll add a `SkeletalMeshComponent` to our `AwesomeComponentActor`. Start by deleting `SpriteComponent`.

15. Now let's add a `SkeletalMeshComponent` to the default properties:

```
defaultproperties
{
  Begin Object Class=SkeletalMeshComponent Name=AwesomeMesh
  SkeletalMesh=SkeletalMesh
    'CH_IronGuard_Male.Mesh.SK_CH_IronGuard_MaleA'
  End Object
  Components.Add(AwesomeMesh)
}
```

16. Compile the code and open `AwesomeTestMap` in the editor. We can see the skeletal mesh, but it's all dark!

17. In order for our Component to be able to receive light, we also need to add a `DynamicLightEnvironmentComponent`. Any subclass of `PrimitiveComponent` can have a light environment assigned to its `LightEnvironment` variable, but they're mainly only used for `StaticMeshComponents` and `SkeletalMeshComponents`. Sprites and other components don't really need lighting calculations.

18. Let's add a `DynamicLightEnvironmentComponent` to our `AwesomeComponentActor`:

```
Begin Object Class=DynamicLightEnvironmentComponent
  Name=AwesomeLightEnvironment
End Object
Components.Add(AwesomeLightEnvironment)
```

19. As we're not changing any of the variables in the light environment declaring one is as simple as those three lines. However, if for example, we didn't want our mesh to cast shadows, we could write it like this if we wanted:

```
Begin Object Class=DynamicLightEnvironmentComponent
  Name=AwesomeLightEnvironment
  bCastShadows=false
End Object
Components.Add(AwesomeLightEnvironment)
```

20. Now that we have the light environment, we can assign it in our `SkeletalMeshComponent`:

```
Begin Object Class=SkeletalMeshComponent Name=AwesomeMesh
  SkeletalMesh=SkeletalMesh
    'CH_IronGuard_Male.Mesh.SK_CH_IronGuard_MaleA'
  LightEnvironment=AwesomeLightEnvironment
End Object
Components.Add(AwesomeMesh)
```

21. Our `AwesomeComponentActor` class should look like the following code snippet:

```
class AwesomeComponentActor extends Actor
  placeable;

defaultproperties
{
  Begin Object Class=SpriteComponent Name=MySprite
    Sprite=Texture2D'EditorResources.S_Keypoint'
      HiddenGame=true
  End Object
```

```
Components.Add(MySprite)

Begin Object Class=DynamicLightEnvironmentComponent
  Name=AwesomeLightEnvironment
End Object
Components.Add(AwesomeLightEnvironment)

Begin Object Class=SkeletalMeshComponent Name=AwesomeMesh
  SkeletalMesh=SkeletalMesh
    'CH_IronGuard_Male.Mesh.SK_CH_IronGuard_MaleA'
  LightEnvironment=AwesomeLightEnvironment
End Object
Components.Add(AwesomeMesh)
}
```

22. Compile the code and open `AwesomeTestMap` in the editor. Now we can see him!

What just happened?

As we can see, Components are primarily used to give our Actors a physical representation. It could just be a sprite whose only use is to let us know where our Actor is in the editor so we can select it, or it could be a character or vehicle mesh that's used in game.

Components are inherited from parent classes just as variables and functions are. But what if we don't want a Component from our parent class? With a function we could just override it in the subclass and empty it out, but with Components there is a function that we can use in the default properties to do this. Taking our example SpriteComponent:

```
defaultproperties
{
```

```
Begin Object Class=SpriteComponent Name=MySprite
  Sprite=Texture2D'EditorResources.S_Keypoint'
  HiddenGame=true
End Object
Components.Add(MySprite)
}
```

Removing it in a subclass would only require one line in the subclass' default properties:

```
Components.Remove(MySprite)
```

This way we have complete control over our Actor's appearance.

Components being inherited can also create a problem that we need to avoid when working with them. In the previous chapter, we discussed compiler errors, and Components have one specifically for them. Let's take a look.

Time for action – Component compiler error

The problem happens when we declare a Component that has already been created in our parent class. To see it we'll create a new class with a Component:

1. Create a new file in `Development/Src/AwesomeGame/Classes` called `AwesomeInfo.uc`.

2. Open `AwesomeInfo.uc` in ConTEXT and write the following code in it:

    ```
    class AwesomeInfo extends Info
      placeable;

    defaultproperties
    {
      Begin Object Class=SpriteComponent Name=Sprite
        Sprite=Texture2D'EditorResources.S_Keypoint'
          HiddenGame=true
      End Object
      Components.Add(Sprite)
    }
    ```

3. Compile the code and we'll get the following error:

    ```
    [0004.20] Log: R:\UDK\UDK-AwesomeGame\Development\Src\
    AwesomeGame\Classes\AwesomeInfo.uc(6) : Error, BEGIN OBJECT: The
    component name Sprite is already used (if you want to override
    the component, don't specify a class):     Begin Object
    Class=SpriteComponent Name=Sprite
    ```

4. This error is telling us that the name `Sprite` is already being used by a Component, and if we take a look at `AwesomeInfo`'s superclass,(`Info`), we can see it in the default properties there:

```
Begin Object Class=SpriteComponent Name=Sprite
  Sprite=Texture2D'EditorResources.S_Actor'
    HiddenGame=TRUE
    AlwaysLoadOnClient=FALSE
    AlwaysLoadOnServer=FALSE
  End Object
Components.Add(Sprite)
```

5. If we didn't want to override this Component, then we would need to choose a different name for our own. However, if we did want to override this Component and change some variables, then we would just need to remove the `Class=` part of our Component:

```
Begin Object Name=MySprite
  Sprite=Texture2D'EditorResources.S_Keypoint'
  HiddenGame=true
End Object
Components.Add(MySprite)
```

6. Compiling that code works, and now we would be able to change the properties of that Component inherited from our parent class.

What just happened?

This is another case of a scary looking compiler error with a simple solution, it all depends on whether we wanted to override the Component or not. The only other compiler error dealing with Components has to do with putting variables in one that don't exist for that Component class, so when working with them, make sure the variables you're setting in the Component actually exist.

Interacting with Components

Being able to create Components is essential, but what if we need to change them during gameplay? To do this, we can create a variable out of the Component and use them in functions, or access their variables directly. Let's try that out now.

Time for action – Components as variables

As our new `AwesomeInfo` class doesn't have any subclasses, we can mess around with it without worrying about breaking anything, so let's keep working there.

1. First, we're going to put a `StaticMeshComponent` in the class, similar to what we did with our `AwesomeEnemy` class. Let's rewrite our `AwesomeInfo` class to look like the following code snippet:

```
class AwesomeInfo extends Info
    placeable;

defaultproperties
{
  Begin Object Class=StaticMeshComponent Name=MyMesh
    StaticMesh=StaticMesh'UN_SimpleMeshes.TexPropCube_Dup'
    Materials(0)=Material'EditorMaterials.WidgetMaterial_Y'
    Scale3D=(X=0.25,Y=0.25,Z=0.25)
  End Object
  Components.Add(MyMesh)

  bHidden=false
}
```

2. As we're using an emissive material, we don't need to set a light environment for the `StaticMeshComponent`. The `Info` class has `bHidden` set to `True`, we need to change it so we can see the `AwesomeInfo` in game.

3. Compile the code, and open `AwesomeTestMap` in the editor.

4. If the `AwesomeActor` is still there, delete it.

5. Select `AwesomeInfo` in the **Actor** tab of the Content Browser (under **Actor | Info**) and place one in the map near the player start. In its properties, make sure **Display | Hidden** is unchecked.

6. Save the map and close the editor.

7. Run the game, and we'll see the `AwesomeInfo` Actor in the game. Exit the game.

8. Now that the `AwesomeInfo` Actor is there, we need a way to interact with it. We can do this by declaring a variable of the Component's class. Add this line to the top of `AwesomeInfo` under the class declaration:

```
var StaticMeshComponent MyMeshComponent;
```

9. Next, we'll add a line at the end of our `Component` declaration in the default properties:

```
defaultproperties
{
  Begin Object Class=StaticMeshComponent Name=MyMesh
    StaticMesh=StaticMesh'UN_SimpleMeshes.TexPropCube_Dup'
    Materials(0)=Material'EditorMaterials.WidgetMaterial_Y'
    Scale3D=(X=0.25,Y=0.25,Z=0.25)
  End Object
  Components.Add(MyMesh)
  MyMeshComponent=MyMesh

  bHidden=false
}
```

10. Setting the variable such that it lets us interact with the component through script. If we wanted to make the `StaticMeshComponent` changeable in the editor, then we could add the parentheses to the variable declaration like the following code:

```
var() StaticMeshComponent MyMeshComponent;
```

This would be useful in, for example, a decorative class that had some UnrealScript functionality behind it, like to for example, if you wanted to have it explode when shot. You'd want the level designer to be able to set the static mesh that it used along with other properties, so you would make the class user editable.

1. Now that we have the variable, let's see if we can use it. We'll use some Kismet to toggle the material that's on it. First, let's declare two variables in our class for the materials. Add the following line to the top, under the class declaration line:

```
var Material GreenMat, RedMat;
```

2. Now let's define their default properties:

```
GreenMat=Material'EditorMaterials.WidgetMaterial_Y'
RedMat=Material'EditorMaterials.WidgetMaterial_X'
```

3. Now for the function that will interact with the Component. We'll use the `OnToggle` function so we can use the Toggle Kismet action on our `AwesomeInfo` Actor:

```
simulated function OnToggle(SeqAct_Toggle Action)
{
  if(Action.InputLinks[2].bHasImpulse)
  {
    if(MyMeshComponent.GetMaterial(0) == GreenMat)
      MyMeshComponent.SetMaterial(0, RedMat);
```

```
        else
            MyMeshComponent.SetMaterial(0, GreenMat);
    }
}
```

In this function, we check if the material on the Component is `GreenMat`, if it is set it to `RedMat`. If it's not, then we know it's `RedMat`, so set it to `GreenMat`.

4. Compile the code.

5. Open `AwesomeTestMap` in the editor.

6. Click on the `AwesomeInfo` Actor to select it, and then open the Kismet editor.

7. Right-click and select **New Object Var Using AwesomeInfo_0**.

8. Right-click above the object variable and select **New Action | Toggle | Toggle**.

9. Connect the Target variable link to the `AwesomeInfo_0` object variable.

10. Close the Kismet editor and select **Trigger** in the **Actor** tab of the Content Browser.

11. Add a Trigger near the `AwesomeInfo` Actor.

12. Double-click to open the Trigger's properties, and uncheck **Display | Hidden**.

13. With the Trigger still selected, open the Kismet editor.

14. Right-click to the left of the other two parts of the sequence and hit **New Event Using Trigger_0 | Touch**.

15. With the Trigger event selected, set its **Sequence Event | Max Trigger Count** to **0**.

16. Connect the Touched output of the Trigger event to the Toggle input of the Toggle action. The Kismet sequence should look like the following screenshot:

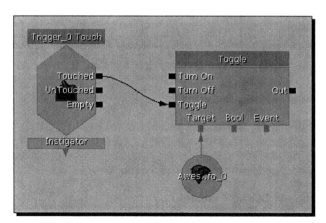

17. Save the map and close the editor.

18. Run the game, and every time you run over the trigger the `AwesomeInfo` Actor will toggle its material.

What just happened?

This was a simple example of interacting with Components, but with a little experimentation this could be used for a lot of different purposes. For example, if we had a vehicle that could be modified with different parts, then we could use the `SetStaticMesh` or `SetSkeletalMesh` functions to change the component appearance.

Have a go hero – Using SetStaticMesh

Using all the knowledge you've gained from the previous chapters, see if you can create an array of static meshes (choose any you can find in the Content Browser, right-click and select **Copy Full Name to Clipboard** to get them for your default properties) and toggle through them when the player runs over a Trigger. Remember that the static mesh component's scale is currently set to 0.25, so you may want to change that as well!

 Hint – Creating an array of static meshes in the default properties will make this task easier.

A practical example

We had the hypothetical example of using Components to customize a vehicle, but let's see if we can come up with something more practical for our `AwesomeGame`. Sprites and meshes aren't the only thing we can use as Components, we can also use lights. Let's see if we can create a toggleable flashlight for our player.

Time for action – Creating a toggleable flashlight

We'll be working in our `AwesomePawn` class for this, but first, let's set the mood.

1. Open `AwesomeTestMap` in the editor.

2. Select all of the lights, and in their properties set **Light | Light Component | Brightness** to **0.3**.

3. Rebuild the map by clicking on the **Build All** button in the top toolbar.

4. Save the map and close the editor.

5. Open `AwesomePawn.uc` in ConTEXT.

6. We'll need a variable to store our light component, so let's add it:

```
var SpotLightComponent Flashlight;
```

7. Now let's add the Component to the default properties:

```
Begin Object Class=SpotLightComponent Name=MyFlashlight
   bEnabled=true
   Radius=1024.000000
   Brightness=1.90000
End Object
Components.Add(MyFlashlight)
Flashlight=MyFlashlight
```

8. Compile the code and run the game. We have a flashlight!

9. Now to toggle it. We can use an already existing function for this, `Use()`. It's in `PlayerController`, so we'll have to override it in our `AwesomePlayerController` class. If it's already there, then change it to the following code snippet. If not, then write the following code in `AwesomePlayerController`:

```
exec function Use()
{
   if(AwesomePawn(Pawn) != none)
      AwesomePawn(Pawn).Flashlight.SetEnabled
         (!AwesomePawn(Pawn).Flashlight.bEnabled);
}
```

10. Compile the code and run the game. Now when you click on **Use** (default key is *E*), the flashlight will toggle!

What just happened?

Now we can see some of the more practical uses of interacting with Components in our classes. Components help keep things organized by avoiding creating unnecessary classes and code. In our flashlight example, the light could be created as a separate Actor that's attached to our Pawn, but keeping it as a Component keeps things simple.

DLLBind

DLLBind gives us a way to interact with code outside of the UDK. It is not a replacement for UnrealScript, but lets us extend the functionality if we find we need to. As an example, as UnrealScript's only interaction with files is through the ini's by way of `config` variables, creating a save game system might be complicated or easily hacked. By using DLLBind, we can send calls to an external file to take care of that. Let's take a look at a simple DLL interaction.

Time for action – Using DLLBind

One thing to note is that currently, DLLBind only works with the 32-bit code. If your ConTEXT or batch files are set up to run the Win64 folder's `UDK.exe`, then you need to change it to run from Win32 for DLLBind to work. You will get a compiler warning about it if you try to compile with the `Win64 UDK.exe`.

First up, we need to create the DLL. I've provided one in the files included with the book, but for reference sake, here is the code inside it:

```
#include "stdafx.h"
#include <stdio.h>

extern "C"
{
    __declspec(dllexport) void DLLFunction(wchar_t* s)
    {
        MessageBox(0, s, L"DLL has been called!", MB_OK);
    }
}
```

Basically, we're creating a function called `DLLFunction` that takes a `wchar_t` (equivalent of a string) and pops up an `OK` box with the string as a message.

1. Grab `AwesomeDLL.dll` from the files included with the book and place the `.dll` in the `UDK-AwesomeGame\Binaries\Win32\UserCode` folder.

2. Now for the UnrealScript side of things. We're going to use our `AwesomeInfo.uc` Actor for this, so let's write it as follows:

```
class AwesomeInfo extends Info
   placeable
   DLLBind(AwesomeDLL);

dllimport final function DLLFunction(string s);

simulated function PostBeginPlay()
{
   local string s;
   s = "Hi DLL!";
   DLLFunction(s);
}

defaultproperties
{
}
```

We use DLLBind as a class keyword with the name of the DLL in parentheses. The DLL function must be declared as `dllimport final`, and we're passing it a string called `s` (the name of the variable is arbitrary).

In `PostBeginPlay`, we create a local string, assign it a value, and then call our `DLLFunction` with it.

3. Compile the code. If the compiler gives you any warnings about the DLL, make sure it is in the right location and the name is the same as in UnrealScript. Furthermore, make sure you're compiling with the Win32 version of `UDK.exe`.

4. We still have the `AwesomeInfo` Actor placed in `AwesomeTestMap`, but open the editor to make sure it's there. You may get a warning about a missing component (we've removed them from the default properties), if so just click on **OK** and save and close the editor.

5. Run the game. We should see a message box pop up as the game starts!

What just happened?

DLLBind is useful when you need some functionality that the UDK doesn't provide on its own, but as I said before it is not a replacement for UnrealScript. If you come into it thinking that any core functionality of your game is going to be through DLLBind, then you need to rethink your approach.

Final Thoughts

No amount of reading books and tutorial is going to explain everything about UnrealScript to you. The lessons you've learned in this book are enough to get you started, but the best way to learn more is by experimenting with the code on your own. I really can't stress enough the importance of reading through the source code. Object, Actor, Controller, and Pawn are the four most important classes to read through. Reading through these classes, taking a look at the functions and variables they have that you can use, and seeing how they do things will help you understand how everything fits together in the UDK world.

Take your time, and be patient. Unless you're coming into UnrealScript with years of experience in another programming language, don't expect to create an entire game in a few weeks or even months. Personally, it took me a few years to get to the point where I felt comfortable programming an entire game using UnrealScript. Start small, creating variations on the weapons that come with the UDK, or altering the rules of the GameInfo a bit. Don't set your initial goals so high that they'll be unattainable, you'll only become frustrated.

And finally, have fun! You are making video games after all.

Other Resources

There are resources available on the internet to help you along. Here are the ones that I use:

- ◆   `http://udn.epicgames.com/Three/WebHome.html`

    The Unreal Developer Network is Epic Games' official site for everything related to developing games with the Unreal Engine and the UDK in particular. There are resources here for everything from UnrealScript to level design to the material editor.

- ◆   `http://forums.epicgames.com/`

    The official Epic forums are a great place to get answers to your UDK questions and show off your work. I post there pretty often, so if your question is answered by Angel Mapper you know you've come to the right place!

◆ http://wiki.beyondunreal.com/

Another great resource for UnrealScripters. The information here spans all versions of the Unreal Engine going back more than 10 years, so make sure the information you're reading applies to Unreal Engine 3!

◆ http://forums.beyondunreal.com/

The Beyond Unreal forums are another great place to post questions and show off your work.

◆ http://www.unrealplayground.com/forums/

My personal favorite hangout. It's not as active as it used to be, but I'm loyal. UP'ers unite!

I hope you've enjoyed reading this book, and I hope the lessons you've learned here will help you make some awesome UDK games. I always love to hear from fans, so if you'd like you can send me an email at rachel@angelmapper.com. I can't wait to see what you create!

Pop quiz – Components and DLLBind

1. How are components created?

   a. As a variable declaration

   b. As a function declaration

   c. In the default properties

2. How are components interacted with through script?

3. What two function modifiers need to be declared in a DLL binding function?

4. How awesome are you now?

Summary

We learned a lot in this chapter about components and DLLBind.

Specifically, we covered:

◆ How Components are created and how to interact with them through script

◆ How to use DLLBind to extend the functionality of the UDK

◆ Other resources you can use in your quest to learn UnrealScript

Now that we've learned about UnrealScript, you're ready to start making games. Have fun!

Pop Quiz Answers

Chapter 1, Project Setup and Test Environments

1	`Content`. The `Content` folder contains all of our game's assets, including the levels.
2	`BaseEngine.ini`. Looking at the top of each `ini` folder for the line `BasedOn` will tell you whether or not the file has a parent.
3	`placeable` makes it so an Actor class can be placed in a level by the level designer.

Chapter 2, Storing and Manipulating Data

1	An integer can only express whole numbers while a float can use fractions.
2	A vector is a struct composed of three floats, X, Y, and Z, used as a location or direction.
3	Add parentheses after var. Example: `var() float MyEditableFloat;`

4	`if(!bWater)`
	
	   `bThirsty = true;`

Chapter 3, Understanding the Class Tree

1	False – Actors are created from a class blueprint, but after placing them in the editor changes we make to them only apply to the ones we change.
2	`Subclass`
3	True – If the variable isn't the class we cast to or one of its subclasses, then the cast will return none.

Chapter 4, Making Custom Classes

1	The `PlayerController` class
2	`Bump`
3	`B – A`

Chapter 5, Using Functions

1	`static` lets us call a function on a class without needing an instance of that class to call it on.
2	Both of these examples would return a Boolean!
3	To skip over an optional parameter, simply add another comma to the function call's parameters.

Chapter 6, Using States to Control Behavior

1	`State, Non-state, Super`
2	`GoToState`
3	Latent functions

Chapter 7, Working with Kismet

1	Actions, Events, Conditions, and Variables
2	Events do not have input links
3	`TriggerEventClass` triggers events linked to Actors through the editor

Chapter 8, Creating Multiplayer Games

1	`Simulated`
2	`Reliable` and `Unreliable`
3	`Repnotify`

Chapter 9, Debugging and Optimization

1	The class is missing a closing curly bracket somewhere: }
2	`if(SomeActor != none && SomeActor.SomeVariable > 8)`
3	Most likely to return false

Chapter 10, Odds and Ends

1	In the default properties
2	By assigning them to a variable
3	`dllimport final`
4	Totally awesome!

Index

Thank you for buying
Unreal Development Kit Game Programming with UnrealScript:
Beginner's Guide

About Packt Publishing

Packt, pronounced 'packed', published its first book "*Mastering phpMyAdmin for Effective MySQL Management*" in April 2004 and subsequently continued to specialize in publishing highly focused books on specific technologies and solutions.

Our books and publications share the experiences of your fellow IT professionals in adapting and customizing today's systems, applications, and frameworks. Our solution based books give you the knowledge and power to customize the software and technologies you're using to get the job done. Packt books are more specific and less general than the IT books you have seen in the past. Our unique business model allows us to bring you more focused information, giving you more of what you need to know, and less of what you don't.

Packt is a modern, yet unique publishing company, which focuses on producing quality, cutting-edge books for communities of developers, administrators, and newbies alike. For more information, please visit our website: www.packtpub.com.

About Packt Open Source

In 2010, Packt launched two new brands, Packt Open Source and Packt Enterprise, in order to continue its focus on specialization. This book is part of the Packt Open Source brand, home to books published on software built around Open Source licences, and offering information to anybody from advanced developers to budding web designers. The Open Source brand also runs Packt's Open Source Royalty Scheme, by which Packt gives a royalty to each Open Source project about whose software a book is sold.

Writing for Packt

We welcome all inquiries from people who are interested in authoring. Book proposals should be sent to author@packtpub.com. If your book idea is still at an early stage and you would like to discuss it first before writing a formal book proposal, contact us; one of our commissioning editors will get in touch with you.

We're not just looking for published authors; if you have strong technical skills but no writing experience, our experienced editors can help you develop a writing career, or simply get some additional reward for your expertise.

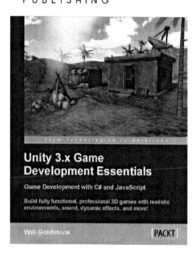

Unity 3.x Game Development Essentials

ISBN: 978-1-84969-144-4   Paperback: 420 pages

Build fully functional, professional 3D games with realistic environments, sound, dynamic effects, and more!

1. Kick start your game development, and build ready-to-play 3D games with ease

2. Understand key concepts in game design including scripting, physics, instantiation, particle effects, and more

3. Test & optimize your game to perfection with essential tips-and-tricks

Adobe Flash 11 Stage3D (Molehill) Game Programming Beginner's Guide

ISBN: 978-1-84969-168-0   Paperback: 412 pages

A step-by-step guide for creating stunning 3D games in Flash 11 Stage3D (Molehill) using AS3 and AGAL

1. The first book on Adobe's Flash 11 Stage3D, previously codenamed Molehill

2. Build hardware-accelerated 3D games with a blazingly fast frame rate

3. Full of screenshots and ActionScript 3 source code, each chapter builds upon a real-world example game project step-by-step

4. Light-hearted and informal, this book is your trusty sidekick on an epic quest to create your very own 3D Flash game

Please check **www.PacktPub.com** for information on our titles

HTML5 Games Development by Example: Beginner's Guide

ISBN: 978-1-84969-126-0   Paperback: 352 pages

Create six fun games using the latest HTML5, Canvas, CSS, and JavaScript techniques

1. Learn HTML5 game development by building six fun example projects

2. Full, clear explanations of all the essential techniques

3. Covers puzzle games, action games, multiplayer, and Box 2D physics

4. Use the Canvas with multiple layers and sprite sheets for rich graphical games

Google SketchUp for Game Design: Beginner's Guide

ISBN: 978-1-84969-134-5   Paperback: 270 pages

Create 3D game worlds complete with textures, levels and props

1. Learn how to create realistic game worlds with Google's easy 3D modeling tool

2. Populate your games with realistic terrain, buildings, vehicles and objects

3. Import to game engines such as Unity 3D and create a first person 3D game simulation

4. Learn the skills you need to sell low polygon 3D objects in game asset stores

Please check **www.PacktPub.com** for information on our titles

CPSIA information can be obtained at www.ICGtesting.com
Printed in the USA
BVOW022257110213

312972BV00003B/151/P